THE MISSION AND EXPANSION OF CHRISTIANITY IN THE FIRST THREE CENTURIES (VOLUME 2)

THE MISSION AND EXPANSION OF CHRISTIANITY IN THE FIRST THREE CENTURIES (VOLUME 2)

Harnack, Adolf Von, 1851-1930 and moffatt, James, 1879- Tr

www.General-Books.net

Publication Data:

Title: The Mission and Expansion of Christianity in the First Three Centuries
Volume: 2
Author: Harnack, Adolf Von, 1851-1930 and Moffatt, James, 1879- Tr
Publisher: London, Williams and Norgate ; New York, G.P. Putnam's sons
Publication date: 1908

How We Made This Book for You
We made this book exclusively for you using patented Print on Demand technology.
First we scanned the original rare book using a robot which automatically flipped and photographed each page.
We automated the typing, proof reading and design of this book using Optical Character Recognition (OCR) software on the scanned copy. That let us keep your cost as low as possible.
If a book is very old, worn and the type is faded, this can result in typos or missing text. This is also why our books don't have illustrations; the OCR software can't distinguish between an illustration and a smudge.
We understand how annoying typos, missing text or illustrations, foot notes in the text or an index that doesn't work, can be. That's why we provide a free digital copy of most books exactly as they were originally published. Simply go to our website (www.general-books.net) to check availability. And we provide a free trial membership in our book club so you can get free copies of other editions or related books.
OCR is not a perfect solution but we feel it's more important to make books available for a low price than not at all. So we warn readers on our website and in the descriptions we provide to book sellers that our books don't have illustrations and may have typos or missing text. We also provide excerpts from each book to book sellers and on our website so you can preview the quality of the book before buying it.
If you would prefer that we manually type, proof read and design your book so that it's perfect, simply contact us for the cost. We would be happy to do as much work as you would be like to pay for.

Limit of Liability/Disclaimer of Warranty:
The publisher and author make no representations or warranties with respect to the accuracy or completeness of the book. The advice and strategies in the book may not be suitable for your situation. You should consult with a professional where appropriate. The publisher is not liable for any damages resulting from the book.
Please keep in mind that the book was written long ago; the information is not current. Furthermore, there may be typos, missing text or illustration and explained above.

1

THE MISSION AND EXPANSION OF CHRISTIANITY IN THE FIRST THREE CENTURIES (VOLUME 2)

(Council of Nic a); together with some brief
ACCOUNT OF THE SprEAD OF CHRISTIANITY THROUGHOUT THE Various PROVINCES 96-306 Â 1. Palestine 97-120 Â 2. Phoenicia 120-125 Â 3. CCELE-SVRIA 125-140 Â 4. Cyprus 140-142 Â 5. Edessa (Osrhoene) and the East (Mesopotamia, Persia, Parthia, and India). 142-152 Â 6. Arabia 153-158 Â 7. Egypt and the Thebais, Libya and
Pentapolis. 158-179 Â 8. Cilicia 180-181 Â 9- Asia Minor in General. 182-192
A. Cappadocia 192-196
B. Armenia, Diospontus, Paphlagonia,
PonTUs Polemoniacus. 196-210
C. BitHYNIA 210-212
D. Galatia, Phrygia, and Pisidia (with Lycaonia). 212-222
E. Asia (Lydia, Mysia, Hellespontus, and Caria) 222-226
F. Lycia, Pamphylia, and Isauria. 226-229 Â 10. Crete and the Islands.,. 229-230 Â 11. Thrace, Macedonia, Dardania, Epirus,
Thessaly, and Achaia. 230-236 Â 12. MCESIA AND PanNONIA, NorICUM AND
Dalmatia 236-239 Â 13. The North and North-West Coasts of

THE Black Sea 239-240 Â 14. Rome, Middle and Lower Italy, Sicily, and Sardinia. 240-257 Â 15. Upper Italy and the Romagna. 257-260 Â 16. Gaul, Belgica, Germany, Rh tia. 260-272 Â 17. Britain 272-274

PAGES Â 18. Africa, Numidia, Mauretania, and
Tripolitana. 274-297 Â 19. Spain 297-306

Appendix I. The Spread of Christian Heretical Unions and of Sectarian Churches. 307-311

Appendix II. The Rise of Differences in the Provincial Churches throughout the Catholic Church 312-316

Appendix III. The Spread of Christianity and the Spread of Other Religions in the Empire (especially Mithraism). 317-323

Chapter IV. Results. 324-337

Addendum. 338

Indexes. â (a) New Testament Passages. 339-342 (b) General 343-348 (c) Geographical. 349-358

Maps. â I. The Spread of Christianity down to 180 a. d.

II. The Spread of Christianity circa 325 a. d.

III.-XI. Special Maps, illustrating the Spread of Christianity down to 325 a. d., in: â III., Palestine, Phoenicia, Arabia; IV., Syria and Mesopotamia; V., Egypt, the Heptanomis, THE Thebais; VI., Asia, Phrygia, Cappa-Docia, etc., Armenia; VII., Thrace, Macedonia, AchAia, Mcesia, Dalmatia, Pannonia; VIII., Italy; IX., Britain, Gaul, Germany, Italia Superior; X., Spain, Africa, Cyrenaica; XI., Numidia, Africa procon-

SULARIS, ZeuGITANA.

Mission and Expansion of Christianity in the First Three Centuries

BOOK IV

THE SPREAD OF THE CHRISTIAN RELIGION

CHAPTER I

GENERAL EVIDENCE FOR THE EXTENT AND INTENSITY OF THE SPREAD OF CHRISTIANITY. THE MAIN STAGES IN THE HISTORY OF THE MISSION.

JosePjuis, the Jewish writer at the close of the first century, completely ignores the Christian movement; for his so-called testimony to Jesus is a Christian interpolation. He may have deliberately ignored it. Nevertheless, we may infer from his silence that Christianity was numerically insignificant among the religious movements of the age. Even at a much later period it was unnoticed by historians. Herodian, for example, who wrote (about 240 a. d.) a comprehensive history of the period between the death of Marcus Aurelius and the accession of Gordian III., neverjneiitionad it.

The following is a chronological list of the more important passages bearing on the outward and the inward spread of Christianity. So far as I know, it has never been attempted before.

Â 1. Paul, 1 Thess. i. 8: ev iravr tottco oi5 ixovov ev t MaÂ: e(5owa Koi 'A aa rj TrctTt? vixihv e exy'fkvdev.

Paul, Rom. i. 8: ttio-th vulwv Karayyewctai ev o u tw Koa-au (cp. XV. 19 f.).

Paul, Coloss. i. 6: TO evayyexiov to nrapov ei vmag Kaocog Kal â v Travti tm kogtului (cp. ver. 23: to evayyexiov to Krjpvxqev ev Tracrr tÂ KTicrei t; utto tov ovpavov).

Â 2. Paul 1 Tim. iii. 16: Xxcrro? ektjpvxotj ev eovecriv, â TntTev6r ev Kocrua).

Â 3. Mark xiii. 10, Matt. xxiv. 14: c;ofx 'creta tovto to evayyexiov tÂ ? Sacrixeia ev oxfj Ttj oikovjuevt ei? ixaptvpiov Tracriv Toh eovetriv, koi TOTe I'j ei to rexo?; cp. x. 18: em yeiiovag Kat acrixet'i ax i'icrecroe evekev eulov ei? fxaptvpiov autof? Kai Toh eoveaiv.

Â 4. Acts vii. 6: ol t V oikovui.â vr v ava(TTatco(ravte9 ovtoi i. e., the Christian missionaries Aral evodse irapeicriv.

Â 5. Acts xxi. 20: Oecopei, Trocrai uvpiaseg eicriv ev to?? 'lovsaioi; Twv TretricrteukOToyv, Kai Travte tjxootai tov vojulov virapxovcriv.

Â 6. John's Apoc. vii. 9: fxeta tuutu elsov Kai isov o Ao? iroxvg ov apiofx crai avtov ovsei esuvatOy â k iravto eovovg koi (puxMv Kai Xawv Kai yxaxrcruiv.

Â 7. Mark xvi. 20: ckelvoi i. e., the disciples of Jesus e exOovre? eki' pv av iravtaxov; cp, the variant appendix: avtOi Si 6 'Itjcrovg airo avatoxrji Ka axpi Stxreuig e atrectTeixev Si avtWv i. e., the disciples to lepov koi aj)6aptov Ki pvyfxa (cp. Matt. xxiv. 9, xxviii. 19, Acts i. 8, and the Preaching of Peter cited in Clem., Strom., vi. 6. 48).

I 8. Clem. Rom. v.: XlaiAo?. Sikaiocruvrjv Sisa a: oxov TOV Koa-fxov " Paul. having taught righteousness to all the world."" â So it is said of Peter in the pseudo-Clementine epistle to James which introduces the pseudo-Clementine Homilies, that he " bore witness to all the world of the good Ring who was to come," toi ecrojuievov ayaoov bxw tw Koajuip p. r)vucrag i ao-ZXea; cp. xlii. 4: ol airoctToxoi. KatO. Xc pa? Kai TToxeif Kt pvcrcrovtei (" the apostles preaching throughout countries and cities"), and lix. 2: 6 apiofxo?. twv ckXekTcov ev oxw T(p Koa-fxu) (" the number of the elect throughout all the world ").

Â 9. Ignatius, Eph. iii.: ol etricrkoiroi ol cotu Ta ireputa i. e., Tov KOCTijLOv opicroei Teg ev 'lr (rov ILpictTOv yicox; eicrlv (" the bishops settled in the utmost corners of the world are in the mind of Jesus Christ").

Â 10. Plin Y s E i.-Â ul-Tra. j. Jicvj â (xcvii.):". visa est enim mihi res digna eonsultatione, maxime propter periclitantium numerum. multi enim omnis aetatis, omnis ordinis, utriusque sexus etiam, vocantur in periculum et vocabuntur. neque civitates tantum sed vicos etiam atque agros superstitionis istius contagio pervagata est; quae videtur sisti et corrigi posse, certe satis constat prope iani desolata templa coepisse celebrari et sacra solemnia diu intermissa repeti pastumque venire victimarum, cuius adhuc rarissimus emptor inveniebatur. ex quo facile est opinari, quae turba hominum emendari possit, si sit paenitentiae locus" (" The matter seemed to me to deserve attention, especially as so many are imperilled. For many of I all ages and ranks, and even of both sexes, are in risk of their lives, or will be. The infection of the superstition has spread not only through cities but into villages and country districts, and yet it seems possible to check it and put it right. At any rate, it is quite certain that temples which were almost forsaken are beginning to be frequented; sacred rites, long fallen into disuse, are being revived; and there is a market for fodder used by the sacrificial victims, whereas up till now buyers had been very scarce. Hence it is easy to imagine what a nmltitude of men could be reclaimed, if they had but a chance of repentance "). Compare also Clem. Ronu vi., and Tacit., Annul., xv. 44, where " a great multitude of the elect" iroxv ttaJOo? ecxecraiv, multi-tudo ingens) is said to have perished by martyrdom in the Neronic persecution. The expression " multitudo ingens" is used in Tertullian's jo. xxi. of the number of adherents personally gained by Jesus. " Christians of the country," first used by Pliny, is a term which occurs fairly often in subsequent documents.

Â livjBIermas, Shnil, viii. 3: to Sevspov tovto to fx ya to (TKeirat ov Tresla ku) oprj Ka iracrav ttjv yrji vojuo' 6eov eanv o oooelf eu oxov tov koctijlov ' 6 Se pouo ovto? vlo? Oeou ectTi Ktjpux eh â '? TO. irepata t? yj?, ol Se vtto Ttjv aketrrju Xaoi ovteif, ol akOucravtC? tov KtjpvyjuLUTO? kui irin-Tevaravte? ef avtov (" This mighty tree which overshadows plains, mountains, and all the earth is God's law given to the whole world; and this law is the Son of God preached to the ends of the earth. The peoples under its shadow are those who have heard the preaching and believed on him"); cp. im ix. 17: ra opt Tavra ra Scoseka SoosfkU (pvxai eicriv at KaroikOvcrai bxov tov Kocrixov' CKtjpvxqv ovv eig tuvtu o vlos tov Oeov Sia twv airoctToxoiv. iravra xa eovt tu vtto tov ovpavov kutoc Kovvta, cikovcravta Koi irkTrevcravta, eiri rw ovoxati ekXyjorjo-av tov vlov tov Oeov (" These twelve mountains are twelve tribes who inhabit the whole world; to these tribes, then, the Son of God was preached by the apostles. All the nations dwelling under heaven are called by the name of the Son of God, once they hear and believe'").

Â 12. Justin's Apology is inscribed thus: virep toou ck-ttuvto yevov avopwtTwv asikW'; nicrovfxevcov kui etrijpea ojieuwi' (" On behalf of those in every race who are unjustly hated and abused"); cp. xxv., xxvi., xxxii., xl., liii., and lyi. where Christians are invariably represented as drawn " from all nations" (ck ttclvtcov TOiv eqvwv) or " from every race of men" (ec TravtO? yei Of? avopoowcov); also Dial, cxvii.: ovse ev yap 0X009 ectTi TL yevo? avopwtTWv, eire ap dpcov eire EAXrwo e're otrxcof (ptipiovu oi ouati irpoa-ayopevofxevociv, rj ajua o cwv = Scythians i) uoikwv Kaxovp-evuiv ev arkijuai KT V0Tp6(pu)v oikOvvtooi', ev oh Sia tov ovop-UTO TOV crtavpco6evt09 'Irjaov evx l. ylvoDVTai (" For thprpjgjint a sipglp tapp f Oiiijna. t beings, barbarians, Greeks, or whatever name you please to call them, nomads or vagrants or herdsmen living in tents, where prayers in the name of Jesus the crucified are not offered up."); cp. xvii., xliii., lii., liii., xci., cxxi., cxxxi., and Apol. I. liii.: Trxelova. tou? e eovcov tcov airo 'lovsatcov KOI lapapewv Xpi(rtiavov9 eisoteg ("more Christians from among pagans than from the Jews or Samaritans").

Â 13. Pseudo-Clem. (= bishop Soter), ad Cor. ii.: ep po9 esokei elvai airo tov Oeov 6 Xaog rjpwv, vvv Se TTiatevcravtei; Trxeioveg eyevofxeoa twv Sokovvtcov exÂ i Oeov (" Our people then seemed to be deserted by God; whereas now, after believing, we ha ve outnumbered t hose i. e., the Jews who seemed to have God").

Â 14. The anonymous author of the epistle to Diognetus, vi.: ecnraptm Kara ttuvtcov tmv rod crwyuatO? ulexcov ' I'X'h "â Â ' pkTTiapo). Kara rag rod koctixov iroxeig ("Through all the members of the body is the soul spread; so are Christians throughout the cities of the world").

15. Celsus (in Orig., VIII. lxix.): vjulwi' Se kuv irxavarai rig en avoavuiv, awa tjrelrai irpog Oavarov Sikijv (" If any one of you transgresses secretly, he is none the less sought for and punished with death").

 16. apylus Mart. Carpi, Papyli., etc., xxxii.): = e iraa-n etrap')(!. a Kal iroxei eicnv juloi reki'a Kara Beov ("In every province and city I have children towards God""'). Compare also the remark of Melito to Marcus Aurelius (in Eus., H. E., iv. 26), that many imperial rescripts had been published in different cities regarding Christianity, and the fact that the rescript of Pius to the Common Diet of Asia, which contains a nucleus of truth, says that " many governors in the provinces have already addressed the emperor on the question of Christianity."

I 17. Iren. I. x. 2: rovro ro Ky' pvyixa irapeik ipvla Kai ravrtjv riv TTiariv rj eccajcrta, Kanrep iv bxw rw Kocrjaw Siecnrapmei'i, etTifxexcog pu acrcrei, cog eva oikov oikOvaa ' Kai ojuoioyg Tricrrevei rovroig, wg ix'iav xfyvxh " c" " 1 avrr v exovcra Kapsiav, kui (Tfx wtw? ravra Ktjpva-crei Kai Sisacrkei Kai Trapasiswcriv, cog eu (Trofxa Kâ Krr ui.â pr ' Kai yap ai Kara rou Kocrfiov Siaxekroi avojuLOiai, aw t Suvafxig rijg irapasocrecog ULia Kai r avrrj' Kai j-oure ai ev Tepfxaviaig ISpvjuLevai ekKXijcriai axXcog iretricrrevkadiv '. ri axXcog Trapasisoacriv, ovre eu raig 'l tjpiaig oure eu K. exroig' ovre Kara rag auaroxag oure eu Aiyutrrw ovre eu A3J oure ai Kara fiecra rou Kocrp-ov ispvmeuai ' axX uxrirep a ijxiog. ej oxo) rep Koa-p-o) etg Kai 6 avrog, ovrco Kai ro Ki pvypa rrjg ax 6eiag-nrauraxf (paiuei ("Though scattered throughout the whole world, the church carefully keeps this preaching and faith which she has received, as if she dwelt in a single house. Likewise she believes these doctrines as if possessed of a single soul and of one heart, proclaiming and teaching and handing them down with unbroken harmony, as if possessed of but one mouth. For although the languages of the world are varied, yet the meaning of the Christian tradition is one and the same. There is no whit of difference in what is beheved or handed down by the churches planted in Germany or in Iberia or in Gaul or in the East or in Egypt or in I ibya or in the central region of the world. Nay, as the sun remains the same all over the world. so also the preaching of the faith shines everywhere"). See also III. xi. 8: Karecnraptai rj ckKXrjcria eiri irua-tj? T9 y79 (" the church is scattered over all-ilie-,Â artll"'"'), II. xxxi. 2: ovk e(TTiv apidfj-ov eitreiv tmv papierijLatociv v kutu iravtO Tov koctjuov r ekKXrjcria wapa Oeov a3ov(Ta, k. t. X. (" It is impossible to enumerate the gifts received by the church from God over all the world," etc.), and III. iv. 1: " Quid autem si neque apostoli (juidem scripturas reliquissent nobis, nonne oportebat ordinem sequi traditionis quam tradiderunt iis quibus coramittebant ecclesias? cui ordinationi assentiunt multae gentes barbarorum eorum qui in Christum credunt, sine charta vel atramento scriptam habentes per spiritum in cordibus salutem (" What if even the apostles had not left us writings."' Would it not be necessary for us then to follow the course of that tradition which they bequeathed to those in whose care they left the churches?â a course adhered to by many nations among the barbarians who believe in Christ, having salvation written in their hearts by the Spirit, without ink or paper").,;, r '-.

 18. Clem. Alex., Protrept. x. (close) and xi. (beginning): " It is no longer necessary to go to Athens, since the Logos is now revealed to all, including Athens and Greece " (Trduru vvv 6 Sisdakoxo Kartjx' i Km to irav tSt 'A-Utjifai kui EXAa?

yeyovev TOO Xoyco); Sfrotn., vi. 18. 16T: o tov Sisaa-Kaxov tov uetepov Xoyo9 OVK efxeivev ev ' ov8ala fiovi, Kabdirep ev Ttj EXAa(5t (pi o(TO(J)la, sxvqi Se ava wacrav Ttjv oikOvmeviji ireiowv EAXjkoj re oJLOv Kui ap apcov cara eoio? kul KU)ii v kui ttoxiv iracrav, o'lkov bxov KUI isia ekuctTOv Twv e7rakt Koot(ioi, Kai avtMU ye Tcov (fixo(T6(f)(i)V OVK oxlyov t'jst eiri axi'fieiav jueoKXTO. (" The word of our teacher did not remain in Judaea alone, as did philosophy in Greece, but was poured out over the whole universe, persuading Greeks and barbarians alike in the various itattons and villages and cities, winning over whole households, and bringing to the truth each individual of those who had believed, as well as not a few philosophers'"').

Â IQ. JPol crates (in Eus. j H. E., v. 24. 7) says that he had " met with Christian brethren from all over the world " (a-vfjijse- 3 r K(0(i TO?? etTO T 9 OlkOVjuevtj'i asâ (f)0?).

Â 20. JTertullian, Apol. ii.: " Obsessam vociferantur civitatem, in agris, in castellis, in insulis Christianos, oranem sexum, aetatem, condicionem, etiam dignitatem transgredi ad hoc nomen " (" The cry is that the State is infested with Christians, in the fields, in the villages, in the lodging-houses! Both sexes, every age and condition of life, rank itself, are gone over "y to The Christian name!"). xxxvii.: " Si et hostes exertos non tantum vindices occultos agere vellemus, deesset nobis vis numerorum et copiarum? plures nimirum Mauri et Marcomanni ipsique Parthi vel quantaecumque unius tamen loci et suorum finium gentes quam totius orbis? hesterni smnus et vestra omnia implevimus, urbes, insulas, castella, municipia, concilia-bula, castra ipsa, tribus, decurias, palatium, senatum, forum, sola vobis relinquimus templa. cui bello non idonei, non prompti fuissemus, etiam impares copiis, qui tam libenter trucidamur, si non apud istam disciplinam magis occidi liceret quam occidere? potuimus et inermes nee rebelles, sed tantummodo discordes solius divortii invidia adversus vos dimicasse. si enim tanta vis hominum in aliquem orbis remoti sinum abrupissemus a vobis, suffudisset utique dominationem vestram tot qualium-cumque civium amissio, immo etiam et ipsa destitutione punisset. Procul dubio expavissetis ad solitudinem vestram, ad silentium verum et stuporem quendam quasi mortui orbis. plures hostes quam cives vobis remansissent. nunc etiam pauciores hostes habetis prae multitudine Christianorum, paene omnium civitatium paene omnes cives Christianos habendo" (" If we wanted to play the part of avowed enemies, not merely of secret avengers, would we be lacking in numbers or resources? Do the Mauri, the Marcomanni, the Parthians themselves, or any nation, however great, belonging to one country and living within its own boundaries, do these, forsooth, outnumber one that is all over the world? SWe are but of yesterday. Yet we havejfilled all the places you fre uentâ cities, lodging-iyx." r- yi- '-r- l â y ; A. v, i-X houses, villages, townships, markets, the camp itself, the tribes, town councils, the palace, the senate, and the forum. All we have left you is your temples. For what war should we not have been fit and ready, even despite our inferiority in numbers, we who are so willing to perish, were it not better, according to our mind, to be killed rather than to kill? We could have fought you even without being rebels, simply by showing our ill-will in separating from your polity. For if such a force of men as ours had broken away from you to some distant corner of the world, why, your empire would have been covered with shame at the loss of so many citizens, no matter who they were; nay, your punishment would have been civic bankruptcy. Undoubtedly you would have shuddered at your desolate condition, at the very silence, and at the stupor as of a world lying in death You would have been left with more foes than citizens; for nowadays it is owing to the multitude of Christians that your foes ai'e fewer, sjnce nearly all the citizens-of nearly all your cities are Christians "). De Corona, xii.: " Et apud barbaros Christus"" (Tertullian has already assumed there were Christians among the barbarians conquered by the Romans). Ad Scap. ii.: " Tanta hominum multitudo, pars paene maior civitatis cuiusque, in silentio et modestia agimus" ("For all our vast numbers, constituting almost a majority in every city, we lead a quiet and modest life"). Ad Scap. v.: " Hoc si placuerit et hie fieri i. e., bloody persecutions, quid facies de tantis milibus hominum, tot viris ac feminis, omnis sexus, omnis aetatis, omnis dignitatis, off'erentibus se tibi? quantis ignibus, quantis gladiis opus erit? quid ipsa Carthago passura est, decimanda a te, cum propinquos, cum contubernales suos illic unus quisque cognoverit, cum viderit illic fortasse et tui ordinis viros et matronas et principales quasque personas et amicorum tuorum vel propinquos vel amicos? parce ergo tibi, si non nobis; parce Carthagini, si non tibi; parce provinciae, quae visa intentione tua obnoxia facta est concussionibus et militum et inimicorum suorum cuiusque " (" Should you determine to carry out this policy here, what will you do with sq many thousands of people, men and women, of both sexes and of every age and rank, all presenting themselves to you? What fires, what swords you will require? What will Carthage herself have to suffer if thus you have to decimate her, since everyone will recognize in their number his relatives and companions, catching sight perhaps of men and women there who belong to your own rank, and recognizing all the principal men of the city, with kinsmen or friends of your own circle? Spare yourself, if you will not spare us! Spare Carthage, if you will not spare yourself! Spare the province, which the sight of your purpose has rendered liable to violent extortion at the hands of the soldiery and of one's private enemies"). Adv. Marc. iii. 0: "Aspice universas nationes de voragine erroris humani exinde emergentes ad deum creatorem, ad deum

Christum Christus totum iam orbem evangelii sui fide cepit (" Look at whj)le nations emerging from the whirlpool of error, to God their creator, to Christ as God Christ has now won the w hole, round world by the faith of his gospel"). J)e Fuga, xii.: " Numquam usque adhuc ex Christianis tale aliquid prospectum est sub aliqua redemptione capitis et sectae redigendis, cum tantae multitudinis nemini ignotae fructus ingens meti posset"" (" Up to the present moment no such gain has ever been made out of any purchase-money paid for a Christian's person and sect, though a rich harvest could be reaped from their, vast numbers, which are well known to everybody""),- dv. Judccos, xii.: "In quern alium universae gentes crediderunt nisi in Christum, qui iam venit? Then follows Acts ii. 9 f. et ceterae gentes, ut iam Getulorum varietates, et Maurorum multi fines, Hispaniarum omnes termini, et Galliarum diversae nationes, et Britannorum inaccessa Romanis loca, Christo vero subdita, et Sarmatarum, et Dacorum, et Germanorum, et Scytharum, et abditarum multarum gentium et provinciarum et insularum multarum nobis ignotarum, et quae enumerare minus possumus" (" On whom else have all the nations of the world believed, but on the Christ who has already come?. with others as well as different races of the Gaetuli, many tribes of the Mauri, all the confines of Spain, and various tribes of Gaul, with places in Britain which, though inaccessible to Rome, have yielded to Christ. Add the Sarmatte, the Daci, the Germans, the Scythians, and many remote peoples, provinces, and islands unknown to us, which we are unable to go over""). In de Anima xv,, philosophers and physicians are first mentioned, together with their followers; then Christians, who are " omnibus plures." De Anhna xlix.: "Nulla iam gens dei extranea est, in omnem terram et in terminos orbis evangelio coruscante" (" No race now lies outside God, the gospel flashing over all the earth and to the world's boundaries "); cp. ch. vii: " Omnes iam nationes ascendunt in montem domini" (" All nations now go up to the hill of the Lord ").

  Â 21. Caecilius, in Minuc. Felix, ix.: "Ac iam, ut fecundius nequiora proveniunt, serpentibus in dies perditis moribus per universum orbem sacraria ista taeterrima impiae coitionis adolescunt" (" And as the fouler a thing is, the faster it ripens, while dissolute morals glide on day by day all over the world, those loathsome rites of an impious assembly are maturing"; also Octavius in xxxi.: " Et quod in dies nostri numerus augetur, non est crimen erroris sed testimonium laudis" ("That OLU' numbers increase daily is a reason, not for charging us with error, but for bearing witness to us with praise"); xxxiii.: " Nee nobis de nostra frequentia blandiamur: multi nobis videmur, sed deo admodum pauci sumus" (" Nor let us flatter ourselves about our numbers. We seem many to our own eyes, but in God's sight we are still few "), 22. Origen, de Prkic, iv. 1. 1 f.: iraa-a 'EXAa? koi dp apo? t Kara. Tr v oikovixevrjv fxcov Xtora? e ei fxvpiov, KaraxitTOVTa toi'9 iratpuiov? v6p. oug cat vofxi op.â VOV9 Oeov, t 9 Ti p ' (Te(t g TWf Mcocreco? voxwv Kai t? uaoijreia to)v ' i)(tov pictTOu Xoyoov. Kai eav eirkTTi'ia-eop. ev, Trto? ep (Tij)ospa oxlyoi') erecri twv oixoxoyouutcov tov j piatiavkTimov eiripovxeuo-peucou, Kai tivwv Sia tovto avaipovp. eiwv, erepoov Se atroxXuvtoov Tag KTi)(Tei;, Sesvvrjtai 6 Xoyog, Kaitoiye ovse twv Sisaa-Kaxcov irxeovai ovtoov Travraxocre Kt pox vai Ttj? oikoviievt, io(ttâ ' See also Hippol., Philos., x. 34; toioctos b-n-epl rh 6e7oy a. 7 Orjs 6yos, S) vopoitTOi "EWrjves re Kcd Bdpfiapoi, Xa 5a7oi re koi 'Aaavpioi, Alyvtmol tâ Kai Aij8iÂ 6s, Ivsoi re koi A. l6iones, Kexrof re koi 01 (rrparrjyovi'Tes Aarlyot, iravres re 01 T-qv Evpwtrr)v, 'Aaiay re Kai Ai vf)v Karoikovvres (" Such is the true word regarding God, O ye Greeks and barbarians, Chaldeans and Assyrians, Egyptians and Libyans, Indians and Ethiopians, Celts and warrior Latins, all ye inhabitants of Europe, Asia, and Libya").

  "EXXÂ; a9 KCLL Bap apovi, arocjiov? re Kai avorjtOvi; irpocroea-Oai TH Sia 'l (Tou Oeotje eia â jmet ov tj Kara uvbpunrov ro Trpdyfia eivai eyeiv ov Sia-Td ojuiev (" All Greece and the barbarian part of our universe contain thousands of zealots who have deserted their ancestral laws and the recognized gods, the observance of the Mosaic laws, and discipleship to the words of Jesus Christ. And if we observe how strong the Word has waxed in a very few years, though those who acknowledged Christianity formed conspiracies, and put some to death on this account, while others lost their property, and that in spite of the small number of its teachers, it was preached everywhere in the world, so that Greeks and barbarians, wise and foolish alike, adhered to the worship that is through Jesusâ we cannot hesitate to say that the result is beyond any human power'"). Horn. ix. 10 wi Josiia (Lommatzsch, vol. xi. p. 100): " Convenerunt reges terrae, senatus populusque et principes Romani, ut expugnarent nomen Jesu et Israel simul. decreverunt enim legibus suis, ut non sint Christiani. omnis civitas, omnis ordo Christianorum nomen impugnat. sed. principes vel potestates istae contrariae ut non Christianorum genus latins ac profusius propagetur obtinere non valebunt. confidimus autem, quia non solum non nos poterunt obtinere visibiles inimici et adversarii nostri, verum etiam velociter Jesu domino nostro vincente conteretur satanas sub pedibus servorum eius. illo etenim duce semper vincent milites sui,"" etc. ("Thejdngs of the. earth, the senate and people and rulers of Rome, assembled to attack the name of Jesus and Israel at once. They have decreed by law that there should be no Christians. Every state, every rank, assails the name of Christians. But. these rulers and powers will not avail to prevent the race of Christians from spreading farther and wider. Our confidence is that not only shall our visible enemies and foes fail to vanquish us, but that soon Jesus our Lord shall conquer and Satan be trodden under the feet of his servants. For under the leadership of Jesus his soldiers will always conquer," etc.). Horn. xv. in Josua (vol. xi. p. 144): " Noster dominus Jesus ipse cepit omnem terram, in eo quod ex omni terra atque ex omnibus ad eum concurrit credentiam multitudo" (" Our Lord Jesus himself has taken possession of ihe-whole earth, since a multitude of believers gather to him from every land and people"), Horn. i. in Psahn. 36 (Lominatzsch, vol. xii. p. 155): "Nos sumus, non gens' (Deut. xxxii. 21), qui pauci ex ista civitate credimus et alii ex alia, et nustjuam gens integra ab initio credulitatis videtur assumpta. non enim sicut Judaeorum gens erat vel Aegyptiorum gens, ita etiam Christian-orum rjenus gens est una vel integra, sed sparsim ex singulis gentibus congregantur " ("We are ' no people," who believe a few from this state or from that; no entire race of unbelievers seems anywhere to have been won over. For the race of Christians is not one people, like that of the Jews or Egyptians formerly; it is not a unity, but gathered sporadically from the separate nations'"). Select, in Ps. 46 (vol. xii. p. 333): iraxal jmev Kvpioi?c ovk e-rrl iraa-av Tr v yt V Koi v lri(TTOii oxyo(9 Koi. (po epo? evxapecriv evapioULjtoi? Kat Bacrixevf ov TroxXoi? koi fxeyag cnravioi'S. vvv Se ttoxXm Trxeiocri ravra iravra etTLv. In Matt. Comment. series 39 (Lommatzsch, vol. iv. pp. 269 f.), on Matt. xxiv. 9 (" Et praedicabitur hoc evangelium regni in universo orbe, in testimonium omnibus gentibus, et tunc veniet finis"): si discutere quis velit, quod ait ' omnibus gentibus," satis inveniet certum, quoniam omnibus etiam in ultimis partibus terrae commor-antibus gentibus odio habetur populus Christi, nisi forte et hie aliquis dicat propter exaggerationem positum ' omnibus' pro 'multis'. et in hoc statu constitutis rebus (sc. in the last days) evangelium quod prius non fuerat praedicatum in toto mundoâ multi enim non solum barbararum, sed etiam nostrarum gentium usque hunc non audierunt Christianitatis verbumâ tunc autem praedicabitur, ut omnis gens evangelicam audiat praedicationem, et nemo derelinquatur qui non audivit, et tunc erit saeculi finis. nondum enim multi proditores de ecclesia facti sunt, et nondum multi falsi prophetae exstiterunt multos fallentes: sic et nondum odio habiti sunt ab omnibus gentibus etiam in ultimis partibus terrae habitantibus, propter nomen Christi: sic et nondum est praedicatum evangelium regni in toto orbe. non enim fertur praedicatum esse evangelium apud omnes Ethiopas, maxime apud eos, qui sunt ultra flumen; sed nee apud Seras nee apud Ariacin" Orientem, edd., but he probably means 'Aptaoy, a region on the western coast of India

"audierunt Christianitatis sermonen. quid autem dicamus de Britannis aut Germanis, qui sunt circa oceanum, vel apud barbaros, Dacos et Sarmatas et Scythas, quorum plurimi nondum audierunt evangelii verbum, audituri sunt autem in ipsa saeculi consummatione. adspice enim quod ait: ' et prae-dicabitur hoc evangelium regni in toto orbe, in testimonium omnibus gentibus, et tunc erit finis." si autem vult quis temere dicere, praedicatum iam esse evangelium regni in toto orbe in testimonium omnibus gentibus, consequenter dicere poterit et quod ait ' tunc erit finis,"" iam finem venisse: quod dicere temeritatis est magnae" (" And this gospel of the kingdom shall be preached in all the world, for a testimony to all nations, and then shall the end come. '"' " If anyone wishes to discuss the meaning of 'all nations" in this passage, he will find it quite clear and sure, since the people of Christ are hated by all nations, even by those dwelling in the uttermost parts of the earth. Unless, it may be, one declares that here too ' all"" is put for ' many' by way of hyperbole Such being the position of affairs i. e. at the end, the gospel, which formerly had not been preached in all the worldâ for many people, not only barbarians but even of our empire, have not yet heard the word of Christâ this gospel will then be proclaimed, so that every race may hear the evangel, leaving none who fails to hear it. And thereafter the end will come For many traitors have not yet arisen from the church. Many false prophets have not yet arisen to deceive many. Nor yet have all the nations dwelling in the uttermost parts of the earth hated us for the sake of Christ"'s name; nor yet has the gospel of the kingdom been preached in all the world. For we are not told that the gospel has been preached among all the Ethiopians, particularly among those who are on the other side of the River: nor among the Serae, nor in Ariace, has the tale of Christ been heard. But what shall we say of Britain or Germany, on the seaboard, or the barbarians, the Dacians, the Sarmatse, and the Scythians, most of whom have not yet heard the gospel, but are to hear it at the consummation of the ages? For see what he saith. ' And this gospel shall be preached in all the world, for a testimony to all nations, and then shall the end be." If anyone would hastily affirm that the gospel of the kingdom had been already preached in all the world as a testimony to all nations, he would also be able to say, of course, ' then shall the end be," the end is now here. Which would be an exceedingly rash assertion""). Hom. in Lnc. xii. (vol. v. p. 128: " Ita fiebat, ut de omnibus gentibus nonnulli proselyti fierent ix., in pre-Christian days, et hoc ipsum angelis, qui gentes habebant subditas, adni-tentibus. nunc autem populi credentium accedunt ad fidem Jesu, et angeli, quibus creditae fuerint ecclesiae, roborati praesentia salvatoris multos adducunt proselytos, ut congre-gentur in omni orbe conventicula Christianorum" ("Formerly some proselytes were gained from all nations, by the aid of the very angels who ruled over these nations. But now multitudes of believers flock to the faith of Jesus, and the angels entrusted with the care of the churches, strengthened by the presence of the Saviour, bring over many proselytes to form gatherings of Christians all over the world"). C. JJels., III. xv.: eirav irdxiv 01 iravti toottw SiaBawovre tov 6yov Tr V aitiav ri?? eiri toctovto vvv crtaaew? ev 7r ' 9et tmv ina-Tevovtoov vojuli-arwcriv etvai, ev tw jl) TrpocrtoxejuLeicroat avrov? vtto toov t yovfj. tvuv 6uloim roh Trdxai xpovot? (" Since those who utter all kinds of calumny against the gospel ascribe the present prevalence of sedition tci, tke multitude of believers, and to the latter not being persecuted by the authorities, as long ago they were "); ibid. III. xxix.: 6 Se TrevV tt? tov 'Irjcrooi Geo? ecxfcra? irairau T) v Tuv SdijuLOvcou etTiSovxrjv etTOu'icre iravtaxov T s" oikovuiâ i'; virep T79 Twv dv6pooirwu etTictTpocpfjg koi Siopouxreoo Kparfjarai TO evayyexiov 'Itjcrov Ka yeuecroai iravtaxov ekKXtja-iais avti-iroxitevofxiua? ekKXrjcria SekTisaijuovcoi' Km akoxacrtoov Kai asikwv see vol. i. p. 264. In III. xxx. we read that the presbyters of the Christian churches were worthy of holding civic offices of authority, e"i Tt? ectTiv ev t(u iravt). Troat? too Oeov (" if there be any city of God in all the world"); VHI. Ixix.: (aixev oti, e'nrep, " dv Suo arvp-cjioovsicriv e ulcciv eiri Ttji yrji irepi iravtOg â 7rpayj. at0i ov eav aitt (TOt)VTai yev aetai avtOi irapa tov ev to; ovpavoh Trarpo? "â t XP vofxi eiv, ei ixr juovov o)? vvv iravv oxlyoi (TVfx(l)(jovoiev dxXd irda-a t viro 'Fwfxatwv upxu'- ("We say that ' if two of us agree on earth as touching anything that they ask, it shall be done for them by the Father in heaven; and what if not simply a handful of people agree, as at present, but the whole-Roman empire?"). VIII. Ixviii.: xao-a xeu 6pr (TKeia Kata uo)')cretai, jmovrj Se rj picrtiavoov Kpatrcrei, rjTi KOI juLOvr TTOre Kparrfcrei, tov Xoyov aei Trxeiova? veuojuievou frux 9 cp. vol. i. p. 263. III. viii.: SXlyoi Kara Kaipovg koi Tpospa â vapi6juLt T0i VTTep T s pictTiavmi OeocreSelas Teoizjkaai, KCoxvovro Oeov to irav ekTroxeurjofji at avtiov eovo (" From time to time a few, who can easily be counted, died for the sake of Christian religion, God refusing to allow the whole people to be exterminated"). III. x.: on jmev ouu crvKplaei tov e fjg Trxi'jooug oxiyoi ijcrav ap ofxevol ptcrttavoi Stjxoi (in reply to Celsus, who had declared that the original number of Christians was extremely small, Origen observes: " It is obvious that Christians at first were few in number, compared to their sub-sequent host"). III. ix.: vvv fxev ovv tolxo, otâ Sia to irxtjoo Twu irpocrepxoij-evwv tm Xoyo) Km irxovcnoi kql tlve twv ev a icofxacri Kai yvvaia to. a pa Kai evyevrj airosexovtai Tovg airo TOV Xoyov, ToxJL)'itâ i T19 Xeyeiv 8ia to So apiov irpo'iaartacroal Tiva Ti cara picrtiavovg SisactKaxiaii cp. vol. i. p. 348. In in Joh., torn. i. 1, we read that "it is not too bold an assertion to say that the number of Jewish Christians does not amount to 144,000"; c. Cels., I. Ivii.: "The number of disciples belonging to Simon Magus all over the world does not amount at present, in my opinion, to thirty. Perhaps that is even putting it too high. They only exist in Palestine, and indeed only in extremely small numbers." For a passage from Origen, quoted by Eusebius H. E. iii. 1), see under Â 27.

Â 23. Cypriaiij ad Dernetrian. xvii: " Inde est quod nemo nostrum quando adprehenditur reluctatur nee se adversus iniustam violentiam vestram quamvis nimius et copiosus noster populus ulciscitur" (" Hence it is that none of us, on being arrested, makes any resistance or avenges himself against your unjust violence, although our people are numerous and plentiful").

Â 24. The pagan (Porphyry) in Macarius Magnes, iv. 3: isov Tracra Trj oikovix-evrf pvp. r tov evayyexlov tv ' eipai ex i 16 MISSION AND EXPANSION OF CHRISTIANITY
Kai TepjuLOve oxoi Kai KO(rULOu irepara to evayyixiov bxov Karexovcri (" Behold, every corner of the universe has experienced the gospel, and the whole ends and bounds of the world are occupied with the gospel").

Â 25. Lucian the Martyr, Orat. (in Rufin, H. E., ix. 6): " Quae autem dico, non sunt in obscuro gesta loco nee testibus indigent, pars paene mundi iani maior huic veritati adstipulatur, urbes integrae, aut si in his aliquid suspectum videtur, con-testatur de his etiam agrestis manus, ignara figmenti" (" But the matters I refer to did not take place in some hidden spot, nor do they lack witnesses. Almost the greater part of the world is now devoted to this truth, whole cities in fact; and if any of these be suspect, there are also multitudes of country folk, who are innocent of guile ").

Â 26. Maximinus Daza's Rescript to Sabinus (in Euseb., H. E. ix. 9): rjvlKa crvvelsov axesov atravtai avopcotrov kqtq-Xekpoelcrr? t 9 tcov Oeociv Oprjcrkeia i tm kovei twv pictTiavwv eavtovg (TvijiijLâ ijilX()Tai (Diocletian and Maximian issued edicts for the suppression of Christianity, " when they saw almost all men deserting the worship of the gods and attaching themselves to the Christian people ").

Â 27. Lactantius, Instit., iv. 26. 35: "Nulla gens tam in-humana est, nulla regio tam remota, cui aut passio Christi aut sublimitas maiestatis ignota sit"" (No race is so uncivilized, (j no region so remote, as to be ignorant of the passion or the lofty majesty of Christ). De Moii. Persec. 2: " Et inde discipuli qui tunc erant undecim. dispersi sunt per omnem terram ad evangelium praedicandum. et per annos xxv. usque ad principium Neroniani imperii per omnes provincias et civitates ecclesiae fundamenta miserunt. " " Nero cum animadverteret non modo Romae sed ubique cotidie magnam multitudinem deficere a cultu idolorum et ad religionem novam transire" (" Thence the disciples, who then numbered eleven, scattered over all the earth to preach the gospel. and for twenty-five years, down to the beginning of Nero's reign, laid the foundations of the church in every province and st ate." " " When Nero noticed that not only at Rome but everywhere a large multitude were daily falling away from idolatry and coming over to the new religion"). 3 (between Trajan and Decius): " Ut iam nullus esset terrarum angulus tarn remotiis quo non religio dei penetrasset, nulla denique natio tarn feris moribus vivens, ut non suscepto dei cultu ad iustitiae opera mitesceret" (" There was now no nook or corner of the earth so remote that the divine religion had not reached it, no nation so rough in life that it was not mellowing to works of righteousness by having accepted the worship of God"). Cp. Arnobius,) Â ii. 5: "lam per omnes terras in tarn brevi temporis spatio "' inmensi nominis huius sacramenta diffusa sunt, nulla iam natio est tam barbari moris et mansuetudinem nesciens, quae non eius amore versa molliverit asperitatem suam et in placidos sensus adsumpta tranquillitate migraverit" ("The sacraments of this great name are now spread all over the earth in so short a time. No nation now is so barbarous and ignorant of mercy, that it has not been turned by this love to modify its harsh ways, and come over to a peaceful temper by the acceptance of peace""), i. 16: "Si Alamannos Persas Scythas idcirco voluerunt devinci, quod habitarent et degerent in eorum gentibus Christiani: quem ad modum Romanis tribuere victoriam, cum habitarent et degerent in eorum quoque gentibus Christiani " si in Asia, Syria idcirco mures et locustas effervescere prodigialiter voluerunt, quod ratione consimili habitarent in eorum gentibus Christiani: in Hispania, Gallia cur codem tempore horum nihil natum est, cum innumeri viverent in his quoque provinciis Christiani " si apud Gaetulos j- cum Aquitanos huius rei causa siccitatem satis x ariditatemque miserunt, eo anno cur messes amplissimas Mauris nomadibusque tribuerunt, cum religio similis his quoque in regionibus verteretur?"

energetic character, and to the fact that the gospel had already reached barbarians, Greeks, and Latins in the course of its diffusion throughout the empire.

Â 3 (Matt. xxiv. 14) contains the general theory of the mission, which is put into the lips of Jesus: " the gospel has to

Are we not to understand the original form of the story of Pentecost (in Acts ii.) in some such sense?â as though the end might come, now that representatives from all the nations were gathered in Jerusalem, and had thus had the gospel brought home to them all.

be preached to all the world for a testimony to the heathen. Then coines the end." The eschatological picture drawn by the author of the Apocalypse (Â 6, Apoc. vii. 9) corresponds to this.

The passages from Paul (1 Thess. i. 8; Rom. i. 8, xv. 19 f.; Col. i. 6. 23) are deliberate rhetorical exaggerations; so in Â 4 (Acts xvii. 6).

The passages in Â 7 (Matt. xxiv. 9, xxviii. 19; Mark xvi. 20; Acts i. 8; Preaching of Peter) and Â 2 (1 Tim. iii. 16, quotation from a hymn) affirm that the disciples of Jesus, or the apostles, received a commission to go into all the world and preach the gospel to all men, and that they discharged this commission. This belief, that the original apostles had already preached the gospel to the whole world, is therefore extremely old; nor, even supposing that Matt, xxviii. 19 is taken as an interpolation, need it be put later than c. 90 a. d. (cp. Acts i. 8). The belief would never have arisen unless some definite knowledge of the apostles' labours and whereabouts (i. e., in the majority of cases) had been current. Both Clemens Romanus (Â 8) and Ignatius (Â 9) assume that the gospel has already been diffused all over the world, the former speaking, with rhetorical exaggeration, of Paul as the missionary who had taught all the M'orld. Finally, as the conception emerges in Hernias (Â 11), it is exceptionally clear and definite; and this evidence of Hermas is all the more weighty, as he may invariably be assumed to voice opinions which were widely spread and commonly received. On earth, as he puts it, there are twelve great peoples, and the gospel has already been preached to them all by the apostles.-

The actual expansion of the gospel during the first century must be deduced from the writings of the New Testament and the earliest extra-canonical literature. With regard to the intensity of its spread, we possess no evidence beyond that of

Cp. what has been already said on this passage in vol. i. pp. 73 f.

I shall not enter into any discussion of the legends underlying the apocryphal Acts of the Apostles, since it is no longer possible to ascertain accurately even the modicum of truth which may have been their historical kernel. A few details will be discussed elsewhere. The legends regarding the distribution of the apostles and their missionary spheres are exhibited by Lipsius in his Apokr. Apostelgeschichten, i. i. pp, 11 f.

the passages cited under Â 5 (Acts xxi. 0) and Â 10 (Pliny). These passages, however, are of extreme importance. The former testifies that among the Palestinian Jews, at the time of Paups last visit to Jerusalem i. e., during the sixth decade), Christians were alrea(lv to be found in tens of thousands. The latter passage yields even richer spoil. It sketches the compass r h, and consequences of the Christian propaganda in Bithynia and k f Pontus during the reign of Trajan; it depicts an activity which V l astounds us and which might dispose us to question Pliny"s statementsâ particularly as he had good reasons for exaggerating the movement, in order to dissuade the emperor from taking any wholesale, bloody measures for its repression. Still, the main points of the governors tale must be correct, and they are i uite enough to justify the opinion that exceptionally strong currents were already flowing in these provinces which told in favour of a religion like Christianity (see below, Sect. III. Â 9 in the third chapter of this Book).

As the statements of Justin (Â 12) and the author of the epistle to Diognetus (Â 14) upon the diffusion of Christianity are mainly due to the theoretical belief that the gospel must have already spread all over the earth, they are of no value, although the evidence of Dial, cxvii. may perhaps be based on some knowledge of the nomadic Arabs having already been reached by the message of Christianity. Justin, as a native of Samaria, might quite well know something about these tribes. In any case, the other notice is of some importance, viz., that by-theage of Justin the Gentile Christians already outnumbered the J ewish Christians. Still more significant, of course, is the statement of pseudo-Clemens (Soter), wa-iting about fifteen years later, to the effect that the Christians were more numerous than the Jews (13). For, even if this notice represents a purely

To be perfectly prudent, one has to take this estimate as applying to the time when the author of Acts wrote (i. e., about thirty years later), not to the days of Paul.

- Just in the same way as he probably exaggerated the effects produced by the measures to which he had himself resorted.

â The figure employed by the author of the epistle to Diognetus, who compares Christians in the world to the soul in the body, presupposes, however, a certain vigour in the expansion of Christianity, even although this vigour may have been largely exaggerated.

subjective estimate, even if it applies in the first instance only to the special circle which the author had in view (i. e., Rome), still it must remain an illuminating fact that a prominent Roman Christian, circa 170 a. d., was under the impression that the Christians were already superior numerically to the Jews.

The language employed by Celsus (Â 15) serves as a welcome corrective of the Christian exaggerations. True, Celsus also exaggerates. But he exaggerates in an opposite direction. He makes out as if Christianity were already in extremis owing to the rigour of the imperial regulations under Marcus Aurelius. This, of course, is not worth serious discussion. Nevertheless, the mere fact that he could give vent to such an idea, proves that there was no question as yet of enormous crowds of Christians throughout the empire.

The general theory, that the church had already spread all over the world, also underlies the assertions of Irenaeus (Â 17) and Clement of Alexandria (Â 18). Nevertheless, the statements of the latter author deserve consideration, for he met with many people from various quarters, and he testifies, moreover, that " not a few" philosophers had betaken themselves to Christianity. The remarks of Irenasus, again, have some weight as regards the churches in Germany and among the Celts at any rate â however worthless they may be as regards Iberia, etc. On the former churches Irenaeus could speak from personal knowledge, and it is they who are meant in his allusions to barbarian tribes who possessed true Christianity, although they had not the scriptures in their own language.

The information given by Polycrates (Â 19), bishop of Ephesus, is independent of any theory, so that it possesses great value. He testifies that he had become personally acquainted with Christians from all parts of the world, i. e., of the empire. This was written circa 190 a. d.

"Already,"' exclaims Tertullian (Â 20), " there are Christians in almost every township"; or again, in language which is somewhat milder but none the less highly coloured with exaggeration, "The larger number in every township are Christian."

The statement made by the martyr Papylus before the magistrate (Â i6) shows that there were Christians in his day in every province and town of Asia.

By 197 A. D. Christianity must have increased extraordinarily in Carthage and throughout the proconsular province, otherwise Tertullian could never have written as he did, nor could he have employed the large numbers of Christians without more ado as a menace to the pagans. Furthermore, we may believe him when he declares that no locality, no quarter of his native city, was destitute of Christians, and that they were to be found in all ranks of society up to the very highest. The substance of the despondent complaints made by the heathen about the increase of Christians is thus reproduced in the very terms in which they were uttered (cp. Caecilius in Min. Felix, Â 21, who finds church buildings and priests in existence, and who therefore must have written a considerable time after Tertullian). Christians were to be encountered at every turn, and people felt restricted and menaced by them in their very homes. Tertullian speaks of " so many thousands" (tantis milibus hominum), and this would be no exaggeration; while, if Christianity went on increasing throughout the following century by the same i-ate of progression in Carthage and the proconsular province, the whole district must have been predominantly Christian by the time of Con-stantine, so that one can understand how that emperor (Â 28) could regard it as substantially a Christian country. Cyprian's activity falls midway between Tertullian's Apology and Con-stantine, and one gets a vivid impression, from his correspondence, that the Carthaginian Christians now numbered many thousands. Cyprian himself asserts Ep. xx. 2) that thousands of litterae pacts, or "certificates,"" were issued daily during the Decian persecution. On the other hand, the enumeration of the barbarian tribes where Christians were to be found (in adv. Jtid. 7) is not based upon reliable information, as is quite plain from the naive addition of the " many islands unknown to us, which we are unable to reckon up" ("insularum multarum nobis ignotarum et quae enumerare minus possumus"). The general

Nevertheless it is noteworthy that Hippolytus also writes Philosoph. x. 34): TOiovtos b Trepl rb Qtiov axridris 6yos, S dvopaiiroi "EWrjvfs re Kal jsdppapot, Xa 5aioi t(koi 'Acravpioi, Alyvtrrtoi re Kal Ai'Siiey, 'Ivsoi re Kal Alolones, K Aroi Tâ Kal oi itpatTf yovvtis Aarlvoi, iravtis re 01 ttjv Eupwn-rjj' 'Aaiav re Kal Ai injy Katoikovvtes, ots crvfi ovxos e'ycb yiyonai (see above, p. lo). This passage does not prove, of course, that there were local Christians in all these districts, but it 28 MISSION AND EXPANSION OF CHRISTIANITY statement that the gospel had reached several barbarian tribes may be accepted as trustworthy, but beyond that we cannot go. Note also how Tertullian supposesâ though he does not base his idea, of course, upon statisticsâ that Christians when put together would outnumber any people (also Cyprian's remark in Â 23).

The evidence of Origen (Â 22) is all the more welcome, as he jonns the Jirst and only Christian narrator ivho testifies to the relative paucity of Christians. Indeed, in witnessing (i) to the fact that there were still a number of nations within as well as without the empire (" non solum barbarae, sed etiam nostrae") to which Christianity had not penetrated, or in which only a very small fraction of people (perhaps the population on the frontiers) had heard the gospel, Origen shakes off the dogmatic theory already mentioned; and this is all the more significant, inasmuch as he accepts the legends about Thomas having gone to the Parthians, Andrew to the Scythians, etc. In the second place (ii) he shows that no such thing as an entirely Christian town was yet in existenceâ for such we must take to be the meaning of the passage in c. Cels., III. xxx. (though it may also be interpreted in a different sense). Thirdly (iii), he admits, in controversy with Celsus, that when Christians are numbered relatively to the citizens of the empire, they are still irdw oxlyoi ("quite few in number"), although, compared to their own original numbers, they now represent a multitude (ttx Oo?). From the large and steady increase of Christians (iv) he infers â not once but over and againâ that their religion will in days to come supplant all others and rule unrivalled. At the same shows how the Christian preacher and author felt he was the teacher of all nations, not in an abstract but in quite a concrete sense, and how already his eye was fixed on every individual. It is Cyprian's age that furnishes us with our first notice of the number of Christians in a Christian community, viz., in that of Rome (Eus., I. E., vi. 43). The notice, of course, is indirect, for the Roman bishop Cornelius merely states the number of the clergy and tlie number of those supported by the church (cp. below, chap. III., sect. 14).

It is instructive to find that among the nations whom he mentions in this connection are some to whom Tertullian oc. cit.) declares that Christianity had penetrated. Origen, however, does not deny that certain individuals from these nations had heard the gospel preached; besides, adopting a looser way of speaking, he writes several times as if Christianity had spread all over the world.

t-?

time (v) he draws attention to the increasing diffusion of Christianity among the rich, among people of good position, and among matrons, observing that the number of Christians is steadily increasing, although the number of (missionary) teachers (is on the decline. He further explains (vi), as against Celsus, that Christian martyrs were hitherto SXlyoi Kara Kcupovg kqi arcpospa evaplOjutjtOi." All these observations show Origen to very great advantage as compared with his predecessors. And even his remarks upon the number of Jewish Christians are of weight. Porphyry's statement is instructive (Â 24), just because it reproduces the impression made upon wide circles of paganism by the expansion of Christianity. Evidently Christians were to be found in all quarters.

In the days of Philip the Arabian, Origen had stated that there was not yet a single town wholly Christian. Two generations later, Lucian the martyr mentions whole cities (" urbes integrae," Â 25) which were Christian. A Syrian himself, he made this statement in Nicomedia, and as a matter of fact we know that at the beginning of the fourth century there were localities in Asia, Phrygia, and Syria which were practically Christian altogether. The impression left by the latter provmces upbn Lucian's mind led him to declare that " pars paene mundi iam maior" belonged to the Christian religion. Note the " paene." Christians still constituted the smaller section of the population in these districts, but in several quarters their numbers were already equivalent to one-half. On this point we can credit Lucian's testimony, while at the same time we are bound to distrust Tertullian, who had made a similar statement 110 years earlier. Lucian's assertion is also borne out by a passage in a rescript of Maximinus Daza (Â 26), who observes, in reference to the same districts (viz., Syria and Asia Minor), that " almost everyone has abandoned belief in the gods and attached himself to the Christian people.""

On this, cp. above, vol. i. p. 511.

This occurs, of course, in a polemical connection which made it natural for Origen to represent the number of Christian martyrs at as small a figure as possible.

Dionysius of Alexandria (in Eus., H. E., vii. 7) had already remarked, with reference to Phrygia and the adjoining provinces, that they included "the most populous churches."

Nothing is to be gathered from the statements of Lactantius (Â 27), for, as we have seen, both Origen and the evidence of the fourth century contradict his assertion that Christianity had penetrated to all the barbarian tribes by the time of Decius. The observations of Eusebius (Â 29), however, deserve some further notice. No doubt he did not, and he could not, give a history of the expansion of Christianity, partly because he had no sources at his disposal for such a task, partly because the dogmatic character of his historical conceptions would not allow him to describe a gradual extension, but simply a more inward expansion. The apostles, according to Eusebius as well, had already made Christianity an extensive movement by distributing amongst themselves the task of spreading it completely over all the world. In fact, Eusebius went a step further in this direction. Christ, he held, had himself filled the world with his holy name, and fxvpioi ocroi had already come to him from regions far remote. In this connection the legend of the correspondence between Jesus and Abgar of Edessa was of supreme importance to him, since it came in as a sort of substitute for the evidence, which otherwise was awanting, of Jesus having widened the range of his activity far beyond the Jews and Palestine (cp. vol. i. pp. 71, 102). Down to the reign of Commodus, Eusebius knew of nothing important enough to deserve mention in this connection; he contents himself with merely repeating over and again how numerous and widely spread the Christians were in all directions; he also notes the entrance of the new religion into the aa-ixeuovaa ttoxi under Claudius, and the attention paid it by pagan authors under Domitian. But for the age of Commodus he was in possession of a special contemporary source (connected perhaps with the Acts of Apollonius); he was aware that the propaganda of Christianity had made a remarkable advance during that period, and that in Rome especially a large number of prominent and wealthy people had gone over to this religion together with all their households

He does mention evangelists (iii. 37. i f.) who had preached to? s trt wdxitav a. v7)K6ois Tov TTjs itictTfoos x6yov after the age of the apostles; this denotes, however, not lands and peoples hitherto unreached, but merely such parts of these countries as had not yet heard anything of the gospel.

and families, He then singles out two other stages in the growth of the propaganda, viz., the period of Philip the Arabian and the decades immediately preceding the last great persecution. As to the latter period, he states (in passages which have not been printed above) that Christians were now to be found occupying the chief places of honour at court and in the state, not excluding the position of governor, while their religion enjoyed high esteem as well as perfect liberty among the Greeks and the barbarians. The number of Christians, whom he describes as the most populous of all nations, had also become so large that the church buildings everywhere were too small; they had to be pulled down in order to make room for new and larger structures. The horizon of Eusebius, we must not forget, s tched from Alexandria over Palestine and Syria nearly to Nicomedia, and we have already ascertained that these were the countries in which Christians were most numerous. Of the West and of Rome Eusebius knew little, so that we cannot absolutely trust his assertion that Maxentius was originally favourable to the Christians in order that he might please and flatter the Roman populace. All that we know of the spread and strength of Christianity in Rome from authentic sources (dating from the fourth century) renders it quite improbable that during the first decade of that century Christians were so numerous in Rome, or had such control of public opinion, that Maxentius was induced to assume for a time the mask of favour to their cause. Eusebius at this point was availing himself of a pragmatism which would apply to the East, but not to Rome. â These remarks would cover all the more important issues suggested by the above collection of passages. As for the stages of the mission and its history, the outstanding revivals subse-yv'quent to the life and labours of Paul are denoted by (1) the era ' of Conmiodus and his immediate successors; and (2) by the years 260-303 a. d. In both of these periods, particularly in the latter, it is obvious that a large increase accrued to Christianity. The earliest period laid the foundation. House churches and town churches were established. The second ' This statement is corroborated by the marriage-laws laid down by Callistus, bishop of Rome, with reference to matrons (cp. vol. i. pp. 171 f.).

period (subsequent to Commodus) saw Christianity a serious factor in the provinces and throughout the empire. In the third period it was prepared, as a universal church, to assume control over the entire sphere of public religion.

The progress of Christianity for almost three centuries suffered no relapses; it hardly ever came to a standstill. We do not take into account the passage in the pseudo-Cyprianic de Singiilaritale Clen'corum, ch. i. ("ecclesia, quae per segnitiem nostram redigitur per dies singulos ad nimiam paucitatem), which asserts that the church was being daily reduced in number. This treatise belongs to the fourth centuiy, and besides, the church in question is that of the Donatists (cp. my study in Texte ii. Uniers., xxiv. 2).â The comparatively slender spread of Christianity, even at the close of the fourth century, might be corroborated by a remark of the Donatist bishop, Vincentius of Carenna in Mauretania, who (cp. Aug., Epist. xciii. 22) wrote: "Quantum ad totius mundi pertinet partes, modica pars est in compensatione totius mundi, in qua fides Christiana nominatur." But this is the word of a Donatist who desires to controvert the oecumenical character of the church, as being the chief argument for its legitimacy. Strictly speaking, he was right, and Augustine calls him, ironically of course, a "learned man" (homo doctus). Christianity had not really reached the majority of the barbarians as yet. But these tribes are outside the reckoning, as we may put it. Augustine replies to him that Christianity has already reached many barbarian people even in this short space of time, so that Christ's prophecy will soon be fulfilled; the gospel will be preached to the whole world. This reply is an admission that the gospel had not yet been preached to all nations by any manner of means.

CHAPTER II
ON THE INWARD SPREAD OF CHRISTIANITY

The inner spread of Christianity comes out primarily and pre-eirnnentty in the sense, felt by Christians, of their own strength. Evidence of this feeling is furnished by the zeal they displayed in the extension of the faith, by their consciousness of being the people of God and of possessing the true religion, and also by their impulse to annex any element of worth and value. These factors have been already noticed. But the inward expansion of Christianity may be verified at other points, and in what follows we shall survey its spread (1) among . the aristocratic, the wealthy, the cultured, and the official! 1 classes; (2) at court; (3) in the army; and (4) among women. ' Â 1. The spread of Christianity among the aristpcratic the. ctdtured, the zcealthi, and the official classes. " You see your calling, brethren,"' writes Paul in 1 Cor. i. 26-27; " not many wise after the flesh, not many mighty, not many of noble birth CtV-?-â nay, the foolish things of the world has God chosen, that he might put the wise to shame; and the weak things of the world has God chosen, that he might put the strong things to shame; and the base things of the world, and things despised, has God chosen, even things that are not, that he might bring to nought the things that are, so that no flesh should glory before him." Other evidence, covering the period between the primitive age and that of Marcus Aurelius, confirms the view that in the contemporary Christian communities the lower classes, slaves, freedmen, and labourers, very largely pre- ' Origen (r. Cels., III. xlviii.) observes, on this passage: "It is possible that these words have led some to suppose that no wise, cultured, or intelligent person embraces the Christian faith."

dominated. Celsus (c. Cels. I. xxvii.; III. xviii., xliv.; VIII. Ixxv., etc.) anctCaecilius (in Minucms Felioc) distinctly assert this, and the apologists admit the fact. Even the officials of the Christian church frequently belonged to the lowest class (see above, vol. i. p. 168).

Even Paul, however, implies that some people who were wise and mighty and of good birth had become Christians. And ' j this is borne out by the book of Acts. The proconsul Sfirgius "si Paulus was brought over to the faith in Cyprus (xiii. 7-12), " ionysius the Areopagite in Athens (xvii. 34), and " not a few women of good position" in Thessalonica (xvii. 4). So with Beroea (xvii. 12). From Rom yi. 23 we learn that Erastus, the city-treasurer of Corinth, became a believer. Priscilla, the coadjutor of Paul, must also be assigned to the upper classes, on account of her high culture (see below, under Â 4); and Pliny informs Trajan that "many of all ranks" (multi omni ordinis) in Bithynia had gone over to the Christian sect. The epistle of James inveighs against hard-hearted Christian proprietors, of whom it draws a melancholy sketch, complaining ' See v., viii., xii.; also Lucian's Peregrin., I2, 13, and Aristides Rhetor, Orat, 46 (Christians do not occupy seats in the civic council).

But they make it out to be an honour to Christianity.

â Cp. Knopf on "The Social Composition of the Primitive Gentile Christian Churches " (Zi?j. yÂ r Theol. u. Kirche, 1900, pp. 325 f.), and the same writer's Nachapostolisches Zeitalter (1905), pp. 64 f., with several sections in von Dobschtitz's Die U7-christl. Geeiiden Kng. trans., Christian Life in the Primitive Churches, 1904. The scarcity of material available for the apostolic and the sub-apostolic ages, however, prevents us from gaining much more information than what might be inferred a priori or deduced from one or two general statements. In his volume on The Share taken by Ch-istians in Public Life during the fre-Constattine Period (1902), Bigelmair also discusses (pp. 76 f., 125 f.) the relation of Christians to the state and to civil offices.

Their conversion was always hailed and recorded with special delight by the churches. Note how even Augustine, in the eighth book of his Confessions, talks of the conversion of Victorinus the famous orator; also his general remark (viii. 4, 9) on notable converts: "Quod multis noti multis sunt auctoritati ad salutem et multis prgeeunt secuturis" ("Because tliose who are known to many influence many in the direction of salvation, and lead the way for many to follow ").

See Lightfoot's article in the Contemporary Review, vol. xxxii. (1878), pp. 290 f., Kellner in the Catholik (18S8), pp. 389 f., and Wendt's commentary upon Acts, pp. 227 f.

Â For Christian merchants who travel, cp. iv. 13 f. The frequent warning against â KKiovi ia. (covetousness) which occurs in the primitive literature may apply primarily to traders.

also that they are unduly favoured even at the services of the church. In Ronie, a. distinguished lady ("insignis femina," Tacit., Ann. xiii. 32), Pomponia Graecina, was converted, followed not long afterwards by the consul Titus Flavius. Clemens and his wife Domitilla (see under Â 2). These and similar results must ere long have attracted a large number of adherents to the local Christian church from the better classes.

Ignatius in his epistle to the Roman church, assumes that it was so influential as to have the power of hindering his ijiartyrdom, a fear which would have been unreasonable had not the church contained members whose riches and repute enabled them to intervene in this way either by bribery or by the exercise of personal influence. The "Shepherd" of Hennas shows that such people did exist at Rome. We read there of Roman Christians who are "absorbed in business and wealth and friendship with pagans and many other affairs of this world " e irecjivpixivoi TToayxareai? Koi ttxovtw kui cpixiai edvikau koi awaii TTowaig irpayiuareiai tou aioovo? rovrou, Aland., x. 1), and of others who "ha e won riches and renown among pagans" irxovtrjcravre? Kal yevoxevol evso oi-wapa toi tdveaiv)."

Hermas frequently has occasion to mention the rich members of the church, and his reproofs of their conduct are severe.

' Dio Cassius relates (lxvii. 14) that many others, besides Clemens and Domitilla who had apostatized to Jewish customs, were condemned by Domitian on the score of "atheism": kox ol fxev airedavov, ol Se ruv yovy ovaiuv ictTrjp-fidricrav â f) 5e Ao U(TjaA. a virepupiffdi ix6vov els Uavsanipetav ("And some were put to death, while others were stripped at least of their property. Domitilla was merely banished to Pandetaria "; cp. Ixviii. i, where we are told how Nerva prohibited accusations of atheism and Judaizing). All these people were evidently Christians, and indeed, to some extent at least, people of property. Cp. the inscriptions found in the catacomb of Domitilla, and de Rossi in Btiuett. (1865), pp. 17 f. 33 f., 89 f.; (1874), pp. 5 f., 68 f., 122 f.; (1875), pp. 5 f. Even Acilius Glabrio, the senator and ex-consul also mentioned by Dio, was possibly a Cltristian (cp. below, p. 46).

' He continues thus: vneprifpaviau ixiya 7 v ivesvcravro Kal v pr) 6(ppovfs iyivovto Kol Karemirov rriv a. i 6imv kou ovk iko-r dr (Ta. v to? s Sikuiois, awa fxera twj idvsiv ffvve 7 (Tav, kox avrr 7) 65hs rjsvrepa avto7s icpaiiero (" They invested themselves with a mighty pride and became high-minded, and abandoned the truth, nor did they cleave to the righteous but held intercourse with pagans. Such was the path of life which seemed more pleasant to them," Sim., viii. 9).

Stm. i.: Ti SSe uxets kroitia ire aypovs Kal Trapard ns Tro vteae7s Kal oiko-Sofias Kal olk fxata ndraia cp. vol. i. p. 97; lys., i. I. 8, ii. 2, iii, 6. 5 f, 36 MISSION AND EXPANSION OF CHRISTIANITY

In the appendix to his Aj ology (II. ii,), Justin describes the conversion of a prominent Roman lady, and the Florinus mentioned by Irenaeus (in Eus., H. E. v. 20, 5) must have been of good position. Christianity also secured men of culture in her apologists. This was conspicuously the case with the best of the so-called "gnostic"" scholars and thinkers. No one can peruse the extant fragments of Valentinus without feeling moved by the lofty spirit and choice culture of the man. And the same holds true of his pupils, Ptolemseus and Heracleon, as may be seen from the former's letter to Flora, and the latter's commentary on the gospel of John. Marciouj too, was so well off that he could present the church of Rome- with 200,000 sesterces (see above, vol. i, p. 156). It is very uncertain whether we are to infer from Aristides Apol. xv. 4) that there were several Christians in the magistracy as early as 150 A. D. h The age of Commodus marks a distinct stage in the movement,

Y Founding on a source which is no longer extant (see pp. 30 f.),

Eusebius relates how the preaching of Christianity spread throughout all classes at this period, coarre 'Stj kq tu)v ein. 'J cofx â u juLfixa ttxovto) Kai yevei Siacpavm irxeiov? eiri t; i' a" v A (Tcpcov ofj-oa-e X' pelv iravoiki re Koi TrayyeiT crcotrjpiai'. This he proceeds to illustrate by the case of Apollonius at Rome, who belonged at any rate to the upper classes, and indeed was in likelihood a senator." Not much later than this, perhaps, we iii. 9. 3 f., iii. II. 3; Matid., viii, 3, xii. 1-2; Sim., ii., iv., viii. S, ix. 20. i f., ix. 30. 4 f,, ix. 31. if.

ilzov ffi afj. itpws Trpaffffovra ev rrj aaixikrj ahxrj koi evdokifi Tv irapa Uoxv-KOLpirti ("I saw thee faring prosperously in the royal court and endeavouring to stand well with Polycarp"). Cp, the expression of Epiphanius JIar., Ixiv. 3) about Ambrose, the Maecenas of Origen: "A Pp. tcov Siacpavaiv iv avxais Pacri tka7s.

' "And if they are judges, they judge righteously." It is not necessary to suppose that this means public judges.

"Cp. on this Klette, Texte it. filters., xv. Heft 2, pp. 50 f., and Neumann op. cit.), p. 80. The Acta Petri cunt Siinone prove the spread of Christianity among the Roman knights since the age of Commodus. Cp. also Clem. Alex., Adtunbr. (Hypotyp,), on I

Pet. v. 13: "Marcus, Petri sectator, praedicante Petro evangelium palam Romae coram quibusdam Caesarianis equitibus, petitus ab eis," etc. Pseudo-Linus 3 presupposes the conversion of senators under Commodus: " Innotuerant hoc eis celeri nuntio qui fuerant ex senatoribus illuminati."

should date the inscription from Ostia (see above, vol. i. p. 426), which proves that some members of the gens Anna? a were Christians; in the same way it is indubitable that a number of the Pomponii had died as Christians by the close of the second century. Tertullian's language tallies with this. He narrates how the pagans complained of people " of all ranks" ("omnis dignitatis," ad Nat. i. 1, Apol. i.) going over to Christianity, and he himself claims that Christianity has gained possession of " conciliabula, castra ipsa, tribus, decurias, palatium, senatum forum"" cp. above, p. 7; also ad Scap., iv.-v.: " Tot viri ac feminae omnis dignitatis. contuber-nales suos illic unusquisque cognoscet, videbit illic fortasse et tui ordinis viros et matronas et principales quasque personas et amicorum tuorum vel propinquos vel amicos Clarissin i viri et clarissimae feminae" (translated above on p. 8). y Similar testimony is borne by Clement and Origen. The ya. J former devoted a special treatise to the problem, "Quis dives salvetur? " and the volume discusses, not rich people who require conversion, but those who are Christians already. Origen tells the same tale. If it had been possible at an earlier period to declare that Christians held no offices, and that they had no seats on a civic council, if they could be 1 See de Rossi, Jioi. sott., ii. tab. 4950, Nos. 22, 27, and tab. 41, No. 48. n

"Tertullian himself was a distinguished lawyer in Rome before he became a JJl t–Christian (Eus., II. E.,"u. 4 '. There is nothing, in my judgment, to prevent the lout e, hypothesis that he is the lawyer whose works are quoted in the Digests.

Clement Strom., vi. 18. 167) asserts that not a few philosophers had already turned Christians; and it must also be taken as a sign of the times, when we find the governor of Arabia asking the prefect of Egypt to send Origen to him that he might listen to his lectures (Eus., H. E., vi. 19). Compare the introduction to pseudo-Justin's " Address to the Greeks," in the Syriac edition, which describes the author as " Ambrosius, a high dignitary of Greece, who has become a Christian," and tells how his " fellow-senators" had raised a protest against him.

Cp. ii. f., The Paedagogus also proves that the church, for which its instructions were designed, embraced a large number of cultured people.

c. Cels., III. ix.: vvv fx-ev oli Toixa, 'dre 5ia rh ttxtjoos twv irpocrepxoixevwv Tf oytfi Kal Trxovffioi Koi Ttves twv (v a iuifmacri Kal yuvata to. a pa koi ev-yev OTTosexovtai tous airh tov xdyov, roafxricni tis eyeiu Sta rh So dpiov irpoiaraffoai Tiuas Trjs Kara XpictTLavoiis SisactKakias; cp. vol. i. p. JJ47; see also II. Ixxix. His friend Ambrosius became a decurion (cp. Exhort, ad Mart, xxxvi.: koi xaaiffta ei Solacrsels kox atrosex f s lirh irkeictTa)! '6(Xwv TrsXewv vvv ii(rirepe'i irox-irevets atpuv rhv (xravphv tov 'Iriffov, lepe 'AjuSpo'crte).

charged once upon a time with " barrenness in practical affairs"" (" infructuositas in negotiis ") and " most contemptible indolence" ("contemptissima inertia"), the day for such reproaches had passed by the middle of the third century. Throughout the larger churches many Christians were to be found who, by birth or wealth, belonged to good society; people who had so much to lose, that a persecution was a doubly severe test of faith, as both Cyprian and Eusebius recognize. The civil service, too, was widely permeated by Christianity. The " Octavius " of Minucius Felix plunges us into that circle at an early stage in the history of the faith, 1 while the second rescript issued by Valerian in 258 against the Christians takes notice of none but the upper classes and the merubers of Caesar's household, outside the clergy (Cypr., Ep. lxxx. 1: " Ut senatores et egregii viri et equites Romani dignitate aniissa etiam bonis spolientur et si adempti faculta-tibus Christiani esse perseveraverint, capite quoque multentur, matronae ademptis bonis in exilium relegentur, Caesariani autem. confiscentur et vincti in Caesarianas possessiones ' descripti mittantur" = " Senators and prominent men and Roman knights are to lose their position, and moreover be stripped of their property; if they still persist in being Christians after their goods have been taken from them, they are to be beheaded. Matrons are to be deprived of their ' In de Lapsis, vi., however, he draws a repulsive picture of the entirely secular life of the rich Christians.

'â Eus., H. E,, viii. 9: i aiperus ekelvoi 6avfj. a(natepot, oi ttkovt fiiv kox evyeyfia koi S6 7, 6yw re Koi pi 0(TO(pia Stairpe pa. vres iravta ye fjirjv SfvTtpa defxivoi TTjs. Trifftioos ("Still more wonderful were those who, though conspicuous for their wealth, birth, and high position, and though eminent in learning and philosophy, yet ranked everything second to their faith "). Even by the time that the Decian persecution broke out in Alexandria, there were many local Christians among the leading people and officials of the city; cp. Dionys. Alex, in Eus., H. E., vi. 41. II: wowox fxev evdeais raiv Trepkpavea-Tepwv 01 xev a. Tffii'Tcov Srjdi6res, 01 Se Sr fxacrievovres iiirh rwv wpa etav r yowo (" And many of the more eminent people came forward at once in terror, while others, in government service, were induced by their public duties").

â ' The notice (in the Acts of Calocerus and Parthenius) of a Christian consul named milianus is untrustworthy, despite the alleged corroboration afforded by the catacombs (cp. Allard's Persl c, iii. pp. 241 f,; Bigelmair's Die Beteil. der Christen am offentl. Leben, 1902, 151 f.). There was a consul of that name in 248 A. D.

property and banished into exile. But members of Caesar's household are to have their goods confiscated and be sent in chains by appointment to the estates of Caesar "). This rescript shows, more clearly than any single passage could, the extent to which Christianity had already spread among the upper classes. From this rank sprang bishops like Cyprian, Dionysius of Alexandria, Anatolius, Paul of Samosata, and Phileas of Thmuis, who bore themselves like prominent statesmenâ Paul of Samosata, moreover, discharging the duties of a ducenarius in addition to his episcopal functions. Jiionysius enumerates (in Eus., H. E. vii. 11. 18), am mg the sufferings he endured for Christianity in the reign of Decius, "Sentences, confiscations, proscriptions, seizure of goods, loss of dignities, contempt of worldly glory, scorn of praise from govenors and councillors " a7ro(pacreig, St ulâ vrâ i?, irpoypacpa, vtrap ovtcav apiraya, a iootxatcoi atrooeaeig, S6 f 9 Kocrutkr oxiyopia, etva'ivwv tjyeij. ovikwv Kai ovxevtikwv Kata(ppovi' crâ i). He also knows of a whole class of Alexandrian Christians whom he describes as '7rpofl)ave(TTâ poi ev T(f Kocruo) (Eus., H. E. vi. 41, viii. 11). Anatolius laboured as a statesman in Alexandria, and was a member of the local city council (Eus., H. E. vii. 32). His fellow-citizens in Alexandria requested him to start a local school for the Aristotelian philosophy (Eus., H. E., vii. 32).

Eusebius (H. E., viii. 1) gives us the position of matters in the reign of Diocletian i. e., down to 303 a. d.) as follows: " The

Cp., e. g., the tale of Astyrius, who belonged to the senatorial order, in Eus., JI.Â., vii. i6f.

Eus., H. E., viii. 9. 6 f., where he continues (see p. 38, note 2): olos ikias TTJs fiovitav evcarjcias (TriakOTros, diairpfipas av))p rais Kara rrjv irarpisa iroatteiais re Kal iitovpyiais, (v re to7s Kara ikocrocpiav 6yois, k. t. A. (" Such a man is Phileas, bishop of the church at Thmuis, a man eminent for his patriotism and for the services he had rendered to his country, a man of philosophic attainments also").

â On this bishop see Gomperz in Afzz. d. k. Wiener Akad., Phil.-Hist., Klasse (1901), No. vii. 2. Another Christian, Eusebius byname, who afterwards became bishop of Laodicea, also played a political role at Alexandria during this period (Eus., H. E., vii. 32). Compare the description of bishop Phileas of Thmuis (viii. 9). If one puts together what is known of Christianity at Alexandria during the last third of the third century and the beginning of the fourth, one gets the impression that the Alexandrian Christians were already a strong and influential party in the city, with which the political authorities had to reckon.

emperors " he says, " even tnisted iir jiiembers zvith provinces to govern (ra? toov eovoiv rjyejuLovlag), and exempted them from the dxdy of offering saaifice."" Unfortunately, Eusebius has not told us what provinces were committed to Christian governors, just as he fails to mention (in viii. 11) the name of that town in Phrygia whose entire population, including officials, were Christians. Only two Christians of high position are mentioned by him, viz., Philoromus of Alexandria, and a certain Adauctus.

We can see, then, how even prior to Constantine the Christian religion had made its way into the government service, just as it had found an entrance, thanlvs to Clement and Origen, into

The latter fact has not even yet been weighed properly in any estimate of the situation previous to Constantine. It looks like a recognid n. of Christianity along administrative lines. On the other hand, the fifty-sixth canon of Elvira permits the acceptance of the duumvirate, but orders the magistrate to keep away from church during his year of office (" Magistratus vero uno anno quo agit duumviratum, prohibendum placet ut se ab ecclesia cohibeat"). This is the final compromise.

â This valuable paragraph runs as follows: llav 7)fiil navtis ol r v troxiv o'lkOvvtes, Xoyifft'fis re avrhs Kal arparriyhs ffvv tois ev rexei iraai cat oay S ip 'X. pkniavovs Tpa. s bfj. oxoyovvtes oii5' birwatLOvv tois TvpoatatTovaiv (l5a o atpf7f iweiodpxovv (" All the inhabitants of the city, together with the mayor, the governor, and all who held office, and the entire populace to boot, confessed themselves Christians, nor would they obey in the least those who bade them worship idols ").

viik.9-: iaopco os apxw Tiva ov tt)v rvxovaap rrjs car' 'AAf duspeiav fiacrixikris Bioik7 afus eykexeiptfrxevos, hs uera rov a iwxatos Koi rfjs 'Poouaikrii Tixris iinh (TTpatidirais 5opv(popovfjieyos ecactTTjs avekpivero rjfiepas (" Philoroniusheld a high position in the imperial government of Alexandria, and dispensed justice daily, attended by soldiers, as befitted his dignity and Roman post of honour ").

' viii. II: Kai ris erepos 'Poi ai'cfjs a ias itreiarmfieyos, ""ASavkTos ovojxa, y4vos Twv trap' 'IraaolS 4in(Trij. wv, Sta iraarjs ZiexQuv dvrip rris irapa fiaaiaevai Tij. ris, ws Kal Tos Ka66 ov SioikTiffeis rrjs Trap' avrots Kaxovfxivqs fmayicrtpoTrjtos re koi Kadokik6rrjros a. jx4fj. TTrws 5ie 6e7v, K. r. K. (" And there was another Roman dignitary, called Adauctus sprung from a noble Italian house, who had passed Jhrough every place of honour under the emperors, so that he had blamelessly filled the general offices of the magistracy, as it is called and of minister of finance ").â Dorymedon was a member of the civic council in Synnada (cp. Aca Dorytn.), and Dativus is described as a senator in the African Acta Sat. et Dativi (cp. Ruinart, op. cit. p. 417)- ' For Christians who took the office of flamen, see the canons of Elvira, and Duchesne's Zd concile ctElvire et les Jlaminefttfi'tiens (1887, Melanges Renier). The council did not prohibit acceptance of this office, but it laid stringent conditions on any Christians who were elected.

ON THE INWARD SPREAD OF CHRISTIANITY 41 the world of learning, although Â liej si majority of the aristo- Â j,2k

Qracy, by birth or position, still continued to be pagan. This-jw is indirectly certified by Porphyry as well, and Arno)iiis writes.â.

(ii. 5) to this effect: " Tarn magnis ingeniis praediti oratores, grammatici, rhetores, consult! juris ac medici, philosophiae etiam secreta rimantes niagisteria haec expetunt spretis quibus paulo ante fidebant" (" Omiors of such high endowments, scholars, rheto. ticians, lawyers, and doctors, these, too, pry into, the secrets of this philosophy, discarding what a little before they relied upon "). We also know a whole series of names of orators and grammarians who came over to Christianity. The

Antiochene " sop hist'" M ajLchioii, " the one man who was capable of refuting and unmasking Paul of Samosata," was a teacher of

Greek learning who had been converted. He seems to have practised his profession even as a Christian (Eus., H. E., vii. 30).

Diocletian had a Latin orator and a grammarian summoned from Africa to Nikomedia, when it was discovered that both were Christians (Lactantius and Flavins; cp. Jerome, de Vir. I

Irilust. Ixxx., and adv. Jovin. ii. 6). Arnobius himself was '- A yu- fx orator, and only became a Christian in his later years. Possibly., câ

Victo rinus of ettau also belonged to this class prior to his Vv- 4

Christian vocation. The author of the song " Laudes Domini"

is to be mentioned in this connection, while in the Gesta apud

Zenophilum (under Diocletian) a converted orator appears, who is also described as a Latin grammarian.

1 This is especially true of Rome. Even about 360 a. d. we find Augustine LA Aa a Ci writing(Cci; j-j'., viii. 2. 3: " sacris sacrilegis tunc tota fere Romana nobilitas inflata 0 inspirabat populo iam et ' omnigenum deum monstra'") of " the sacrilegious rites ' J I to which at that time almost all the Roman nobility were addicted. They inspired the common people too with a passion for monstrous gods of all sorts."

About seventy years after Diocletian, the author of the pseudo-Augustinian Qiiastiones in Vehts et Novum Testa? nentiim writes (nr. 114 at close): " Quodsi odio digna res esset aut aliquid haberet fallaciae, quotidie ex Christianis fierent pagani.

porro autem, quoniam haec Veritas est, quotidie omni hora sine intermissione deserentes Jovem, inter quos sophistae et nobiles mundi, qui eum deum confessi erant, confugiunt ad Christum" ("If Christianity were deserving of hatred or had any element of falsehood in it, Christians would daily turn to paganism. Whereas, just because it is the truth, pagans turn to Christ at every hour of the day, unceasingly, abandoning Jove; amongst them sophists and nobles who rmerl)? worshipped Jove as God "). This was true of the period circa 300 A. dt'

It need not be said that the conversion of a dozen or two orators and professors meant nothing either way. The really decisive factor was the development of Christian learning at Alexandria and Caesarea. It adhered to the church. But it won over the educated classes to Christianity, and provided the Neoplatonist philosophers with serious rivals. In the West, where the full strength of Christian learning was not felt, the full strength of learning in general was conspicuous by its absence. Here the upper classes were brought over to the faith by the authority and stability of the church.

y Sr7 TJiÂ spread of Christianity at coiirt. Let me preface this section with a brief reference to the Jews a t thfi-imperial court. We find them there even in the 3ays of Augustus; indeed, inscriptions tell us that they were so numerous as to possess a sj-nagogue of their own. As we find inscriptions of Jewesses at Rome called Flavia Antonina, Aurelia, and Faustina, or of Jews called Aurelius, Claudius, and Julianus, it is natural to conjecture that they included many slaves or freedmen from the court, or their descendants. And they had great influence. It was through the good offices of Alityrus, the Jewish actor, vrho was a great favourite with Nero, that Oi? Josephus was presented to the empress Poppaea in Puteoli, and obtained, by her help, the liberation of some Jewish priests (Joseph., Vita iii.). The queen herself seems, in factjjtq ave been a kind of proselyte (Joseph., Antiq. xx. 8. 11). As has 1 Cp. V. Engestrom's Om Judarne i Rom undre iildre tider och deras kata-CwÂ 5 r (Upsala, 1876).

2wa7(077? Auyuva-r-na-Looy: C. I. G., 9902, 9903; cp. Fiorelli's Catalogo delmuseo Nazionale, Iscriz Lat., 1956, i960; Orelli,- 222 â Q, z. x xzz, Dissertaz., ii. 162. 12. Engestrom, Nos. 3, 4, p. 31. Besides this, there was a awarfta' 'Aypnrit-na-iwy in Rome C.. G. 9907; Engestrom, No. 2, p. 31), connected, probably, with Agrippa, the friend of Augustus. For other Jewish synagogues in Rome, consult Engestrom; and above, vol. i. p. 443.

Flavia Antonina: Engestrom, No. 3. Quintus Claudius Synesius, No. 8; Annianus, son of Julianus, No. 9; Julianus, son of Julianus, No. 10; Lucina, No. 16; Lucilla, No. 44; Alexander, son of Alexander, No. 18; Valerius, husband of Lucretia Faustina, No. 19; Gaius, No. 24; Julia, No, 27; Alexander, No. 34; Aurelia Camerina, No. 35; Aurelius Joses, husband of Aurelia Anguria, No. 36; Aelia Alexandrina, daughter of Aelia Septima, No. 37; Flavia Dativa Flavise, No. 38; Marcella, No. 41. On the Jews at the imperial court, see Renan's Ant(christ, p. 9 n. 2, pp. 125 f. (German ed.), Eng. trans., pp. 4 f., 62 f.

been already observed (vol. i. pp. 58, 488), the Jews were probably the instigators of the Neronian outburst against the Christians; the Samaritan Thallus, a freedman of Tiberius, was able to lend the Jewish king, Herod Agrippa, a million denarii; the relations between the Herodians and the emperors of the Julian and Claudian dynasties were close; ' and so on. Previous to the great war, there were certainly many linl between the Palestinian Jews and the imperial court, although subsequently, during the next hundred years, they must have become fewer, and finally disappeared altogether. Neither then nor afterwards had they any direct bearing upon the connection of Christians and the court.

This latter connection has been overgrown by a luxuriant tangle of legend and romance. Peter and Paul are said to have stood before Nero, while John was condemned by Domitian in person, and dozens of their contemporaries at the
  Jos., Antiq., xviii. 6. 4. For the court intrigues of Acme, the Jewish slave-girl of the emperor Livia, see Anliq., xvii. 5. 7 f., Bell. Jud., i. 32. 6 f.

"Caracalla is reported to have had a Jewish playmate (Spart., Caracall., i.).

No attempt has yet been made to collect the opinions of Christians on the personal character and regulations of the various emperors, although ample material lies in the apologists Melito, Tertullian, Origen, Lactantius, Eusebius, etc., as well as in the Sibylline Oracles and the Apocryphal Acts.

So the Acta Petri et Pauli (Kenan's Antichrist, ibid.); cp. especially c. 31. 36 f., 84. The legend assumes varied forms in many writers (cp. also the pseudo-Clementine literature, which, in its extant shape, is not perhaps earlier than the opening of the fourth century), and somewhere in the course of the sixth century it was finally shaped in the Acta Psettdo-Lini and the Acta Ner. et Achill. In the first book of the former Acts, Nero is only mentioned incidentallyj but many n oble lad ies are described as converted, including four concubines of the prefect 'Sgrippa (Agrippina, Eucharia, Euphemia, Dionis), and Xandippe, the wife of Albinus, "Caesaris amicissimi." According to Book II., however, the preaching of Christianity proved far more efficacious: "Paul was visited by a mighty con- j: ourse from the imperial household, who believed in the Lord Jesus Christ

And besides, the instructor of the emperor i. e., Seneca was closely knit to him by ties of friendship, recognizing that he possessed the mind of God " (" Concursus quoque multus de domo Caesarii fiebat ad Paulum, credentium in dominum Jesum Christum. sed et institutor imperatoris adeo est illi amicitia copulatus, videns in eo divinam sententiam"). A magister Caesaris reads aloud Paul's writings, and many of Nero's personal retinue (" ex familiari obsequio Neronis") follow the apostle. Patroclus, a former page of the emperor, who was then "ad vini officium" (acting as wine-bearer), becomes a Christian. Barnabas, Justus, a certain Paul, Arion Cappadox, Festus Gallata, are all Christian servants of Nero, while a distinguished lady, named Plantilla, is a friend of Paul. A section of imperial court are alleged to have become Christians. All this we must simply ignore. More serious attention perhaps should be paid to Tertullian's statement about Tiberius (in Apol. v., reproduced in Eus., H. E., ii. 2), but in the end one is obliged to dismiss the whole account as unauthentic.

Paul's epistle to the Philippians closes with these words: aa-Trd ovrai vjuLcig Trdvres ol dyioi, juLaxicrra Se ol ec t?? Katcrapos oikia (iv. 22). This implies that the Roman church contained a special group of Christians who belonged to the household of the Caesar, people who either had had some previous connection with the Philippian church or had recently formed a connection with it by means of Epaphroditus, the Philippian envoy.

Several years before Philippians was written, Paul wrote the epistle to the Romans. Within the ample list of greetings in the sixteenth chapter, Paul groups two sets of people: the

Nero's court is thus represented as having been Christians. In Fsetido-Lmus, and still more in the Acta Ner. et Achill., which would more aptly be described as Acta Domitillce, many historical names of Christians belonging to the second and third centuries (in the capital and from a wider environment) have been employed, but all the allusions to the court are imported, as is shown by the ancient martyrologies, which know nothing of such a phase (cp. Achelis in Texte ti. Unters., xi. 2). It was the historical fact of Clement and Domitilla being relatives of Domitian which fired this train of fantasy, although, so far as we know, it did not start till the close of the second century. Thereafter relatives of the emperor are part of the regular stock-in-trade of the apocryphal rrck Â Peter and Paul (cp. also the Acta Barnabce auctore Marco, e. 23: 'lejsovir- (Tolos., (Tvyyeyrjs Nepcovos). Even Livia, Nero's consort, was reported to have been v"- a convert. It is just possible that several Roman Christians, mentioned in the oldest Acta Petri (Vercell.), were historical personalities. In chap. iii. we read: " Dionysius et Balbus ab Asia, equites Romani, splendidi viri, et senator nomine Demetrius adhaerens Paulo. item de demo Caesaris Cleobius et Ifitus et Lysimachus et Aristeus, et duae matronae Berenice et Filostrate cum presbytero Narcisso." And in chap. viii.: Marcellus senator. In the Acts of Paul, the oldest member of this class of literature (dating from the second century), a ttoau irkr dos ec ttjs Kaiaapos ohias is mentioned as having listened to the preaching of the apostle and been converted. The emperor's cup-bearer, Patroclus (see above) is specially mentioned; also 01 irpsitoi rod Heptavos, Barsabas Justus, 6 irxatvtrovs, Urion of Cappadocia, Festus of Galatia, the prefect Lagus, and the centurion Cestus.

Perhaps they had entertained him. But one must bear in mind that the town of Philippi was almost entirely Latin (or Roman), and that it would therefore be in intimate relations with the capital (cp. Acts xvi. 21).

- Many scholars separate this chapter from the rest of the epistle, and take it as a note to Ephesus. But the reasons for such a tour deforce do not appear to me convincing.

â vÂ-

Christians belonging to the household of Narcissus, and those belonging to that of Aristobulus (10-11). These Christians must therefore have been members of the households of two distinguished men who were not Christians themselves. Now, as we know that during the reign of Claudius no one in Rome was i') so powerful and so intimate with the emperor as a certain ' "" 'Â. Narcissus, and also that a certain Aristobulus (an uncle of, Herod the Great) was living then at the capital as a confidential–"S S friend of Claudius, it seems likely that these were the very two persons whose households are mentioned here by the apostle.

At the close of their epistle to Corinth (the so-called First Epistle of Clement), in 95-96 a. d., the Roman Christians explain how they entrusted the delivery of the epistle to two– seniors who had lived blameless lives among them from youth upwards. At the latest, then, these men must have become Christians by 50 a. d. They were called Claudius Ephebus and Valerius Bito, and Lightfoot rightly assumes that they were membei: s of the retinue of the emperor, as the wife of Claudius, (Messalina) belonged to the gens Valeria. Thus they would be f among the Christians who sent greetings in Paul's letter to the Philippians. V, j ' Narcissus died in 5455, and in my opinion Romans was written in 5354 T" T (though the majority of critics put it four or five years later). On Narcissus, the pu– freedman and private secretary of Claudius ("ab epistulis"), see Prosopo:, lj

"â P- 397 and Lightfoot's Philifipians (third ed.), p. 173: "As was usual in such ' " "-cases, his household would most probably pass into the hands of the emperor, still, however, retaining the name of Narcissus. One member of the household apparently is commemorated in an extant inscription: TI. CLAVDIO. SP. F. NARCISSIANO (Murat., p. 1150, 4)." See also Hirschfeld's remark in the Beitrdge zur alten Geschichte, ii. 2, p. 294: "The Trpsrepov tiapkiffffov ovcria which passed to the emperor (Wilcken's Osraca, i. 392 f.) is rightly referred to the private secretary of Claudius." Thus the Christians of Caesar's household mentioned in Philippians might be the members of the household of Narcissus mentioned iÂ Romans. Aristobulus was still alive (according to Josephus, Antiq., xx. i. 2) in 45 A. D. at any rate, but the year of his death has not been preserved. His domestic establishment also may have been transferred to the imperial household (see Lightfoot, loc. cit.). r

I pass over the alleged relations between Seneca and Paul and their forged yj Q vvft-c ' correspondence; nor does it prove anything for our present purpose to find that some members of ihsge7is Annsea subsequently became Christians (see vol. i. p. 1 426). There is no warrant for claiming Acte, one of Nero's favourite slaves, as a ("rtaj ' Christian, and it is a matter of really no moment if names (such as Onesimus, Stephanus, Phcebe, Crescens, Artemas) occur in this environment which also recur

T. Flavius Clemens and his wife Domitilla, who were closely related to Domitian, were certainly Christians, and it was as

Christians that they were punished in 95-96. Their sons, the presumptive heirs to the throne, were brought up by a Christian mother. The contemporary presbyter-bishop of Ronier i nrerrfc, is in all likelihood different from the consul of that name; nevertheless, he may have belonged to the royal household.

The murderer of Domitian, a member of Domitilla's household, need not have been instigated by the church, although he is said to have carried out his plot in order to revenge his mistress, Of his Christianity nothing whatever is known.

The traces in Hernias of Christians at court are dim.

Hadrian, that inquisitive searcher into all manner of novelties ("omnium curiositatum explorator"), may have busied himself, among other things, with judicial proceedings against Christians, but his letter to Servian is probably a forgery (Vopisc, Saturn. 8), and the statement that he wished to erect a temple to Christ is quite untrustworthy. His freedman Phlegon, who composed a chronicle of the world, perhaps with some assistance from his master, betrays indeed a superficial acquaintance with the life and miracles of Jesus, but he mixes up Christ and Peter (Orig., c. Cels., II. xiv.), in the New Testament. On the other hand, we may note, at this point, that the early (though, of course, entirely fictitious) Aca Paidi of the second century mention a queen Tryphsena in Asiatic Antioch, who shows motherly kindness to the Christian Thekla. She is described, and described correctly, as a relative of the emperor; for Tryphsena, the consort of King Polemon of Asia Minor (in the middle of the first century), was connected with the Emperor Claudius (v. Gutschmidt, Rhein. Museutn, 1864, pp. 176 f.).

- Dio Cassius, Ixvii. 14; Suet., Domit. 15; Eus., H. E., iii. 17; Bruttius, in Eus., H. E., iii. 18. 5. Domitilla's person, lineage, and place of exile are matters of dispute. Perhaps there were two Christian Domiiillas, both of whom were exiled (?). For her lineage, see C. I. L., vi. i. No. 948.

2 Suet., Domit., 15. 17; Dio Cassius, Ixvii. 15-17; Philostr., J ita Apoll, viii. 25.

On the other hand, Acilius Glabrio, whom Domitian punished, was perhaps a Christian (Suet, Domit. 10: " Complures senatores, in iis aliquot consulares, interemit, ex quibus Salvidienum Orfitum, Acilium Glabrionem in exiho quasi molitores no 'arum rerum "). There is a burial-niche of the Acilii in the catacombs, but the iionnection of this with Acilius Glabrio is uncertain.

Lamprid, Alex, 43: " Christo templum facere voluit eumque inter deos recipere. quod et Hadrianus cogitasse fertur, qui templa in omnibus civitatibus sine simulacris iusserat fieri which is possible, quae hodieque idcirco quia non

In the proceedings taken against Justin at Rome during the early years of M. Aurelius, one of his pupils is also implicated, Euelplstus by name. He describes himself as an imperial slave (Acta Justini, 4), so that Christianity had evidently not died out among the members of the imperial household. Perhaps the Palatine caricature of a crucifix (Mus. Kircher) also belongs to this period; but probably it is later (reign of Alex. Severus). It proves that Christians were still to be found among the royal pages.

Under Commodus we hear of Carpophorus, a Christian " of the emperor's household,"'"' whose slave rose to be bishop Callistus (Hippol., Philos. ix, 12). And Irenaeus writes (iv. 30. 1) as follows: " Quid autem et hi qui in regali aula sunt fideles, nonne ex eis quae Caesaris sunt habent utensilia et his qui non habent unusquisque eorum secundum suam virtutem praestat?"" (" And what of those who in the royal palace are believers? Do they not get the utensils they use from the emperor"'s property? And does not each one contribute, according to his ability, to those who have no such utensils?"'"'). Which proves that there was quite a group of Christians at court, and that their circumstances were good. For a number of years, too, the royal concubine Mama (ovcra (pixooeog Trawakrj Kojuosov) was habent numina dicuntur Hadriani, quia ille ad hoc parasse dicebatur" ("He wished to erect a temple to Christ and to enrol him among the godsâ a project which Hadrian also is said to have entertained. For that emperor had ordered temples without images to be erected in every city, and these are to this day called ' Hadrian's," since they have no idols, and since they are said to have been raised by him for this purpose "). What follows may apply to Alexander rather than to Hadrian. The legend may have arisen, not earlier than the third century, in order to explain the Hadrianic temple nullius dei.

' Wiinsch Se Amm'sche Verfluchungstafeln ans Rom., 1898, pp. 112 f.) refuses to regard this as a caricature; he holds it is a sacred symbol of the Sethian gnosis. But this is very doubtful. Our knowledge of the Sethians during the second and third centuries is far too limited to justify us in making such a deduction. The ass's head may refer to the Typhon Seth. But what of the crucifixion?

This Carpophorus is probably the Carpophorus who erected a monument or tomb at Rome to himself, his household (brother, nephews, foster-son Seleucus their freedmen and freedmen's offspring), and his male and female freed slaves with their offspring (cp. C. I. L., vi. 13040). The date agrees, and no trace of paganism occurs in the inscription. Besides, as O. Hirschfeld kindly points out to me, the generosity which embraces so many persons on a monument is unusual in one who is not a Christian.

the most influential person at court during this period; as Hippolytus relates, the Roman bishop Victor had free access to her presence, while it was through her mediation that he secured the release of Christians who were languishing in the mines of Sardinia.

As for the age of Septimius Severus, Tertullian Apol. xxxvii.) testifies to the presence of Christians in the royal palace; and in ad Scapiilam, iv., he writes as follows: " Even Severus himself, the father of Antoninus, was mindful of the Christians. For he sought out Proculus the Christian, surnamed Torpacion, the agent of Euhodia, who had once cured him by means of oil, keeping him in the palace to the day of his death And both uien and women of the highest rank, whom Severus knew to be members of this sect, were not merely exempted by him from injury, but also had open testimony borne them by himself, and were publicly restored to us out of the hands of a raging mob" (" Ipse etiam Severus, pater Antonini, Christianorum memor fuit; nam et Proculum Christianum, qui Torpacion cognominabatur, Euhodiae procuratorem, qui eum per oleum aliquando curaverat, requisivit et in palatio suo habuit usque ad mortem eius. sed et clarissimas feminas et clarissimos viros Severus, sciens huius sectae esse, non modo non laesit, verum et testimonio exornavit et populo furenti in nos palam restitit "'"). His son, Caracalla, also was on intimate terms with this Christian (" optime noverat"), and Tertullian proceeds to describe him as having had a Christian wet-nurse ("lacte Christiano educatus"). Under him died the Christian high chamberlain Prosenes in 217 a. d.; for de Rossi is probably right in concluding from the inscription set up for him by his slaves Inscr. Christ, i. No. 5, p. 9) that he died a

For Marcia, see Neumann, o. cL, pp. 84 f. Iler friendliness to Christians is attested also by Dio Cassus, Ixxii. 4. 6 dpecpas ttjs Mapkias was a Christian presbyter called Ilyacinthus, according to Hippolytus. He negotiated between the royal lady and the Roman church, so that he probably lived at court.

â We know nothing of this lady. Tertullian speaks of her as a familiar figure, but the text is uncertain.

2 Tertullian de Corona, xii.) seems to suggest that there were also Christians in the imperial bodyguard.

The Acta Charalampi (Bolland., loth Feb., pp. 382 f.) mention a daughter of Severus who was a Christian.

Christian. During the third century the court officials became more powerful than everâ although even in the first century individual freedmen of the imperial house had come to exercise a commanding influence in the management of the state. Originally the court appointments and the offices of state were sharply distinguished. While the latter could not be held save by freemen of knightly or senatorial rank, the former were filled up with imperial freedmen and slaves. But gradually the knights invaded the imperial household, while, on the other hand, freedmen and slaves were ennobled and admitted to the higher branches of the civil service. It was still customary, however, for imperial freedmen or the " Caesariani" to hold the court appointments (in which a graduated hierarchy of offices also obtained), and frequently they became the most influential persons in the state. Thus even a Christian, if he possessed the confidence of the emperor, could become a man of importance in the empire.

Some of thesyrian royal ladies were favourably disposed to Christianity. Julia Mammaea, we are told, summoned OrigÂ rlâ to Antioch, and Hippolytus dedicated a volume to her. i f l J ' ' Orosius, therefore, dubs her a Christian (vii. 18). The court of her son, the emperor Alexander, was composed of many Christians, and he himself was so favourable to them that he was celebrated by the Christians not long after his death as one who had been secretly a fellow-believer. His sayings prove that this "Syrian chief of the synagogue"" (Lamprid., Alex. 28) 1 As the Christianity of Prosenes simply is an inference from the words " receptus ad deum " and from the lack of any pagan phrases, it is not ce rtain. Besides, Prosenes himself did not use these words.

2 For details, see Hirschfeld's Die Kaiseruchett Verwaltungsbeaniten bis auf Diocletian (2nd ed., 1905), especially pp. 471 f., on the " Caesariani." The later group of " Ccesariani" (or " Catholiciani") is to be distinguished from the "Csesariani" in general. The former had to look after the seizure of confiscated goods. They are referred to in Valerian's decree against Christians.

Eus., H. E., vi. 21. On Hippolytus and Mammsea, see my History of Christian Literature, i. pp. 605 f. We do not know who the Severina is, mentioned on the statue of Hippolytus; some have wrongly thought of Aquilia Severa, the consort of Elagabalus.

â Eus., H. R., vi. 28: irpbs rbj 'AA6 at'5poiÂ oikov sk iraâ i6vav Tricrtwv avveatuira. Hence Orosius (vii. 29) speaks of a " familia Christiana Alex."

really busied himself with the Christian religion. The Christian author Julius Africanus was a friend of his.

The state of matters remained the same under Phjup-the Arabian, who also was claimed ere long as a secret Christian (Eus., H. E. vi. 34). Origen wrote to him and to his consort Severa (Eus., H. E., vi. 36). And Cyprian, looking back on this period, writes angrily that "the majority of the bishops, scorning the stewardship of God, became stewards of earthly monarchs" (" episcopi plurimi divina procuratione contempta procuratores regum saecularium facti sunt," de Lapsk, vi.). So that it was not merely the laity, but the very bishops as well, who pressed forward into the most influential and lucrative appointments at the royal court!

Like Maximinus Thrax, both Decius and Valerian after him purged the court of Christians. At the opening of Valerian's reign their number had again increased. " For the emperor was A friendly and favourable to the servants of God; none of the previous emperors, none even of those who were said to be Christians, ever behaved with such kindness and favour to them as did Valerian. He treated them with quite undisguised friend- liness and goodwill at the commencement of his reign; his xvhole

' We knew already thai Julius Africanus had dedicated his Kecrroi to the emperor, but now Grenfell and Hunt Oxyrhynckus Papyri, vol. iii., 1903, pp. 36 f.) have discovered the conclusion of the eighteenth book of the Keo-rot on a papjrus which seems to have been written between 225 and 265. We read here that "(thou wilt find these Homeric verses) iv 'Pwf. y irphs Ta7s 'AXe avspov depfxais

Africanus was also a friend of Abgar, king of Edessa, but he and his court had been avowedly Christian since the beginning of the third century (cp. the local Christian thinker and poet, Bardesanes).

- Naturally, there was a constant interchange between royal officials in the capital and throughout the imperial possessions in the provinces. â For the landed property of the emperors during the first three centuries, see Hirschfeld's study in the Beitrcige z. alien Gesckkhe, Bd. 2, H. I, pp. 45 f., H. 2, pp. 284 f. "The imperial property in the provinces was far more valuable than it was in Italy. Egypt deserves mention primarily in this connection, since Augustus had taken it over in his capacity of assignee of the Egyptian kings But of all the provinces of the empire (p. 295), none had so enormous an imperial property to show as Africa."

3 In the Martyrdom of St Cotton (under Decius) it is stated that he was a gardener in the royal garden at Magydus in Pamphylia (cp. von Gebhardt's Acta Mart. Selecta, p. 130).

court was full of pious people; it ivas a veritable church of God" (Dionys. Alex, in Eus., H. E. vii. 10). But this did not continue. And in the second rescript of 258 a. d. against the Christians, the following allusion to the " Caesariani"" occurs: " Caesariani quicumque vel prius confessi fuerant vel nunc confessi fuerint confiscentur et vincti in Caesarianas possessiones descripti mittantur " (Cypr., Ep. Ixxx.; sec above, p. 49).

The persecution, however, did not last. Under his son Gallienus, the Christians already made their way back into the court, and now increased at such a rate that under Diocletian (whose wife and daughter were Christians) the court at Niconiedia consisted largely of Christians. The early rescripts of Diocletian were specially designed to purge the court of them. Eusebius also states that there were Christians at the court of Constantius Chlorus Vita Const., i. 16), and the same holds true of the court of Licinius."

This sketch, which makes no pretension to be complete, may serve to indicate how Christians made their way into the court

It is pure fantasy to assert, as has been quite recently done, that his consort Cornelia Salonina was a Christian; all we know is that she was a friend of Plotinus, as Porphyry relates (Ufa Plotin. 12). No satisfactory explanation has been offered, however, of the legend on several of her coins, "Augusta in pace" (Schiller's Gesch. d. Rom. Kaiserzeit, i. 2, p. 908).

'â We hear, for example, of Dorotheus, the presbyter of Antioch, being appointed to superintend the imperial dye-works at Tyre (Eus., H. E., vii. 32). Incidentally, Eusebius remarks (vii, 16) that Astyrius, a Christian of senatorial rank, "was very highly esteemed by the emperors." He gives an instance of his great candour.â The position of Paul of Samosata, bishop of Antioch, under Zenobia is well known. He filled a high office of state. Was Zenobia a Jewess?

â Perhaps P lavia Maximiana Theodora, the second consort of Constantius Chlorus, was also a Christian. She was Maximian's step-daughter; cp. v. Schultze in Protest, Real-Encykl, x. pp. 758 f. One of their daughters was called Anastasia, and the cross appears on one of her coins (after 328) alongside of her likeness. We are no longer able to ascertain how near Constantius Chlorus drew to Christianity.

â Eus., H. E., viii. 11. Compare the parallel passage in Lactantius, de Morte Persec. 15; also the stories of the courtiers Dorotheus and Gorgonius (Eus., viii. 6) and the pagan Petrus. We may accept the death of the two martyred courtiers Sergius and Bacchus as historical, though their Acta are unauthentic.

The epistle of Theonas, which tells of a Christian librarian of Diocletian, is a forgery; cp. my study in Texte u. Unters., xxiv. 2.

" See Jerome's Chron. ad ann. 2337: " Licinius Christianos de palatio suo p ellit " (" Licinius expels the Christians from his palace ').

at an early period, and how they became a factor which was occasionally quite important.

Â 3. The spread of Christianity in the army The position of a soldier would seem to be still more incompatible with Christianity than the higher offices of state, for Christianity prohibited on principle both war and bloodshed. Yet officers under certain circumstances were responsible for the death-penalty, like the higher state officials, while the rank and file, even apart from manslaughter in battle, had to do all they were told. Furthermore, the unqualified military oath conflicted with the unqualified duty of a Christian to God. Then again, the imperial cultus came specially to the front in the army; it was almost unavoidable for each individual soldier. The officers had to sacrifice, and the soldiers had to take part. The regimental colours also seemed like pagan " sacra," so that veneration for them was a sort of idolatry. Even military distinctions (like crowns, etc.) appeared to strict Christians to be tainted with idolatry. And, finally, the conduct of soldiers during peace (their extortion, their license, their police duties) was as opposed to Christian ethics as their wild debauchery and sports e. g. " the Mimus") at the pagan festivals. Christianity therefore, never became a 7'eligion of the camp, and all representations of Christianity which make out as if it had diffused itself H specially by means of soldiers are to be set aside (see vol i. pp. t 308, 368). Upon the other hand, there were Christian soldiers from a very early period, perhaps from the very first, though the " military " problem did not become acute for Christians till about the reign of Marcus Aurelius or Commodus. It is easy to understand why this was so. Down to that period Christian soldiers were still few and far between. Christianity had won them when they were soldiers already. The rule held good, "Let every one remain in the calling wherein he was called." Other callings had also special dangers of their own. Besides, the end was coming soon. Later on, however, Christianity

Cp. my study, Militia Christi in den ersteii drei Jahrhiinderten (1905), Bigelmair's Die Beteiligung der Christen am '6 ffentlichen Leben in zwconstant. Zeit (1902, pp. 164 f.), de Jong's Dietistweigerimg bij de oiide Christenen (Leyden, 1905), and Guignebert's Terttdlian, tude sur ses sentiments d P gard de rempire et de la sociit civile (Paris, 1901, pp. 189 f.).

permeated the army more thoroughly, especially in the East (perhaps in Africa also). Even Christians took service freely or compulsorily, and the idea of a speedy annihilation of all things faded away. The " military " problem now emerged: Can a Christian become or remain a soldier? And if so, how is he to conduct himself in the army? The strict party of believers tried to demonstrate that the Christian religion and the military calling were inconsistent, claiming that Christian soldiers ought to leave the service or else suffer martyrdom. They exulted over every case in which a soldier, under the impulse of his Christian conscience, deliberately committed a breach of military discipline and was marched off' to prison for his offence. Yet such cases were rare. One or two resignations certainly did take place, as well as acts of blunt insubordination; but Christian soldiers considered that it was quite permissible for them to observe the regulations and ceremonies current in the service, while the church, relying on Luke iii. 14, and on the centurions of Capernaum and Caesarea (cp. also the centurion at the foot of the cross), shut one eye to such matters from the very first. In fact, by the opening of the third century, the large body of Christians took it amiss if any soldier endangered his fellow-soldiers (or, under certain circumstances, the whole of the local church) by any outburst of Christian fanaticism. As for the rigorous party, they hardly made anything of their prohibitions. Why, in the prayers of the church the army was regularly mentioned next to the emperor!

A good deal in Christianity would appeal to soldiers: the rule of the one God, His mighty acts of warfare as told by the Old Testament, the case with which the religion could be transported from place to place, since it needed neither temple nor images, the close bond which knit the adherents, etc.

' Of course, it was something to have the power of Christ displayed in the devil's camp!

Cp. T rt, Apol. XXX.; Cyprian, ad Demetr. xx.; Arnob., iv. 36; and the Acta Sebastiani. The bearing of the church's prayers upon this question need not be exaggerated, however, since prayer was offered even for one's enemies, and since one could have very different ideas about the " salus Romani exercitus" and the army itself. Besides, the prayer for the army formed part of the " vota pro Csesare." The emperor, even from the apocalyptic standpoint, had a certain divine right of existence as a bulwark against anarchy and the barbarian hordes; for the "pax terrena" was a relative good, even from the strictest Christian standpoint, as being bound up with the desired "mora finis" (in the sense of 54 MISSION AND EXPANSION OF CHRISTIANITY

And yet, even though he managed to come to some terms about the necessary regulations, the Christian soldier occupied a more perilous position than the ordinary Christian. At any moment his connection with the forbidden sect might occasion summary proceedings against him; besides, he might be expected to perform actions which even the laxer Christian conscience forbade. Martyrs in the army therefore appear to have been relatively more numerous than among civilians; at any rate,

I A-j they are to be met with even during periods which have no r record of any other martyrs. The number of Christian officers fjyj and soldiers in the army gradually increased, however, after the)i reign of Gallienus; so much so that the military autiioritie began to connive at Christianity; they made allowance for it, and 4js looked on quietly while Christian officers made the sign of the cross at the sacrifices. Moreover, they often dispensed silently with their attendance at these sacrifices. It was only in the case of a triumph that strict measures were taken. The emperor . Galerius, who was a pagan fanatic, would not tolerate this position of affairs any longer. Incited by the priests, he tried to check the clandestine process by means of which the army was being Christianized and the gods more and more affronted.

Â He made Diocletian agree to introduce repressive measures.

r. The great persecution which ensued was directed primarily V v against- Christian soldiers, and Licinius followed it up by a "" special edict against them. Conversely, the public toleration and preferential treatment of the Christian religion began with the affixing of the cross to the colours of the regiments (by Con- stantine during his expedition against Maxentius).

Such is, in brief, the scope covered by the theme "the punitive judgment). Now the emperor needed soldiers to maintain this "pax terrena." They were part and parcel of the "sword" which (Rom. xiii. 4) is recognized as a divine attribute of authority, and which no church-father ever dared to deny, in so many words, to the emperor. â. 1 Cp. below on Eus., vii. 15, and, on the other hand, Lact., de Mori. x. The iijJfix church also abstained from making the soldier question acute by means of vj casuistry or decisions on the principle involved. At the great Spanish Council of Elvira, held shortly before the outburst of the Diocletian persecution, an eloquent silence prevailed on this question, though the council otherwise laid down rules for the relation of the church to the state, the community, and society in general.

Christian and the soldier" during the pre-Constantine period. A concise collection of the most important items now falls to be subjoined.

In 2 Tim, ii. 3 f. and Clem. Rom. jcxxvii., the career or organization of the military profession is quite frankly adduced as a pattern for Chiustians.-â The oldest evidence for Christians, and indeed for a fairly large number of Christians, in a legion is furnished by the contemporary accounts of the inira cle o f the rain under M. Aurelius (Apollinaris and Tertullian in Eus., H. E., V. 5). The legion in question was that of Melitene (the 12th), and it is not surprising that of all legions it should contain a considerable percentage of Christians, since it was recruited from districts where Christians were particularly numerous. Neither then nor subsequently did any Christian censure these soldiers for their profession. Indeed, Clement of Alexandria plainly assumes that the military vocation is consistent with the confession of the Christian faith. Tertullian was the sternest of the strict party who held that the army and Christianity were irreconcilable; yet not merely does he testify to the presence of Christians in the army during his own day, but he was enough of a politician at the same time to lay a satisfied stress upon this very fact before civil governors. Did it not refute the accusation that Christians were idle anchorites and ' On the church's use of figures and descriptions drawn from the military calling, see vol. i. pp. 414 f. The possibility of the language of the camp having influenced the ecclesiastical dialect in Africa must be left an open question.

- Among the charges brought by Eusebius against Maximinus Daza H. E., viii. 14. 11) is that of having rendered the army effeminate. Eusebius's feelings thus are those of a loyal citizen of the empire.

Even at a later period the legion still had Christians in its ranks; cp. Eus., H. E., v. 5. I, and Gregory of Nyssa's Oral. II. in XL. Alartyras (opp. Paris, 1638, t. iii. p. 505 f.). The forty martyrs (see below) also belonged to this legion. See my essay on this miracle of the rain in the Sitzimgsber. d. k Pr. Akad. d. IFiss., 1894, pp. 835 f.

â Prolrept. x. 100: (rtpa, Ti ji)jxiviv ire Ka, Tâ i ri(pev tj yvsicns, toc S'lkaia arnj-ai-vovtos Kove (TTpatriyov ("Has knowledge come upon you in military service? then listen to that Commander who gives righteous orders"), which does not, of course, mean that one must give up the army. Cp. Paed. ii. ii. 117, ii. 12. I2r, iii. 12, 91.

Tatian's Orat, xi.) phrase, â t) v fftparriyiat' TrapptT ai ("I renounce the office") refers to the prsetorship, but he, too, was undoubtedly opposed to the military calling.

gymnosophists? Nevertheless, the incompatibility of the higher positions in the army with the Christian vocation was settled for Tertullian by one consideration, viz., that such officers had to perform j udicial duties amongst others; w hile surely the private soldier, he argues, cannot be a Christian, since a man cannot be in two camps at the same timeâ in that of Christ and in that of the devilâ nor can a man serve two masters by the " sacramentum," or oath of loyalty. Furthermore, in disarming Peter, Christ stripped every Christian of his sword, and this renders every appeal to the soldiers who came to John or to the centurion at Capernaum quite untenable (de Idolol. xix.). The soldier who (in 211 a. d.) refused a military crown and was executed for his refusal, was hailed with triumph by Tertullian. He devoted a special treatise to this caseâ which plainly proves that the case was quite unique, and that other Christians in the army accepted the military crown without any hesitation. Qr igen, too, was one of the stricter party. When Celsus

Apol. yixxy.: " Vestra omnia implevimus. castraipsa," xlvii.: " Non sumus Brachmanae aut Indorum gymnosophistae. mililamus vobiscum " cp. vol. i. p. 270. For Christians in the arm t Lambesej see ad Scap. iv. Here, however, he is concealing his own opinions (just as in the Apologia, where he simply says that Christians pray "pro mora finis'"'; he is also concealing that fervid longing for the advent of Christ's kingdom which finds expression in his exposition of the words, "Thy kingdom come"). His private views on the army are given in de Idolol, xix. and de Co7-otia Militis (cp. also de Pallio, v.: non milito).

Probably this soldier, who would not break any other military rules, really wanted to secure for Christians in the army the same consideration as was shown to adherents of Mithra; cp. my Militia Christi, p. 68.

This is brought out with still greater clearness in that view of the subject which was current in Christian circles (ch. i.). " Abruptus, praeceps, mori cuiiidus," such a soldier was dubbed ("headstrong, rash, and eager for death"). " Mussi-tant denique tam bonam et longam sibi pacem periclitari. ubi prohibemur coronari?" ("They murmur at their prolonged and happy peace being endangered Where, they ask, are we forbidden to get crowned?"). In ch. xi. Tertullian expounds still more sharply than in the treatise de Idololatria, the incompatibility of Christianity and the military calling. Here, too, he discusses the question, What is a soldier to do who is converted when a soldier? At one moment it seems as if he might remain a soldier (Luke iii. 14; Matt. viii. 10; Acts x. I f.). There is always the possibility that one might take all precautions against committing any irreligious action as a soldier. But Tertullian recommends only two ways out of the difficulty: either resigning one's post ("ut a multis actum " =as has been done by many) or suffering martyrdom.

demands that Christians ought to aid the emperor by entering the army, Origen answers by pointing out that they do so by their prayers; martial service is no more to be expected from them than from priests."- " We do not accompany the emperor to battle, not even when we are required to do so. But we do battle on his behalf, since we form an army of our own, an army of piety, by our prayers to God." Finally, Lactantius was another rigorist (Listit., vi. 20. 16): "â Militare iusto non licebit, cuius militia est ipsa justitia, neque vero accusare quemquam crimine capitali, quia nihil distat utrumne ferro an verbo potius occidas, quoniam occisio ipsa prohibetur " (" It shall not be lawful for the righteous man to engage in warfare. His true warfare is righteousness itself. Nor will he be right in accusing anyone on a capital charge, since there is no difference between killing a person by word or by the sword. Killing itself is prohibited""").

But these rigorists effected no change whatever in the actual situation. There were Christians in the Melitene lesion and at Lambese, and Christians were to be found in other legions also. It turned out that the soldier who led Potamiaena to martyrdom in Alexandria (2023 a. d.) was attached to the Christian faith, though he had not yet received baptism. A similar instance occurred once more in Alexandria under Decius (cp. Dionys. Alex, in Eus., H. E., l 41. 16); but still more significant is the account given by Dionysius of the Decian

It is quite obvious from this that Christians were charged with a disinclination to serve in the army, and the charge was undoubtedly well founded. In actual life, however, collisions of this kind were rare, for there can hardly have been many cases of Christians being impressed against their will. See Mommsen's J? om. Staatsrecht, ii, 2' ', pp. 849 f.; and in Hennes, xix. (1883), pp. 3 f.; also Neumann, op. cit., i. pp. 127 f.

c. Cels., VIII. Ixxiii. For Christians as "priests of peace " (sacerdotes pacis), see also Tert., de Sped. xvi.

The story of his martyrdom corresponds to that of the soldier in the treatise de Corona, For some reason or another, Basilides (such was his name) was challenged by a fellow-soldier to take an oath, which, as a Christian, he refused to do. His refusal was at first construed as a jest. But when he persisted in it, proceedings were instituted against him (Eus., H. E,, vi. 5).

A somewhat similar incident is already told by Eusebius (vi. 41. 16) in connection with the death of the apostle James, It is taken from Clement of Alexandria.

persecution in the Egyptian capital, where the whole of a small commando (Tvvrayij. a a-rparicotikov), which had been mustered for the trial of some Christians, turned out to be composed either of Christians or of their friends. " And when one who was being tried as a Christian inclined to deny his faith, they gnashed their teeth, made signs to him, held out their hands, and made gestures with all their limbs. Whereupon the attention of everybody was directed to them, but, before they could be seized by anyone, they rushed to the dock and avowed that they were Christians" (Eus., H. E., vi. 41. 22 f). As there had not been any intention, of course, of specially selecting Christian soldiers for this judicial duty, the incident shows how widely Christianity had spread throughout the army in Egypt. When the Diocletian persecution had passed, and when the question arose of subjecting the " lapsi" to a penitential discipline, the soldiers who had offered sacrifice were mentioned in Egypt as a special class by themselves (Epiph., Har., Ixviii. 2).

The account given by Eusebius (vii. 15) of an officer called Marinus, who was stationed at Caesarea in Cappadocia, is most instructive. He distinctly states that at this time (during the reign of Gallienus) the Christians were enjoying peace. Marinus was to be promoted to fill a vacant position as centurion. But another person stepped forward and declared that Marinus was a Christian, and therefore could not, " according to ancient law," hold any Roman office, since he did not sacrifice to the emperors. A trial ensued, and the judge gave Marinus, who had avowed his Christianity, some time to consider his position. On leaving the tribunal, he was taken by the bishop into church. Then, holding out the volume of the gospels and at the same time pointing to his sword, the bishop bade him decide which he meant to choose. The officer grasped the gospels. On reappearing before the judge, he adhered steadfastly to his faith, and was executed. The story shows that among officers in the army the profession of Christianity was not tolerated, and it would even seem as though express regulations

Compare also the other statement of Dionysius (vii. ii. 20), to the effect that soldiers were included among the victims of Valerian's persecution in Egypt.

on the subject were in existence. But it shows also that in practice Christianity was connived at. The authorities always waited for some occasion of conflict to arise.

"The first objects of the persecution were believers in the army,"' says Eusebius (H. E., viii. 1. 7), as he opens the story of the Diocletian persecution. Lactantius agrees with him: " Datis ad praepositos litteris etiam milites court officials having been previously mentioned cogi ad nefanda sacrificia praecepit, ut qui non paruissent, militia solverentur. hactenus furor eius et ira processit nee amplius quicquam contra legem aut religionem dei fecit ' de Mort. x.: " By instructions issued to the officers, he also had soldiers forced to offer accursed sacrifices, so that those who disobeyed were discharged from the army. Thus far did his fury and anger go. Nor did he do anything further against the laws and religion of God"). Hitherto, Christian officers had been tacitly, though not legally, tolerated. The formal exemption from the duty of sacrificing which had been accorded to Christian officials by Diocletian (cp. above, p. 40) hardly applied, of course, to officers. Still, they were exempted tacitly in many cases, it may be. Besides,

Cp. viii, 4 â irxfictTovs Tvaprjv rsiv iv arpatiiais Spay aafxevecrrara rhv ISiuitLKhi Trpoa(nra ofj. evovs iov, ws av fxrj apuoi y voivro tyjs irepl rhv tuv oxwv St ixiovpyhu ivaeffiias ' iis yap 6 (7Tpatoirisdpxr s, '6(Ttls irore i v ike7vos cp. Jerome's CIuov. ad ann. 2317: " Veturius niagister militiae Ciiristianos milites persequitur, paulatim ex illo iam tempore persecutione adversus nos incipiente " = Veturius, the military chief, persecutes Christian soldiers, and the persecution now gradually begins to be directed against us, apri irputov 6Vf; 6ipâ t tc Kara twv atpanvfiartov Stonyjji.(p, (pvkokpivwv Kol StuKadaipccv tovs ev to7s (rrpatOTresois ava(pepofj. ii'ovs, alpeaiv Tt Sisois ireioapxovffiv its fierriv avtois airoxaveiy rifmris â?) rovvavtiov (TTepearoai ravtr s, el avmartOivto tw â Kpoffrd. yp. ati, â KKtlffroi 'dcroi ttjs Xpiatov aat t'tas (TTpatisitat. rrjv eis avrhv 6J. o oyiay, j-t xiwriaai'Tes, rrjs Sokovcrris 5(7js Kal (virpayias, tjs dxov, avafx(pi 6yÂ s â Kpovrinriaai' ("Many soldiers were to be met with who cheerfully accepted the private life of civilians that they might not deny the reverent piety due to the creator of the universe. For when the general, whoever he was, started his persecution of the soldiers, separating them into tribes and purging those enlisted in the army, he gave them a choice: either they were to obey and thus reap the honour which was their due, or else to lose that meed of honour if they disobeyed orders. Whereupon a vast number of soldiers belonging to the kingdom of Christ unhesitatingly made up their minds at once to prefer his confession to the seeming glory and good fortune which they were enjoying"). Presently executions commenced, which had not originally been contemplated. In Mari, Fa., xi. 20, Eusebius incidentally mentions one confessor from the army.

they knew of one expedient at any rate. When the sacrifice began they made the sign of the cross, and thereby safeguarded themselves and their position. This, however, gave a handle to the priests, especially when the sacrifices proved unfavourable; and also to Galerius, with his zeal for strictness. The offence was no longer to be tolerated. Hence it vvas, according to Lactantius, that the persecution arose; and his account bears all the marks of internal probability. The court and the army, the two pillars of the throne, were to be purged of Christians. This determination shows how numerous Christians were in the army, and consequently the dismissal or the martyrdom of soldiers was particularly common during this persecution, while many soldiers of course came also to deny their faith and often to sacrifice. In Melitene and Syria the army was driven to partial rebellion, and it appears that Diocletian scented the plotting of Christians at the back of this (Eus., H. E. viii. 6. 8).

Eusebius also relates how Licinius specially purged the army of Christians during his final efforts to hold out against Con-stantine (H. E., x. 8, Vita Const., i. 54). It was then that the forty soldiers of Sebaste were martyredâ one further witness to the existence of many Christians in the ranks of the 12th Thundering (" fulminata ") legion.

Soldiers play an important role in the Acts of the martyrs. Some instances of this have already been noted, and it would lead us too far afield to state the evidence completely, especially as forgeries were extremely plentiful in this province of literary effort. Reference need only be made to Getulus,

Cp. Acta S. Maximiliani (Ruinart's Acta Martyr., Ratisbon, 1859, p. 341): " Dixit Dion proconsul: in sacro comitatu dominorum nostrorum Diocleliani et Maximiani, Constantii et Maximi milites Christiani sunt et militant,"

- Those aimed at, in the first instance, were the Kara. Tr6 ty (XTparisirai (the soldiers in the cities), i. e., the police-officers and guardians of the peace, whose importance, like that of the court officials, became steadily superior with every decade to that of the civil service.

No passage in this Testament indicates that it was written by, or that it originated with, soldiers (cp. Bonwetsch, Neue kirchl. Zeitschrift, iii. 12, pp. 705 f.; Haussleiter, ibid., pp. 978 f.; Bonwetsch, Stiidien z. Gesck. d. Theol. n. Kircke, i. pp. 75 f.; and von Gebhardt's Acta Mart. Selecta, 1902, pp. 166 f.). The record of the martyrdom, which must be used with care and caution, is printed on pp. 171 f. of von Gebhardt's volume.

ON THE INWARD SPREAD OF CHRISTIANITY 61 the husband of Symphorosa, and his brother Amantius, to the famous "passio" of Mauricius and the Thebaic legion, etc. Nereus and Achilles (cp. Achelis, in Texte u. Unters., xi. 2. 44), Polyeuctes,- Maximilianus, Marcellus, Julius the

Repeated efforts have been made to save some part of the legendary material; cp. Bigelmair, op. cit., pp. 194 f., as against Hanck's Kirchengesch. Deutschlandi, Pi, p. 9, note I; p. 25, note i. One or two martyrdoms of soldiers may underlie the legend (cp. Linsenmayer's Die Bekdnipfung des Christentums ditich d. rom. Staat, 1905, pp. 181 f.), but even this is doubtful.

"Of the Meljtene Jegmn; eg. Conybeare's Apol. and Acts of Apouonius (1S94), pp. 123 f. V– â– â â â â â ' f : ' â â â"

Cp. Ruinart, op. cit., pp. 340 f. ("Thevesti in foro" = Before the court at Theveste). " Fabius Victor temonarius est constitutus cum Valeriano Quintiano praeposito Caesariensi cum bono tirone Maximiliano filio Victoris; quoniam probabilis est, rogo ut incumetur Maximilianus respondit: Quid autem vis scire nomen meum? mihi non licet militare, quia Christianus sum. Dion proconsul dixit: apta ilium, cumque aptaretur, Maximilianus respondit: non possum militare, non possum maleficere, Christianus sum. Dion proconsul dixit: Incumetur. cumque incumatus fuisset, ex officio recitatum est: Habet pedes quinque quinos?, uncias decern so that he was able-bodied. Dion dixit ad officium: signetur. cumque resisteret Maximilianus, respondit: Non facio; non possum militare" ("Fabius Victor, collector of the military exemption tax, was brought up with Valerianus Quintianus, prefect of Csesarea, and with Maximilianus the son of Victor, a good recruit. ' As he is a likely man, I ask that he be measured.". M. answered, 'But why do you want to know my name? I dare not fight, since I am a Christian." ' Measure him," said Dion the proconsul; but on being measured, M. answered, ' I cannot fight, I cannot do evil; I am a Christian." Said the proconsul, ' Let him be measured." And after he had been measured, the attendant read out: he is five feet ten. Then said Dion to the attendant, 'Enrol him." And M. cried out, 'No, no, I cannot be a soldier'"). See also what follows. " Milito deo meo; non accipio signaculum; iam habeo signum Christi dei mei si signaveris, rumpo illud, quia nihil valet non licet mihi plumbum collo portare post signum salutare domini mei" ("I am a soldier of my God. I refuse the badge. Already I have Christ's badge, who is my

God. If you mark me, I shall annul it as invalid I cannot wear aught leaden on my neck after the saving mark of my Lord '"). To the proconsul's question as to what crime soldiers practised, Maximilianus replied, "You know quite well what they do" (" Tu enim scis quae faciunt ").â Here we have a scene of forcible conscription.

â Cp. Ruinart, pp. 343 f. ("in civitate Tingitana"). On the emperor's birthday, when everybody was feasting and sacrificing, "Marcellus quidam ex centuri- onibus legionis Traianae reiecto cingulo militari coram signis legionis, quae tunc aderant, clara voce testatus est, diceus: Jesu Christo regi aeterno milito. abjecit quoque vitem et arma et addidit: ex hoc militare imperatoribus vestris desisto et deos vestros ligneos et lapideos adorare contemno. si talis est condicio militantium, ut diis et imperatribus sacra facere compellantur, ecce proicio vitem et cingulum, renuntio signis, et militare recuso " ("A certain Marcellus, belonging to the centurions of the Trajan legion, threw aside the military belt in veteran, Typasius the veteran, Theodorus (Ruinart, pp. 506 f.: of Amasia in Pontus), Tarachus, Marcianiis and Nicander," Dasius, front of the regimental standards, and testified in clear tones that he was a soldier of Jesus Christ, the King Eternal. He also threw away the centurion's staff and arms, adding, ' Henceforth I cease to be a soldier of your emperors. I scorn to worship your gods of wood and stone. If it be a condition of military service to be obliged to do sacrifice to your gods and emperors, then hereby I throw off my staff and arms. I give up the colours, I refuse to be a soldier'"). When on trial, he added that it was unbecoming for a Christian, who served his captain Christ, to serve in secular engagements ("non decebat Christianum hominem molestiis secularibus militare, qui Christo domino militat ").

1 Cp. Analed. Bollatid., x. (1891), pp. 50 f. Militia Christi, pp. 119 f.): " Maximo praeside Dorostori Moesiae. non possum praecepta divina contemnere et infidelis apparere deo meo. etenim in vana militia quando videbar errare, in annis xxvii nunquam scelestus aut litigiosus oblatus sum judici. septies in bello egressus sum, et post neminem retro steti nee alicuius inferior pugnavi. princeps me non vidit aliquando errare " ("I cannot set at naught the commands of God, and appear disloyal to my God. For even during all the twenty-seven years of my vanity and military service, I was never shown to the judge as a scoundrel or quarrelsome fellow. Seven times I took the field, and never yielded place to anyone, nor fought less bravely than anyone else. My captain never saw me going wrong").

Cp. Analect. Boiland., ix. (1890), pp. Ii6f.: Tigabis in Mauretania, The Acts are of doubtful authenticity.

Cp. Ruinart, pp. 451 f. (The Acts are late and poor.) When the judge asked what was his position, he replied: crrpatLOitikris â â â â dia Se rh Xpiatiavsi- it e flvai v)v ircfyaviveiv yperrjadxriv ("That of a soldier But as I am a Christian, I now choose to wear ordinary dress "). To the further question, how he had ever gained his freedom, Tarachus replied: "I besought Fulvian the taxiarch, and he dismissed me " ise-fidrji' ovx iovos tov Ta idpxov, koi avfxvae fj. t). He met the threats of the judge with the remark (p. 464): et cal to fxamffra oiik? â (rti (Tot Kara rod ffdxarss fxov, arparidirikhv ovra ovroos irapavducos Pacravlc eiv cp. the rescript of Diocletian to Salustius, ir v oh trapairovrnai crov ras airoyoias, TTparre h de eis ("Though it were ever so unlawful for you to put my body to the torture, yet I do not deprecate your insensate breach of military law. Wreak your will on me ").

â Cp. Ruinart, pp. 571 f. (The Acts are untrustworthy.) Upon the judge remonstrating that the emperor had ordered sacrifices, Nicander replies: "This injunction is designed for those who are willing to sacrifice. But we are Christians, and we cannot be bound by an injunction of this kind " (" Volentibus sacrificare haec praeceptio constituta est, nos vero Christiani sumus, et huiuscemodi praecepto teneri non possumus "). To the further question as to why they would no longer draw their pay, Nicander answers, "Because the coin of the impious taints those who desire to worship God" ("Quia pecuniae impiorum contagium sunt viris deum colere cupientibus ").

Cp. Analect. Bolla7id., xvi. (1897), pp. 5 f. Dasius declined to participate in the dissolute military celebration of the Saturnalia. Cp. Parmentier in Rev. de Philol., xxi. (1897) pp. 143 f.; Wendland in Hermes (1S98), 175 f.; and Reich's Der Konig?iit der Dornenkrone (1904).

the famous Pachomius Laurentinus and Egnatius, etc., were all soldiers.

This account of the relations between the church and military service misht be contested on the basis of the twelfth canon of Nicaea, which runs as follows: " Those who are called by grace and have displayed early zeal and laid aside their military belts, but have subsequently turned back like a dog to his vomitâ some even spending sums of money and securing military reinstation by dint of presentsâ these are to remain, after their three years as ' hearers," for the space of ten years further among the ' kneelers,"" etc. It might be inferred from this that the synod considered Christianity incompatible with the military calling. But, on the other hand, as Hefele has rightly pointed, out, in the main Konzilien-Gesch. i.""' pp. 414 f, Eng. trans., i. pp. 417 f), the passage has nothing whatever to do with soldiers in general, but only with such soldiers as had resigned their position for the sake of their Christian confession and had subsequently gone back to the ranks. In the second place, the canon refers to soldiers serving in the army of Licinius, who had given up their military belts when the emperor purged the army of Christians (which is perhaps alluded to in the expression

Pachomius served (cp. his "Life") in the army of Constantine that fought Maxentius. He is said to have been won to Christianity by the brotherly love which the Christian soldiers showed. Thereafter he became a monk, and the founder of the famous monastic settlement at Tabennisi.-â The Acta Arcieai open with a narrative in praise of Marcellus at Carrhse. This wealthy Christian is said to have ransomed over 7700 military prisoners of warâ an act which made a deep impression upon them. " lui admirati et amplexi tarn immensam viri pietatem munificentiamque et facti stupore permoti exemplo misericordiae commonentur, ut plurimi ex ipsis adderentur ad fidem domini nostri Jesu Christi derelicto militiae cingtdo, alii vero vix quarta pretiorum portione suscepta ad propria castra dis-cederent, caeteri autem parum omnino aliquid quantum viatico sufficeret accipientes abirent" ("Astounded with admiration for the man's extraordinary piety and generosity, which they enjoyed, and overcome by his example of humane kindness, the most of them were led to join the faith of our Lord Jesus Christ, by casting away the jnilitary belt; others made off to their own camp after little more than a fourth part of the money had been paid, while almost all the rest took as much as they needed for their journey, and departed "). The story is fiction, in all likelihood; still, it is not without value.

Cp. Cypr., Ep. xxxix. 3 (on Celerinus): "Item patruus eius et avunculus Laurentinus et Egnatius in castris et ipsi quondam saecularibus militantes, sed veri et spiritales dei milites, dum diabolum Christi confessione prosternunt, palmas domini et coronas illustri passione meruerunt."

Tt i Trpwtiju opjuijv evsel acroai), and then gone back to the army, thus denying their faithâ since this army was practically pagan and engaged in combating Constantine, That this is the sense in which the canon is to be taken, is shown by its close connection with the eleventh canon, which treats of those who fell away eirl r? rvpavviso? Aikiviov (" during the reign of Licinius "). Our canon fits in very closely to this one. The relation between the church and the state, as regards the army, concluded with the enactment of the church in the third canon of the great synod at Aries: " Those who throw away their weapons during peace shall be excluded from communion " (cp. Militia Chiisti pp. 87 f.). Constantine also decreed Vita Const. W. 33) that those who had resigned their commissions for religious reasons should have the alternative of rejoining the service or remaining where they were, with honour.

Â 4. The spread of Christianity among women No one who reads the New Testament attentively, as well as those writings which immediately succeeded it, can fail to notice that in the apostolic and sub-apostolic age women played an important role in the propaganda of Christianity and throughout the Christian communities.- The equalising of man and woman before God (Gal. iii. 28) produced a religious independence among women,

Cp. the discussions on " Widows " and " Deaconesses "; also Zscharnack, Der Diejist der Fraic in d. ersten Jahr. d. christ, Kirche (1902); Achelis, Virgines szibintrodiutae (1902); von der Goltz, Der Dienst der Fran in der christ I. Kirche (1905); and Knopfs Nachapost. Zeitalter, pp. 72 f. On Christian women as martyrs and oti virgins, with their treatment by criminal law, cp. Augar in Texte Â. Unters., xxviii. 4.

- Even within Judaism there were many women proselytes, especially from the upper classes. Josephus Bell. Jitd., ii. 20. 2) says that the women in Damascus were almost all inclined to Judaism. Cp. Acts xiii. 50: ol 5e 'loiSaroi irapwrpwav tas ai oixivas yvvolKas ras eiia'X'h ovas Kal tovs Trpwrovs ttjs nokeccs (Antioch in Pisidia), koi in'fiyeipai' Siccyfxhy eirl rhv Tlav ov koi Bapva av, also Acts xvi. 13 (Philippi in Macedonia). Cp. Strabo's generalization upon women as the leaders in religious superstition (i. 7. p. 297): a-Kavtis yap rfis Setaisatfioyias apxvyovs olovrat ras yvvalkas. Clement of Alexandria emphasizes their important role in the mission of the apostolic age StroÂ i., III. vi. 53): 5ta tcsv yvvaikSv koi eh rriv yvvaikuv7riv asta Xrjtws irapfiffesvero rj rod Kvpiov Si5o(rkaa. i'o (" Through women the teaching of the Lord made its way, without any reproach, even into the women's apartments").

Cp. Clem. Alex., Paedag., i. 4:. tti o.)t) v oper j' h. v p'bs koi ywaikhs flvai i'evo7 K6Tfs. el yap afx. po7v 6 dehs ets, ejs Se Ka 6-rraisayooyhs afjifo7v. fx'ia ON THE INWARD SPREAD OF CHRISTIANITY 65 which aided the Christian mission. Jesu4 hij3iselÂ. had-a-circle of women among liis adherents, in addition to the disciples; and a very ancient gloss on Luke xxiii. 2 makes the Jews charge him before Pilate with misleading women.

From 1 Cor. vii. 12 f. we learn that there were mixgji marriages in Corinth, although it is impossible to ascertain whether it was more usual for a pagan to be wedded to a Christian woman, or the reverse. It is quite clear, however, that women appeared in the local assemblies of the church, with yvV- the consent of the apostle, and that they prayed and prophesied A-+â y in public (xi. 5 f.). This fact and this permission may seem to XM v-U contradict the evidence of xiv. 34 f. (" Let the women keep 'v je (ii silence in the congregations: for they are not allowed to speak," r but are to be in subjection, as also the law enjoins. If they wish to learn anything, let them ask their own husbands at home, for it is a scandal that any woman should speak in the congregation"); and, indeed, the one way of removing the contradiction between these two passages is to suppose that in Avvv A- the former Paul is referring to prayers and prophecies of the ecstatic state, over which no one could exercise any control, while the speech axeiv) which is forbidden in the second passage denotes public instruction. At any rate, the apostle is censuring Christian women for overstepping their bounds, not only by attempting to teach in the churches, but also by claiming to appear unveiled at worship.- In- vi. 19 Aquila ikKKi aia, fxia ffcccppocrvvr), alscbs fxia, t rpo(p KOiv, ydfios crv0yios, avanvo, otpis, clKoii, jvwcris, fkTris, virakO'fi, aydirri, 3ioia irdpta. S)v Se Koivhs fxev lss, Kotv Se ri xdpts, Koiv) Se Koi T) ffcotripia, kolv)) tovtuv koi t) aperrj koi r) ayooyi) (" Our judgment is that the virtue of man and of woman is one and the same. For, if the God of both is one, the Instructor of both is also one: one church, one temperate self-control, one modesty, common food, marriage an equal yoke; breath, sight, hearing, knowledge, hope, obedience, loveâ all things are alike to them. Those whose life is common have also a common grace and a common salvation; their virtue and their training are alike").

Luke xxiii. 2 Kwxvovra (p6povs Kaiaapi Sis6pai) Kal airoarpicpovrci, ras ywaikas Koi TO. rekva. The gloss occurs in Marcion's text and the Latin MSS., Palat. and Colbertinus.

' Cp. Tertullian's de Virginibus Velafidis (and the Liber Pontif., s. v. Linus: " Hie ex praecepto beati Pauli constituit, ut mulier in ecclesia velato capite introiret" = This he ordained by the injunction of the blessed Paul, that women must come to church with veiled heads),

VOL. II.

and Prisca (Priscilla), together with the church in their house at Ephesus, send greetings. This passage already mentions the wife along with the husband (although after him), which is noteworthy, for as a rule the husband alone is mentioned in such cases. The woman must therefore have been of some importance personally and in the church at their house, a fact on which some light is presently thrown by the epistle to the Romans.

In Rom. xvi. 1 f. a certain Phoebe is commended, who is described as "one who ministers to the. church at Cenchreae." From the subsequent description of her as one who " has proved herself a succourer of many and of myself" (Trpoarrati? ttoxXcop eyevrjori Kai exov avrov), it is likely that she was a woman of property and a patroness (not an employee) of the church at Cenchreae. This recommendation is followed by the charge to " greetjPrisca and Aquila, my fellow-labourers in Christ Jesusâ who laid down their necks for my life, and to whom not only I but all the Gentile churches render thanks. Greet also the church in their house" (Rom. xvi. 3 f.). Here the name of Prisca stands first, as also is the case, we may add, in 2 Tim. iv. 19. Plainly the woman was the leading figure of the two, so far as regards Christian activity at least. It is to her that thanks and praise are offered in the first instance. She was a fellow-labourer of Paul, i. e., a missionary, and at the same time the leader of a small church. Both of these injunctions imply that she taught, and she could not take part in missionary work or in teaching, unless she had been inspired and set apart by the Spirit. Otherwise, Paul would not have recognized her. She may be claimed as r) atrocrroxog, therefore, although Paul has not given her this title. Further greetings in Rom. xvi. (6 are addressed to a certain Mary ijri? ttoxXci ekOwlaa-ev etv ' In I Cor. i. 11 Paul mentions ol ttjs X 6t s, who brought him special information about the state of matters'ln the Corinthian church; but we do not know if Chloe was herself a Christian, nor can we tell where to look for her.

Further details on Prisca in my essays on " The two Recensions of the Story of Prisca and Aquila in Acts xviii. 1-27 " Siizungsb. d. Freuss. Akad. d. Wiss., 1900, January ll), and " Probabilia uber die Adresse u. den Verfasser des Hebraerbriefs," Zeits. f. d. NTlicht Wissensch., i. (1900), pp. 16 f.). Cp. above, vol. i. pp. 79, 433.

vxag to Tryphena and Tryphosa rag Koiriovaa ev Kvpiw (12),, n, to Persis ifaya-irrjtTi, j'jri? ttoxXo. ekOTrlaarev ev Kvpiw (12), to the mother of Rufus, whom Paul also describes as his own mother ' (13), to Julias, probably the wife of the Philologus with whom she is mentioned (15), and to the Â iter of Nereus (15). Thus j no fewer than fifteen women are saluted, alongside of eighteen CV7? f' men, i and all these must have rendered important services to w the church or to the apostle, or to both, in the shape of the -y work with which they are credited.

From Col. iv, 15 we learn that there w as a conventicle at Colosse, presided over by a woman called Nymphe; for it was in her house that the meetings took place.

In Philippians, which contains few personal items, we read (iv. 2): "I exhort Euodia and I exhort Syntyche to be of the same mind in the Lord. Yea, I pray thee also, true yokefellow, to help these women, for they have wrought with me in the service of the gospel, together with Clement and the rest of my fellow-workers, whose names are in the book of life." These two women, then, had helped to found the church at Philippi, and consequently occupied a position of high honour still (perhaps as presidents of two churches in their houses, like Nymphe at Colosse). They had at present fallen into dissension, and the apostle is careful to avoid siding with either party. He would have them find the right road themselves, with the further aid of the husband of one of them (i. e., of Syntyche)â the other being perhaps a widow, or married to a pagan, or unmarried. The affair would certainly have never been mentioned in the epistle, had it not been of moment to the whole community.

Both in Col. iii. 18 and in Eph. v. 22 the apostle insists 1 Counting Junias, next to Andronicus (xvi. 7), as a man. Chrysostom, however, took the name as feminine (=Junia).

2 The overwhelming probability is that Pomponia Grrecina was also a Christian but this question has been so frequently and fully discussed that it needs no further investigation. Cp, above, p. 35.

'Affiria-aa-df. T! vfi.(pav Koi Tr; v Kar' oikov avrrjs ikKX-qfflav. In the note to Philemon, whose destination was also Colosse, Philemon's wife Apphia is mentioned (but no more) along with himself in the opening address, as the note referred to a domestic affair in which the mistress of the household also had some say.

that wives are to be subject to their husbands, and the injunction becomes doubly intelligible when we observe how natural it was for Christian women to strike out on a line of their own. The book of Acts fills up the outline sketched by Paul. In the church of Jerusalem (i. 14) Christian women were already to the front; a daily meeting was held at night in the house of Mary the mother of Mark (xii. 12). The accession of women as well as of men to the church is expressly noted (v. 14). We hear of Tabitha at Joppa (ix. 36 f.), of Lydia at Philippi, the first Christian woman we know of in Europe (xvi. 14), of Damaris at Athens side by side with Dionysius (xvii. 34), of the four daughters of Philip who were prophetesses (xxi. 9), and of the special share taken by women of the Diaspora in the new movement (xiii. 50, at Antioch. of"Pisidia, ot 'lovsaioi n I

Trapdotpvvav Tag a-ejsojuLevaf yvuaikag ra? â V(rx' juovag Kai Tovg rf TrpootOvg T TToxeco?: xvii. 4, at Thessalonica, irpoa-ekXrjpoootjaau T60 Hav (p Koi T(p 2 a, tcov re cre3oiewj OO rjiwv irxtjoo? TToxv yvvaikwv re rcov Trpwrcov ouk oxlyoi: xvii. 12, at Beroea, TToxXo) e7ri(TTâ vtav KOI TM EXXÂ yv(5a)j yvpaikMV twv evcrx'll ovoiv KOI avspcov note the precedence of the women ovk oxlyoi). Priscilla also is mentioned, and mentioned in a way that corresponds entirely with what Paul tells us. She and her .3' husband- stand independently alongside of Paul (xviii. 2 f.). At Corinth, Ephesus, and Rome they carry on a mission work

A, v-vvU in combination with him, but in virtue of their own authority. Yet in Acts also (xviii. 18, 26) the woman is first, and it was the woman whoâ as Chrysostom rightly infers from xviii. 26 â converted Apollos, the disciple of John the Baptist. As the latter was a cultured Greek, the woman who was capable of instructing him (akpibecrtepov ekOeipai rtjv osov tou Oeov) must have been herself a person of some culture. She w as not merely the mother of a church in her house. As we find from Paul ' Three women, therefore, took part in the founding of the church at Philippi â Lydia, Euodia, and Syntyche. Lydia, however, may be a cognomen, in which case she might be identified with either Euodia or Syntyche.

Aquila alone is described as a Jew from Pontus. Does this mean that his wife was of other and higher origin?

as well, she was a missionary and a teacher. The epistle to the Hebrews probably came from her or from her husband.

In First Peter, women are also exhorted to be submissive to their husbands, but a special motive for this is appended (iii. 1): "iva Km el Tive aireidovcriv tw Xoycp, Sia t 9 tcoi yvvaikwv avacrtpo rjg aveu oyou KepsrjojcropTai, eirotTTevcravte rriv ev (poBw ayi rju auaarpo( )r v vficov. Unbelieving husbands are to be converted by the behaviour of their wives, not by sermons" aind instruction from them. This presupposes mixed marriages, in which it was the women who were Christians.

In the Apocalypse we hear of a Christian, though heretical, prophetess at Thyatira, called Jezebel, who seduced the church. Which tacitly presupposes that women could be, and actually were, prophetesses. Clement af. Rome- celebrates some women who were Christian martyrs.

After staying some time at Smyrna, in the course of his, journey to Rome, Ignatius sends greetings in the two letters which he addressed o he "local church (ad Smyrri. ad Polyc.) from Troasâ letters which otherwise contain very few greetings indeedâ to a certain Alke, ro tto j tov xot opoma ("a name right dear to me "); in one letter he also salutes " the hoasehpld of Gabia, praying that she may be grounded in faith and love" (tou oikov Vaovtai;, i u euxofxai espacroai TTLcrrel Koi ayd-wrj while in the other he sends greetings to t v rod einrpotrov so I, read, following what seems to me to be a probable conjecture of " Lightfoot instead of 'ETrtrpotroi' avv oxw tm o ku) avtrj kuc twv rekvwv rols tckvoi? (" the wife of the governor, with all her household and her children's her children? "). There is some-

In Heb. xi. women are included among the heroic figures of the faith, e., Sarah and Rahab the harlot; cp. the remarkable verse 35.

"' Clem. Rom., vl 2j. Sia rjxos Siaix ertrat yvvaikâ s Aava'ises Koi Aipkai. i. e., Christian women whom Nero murdered by making them appear in these mythological displays, alkiafxara Seiia koi a, v6ffia iradovcrat, iirl rbv rrfs iritrteuis e aiov Sp6fji, oy Kat7 VTTi crav Koi exafiou yepas yivfoiov at acroevtls rep crcofxari (" By reason of jealousy women were persecuted, and after suffering fearful and unholy insults as Danaids and Dircae, attained the goal of faith's course, receiving a noble reward, though weak in body "). Cp. also Iv. 3: ttoaAoi yvvaikes fvsvyaixude7rai Sia T s xÂ-P'-' Â """' "" etrfrexe(ravro irowa avspeta. Their prototypes were Judith and Esther.

"This reading is more probable than Tai'ias.

thing very attractive, too, in Lightfoofs further conjecture th t Gabia is to be identified with the wife of the procurator (" mention is made in the inscriptions at Smyrna of an officer called eirctpotrog crtparriyo? or eiritpoiro Ttjs crtpattjyias; another Smyrnaean inscription speaks of etrlrpotrog rov Se ao-ror;, see Boeck, C. I. G., 3151, 3162, 3203"). This would make the procurator's wife Gabia a Christian, while he himself was a pagan (a typical case, to which we are able to bring forward many a parallel). It would also give her a prominent position in the church. Such a position, and in fact even a more prominent one, must have been also occupied by Alke. Ignatius li does not go into more detail upon the matter. In the epistle - A of the Smyrnaeans upon the death of Polycarp (c. xvii.), however, - we read of an opponent of the Christians, called Nicgias, who

JCSL " Alkc's brother,"" a description which would be meaningless -7 if Alke herself had not been a very prominent lady not only in

Smyrna but also in Philomelium (to which the epistle is

VL addressed). Both of these passages from Ignatius, in short, ' ' throw light upon the fact that she was a Christian of particular influence and energy in Smyrna, and that her character was familiar throughout Asia. By the year 115 a. d. she was already

I labouring for the chui'ch, and as late as 150 a. d. she was still n well known and apparently still living. Her brother was an energetic foe to Christianity, while she herself was a pillar of the church. And so it was with Gabia. In both cases the men were pagans, the women Christians.

A prominent position in some unknown church of Asia must also have been occupied by the woman to whom the second epistle of John was written, not long before the letters of Ignatius. She appears to have been distinguished for exceptional hospitality, and the author therefore warns her in a friendly way against receiving heretical itinerant teachers into her house.

The reaction initiated by Paul at Corinth against the forward position claimed by women in the churches, is carried on by the author of the pastoral epistles. In Tim. ii. 11 f. he

Though many expositors find a local church here, not a woman at all. " Also by an earlier editor of Acts; cp. my remarks in the Sitzungsberichte (as above), p. lo, note 5. Probably Clement of Rome is also to be included in this peremptorily prohibits women from teaching. Let them bear children and maintain faith, love, and holiness. The reason for this is explicitly stated; it is because they are inferior to men.

Adam was first formed, then Eve. It was Eve, not Adam, who was seduced by the serpent. These sharp words presuppose serious encroachments on the part of Christian women, and already there had been unpleasant experiences with indolent, lascivious, and gossiping young widows op. cit., v. 11 f.). As 2 Tim. iii. 6 shows, it was very common for such women especially to succumb to the seductions of fascinating errorists.

One fresh feature in the pastoral epistles is that the existence of a class of ecclesiastical " widows" is taken for granted, and in this coimection special instructions are laid down (1 Tim.

V. 9 f.). Pliny's letter to Trajan mentions Christian women who were called by their fellow-members " deaconesses" (ministras), and there was also an order of regular female ascetics or category. His exhortations to women (Clem. Rom., i., xxi.) are meant to restrict them within their households, and the same holds true of Polycarp ad Phil. iv.). In the " Shepherd " of Hermas, women play no part whatever, which may suggest that they had fallen more into the background at Rome than elsewhere.

' Aisao-KCij â vva. i. Ki. ovk evitpevco. This seems to conflict with Tit. ii. 3, where it is enjoined that Trpecrfivrisas ehai â â â â caaosisacrcaaovs. We must take in the next clause, however ('lya crwcppovi oicriv ras veas (piawspovs elvai, (pixorekvovs, K. T. K.), which shows that the writer does not mean teaching in the church.

This voiced an idea which operated still further and was destined to prove disastrous to the Catholic church. Tertullian already writes thus de Ctdtii Femifi., I. i.): " Evam te esse nescis? vivit sententia dei super sexum istum in hoc seculo: vivat et reatus necesse est. tu es diaboli janua, tu es arboris illius resignatrix, tu es divinae legis prima desertrix, tu es quae eum suasisti quem diabolus aggredi non valuit. tu imaginem dei, hominem, tarn facile elisisti. propter tuum meritum, id est mortem, etiam filius dei mori habuit" (" Do you not know you are an Eve? God's verdict on the sex still holds good, and the sex's guilt must still hold also. You are the devips gateway. You are the avenue to that forbidden tree. You are the first deserter from the law divine. It was you who persuaded him whom the devil himself had not strength to assail. So lightly did you destroy God's image. For your deceit, for death, the very Son of God had to perish"). The figure of Mary the mother of Jesus rose all the more brilliantly as a foil to this. The wrong done, in this view, to the whole sex, was to be made good by the adoration paid to Mary. But it must not be forgotten, apropos of Tertullian's revolting language, that his rhetoric frequently runs away with him. Elsewhere in the same book (II. i.) he writes: " Ancillae dei vivi, conservae et sorores meae, quo iure deputor vobiscum postremissimus equidem, eo iure conservitii et fraterni-tatis audeo ad vos facere sermonem" (" O handmaidens of the living God, my fellow-servants and sisters, the law that sets me, most unworthy, in your ranks, emboldens me as your fellow-servant to address you").

"virgines," who are perhaps referred to as early as 1 Cor. vii. 36 f. The original relation between the church-widow, the deaconess (unknown in the Western church), and the "virgin" lies in obscurity, but such directions show at any rate that ecclesiastical regulations for women were drawn up at a very early period. This was quite a unique creation of the church. But even in antiquity it does not seem to have turned out a success; it soon waned, and indeed it never had any general or uniform popularity.

In the romantic but early Acta Pauli, women also played a prominent role. We are told of a prophetess in the church of Corinth, called Theonoe, of another prophetess in the church called Myrte, ' of Stratonike (the wife of Apollophanes) at Philippi, on account of whom Paul was imprisoned (she is thus the fourth woman mentioned by tradition in connection with that city), of Eubulla and of Artemilla at Ephesus, of Phila at Antioch, of the royal matron Tryphasna, of Nympha at Myrrha, of Aline (Alype?), of Chrysa, of Phirmilla and Phrontina, of 1 Recently this passage has been often discussed, e.:, by Grafe in Theol. Arbeit, aus d. rhein. Pi-edigerverein, N. F., Heft 3 (1899), pp. 69 f, and Julicher in Archiv f, Religionswiss., vii. (1904), pp. 373 f. ("Spiritual Marriages in the Early Church"). But the spiritual and ecclesiastical interpretation of " virgines " has not been uncontested. The bitter sneer of Porphyry the pagan in Mac. Magnes, III. xxxvi., on the Christian "virgins" is interesting: kcx-irws nyes wapbevevovixat ws j-eya ri KOfnrdcovffi Kal Xeyovcri Trvevxatos ayiov in-KXripaxtBai. 6fj. oiws TT) Te afievr) rhv '1-qcrovv; (" How can some of these ' virgin ' women boast so loudly of the fact, declaring they are filled with the Holy Ghost like her who bore Jesus? ").

Thorough studies by Dieckhoff, Uhlhorn, Zscharnack, von der Goltz, and Achelis on "Die Syr. Didascalia" Texte u. Unters., xxv. 2. pp. 274 f.). The differences between the provincial and the local ecclesiastical arrangements must have been specially sharp in this respect. We must beware, therefore, of any generalizations on the subject. Occasionally we hear of a girl under twenty being admitted to the " ordo viduorum " (as, e. g., in Africa, at Carthage?). Cp. Tertull., de Virgin. Vel, ix.

The " mater synagogge" of Judaism is not a parallel; it is a title of honour (cp. Schiirer's Gesch. d, jiid. Volks, iii. ' pp. 50, 55; Eng. trans., ii. 2. 252).

Cp. K. Schmidt, Acta Pauli)Oi,, 2nd ed. 1905). So the Coptic text.

The scraps of papyri prevent us from ascertaining where she is to be located. Like Theonoe, she predicted Paul's fate for him; her role is parallel to that of Agabus in the canonical Acts. The substitution of a woman for a man is characteristic of the author of these " Acts of Paul" for womenâ for such we may term the Acta Paidi.

ON THE INWARD SPREAD OF CHRISTIANITY 73

Lectra in Iconium, and above all of the " apostle" Thekla at

Iconium. We are told that Thekla baptized herself, and that she afterwards laboured and died as a missionary," after enlightening many with the word of God"'"' irokKov (pootia-atra tic Xoyo) Oeov).

It is unlikely that the romancer simply invented this figm-e. I' r

There must have really been a girl converted by a Paul at j a

Iconium, whose name was Thekla, and who took an active part in AA- the Christian mission. As for the later apocryphal Acts of the C ""'

Apostles, they simply swarm with tales of how women of all ranks a were converted in Rome and in the provinces; although the CV details of these stories are untrustworthy, they express correctly enough in general the truth that Christianity was laid hold of by women in particular, and also that the percentage of Christian women, especially among the upper classes, was larger than that of Christian men. " Both sexes â " (" utriusque sexus ") are emphasized as early as Pliny's letter, and other opponents of the faith laid stress upon the fact that Christian preaching was specially acceptable to widows and to wives. This is further attested by the apologists, who have a penchant for insisting that the very Christian women, on account of whom Christianity is vilified as an inferior religion, are better acquainted with divine things than the philosophers. Women who read the

Bible are frequently mentioned. The apologists and Christian teachers numbered women among their audience. A woman called

Charito belonged to Justin's pupils Acta Justini, iv). Dionysius ' Against K. Schmidt.

Cp. Celsus in Orig., c. Cels., III. xliv. Porphyry, too, still held this view (cp. Jerome, iti Isai. 3, Brev, in Psalt. 82, and August., de Civit, Dei, XIX. xxiii.). The woman whom Apuleius describes as abominable Metam., ix. 14) seems to have been a Christian see vol. i. p. 211.

So still Augustine, e. g., de Civit. Dei, X. ii.: " Difficile fuit tanto philosopho sc. Porphyry cunctam diabolicam societatem vel nosse vel fidenter arguere, quam quaelibet anicula Christiana nee cunctatur esse et liberrime detestatur" ("Hard was it for so great a philosopher to understand or confidently to assail the whole fraternity of devils, which any Christian old woman would unhesitatingly describe and loathe with the utmost freedom ").

â â Cp.,., Jerome's remark on Pamphilus (y?. adv. Libros Ruji7ii, i. 9): " Scripturas sanctas non ad legendum tantum, sed et ad habendum tribuebat promptissime, non solum viris, sed et feminis, quae vidisset lectioni deditas " (" He readily provided Bibles, not only to read but to keep, not only for men but for any woman whom he saw addicted to reading ").

of Corinth wrote a letter to a certain Chrysophora, TncrtOTdrrjv ase (p v (" a most faithful sister,"" Eus., H. E., iv. 23). Ptolemaeus the gnostic wrote a profound theological letter to a woman named Flora (Epiph., Hcer., xxxi. 3 f.), which gives a high impression of her culture. Probably he was the same Ptolemaeus who converted a prominent lady in Rome. Origen's women-pupils are often mentioned; he even dedicated his essay on prayer to a woman called Tatiana (Koa-fxiwrdrt koi avspeiotarij). Marcella, the wife of his great friend Ambrosius, also shared his s'tudies. He spent two years in Caesarea (Cappadocia), in the house of a lady called Julia, who evidently had literary interests in Christianity (Eus., H. E., vi. 17, Palladius, Hut. Lmis., 147). Methodius dedicated his treatise on the distinction between foods to a lady (cp, Bonwetsch, Methodkis, i. p. 290), and opened with the remark: " Thou knowest, Frenope, as thou hast shared our conflict and partaken with us in much labour and prayer and fasting How much thou hast been with me in every struggle!""

Even after the middle of the second century women are still prominent, not only for their number and position as widows and deaconesses in the service of the church, but also as prophetesses and teachers. The author of the Acta Theclce is quite in love with his Thekla. It never occurs to him to object to her as a teacher. He rather extols her. As we know from Tertullian that this author was a presbyter of Asia Minor, it follows that there were even ecclesiastics about 180 a. d. who did not disapprove of women teaching and doing missionary work, or of them acting as prophetesses in the gatherings of the church. Even prior to the rise of monasticism we hear of women who gave up all they possessed in order to live in voluntary poverty. As Porphyry put it angrily (Macar. Magnes., III. v.): "Not in the far past, but only yesterday. Christians read Matt. xix. 21 to prominent women, and persuaded them to share all their possessions and goods among the poor, to reduce

For the wealthy woman who adopted him as a boy and had theological lectures delivered in her house, cp. Eus., H. E., vi. 2.

2 The "rights" of women in the early church have been most thoroughly investigated by Zscharnack, perhaps from rather too modern a point of view.

themselves to beggary, to ask charity, and thus to sink from independence into unseemly pauperism, reducing themselves from their former good position to a woe-begone condition, and being finally obliged to knock at the doors of those who were better off."

At Hierapolis in Phrygia the prophetic daughters of Philip enjoyed great repute; Papias, amongst others, listened to their words. Not long after them there lived an Asiatic prophetess called Ammia, whose name was still mentioned with respect at the close of the second century (Eus., H. E., v. 17). The great Montanist movement in Phrygia, during the sixth decade of the i second century, was evoked by the labours of Montanus and two;' j prophetesses called Maximilla and Priscilla. Later on, a pro-v ' f phetess known as Quintilla seems to have made her appearance YJ f" in the same district," while during the reign of Maximinus Thrax f-);' a certain prophetess caused a sensation in Cappadocia (cp. Firmilian, in Cypr., Ep. lxxv. 10).

Among the gnostics especially women played a great role, ij J for the gnostic looked not to sex but to the Spirit. Marcion T v-v v; was surrounded by " sanctiores feminas." Apelles in Rome listened to the revelation of a virgin called Philumena (Tert., de Præscr. xxx., etc.). Marcellina, the Carpocratian, came to Rome, and taught there. Marcus, the pupil of Valentinus and the founder of his sect, had a i: emarkable number of women among his adherents; he let them pronounce the benediction, and consecrated them as prophetesses, thereby leading many

Tertullian de Anima, ix.) writes: " We have with us a sister who has had a share in the spiritual gifts of revelation. For in church, during the Sabbath worship, she undergoes ecstasies. She converses with angels, at times even with the Lord himself; she sees and hears mysteries, pierces the hearts of several people, and suggests remedies to those who desire them." From Aposi. Constit. (cp. Texie u. Inters., v. part 5, p. 22) it is plain that in the case of the church-widows special endowments of grace were looked for, through the Spirit. Even otherwise visions occurred amongst widows; cp. the case of Augustine's mother Confess., vi. i, vii. ' Â, 13, etc.). For the appearance of white-robed women, carrying torches, in the yj Fi '."? Montanist church, cp. Epiph., Hcer., xlix. 2; they were prophetesses and preachers of repentance.

Epiph., Hcbr. xlix. But her personality is uncertain.

Leaving out of account, of course, the Helena of Simon Magus.

Jerome, Ep. xliii.

Â Iren., i. 25: " Multos exterminavit " (" many she led away ").

astray in Gaul. The Coptic gnostic writings show the importance of women in the conventicles of the heretics. On Flora, see above, page 74. And in general the women who belonged to the heretical societies are described by Tertuuian as follows (de Præscr. xli.): " Ipsae mulieres haereticae, quam procaces! quae audeant docere, contendere, exorcismos agere, curationes repro-mittere, forsitan et tingere " (" The very women of the heretics â how forward they are! They actually dare to teach, to debate, to exorcise, to promise cures, probably even to baptize "). It was by her very opposition offered to gnosticism and Montanism that the church was led to interdict women from any activity within the churchâ apart, of course, from such services as they rendered to those of their own sex., Tertullian's treatise upon baptism (de Baptismo) was occasioned by the arrival at Carthage of a heretical woman who in her teaching disparaged baptism. In commencing his argument, Tertuuian observes that even had her teaching been sound, she ought not to have been a teacher. He then proceeds to attackâ thoseâ members of the church (for evidently there were such) who appealed to the case of Thekla in defending the right of women to teach and to baptize. First of all, he deprives them of their authority; their Acts he declares are a forgery. Then he refers ;â Â Â., i. I3. 2: yvvaikas eiixopkrrerj' ijkfkivsrai irapectrwtos ahrov. fjiakicrra Trepl yvvaikas a(r; oaertai, Kot tovto ras evnapifpovs koi â irâ pnroppvpoui Koi-rrxova-iaitaras ("He bids women give thanks even in his presence. he is most concerned about women, and that, too, women of rank and position and wealth"). i. 13. 7 'â v roiis kub' 7 fj. as KAifiacri ttjs 'Posafovaias irowas e r)ira-riikaffi yvpalkas ("In our district of the Rhone they have deluded many women"). On the compulsory consecration of women to the prophetic office, till they actually felt they were prophetesses, see i. 13. 3.

The fj. a6i rptai play a role of their own in these writings, alongside of the fiadrjtai of Jesus, which may suggest the importance of the feminine element in these sects. â Jerome (Â . cxxxiii. 4) has put together all that was known of the prominent heretical women: "Simon Magus haeresim condidit, Helenae meretricis adiutus auxilio. Nicolaus Antiochenus, omnium immunditiarum repertor, choros duxit femineos. Marcion Romum praemisit mulierem, quae decipiendos sibi animos praepararet a fact otherwise unknown. Apelles Philumenam suarum comitem habuit doctrinarum. Montanus immundi spiritus praedicator multas ecclesias per Priscam et Maximillam nobiles et opulentas feminas? primum auro corrupit, deinde haeresi pouuit Arius, ut orbem deciperet, sororem principis ante decepit. Donatus per Africam, ut infelices quosque foetentibus pollueret aquis, Lucillae opibus adiutus est. In Hispania Agape Elpidium, mulier virum, caecum caeca, duxit in foveam, successoremque qui Priscillianum," etc.

to 1 Cor. xiv. 34 to prove that a woman must keep silence. Even as a Montanist, it is to be noted that Tertullian adhered to this position. " Non permittitur mulieri in ecclesia loqui, sed nee docere, nee tingere, nee offerre, nee ulhus virilis muneris, nedum sacerdotalis officii sortem sibi vindicare de V'lrg. Vel. ix.). Even the female visionary in the Montanist church did not speak " till the ceremonies were done and the people dismissed " (" post transacta solemnia dimissa plebe," de Anima, ix.). Origen also forbids women to teach, and rejects the appeal to Deborah, Miriam, Huldah, Hannah, and the daughters of Philip (Cramer, Cat. in Ep. I. ad Cor., p. 279).

Nevertheless, women still continued to play a part in some of the subsequent movements throughout the church. Thus a sempstress in Carthage, called Paula, had to be excommunicated for agitating against Cyprian Ej). xlii.), whilst " that factious woman"" (" factiosa femina"") Lucilla "- was also responsible for poisoning the Carthaginian church with the Donatist controversy at the very outset. Even by the end of the third century we hear of a famous woman teacher in the church, whose lectures were well attended, while the Iberians in the remote Caucasus reported (in the fifth century, cp. Sozom., ii. 7) that they owed their Christianity to a woman who was a prisoner of war.

1 " No woman is allowed to speak in church, or even to teach, or baptize, or discharge any man's function, much less to take upon herself the priestly office." Tertullian frequently discusses the Christian problem of women in his writings; it gave rise to many difficulties. Obviously at the bottom of the legend of the so-called "Apostolic Constitutions" on Martha and Maryâ a legend which is dominated by tendencyâ there lies the question whether or no any active part is to be assigned to women in the celebration of the Lord's supper (cp. Texte tt. Unters., ii. 5- PP- 28 f.: Sre rr (Tiv 6 Stsdffkaaos rhv 6, ptov Kot rh irotriptov Kal 7 v 6yri(Tev avra A yoop â tovt6 eari rh ffcaxa jxov koi rh atfia, ovk iirerpexpe tois yvvai l ffvarrivai 71'= "When the Lord asked for the bread and the cup and blessed them, saying, This is my body and my blood, he did not bid women associate themselves with us ").

Cp. Optat., i. 16; August., Ep. xliii. 17. 25 (ironically): "An quia Lucillam Caecilianus (bishop of Carthage) in Africa laesit, lucem Christi orbis amisit?" ("Was it because Caecilianus injured Lucilla that the world lost the light of Christ?").

Methodius (cp. Bonwetsch, op. cit., i. p. 383; cp. also his study mabhandl. f. a. V. Oettingen, 1898, p. 323): "Come and let me tell you what I once heard in Lycia. The virtue of a woman who was learned in the Scriptures, self-controlled i. e., ascetic), and a philosophic teacher of the Lord's doctrine," etc.

The number of prominent women who are described as either Christians themselves or favourably disposed to Christianity is extremely large. In addition to those already mentioned, mention may be made especially of Domitilla, the wife of T. Flavins Clemens, of the empress Marcia, of Julia Mammaea, of the consort of Philip the Arabian, of the distinguished Roman martyr Soter (of whom Ambrose was proud to be a relative), of the sisters Victoria, Secunda, and Restituta (who belonged to a senatorial family in Carthage), of the Roman matron liucina, who apparently in 258 a. d. had the remains of Paul removed to their position on the road to Ostia, of the wife and daughter of the emperor Diocletian, of St Crispina "most noble and highly born "(" clarissima, nobilis genere""). Tertullian (ad Scap. iv., etc.) speaks of " clarissimae feminae," while Christian " matrons," who were to be exiled, are mentioned in the second edict of Valerian. Juliana, with whom Origen stayed for two years in Caesarea (Cappadocia), and to whom the Jewish Christian Symmachus bequeathed books (Pallad., Hist. Lmis. 64, Eus., H. E. vi. 17), must have been a learned lady. Origen emphasizes the fact that even titled ladies, wives of high state-officials, embraced Christianity (c. Cels., III. ix.). The story of Pilate's wife, who warned him against condemning Jesus (Matt, xxvii. 19), may be a legend, but it was typical in after-days of many an authentic case of the kind. Tertullian tells us how " Claudius Lucius Her-minianus in Cappadocia treated the Christians cruelly, in hot 1 From Tertullian's treatise de Cidiu Feniinarum, as well as from the Paedagogns of Clement, it becomes still more obvious that there were a considerable number of distinguished and wealthy women in the churches of Carthage and Alexandria. In the second book (c. i.) of the former work Tertullian declares that many Christian women dressed and went about just like " women of the world" ("feminae nationum"). There were even women who defended their finery and display on the ground that they would attract attention as Christians if they did not dress like other people (II. xi.). To which Tertullian replies (xiii.): " Ceterum nescio an manus spatalio circumdari solita in duritiam catenae stupes-cere sustineat. nescio an crus periscelio laetatum in nervum se patiatur artari. timeo cervicem, ne margaritarum et smaragdorum laqueis occupata locum spathae non det" ("Yet I know not if the wrist, accustomed to be circled with a palm-leaf bracelet, will endure the numb, hard chain. I know not if the ankle that has delighted in the anklet will bear the pressure of the gyves. I fear that the neck roped with pearls and emeralds will have no room for the sword ").

anger at his wife having gone over to this sect" (" Claudius L. H. in Cappadocia indigne ferens uxorem suam ad hanc seetam transisse Christianos crudeliter tractavit," ad Scap. iii.). Hippolytus narrates how some Christians who had gone out into the desert in an apocalyptic frenzy, would have been executed as robbers by a Syrian governor, had not his wife, who was a believer (oucra-irlcrtu), interceded on their behalf (Comw. in Dan., iv. 18). From the Acts of Philip (bishop of Heracl.) we see that the wife of Bassus the proconsul was a Christian (ch. viii., cp. Ruinarfs, Act. Mart., Ratisbon, p. 444). Eusebius has preserved for us the story of the Christian wife of the prefect of Rome under Maxentius H. E., viii. 14; Vit. Const., i. 34), who, like a second Lucretia, committed suicide in order to avoid dishonour. And Justin (Jpol, II. ii.) tells of a distinguished Roman lady who had herself divorced from a licentious husband. In all these cases the husband was a pagan, while the wife was a Christian. Neither in the pre-Decian period nor in subsequent years was there any difference made between men and women in a persecution. This is one of the best-established facts in the

Cp. also Mart. Saturn, et Z)a!zvi (Ruinart, p. 417): " Fortunatianus, sanc-tissimae martyris Victoriae frater, vir sane togatus, sed a religionis Christianae. cultu. alienus " (" F., the brother of that most holy martyr, Victoria, was indeed a Roman citizen, but he was far from sharing in the worship of Christian religion"). The emperor Julian bitterly complained that the wives of many pagan priests were Christians (Soz., v. 16: ohx Kia-ra x """" iÂ '- ttowcov Upewv Xpt(TTiavi eiu OLKOvuiv ras ya eras). In Porphyry's treatise, 7 ik Koyiaiv (pixocrotpia (cp. Aug., de Civit Dei, xix. 23), an oracle of Apollo is cited, which had been vouchsafed to a man who asked the god how to reclaim his wife from Christianity: "Forte magis poteris in aqua impressis litteris scribere aut adinflans leves pinnas per aera avis volare, quam pollutae revoces impiae uxoris sensum. pergat quo modo vult inanibus fallaciis perseverans et lamentari fallaciis mortuum deum cantans, quem iudicibus recta sentientibus perditum pessima in speciosis ferro vincta mors interfecit" ("Probably you could more easily write on water or manage to fly on wings through the air like a bird, than win back to a right feeling the mind of your polluted impious spouse. Let her go where she pleases, sticking to her idle deceptions and singing false laments to her dead god, who was condemned by right-minded judges and who perished most ignominiously by a violent death "). The difficulties met by a Christian woman with a pagan husband are dramatically put by Tertullian, ad Uxor., ii. 4 f. (partly quoted above, vol. i. pp. 160, 385). Cases in which the husband was a Christian, while his wife was pagan, or nominally Christian, must have been infrequent; cp., however, the Acta Marciani et Nicandri and the Acta Irencei (above, vol. i. pp. 397 f.).

Cp. Augar loc. cit.). Origen Horn, in Jud., ix. i, Lomm., vol. xi. p. 279) writes: "We have often seen with our own eyes women and girls of tender age

Ai history of early Christianity. Consequently the number of I 1 female martyrs is, comparatively speaking, very significant. â r Thekla passed as the first of these, though it was said that she Kf was miraculously preserved. After her, in the ranks of women " martyrs, came JDomitilla, Agnes, and Cecilia in Rome,

Blandina and Biblias in Lyons, Agathonice in Pergamum, Chionia and Agape in Thessalonica, Marcella, Potamiaena, Herais, Quinta, Apollonia, two women called Ammonarion, Mercuria, Dionysia in Alexandria, Perpetua and Felicitas with Celerina the grandmother of Celerinus the confessor, besides Fortunata, Credula, Hereda, Julia, Collecta, Emerita, Calpurnia, Maria, Januaria, Donata, Dativa, Quartillosia in Carthage, the five martyred women of Scili, the Numidian martyrs, viz. Tertuua and Antonia, the eighteen specially famous African women who were martyred under Diocletian, Dionysia in Lampsacus, Domnina Donuina and Theonilla in Egas, Eulalia in Spain, and Afra in Augsburg. But it would lead us too far afield to enumerate even the women of whom we have authentic information as having suffered martyrdom or exile, or having abandoned lives of vice.2 They displayed no less fortitude and heroism than did the men, nor did the church expect from them any inferior response. In her commemoration of the martyrs, she even reckoned these triumphant women worthy of double honour. In the last persecution (that of Licinius) an additional and extremely striking prohibition was put in force, relating to women. The emperor decreed that (1) men and women were not to worship together; that (2) women were never to enter places of worship; and (8) that women were to be taught religion by women only, instead of by bishops (Euseb., Vita suffering torture and being martyred by tyrants; their unripe years and their sex were a twofold source of weakness to them" ("Oculis nostris saepe vidimus mulieres et virgines primae adhuc aetatis pro martyrio tyrannica pertulisse tormenta, quibus et infirmitatem sexus novellae adhuc vitae fragililas addebatur "). Cp. also Cyprian, Ep. vi. 3, de Lapsis, ii., etc.

1 Theonilla (Ruinart, Ada Mart., p. 311) describes herself as a "woman of good birth" ("ingenua mulier"). When she had to let herself be stripped before the magistrate, she declared, "Thou hast put shame not on me alone, but through me, on thine own mother and thy wife" ("Non me solam, sed et matrem tuam et uxorem confusionem induisti per me").

2 For an excellent survey, cp. Zscharnack, pp. 27-37.

Const. I. liii.). The reasons for these orders (which were "generally derided") remain obscure. Concern for feminine morality cannot have been anything but a pretext. But what, then, it may be asked, was their real motive? Are we at liberty to infer from the decree that the emperor considered the stronghold of Christianity lay in women?

It remains to say something about the mixed marriages which Paul had discussed at an earlier period (see above, pp. 65 f.). The apostle did not demand their dissolution. On the contrary, he directed the Christian spouse to adhere to the union and to hope for the conversion of the pagan partner. But Paul was certainly assuming that the marriage was already consummated by the time that one of the partners became a Christian. Not until a comparatively late period do we hear of marriages being concluded between

Christians and pagans. At first, and for some time to come, these unions were never formed at all, or formed extremely seldom; but by the close of the second century such mixed marriages were no longer unheard of. Tertuuian wrote the whole of the second book in his treatise ad Uocorem in order to warn his wife against marrying a pagan, if she became a widow; in the first and second chapters he expressly states that such unions were being consummated. He not merely looks askance at them,

Cp. pseudo-Cyprian, de Singul. Cleric, xiii. f.: " Forsitan aliquis dicat, ergo nee ad domum orationis debemus pariter i. e., men and women convenire, ne aliquis aliquem scandalizet?" (" Perhaps one will say, Then ought we not to go together to the house of prayer, for fear of giving offence to anyone?").

' It is a moot point whether I Cor. vii. 39 fi6vov ev Kvpitf) definitely excludes the marriage of a Christian woman with a pagan. Despite Tertullian's opinion and the weighty support of those exegetcs who advocate this interpretation, I am unable to agree with it. Had the apostle desired to exclude such unions, he would probably have said so explicitly, and noticed the case of a husband as well as of a wife. Or can it be that he is merely forbidding a Christian woman to marry a pagan, and not forbidding a Christian man to choose a pagan girl? This is not impossible, and yet such a view is improbable. The ix6vov ev Kvpicf ("only in the Lord ") means that the Christian standpoint of the married person is to be maintained, but this could be preserved intact even in the case of marriage with a pagan (cp. vii. 16). Besides, the presupposition naturally is that the Christian partner is desirous and capable of winning over the pagan.

Ignatius (ad Polyc. v.) gives a decision in the matter of divorce, but clearly he is only thinking of marriages in which both parties are Christians. No other cases seem to have come under his notice.

but severely reprobates them ("Fideles gentilium matrimonia subeuntes stupri reos esse constat et arcendos ab omni com-municatione fraternitatis," iii.). To his sorrow, however, he has to record the recent utterance of one brother, who maintained that while marriage with a pagan was certainly an offence, it was an extremely trivial offence.

On this subject the church was at first inclined to side with the rigorists. In his Testimonial Cyprian devotes a special section (iii. 62) to the rule that " no marriage-tie is to be formed with pagans" (" matrimonium cum gentilibus non iungendum"),- while it was ordained at the synod of Elvira (canon xv.) that "because Christian maidens are very numerous, they are by no means to be married off to pagans, lest their youthful prime presume and relax into an adultery of the soul" (" Propter copiam puellarum gentilibus minime in matrimonium dandae sunt virgines Christianae, ne aetas in flore tumens in adulterium animae resolvatur "). No punishment is laid down, however. See also canons xvi. and xvii. (" If heretics are unwilling to come over to the catholic church, they are not to be allowed to marry catholic girls. Resolved also, that neither Jews nor heretics be allowed to marry such, since there can be no fellowship between a believer and an unbeliever. Any parents who disobey this interdict shall be excluded from the church for five years " (" Haeretici si se transferre noluerint ad ecclesiam catholicam, ne ipsis catholicas dandas esse puellas;

"It k agreed that believers who marry pagans are guilty of fornication, and are tp. Jbe excluded from any intercourse with the brotherhood "; cp. de Corona, xiii.: " Ideo non nubemus ethnicis, ne nos ad idololatriam usque deducant, a qua apud illos nuptiae incipiunt" ("Therefore we do not marry pagans, lest they lead us astray into that idolatry which is the very starting-point of their nuptials"). The allusion is to the pagan ceremonies at a wedding.

'â The passage in de Lapsis vi. proves, of course, that the church could not always interfere; at any rate, she did not instantly excommunicate offenders. In the gloomy picture drawn by Cyprian de Lapsts, vi.) of the condition of the Carthaginian church before the Decian persecution, mixed marriages do not fail to form one feature of the situation (" Jungere cum infidelibus vinculum matrimonii, prostituere gentilibus membra Christi " = Matrimonial ties are formed with unbelievers, and Christ's members prostituted to the pagans).

These are strict canons. Jews and heretics are worse than pagans; worst of all are pagan priests, of course, since the Christian position of their wives was hopelessly compromised.

sed neque Judaeis necjue haereticis dare placuit, eo quod nulla possit esse societas fideli cum infidele: si contra interdictum fecerint parentes, abstineri per quinquennium placet"). " Should any parents have married their daughters to heathen priests, resolved that they shall never be granted communion" (" Si qui forte sacerdotibus idolorum filias suas iunxerint, placuit nee in finem eis dandam esse communioneni """).

"Because Clnistian girlsarg very numerous"" (" propter copiam puellarum "). This implies that girls, especially of good position, outnumbered youths in the Christian communities. Hence Tertullian had already advised Christian girls who possessed property to marry poor young men ad Uxor., II. viii.). Why, he exclaims, many a pagan woman gives her hand to some freedman or slave, in defiance of public opinion, so long as she can get a husband from whom she need not fear any check upon her loose behaviour! These words were in all probability read by Callistus, the Roman bishop; for even in Rome there must have been a great risk of Christian girls in good position either marrying pagans or forming illicit connections with them, when they could not find any Christian man of their own rank, and when they were unwilling to lose caste by marrying any Christian beneath them. Consequently, Callistus declared that he would allow such women to take a slave or fr ee jnan, without concluding a legal marriage with him. Such sexual unions he would be willing (for ecclesiastical considerations) to recognize (Hipp., PAio., ix. 12; cp. above, vol. i. p. 171). The church thus created an ecclesiastical law of marriage as opposed to the civil, and she did so under the constraint of circumstances. These circumstances arose from the fact of Christian girls within the church outnumbering the youths, the indulgence of Callistus itself proving unmistakably

The " forte " shows, or is meant to show, that this case is unheard of.

At the jynod of Aries the church was content with a mild form of repression; cp. canon xi.: " De puellis fidelibus, qui gentilibus iunguntur, placuit, ut aliquanto tempore a communione separentur" ("Concerning Christian maidens who have married pagans. Resolved, that they be excluded from communion for a certain period ").

Cp. the sarcastic remark of Tertullian the Montanist (in de Vifg. Vel. xiv.): " Facile virgines fraternitas suscipit."

Hippolytus notices the bad effects of this extremely questionable dispensation.

that the female element in the church, so far as the better classes were concerned, was in the majority. The same fact is plain from the eighty-first canon of the synod of Elvira: " Ne feminae suo potius absque maritorum nominibus laicis scribere audeant, quae fideles sunt, vel litteras alicuius pacificas ad suum solum nomen scriptas accipiunt (" Women must not write in their own name to lay Christians, or receive letters of friendship from anyone addressed only to themselves ").

The history of the church's inward growth is reflected in the rise and development of special buildings for the churches. No evidence for any such is to be found prior to Commodus. Possibly some were in existence, but we know nothing of them, and it is unlikely that there were any at all. People met in private houses, while a teacher, like Paul at Ephesus (Acts xix. 9), might hire a school for his lectures. The " domus " of the private house or, where this was not available, the " atrium," may have been devoted to this purpose. The former was usually too small to accommodate more than a couple of dozen people. Hence, when the congregation numbered a hundred or more members, arrangements had usually to be made somehow for room enough to accommodate fifty or more.

Nevertheless, we must consider it certain that the Christians in any of the larger cities soon found it impossible to meet all in one spot. Our earliest evidence, in fact, shows that, as

Cp. Nik. Miiller's article in Protest, Real-Ettcyklm, vol. x. pp. 774 f., where an excellent bibliography is given. For a philological account of " church " = church-building, cp. Kretschmer's remarks in Zeitschr. f. vergleichende Sprach-forschung, xxxix. pp. 539 f.

'â In Chrysostom's age, one church at Antioch was said to reach back to the apostolic age (cp. Chrys., Opp., ed. Montfaucon, iii. p. 60). It is not impossible that the place on which it stood was a Christian house or site even in the first century, for the Christian tradition at Antioch was uninterrupted.

Many items of evidence from the very beginning of Christianity prove this.

Tradition affords no secure basis for the view that worship was usually held in hired or bought school-buildings (trxoxot), so that the form of such buildings determined the later structures of the churches. 'EKi; j 3yria and a. aka. CLov were always distinct from one another, though the distinction tended sometimes to be tlurred (cptvol. i. pp. 357 f.).

far back as we can go, several meeting-places are to be found. How the unity of the church was preserved under these circumstances, we do not know. All that can be said on this point partakes of the nature of a priori conjecture. One thing is clear, and that is, that the idea of a special place for worship had not yet arisen. The Christian idea of God and of divine service not only failed to promote this, but excluded it, while the practical circumstances of the situation retarded its development.

After the close of the second century, things were different. Our information about Edessa, and the writings of Tertullian, Hippolytus, Minucius Felix, Origen, and Cyprian,- show that henceforth there were special places or buildings for worship, called " domus dei," " ecclesia," or " dominicum " (Kvpiakov)-The period of their rise in all probability coincides with that of the church's gi-eat expansion during the reign of Commodus, as well as with the organization of the priestly hierarchy and the "a parallel movement for the consecration of objects and places.

. lie oldest definite church-building bhat we know of is the hurch of Edessa, which was destroyed by a flood in A. n. 201. Whether special buildings for worship were built or selected, their size was always restricted, partly by the amount of means at the disposal of Christians, partly by the need of avoiding remark. Eusebius expressly observesâ and his words have a general bearingâ that the churches were small down to the 1 The passage in the Acts of Justin (ch. iii.) is explicit on this point. The prefect Rustian asks, nov ffwepx crdi (" Where do you meet?"). Justin replies: vda fkaarcfi Trpoaiptcris Ka Sivaj-LS iffri. â iravtois yap voiii tts iirl rh aiirh Tvv4p-X ffdai rifxas-wavtas i. e., we Roman Christians); ovx ovtoos 5e (" Wherever each chooses and can. Do you imagine we all assemble together? By no means"). God is not confined to one spot; prayer can be offered to him anywhere. The prefect retorts: eitre, ttov (Twepx o'S f'J irotoy rsirov aopol fis tovs iadr Tas (Tov; Justin answers, â 701 evava) fxevoa rivhs Mapriyov tov Ttnodiuov axavdov, (cat Trapa iravtO. rhv XP '" tovtov oii yiyvuffkw riv rtva (Tvvfkevaiv (I fxri ttjv tkiivov cp. abovcj vol. i. p. 357. This passage throws light on the well-known passage in the Apol., I. lxvii. (ttj tov tjkIov Xsyofievri riixfpa Trdvrwv Kara. irsKtis fl ypovs ix(v6vro v iirl rb aiirh cvvi ivais y vitai = Oi Sunday, all who stay in the towns or the country gather together). Nothing is said of one or more meetTiig-places for worship in a town.

'" Passages in Muller; only one or two can be added, viz., Orig., Horn. ix. in Levil., c. 9, and Minuc., Oct, ix.

ON CHURCH-BUILDING reign of Gallienus (H. E., viii. 1). Thus in the larger towns it was impossible to think of building an edifice to hold all the local members. The old custom of separating the church into sections for the purpose of worship had to be kept up. On the other hand, the smaller churches, perhaps those of medium size also, found it possible to keep strictly together in their worship, and this plainly was an excellent safeguard against schism and the insinuation of heresy, as well as a powerful lever for the bishop in gathering and controlling the local community. The stricter development of catholicity and the unity of the individual and the general church certainly presupposed, among other things, special edifices for worship. Even where there were a number of churches in one city, the church in which the bishop officiated naturally assumed a special prominence. The rest were superintended by presbyters. Traces of this arrangement are to be found in our extant sources. The building itself was a simple oblong with a niche on one side; examples of this are still to be seen in one or two sites and ruins throughout the East and in Africa (and Rome?).

These hall-churches did not last beyond the reigu., of Gallienus. The growth of the Christian congregations, the ecclesiastical consciousness, and the complicated requirements of the priesthood and. the cultus (which approximated more than ever to those of paganism), involved not only larger buildings but buildings for special purposes e. g., chapels for the martyrs)."- The age admitted of their erection, for an almost unbroken peace reigned from Gallienus to the beginning of the fourth century.

Partly on ground which belonged to private individuals, partly on sites which were the property of the

Cp. the interesting remark of the pagan (Porphyry) in Mac. Magnes, IV. xxi: 0AA.0 Kal ol XptctTiavol ixiixovjifvoi tos KaractKivas tsiv vasiv fiiylcrrovs oxkovs olkosofxovitiv, fis ovs (Tvuiovtis itixovtUi, Ka'itOi f. r Sivhs Kcoavovtos er Tais olkiats Tovto â Kpa. TTiiv, Tuv Kvp'iov Sjjao Jti iravtax f olkovovtos ("Christians too, imitating the temple edifices, construct large buildings, where they meet for prayer, though there is nothing to hinder them from meeting in their own homes, since their Lord is confessedly able to hear them anywhere ").

Cp. especially Eus., Mar. Pal. p. 102 (Violet in Texte ii. Uniers., xiv. 4), and Sozom,, V. 20. From the latter passage we can see that several oikoi eiikT-fjpiot were erected on one site, so that they must have been often quite small chapels.

church (for such were certainly in existence during the second half of the third century), large churches now arose, in the shape and under the name of basij cas. Eusebius says ex- . plicitly (and we could infer it even apart from his evidence) that this was going on from the time of Gallienus. Naturally, it was not done all at once; it was very gradual, so much so that even decades afterwards many congregations had only quite

"). modest buildings. The basilica was not a product of the age of Constantine; it had already made its appearance within ii Christian architecture. The origin of the form would never have occasioned so much perplexity, had it not been for the word

"basilica," which even yet has not been satisfactorily explained."

The basilica itself rested on the hall-church, just as that in its turn went back to the simple chamber or atrium.

-+-. Let me only add that this survey brings out the fact that no

U conclusions upon the size of any Christian congregation can be drawn from the small size of its church-buildings, even when the existence and use of such buildings can be proved for any- Â given period. Even when a church edifice can be shown to

VL have been the only one in the town, no such inferences can

J A i-U v" " " safely be drawn (down to the beginning of the third century); for we do not know whether worship may not have been also conducted in private houses, as a makeshift, nor do we know, as a rule, the special circumstances which may have induced a congregation to endure privation for a time and to make a poor building serve their purposes. On the other hand, the establi shm ent of numerous churches in a town is a fact of great importance for the history of the spread of Christianity. Anything that is known about the separate churches will be found in the following pages, in connection with their respective towns.

1 The name "basilica" was not confined lo a church of some size; it denoted small churches as well.

- Large, stable, and sumptuous basilicas weie jiot erected, of course, prior to Constantine; the great church in Nicomedia could be demolished in a few hours, (cp. Lact., de Mort. 12, and Socrat., ii. 38, where we are told how rapidly a church was removed from one place to another). The. age pf Constantine thus marks a, certain epoch in the history of ecclesiastical buildings; cp. the description of the buildings in Tyre, by Eusebius H. E,, x. 4).

In this chapter I s hall keep strictly within the limits indicated by the title, excluding any place which cannot actually be verified until after 325 a. d. Owing to the fortuitous character of the traditions at our disposal, it is indubitable that many, indeed very many, places at which it is impossible to prove that a Christian community existed previous to the council of Nicaea, may nevertheless have contained such a community, and even a bishopric. But no one can tell with any certainty what such places were. Besides, although unquestionably the age of Constantine was not an era, so far as regards the East, during which a very large number of new bishoprics were createdâ since in not a few provinces the network of the ecclesiastical hierarchy appears to have been already knit so fast and firm that what was required was not the addition of new meshes but actually, in several cases, the removal of one or two â despite all this, it is certain that a large number of new Christian communities did originate at that time. Iit the West a very large number of bishoprics, as well as of churches, were founded during the fourth century, and the Christianizing of not a few provinces now commenced upon a large scale (cp. Sulp. Severus,

I should hold it proven, with regard to the provinces of Asia Minor, that the network there was firm and fast by the time of Constantine. There were about four hundred local bishoprics by the end of the fourth century, so that if we can prove, despite the scantiness and fortuitous nature of the sources, close upon one hundred and fifty for the period before 325 a. d., it is highly probable that the majority of these four hundred were in existence by that time. This calculation is corroborated by the fact that during the fourth century Asiji Minor yields evidence of the chor episcopate being vigorously repressed arid dissolved, but rarely of new bishoprics being founded.

90 MISSION AND EXPANSION OF CHRISTIANITY

Chron., ii. 33: "Hoc temporum tractu mirum est quantum invaluerit religio Christiana " = during this period the Christian religion increased at an astonishing rate). As for the extent to which Christianity spread throughout the various provinces, while the following pages exhibit all that really can be established on this point, no evidence available upon the number of the individual churches (or bishoprics) would make it possible to draw up any accurate outline of the general situation; our information is better regarding some provinces, inferior in quantity as regards others, and first-rate as regards none. Had I drawn the limit at 381 a. d., or even at 343 a. d., a much more complete conspectus could be furnished. But in that case we would have had to abandon our self-imposed task of determining how far Christianity had spread by the time that Constantine granted it toleration and special privileges.

One of the most important aids to this task is the list of signatures to the council of Niccea in 325 a. d,, an excellent critical edition of which has recently appeared Patrum Nicanortitn nomina latine, grace, coptice, syriace, arabice, armeniace, by H. Gelzer, Hilgenfeld, and O. Cuntz; Leipzig, 1898; cp. also C. H. Turner's edition based on independent researches, Eccl. occidentalis niomi-menia iiiris antiqiiissimi. Canonum et conciiiorum Gracoi-um interpretationes Latincb, Oxford, 1899). For a critical estimate of the list in its bearings upon the metropolitan parish, cp. Liibeck's Reichseinteiltitig unci kirchliche Hierarchie (1901). The Nicene list is to be compared also with the documents dating from the rise of the Arian controversy (cp. Schwartz, Ztir Gesck. des Athanashis, v., vi., 1905). Schwartz (pp. 265 f.) has translated into

Greek the Syriac excerpt from the riyios of Alexander (Pitra, Anal. Sacra, iv. 196 f.). The following are the provinces on the list: Egypt, Thebais, Libya, Pentapolis kol ol vw tottoi, Palestine, Arabia, Achaia, Thrace, the Hellespont, Asia, Caria, Lycia, Lydia, Phrygia, Pamphilia, Galatia, Pisidia, Pontus Polemoniacus, Cappadocia, and Armenia. Schwartz is perhaps right in regarding the additional provinces of Mesopotamia, Augustoeuphratesia, Cilicia, Isauria, and Phoenicia as interpolations. Another even more important piece of evidence which he adduces (pp. 271 f.) is thexeco. rd (which he has discovered of an Antiochene synod of 324 A. D,, containing a number of episcopal names, which may for the most part be identified by aid of the Nicene list. Seven, however, representing seven bishoprics, unfortunately remain unexplained. The number of bishops in attendance at Nicaea (which, according to Eusebius, our best witness, Vii. Const., iii. 8, exceeded two hundred and fifty) gives no clue to the spread of the episcopate, let alone the Christian religion, for extremely few bishops were present from Europe and North Africa, and a large number even from the East failed to put in an appearance (The Antiochene list agrees remarkably with the Nicene so far; but even this gives no sure clue to the number of bishops in the respective provinces.) The assertion made by the Eastern sources that over two thousand clergy were present, is credible, but immaterial. One is strongly tempted to bring in the extant signatures

For the purpose of surveying the localities where Christian communities can be shown to have existed before 325 a. d., I shall begin by printing two listsjjlthe places where there were Christian communities before Trajan (or Commodus). "T '

T. Places in which Christian communities or Christians can be traced as early as the first century (previous to Trajan). T i

Jerusalem. Antioch in Syria (Acts xi., etc.).

Damascus (Acts ix.). Tyre (Acts xxi.).

Samaria (Acts viii.; also Samari- Sidon (Acts xxvii.).

Ptolemais (Acts xxi.). Pella3 (Eus., H. E., III. v.; for other Palestinian localities where even at an early period Jewish Christians resided, see under III. i., Palestine).

tan villages, ver. 25). Lydda (Acts ix.). Joppa (Acts ix.). Saron, i. e., localities in this plain (Acts ix.). Caesarea-Palest. (Acts x.).

of the synod of Sardica, which prove the existence of many bishoprics hitherto unattested. But as it is certain that several bishoprics were founded in the twenty years between Nicka and Sardica, we must regretfully put the Sardica list aside.â Cumont's remark upon the Christian inscriptions of the East is unfortunately to the point: "Je ne sais s'il existe une categorie de textes epigraphiques, qui soit plus mal connue aujourd'hui que les inscriptions chretiennes de l'empire d'Orient" Les Inzer, chrit. de HAsie mineure, Rome, 1895, p. 5). For learned classifications of early Christian cemeteries, cp. Nik. Muller's article (1901) s. v. m Protest. Real-Encykls' 'i x. pp. 794-877, and C. M. Kaufmann's IJandlnich d. christl. Archdologie (1905), pp. 74-107 (" Topographie d. altchristl. Denkmaler"). For the topographical materials, cp. also Liibeck op. cit.), and Bruders, Verfassung der Kirche in den zweiten ersten Jahrhund. (1904).

I content myself with a mere enumeration, as the subsequent section, arranged according to provinces, gives a sketch of the spread and increase of Christianity in the respective provinces. In this chapter I have not entered, of course, into the special details of the history of Christianity throughout the provinces, a task for which we need the combined labours of specialists, archæ-ologlitf, and architects, while every large province requires a staff of scholars to itself, such as Africa has found among the French savants. This will remain for years, no doubt, a pious hope. Yet even investigations conducted by individuals have already done splendid service for the history of provincial and local churches in antiquity. Beside de Rossi stand Le Blant and Ramsay, Duchesne, Wilpert, Nik. Mtiller, etcj The modestj)ages which follow, and which I almost hesitate to publish, will serve their purpose if they sketch the general contour accurately in th"e main.

Cp. on Map I.â Note how not n y Acts but also Paul at an earlier-period groups together the Christians of individual provinces, showing that several churches or Christian groups must have already existed in each of the following provinces: Judaea, Samaria, Syria, Cilicia, Galatia, Asia, Macedonia, and Achaia.

Grand-nephews of Jesus (grandchildren of his brother Judas), whom Domitian wanted to punish (according to the tale of Hegesippus), lived in Palestine as

Arabia.
Tarsus (Acts ix., xi., xv.).
Syria (several churches, Acts xv.).
Cilicia (Acts xv.).
Salamis in Cyprus (Acts xiii.).
Paphos in Cyprus (Acts xiii.).
Perga in Pamphylia (Acts xiii., xiv.). Antioch in Pisidia (Acts xiv.). Iconium (Acts xiii.-xiv.). Lystra (Acts xiv.). Derbe (Acts xiv,). Unnamed locahties in Galatia (Gal.; 1 Pet. i. 1). Unnamed localities in Cappa- docia (1 Pet. i. 1). A number of churches in Bithy- nia and Pontus (1 Pet. i. 1;

Pliny's ep. to Trajan)."-Ephesus (Acts, Apoc, Paul's epp.).3

Colosse (Paul's ep.). Laodicea (Paul's ep.). Hierapolis in Phrygia (Paul's ep.). Smyrna (Apoc. John). Pergamum (Apoc. John). Sardis (Apoc. John). Philadelphia in Lydia (Apoc.

John). Magnesia on the Maeander (Ignat.). Tralles in Caria (Ignat.). Thyatira in Lydia (Apoc. John). Troas (Acts xvi., xx.; 2 Cor.

ii. 12). Philippi in Macedonia (Acts xvi.; Paul's epp.). Thessalonica (Acts xvii.; Paul's epp.). Berea in Macedonia (Acts xvii.;

Paul's ep.).

peasants. Relatives of Jesus presided over several of the Palestinian churches (for Mesopotamia, see below).

Here Paul laboured after his conversion (Gal. i. 17), we do not know for how long; the " three years" of Gal. i. 18 include his residence at Damascus as well as his stay in Arabia. Holsten's view is that Paul in Arabia was simply reflecting on the relation of the gospel to the Old Testament, but the inevitable inference to be drawn from Gal. i. 16 is that Paul had already preached to pagans in Arabia. Still, this is not quite certain. Luke, at any rate, does not hold that the Gentile mission had now begun (Acts ix. 19-29, xi. 20 f.). It is likely that Paul was referring primarily to Arabia when he spoke (Rom. xv. 19) of his preaching avh 'itpovaaxrjij. Kal kvk ci â for KVK cf), in spite of all that the excellent Antiochene expositors urge, can hardly mean "in a circle as far as luyria." Jerusalem he neither could nor would ignore as his starting-point; but as he really never laboured there in the role of a missionary, he adds ev kvkxcc, which may quite well denote Arabia, whose boundaries (viewed from a geographical elevation) adjoined Jerusalem and which included Jews among its population.

- Ramsay Ciurci in the Roman Empire, 1S93, pp. 211, 235) shows the likelihood of Amisus having contained Christians at this period.

"Acts xix. 10; Paul laboured here for two years, Scrr tra. vto. s tovs KarolKovvras rrfv 'Affiav a. Kov(Tai rhv oyov tov Kvpiov, lovsaiovs re Kal "E Ar vas. " It may therefore be regarded as practically certain that the great cities which lay on the important roads connecting those seven leading cities i. e., of the Apocalypse with one another had all ' heard the word," and that most of them were the seats of churches when these seven letters were written" (Ramsay on "The Seven Churches of Asia," Expositor, vol. ix. p. 22).

CHRISTIANITY DOWN TO 325 A. D. 93

Nicopolis in Epirus (Titus iii, 12). 1 Athens (Acts xvii.; Paul's ep.). Corinth (Acts xviii.; Paul's epp.). Cenchrese, near Corinth (Paul's ep.).

Crete (ep. to Titus). Illyria(Roni. xv. 19). Dalmatia (2 Tim. iv. lo). Rome (Acts xxvii. f.; Paul's epp.; Apoc. John.). Puteoli (Acts xxviii.).

This is not quite certain: (nrovsacrov faOe?!" irpos fie els 'Niksitokiv exf? y p Kekpika irapaxi f O'O-ai. An early note appended to the epistle to Titus runs: (ypd(pri airh 'Nikon-6 e(Ds t s Makesofias.

' We do not know when Paul reached Illyria; probably it was during a visit to Macedonia, or during his long residence at Corinth. It is not even certain that he visited Illyria at all, for the passage admits of being read in such a way as to mean that he reached the borders of Illyria by his presence in Macedonia. Besides, rh 'l vpik6v, as Renan points out Si Paid, pp. 492 f. Germ, ed., p. 417), is a very general geographical term.

Titus went to Dalmatia on his own initiative, against Paul's wishes. It is not said whether his errand was connected with the gospel; the previous allusion to Demas, in fact, practically excludes this.

â Babylon (i Pet. v. 13) is probably Rome,

The trace of Christianity said to have been found at Pompeii on a mutilated and illegible inscription (HRICTIAN?) is to be left out of account. " The reading is quite uncertain. Eveirirth word ' Christian ' actually did occur, it would simply prove that Christians were known to people at Pompeii, not that there were Christians in the city." This is the opinion of Mau, who also notices Pompeii in Leben und Ktinst, 1900, p. 15) the inscription, first deciphered by himself in 1885, which is scratched upon a wall in a small house (ix. i, 26): " Sodoma Gomora" (cp. Bull, deli' Instit., 18S5, p. 97). "Only a Jew or a Christian could have written this; it sounds like a prophecy of the end."' Is this the stern judgment of a Jew or a Christian on the city? Or did some Jew or Christian write it when the shower of ashes had begun to rain ruin on the city (cp. Herrlich's statement of his interpretation in Berliner-philol. Wochenschrifi, 1903, pp. I151 f.)? Or are we to think of Matt. x. 15 in this connection (so Nestle, Zeits. f. nentest. IViss., 1904, pp. 167 f.)? The existence of Christians at Pompeii cannot therefore be maintained. But, on the other hand, it is deferring too much to lertuuian to infer from y4pol. xl. that there were no Christians in Campania and Etruria previous to 73 a. d. Tertullian does affirm this, but simply because it suits his convenience; he can hardly have had any information on the subject, for Africa possessed no knowledge of Christians in these provinces in Tertullian's day. â A terra-cotta lamp has recently been dug up at Pompeii with the "Christ" monogram. Sogliano's account of it has been reproduced in many journals. But Labanca (Giornale d" Italia, 1.4th Oct. 1905) and others have justly expressed their scepticism on the discovery. In my judgment, it simply corroborates the old suspicion that this monogram was of pagan origin.â It is impossible to prove that,., there were Christians at this period in the towns mentioned in Acts (Ashdod in r- l Philistia, Seleucia, Attalia in Pamphylia, Amphipolis, Apollonia, Assus, Malta, 'V Aftu Mitylene, Miletus, etc.) which have been omitted from the above list. Domitilla was banished to the island of Pontia (or Pandataria?).â I ignore, as uncertain, all the place-names which occur only in apocryphal Acts, together with all provinces y v-V-v

94 MISSION AND EXPANSION OF CHRISTIANITY

Spain.1

Alexandria (no direct evidence but the fact is certainly to be, infeited from later allusions).-

During Trajan's reign, then, Christianity had spread as far as the shores of the Tyivhenian sea, perhaps even as far as Spain itself. Its headquarters lay in Antipch., on the western and north-western shores of Asia Minor, and at Itoms. where, as in Bithynia, it had already attracted the attention of the authorities. " Cognitiones de Christianis," judicial proceedings against Christians, were afoot in the metropolis; Nero, Domitian, and Trajan had taken action with reference to the new movement. Apropos of Rome in Nero's reign, Tacitus speaks of a " multitudo ingens," while Pliny employs still stronger terms in reference to Bithynia, and Ignatius ad Ephes. iii.) describes the Christian bishops as caret Tct irepara opia-Qevre, "settled on the outskirts of the earth." Decades ago the new religion had also penetrated the imperial court, and even the Flavian house itself.

II. Places where Christian communities can be traced before 180 A. D. i. e., before the death of Marcus Aurelius). 3

To those noted under I., the folio wins; have to be added:

A number of churches in the environs of Syrian Antioch (Ignat. ad Philad., 10), whose names are unknown, though one thinks of Seleucia in particular (cp. Acta Pauli): a number of chui'ches in the environs of Smyrna (Irenaeus, in Eus., H. E., v. 20. 8), and many Asiatic churches ibid.,

V. 24). Edessa (Julius Africanus, Bai- desanes, etc.). Churches in Mesopotamia or on the Tigris (see below, under

III).

and countries described there and nowhere else as districts in which missions are said to have existed as early as the apostolic age.

It is disputed whether Paul carried out his design (Rom. xv. 24, 2S) of doing missionary work in Spain. To judge from Clem Rom. v. and the Muratorian fragment, I think it probable that he did. See also Acfa Petri (Vercell.), vi. We should have to include Gaul here, if Fawlav (Sinait., C. minuscc. and Latt.) were the true reading in 2 Tim. iv. 10, or if Faaaria were European Gaul (so Euseb., Epiph., Theod., and Theodoret). But the reading is uncertain. Cp. Lightfoot's edition of Galatians (5th ed.), p. 31.

Some well-known scholars, like Pearson and Vitringa, would take " Babylon " (in I Pet. V.) as the Egyptian town of that name. But, in spite of the tradition that Mark laboured in Egypt (he is mentioned with Babylon in i Peter), this hypothesis is quite baseless.

Cp. below, on Map I.

CHRISTIANITY DOWN TO 325 A. D.

Caesarea in Cappadocia (Alexander the local bishop, Clem. Alex.).

elitene (where the local legion, the "Thundering," contained a large number of Christians, as is proved by the miracle of the rain, narrated by Eus. V. J?", in the reign of M. urelius).

Laranda in Xsaiuaarlâ

Philomelium in Pisidia (Mart. Polyc).

â Parium in Mysia (probably, ace. to the Acta Oiiesiphori).

Nicomedia (Dionys. Cor., in Eus., H. E., iv. 23).

Otrus in Phrygia (anti-Mon-tanist, in Eus., H. E., v. 16).2

Hieropolis in Phrygia (probably, ace. to the inscriptions of Abercius).

Pepuza in Phrygia (Apollonius, in Eus., H. E., V. 18).

Tymion (= Dumanli?) in Phrygia ibid. y

Ardabau = Kdp8af3a? iv rrj Kara

TTjv pvytav Mticrta (Anti-Mon- tanist, in Eus., H. E., v. 16; see Ramsay's Phrygia, p. 573.

Only known to us as the birthplace of Montanus). Apamea in Phrygia (Eus., v. 16). Cumane, a village in Phrygia (Eus., V. 16). Eumenea in Phrygia (Eus., v.

16). Synnada in Phrygia. Ancyra in Galatia ' (Eus., vi. 16). Sinope (Hippol., in Epiph., Hce-., xlii.). Amastris in Pontus (Dionys.

Cor., in Eus., H. E., iv. 23). Debeltum in Thrace (Serapion, in Eus., V. 19). Anchialus in Thrace (ihid.). Larissa in Thessaly (Melito, in

Eus., iv. 26). Lacedaemon (Dionys. Cor., in

Eus., H. E., iv. 23). Cnossus in Crete (ibid.). Gortyna in Crete (ibid.)."' 1 The proximity of Derbe and Lystra, as well as the remarks of Eusebius H. E. vi. 19), make it highly probable that a Christian community existed here before 180 A. D.

2 Ramsay (5 Paul the Traveller, etc., third ed., 1897, pp. vii. f.): "Christianity spread with mar vellous rapid ity at the end of the first and in the second century in the parts. pi-Hirygia that lay along the road from Pisidian Antioch to Ephesus, and in the neighbourhood of Iconium, whereas it did not become powerful in those parts of Phrygia that adjoined North Galatia till the fourth century."

Though this church is not mentioned till afterwards (Alexander in Eus., H. E., vi. 19), our information about it, together with the size of the town, justify its position as above. Cp. also the remarks of Dionysius in Eus., H. E., vii. 7.

Myrra in Lycia perhaps had a Christian community (cp. Acta Paiili).

'H 6fc rjcria r ira. poikOvaa."'h. fj. a. a-rpiv dxa rais Kara Uovtov ikKXTjaiats. Thus Dionysius proves that several Pontic churches were in existence by 170 a. d.

Byzantium, too, had probably a church of its own (cp. Hippol., Philos., vii. 35; perhaps one should also refer to Tert., ad Scap., iii.).

"'H ekKX crla ri irapoikovcra TSptwav axa rats oiira7s caret Kptjrrjt' irapoikiats â evidently there were a number of churches in Crete by this time. It is highly prob-
Same in Cephallenia (Clem. Lyons (epistle of local chm'ch
Alex., Strom., III. ii. 5). in Eus., v. 1 f.; Irenaeus).

A number of churches in Egypt I Vienne (Eus., v. 1 f.).

(cp. Iren., i. 10, the activity of Basilides and Valentinus there, and retrospective inferences: details in III.). Naples (catacombs of St Gen- naro). Churches in Greater Greece. Syracuse (catacombs, but not
Carthage (certain inferences retrospectively from Tertullian).
Madaura in Numidia (martyrs).
Scilium (Scili) in Noi'th Africa (martyrs).
Churches in Gaul (among the Celts; Iren.).3
Churches in Germany (Iren.)."
absolutely certain). j Churches in Spain (Iren.)

Already there were Christians in all the Roman provinces, and in fact beyond the limits of the Roman empire. And already the majority of these Christians comprised a great federation, which assumed a consolidated shape and polity about the year 180.

! III. A list of places where Christian communities can be -i shown to have existed previous to 325 a. d. (the council of Nicaea); together with some brief account of the spread of Christianity throughout the various provinces.-. T able also that Christian churches existed in Cyrenaica before i8o a. d. (cp, belosv, under " Cyrenaica "). Kt; p j'jj occurs in the Acta Paiiu (Coptic, K. Schmidt's ed., p. 65) beside Syria, but the context is in too bad a state to permit of any inferences being drawn from it.

In greater Greece, Clement of Alexandria (f. 160?) met a Christian teacher from Syria and another from Egypt Strom., I. i. 11). Hence there must have been Christians in one or two of the coast towns of Lower Italy, otherwise no Christian teachers would have stayed there.

It is extremely probable that Uthina, Lambese, Hadrumetum, and Thysdrus should also be included, since Tertullian de Monog. xii. ad Scap. iii.-iv.) implies that there were churches there. Cirta, too, would have to be added to their number.

Renan Marc. Aurcle, p. 452) declares: " Le Bretagne avait sans doute deja .Â., before 180 a. d vudes missionnaires de Jesus." But his evidence, the Quarto-deciman controversy, is quite insufficient. " Sans doute " has a " possible," like itself. "II est possible que les premieres eglises de Bretagne aient dil leur origine a des Phrygiens, a des Asiates, comme ceux qui fonderent les eglises de Lyon, de Vienne." "Possible"! Why not? One needs to be a Breton to lay any stress on such an abstract possibility.

So that perhaps Cologne (possibly Mainz also?) had a church.

Â 1. Palestine.

The first stages in the diffusion of the gospel throughout Palestine (Syria-Palestina) are described, though merely in salient outline, by the Acls iif the Apostles, whose narrative I presuppose as quite familiar to my readers. From the outset it was Jerusalem (not the towns of Galilee, as one might imagine) that formed the centre of Christendom in Palestine. It was in Jerusalem that James, the Lord's brother, took over the government of the church, after the twelve disciples had finally realized that their vocation meant the mission-enterprise of Christianity (probably twelve years after the resurrection, as one early tradition in the Preaching of Peter has it, and not immediately after the resurrection). The choice of James was determined by his relatioqship to-Jesus. He, in turn, was succeeded (6061 or 6162) by another relative of Jesus, namely, hisaiousiii Simeojx,-the son of Cleopas, who was martyred under Trajan at the great age of 120. Thereafter, according to an early tradition, thirteen Jewish-Christian bishops covered the period between (the tenth year of?) Trajan and the eighteenth year of Hadrian. This statement cannot be correct, and the likelihood is that relatives of Jesus or presbyters are included in the list. All ihesebjshops were circumcised persons, which proves that the church was Jewish Christianâ as indeed is attested directly for the apostolic age by Paul's epistles and the book of Acts (xxi. 20). It cannot, however, have adhered to the extreme claims of the Jewish Christians; that is, if any basis of fact, however late, underlies the decision of Acts xv. 28 f. At the first investment of Jerusalem the Christians forsook the city (Eus., H. E., iii. 5, and Epiph., Hcer., xxix. 7, 1 Cp. Map III.â See Schiirer's Gesch. d. jiid. Volkes, 1.(3) (1900), II.3) (ij Mommsen's Rom. Geschichte, v. pp. 487 f. Eng. trans., vol. ii. pp. 151 f.; Marquardt's Rom. Staatsverwaltimg, i. pp. 247 f.; and the map in Klostermann's edition of the Otioniasticon of Eusebius (1904).

' His episcopal chair was still shown in the days of Eusebius H. E,, vii. 19).

Details in my Chronologic, i. pp. 129 f., 218 f.

â â Zahn's Forschwtgen, vi. 300) idea is that the number includes the names of contemporary bishops throughout Palestine.

Cp. Knopf, Nachapost. Zeitalter, pp. 25 f. VOL. II.

de Mens, et Pond, xv., after Hegesippus or Julius Africanus), and emigrated to Pella; it was only a small number who eventually returned after the city had once more risen from its ruins, In any case, the local church was small. We have no means of ascertaining its previous size, but the exodus of 68 a. d. precludes any large estimate, All we know is that it comprised priests (Acts vi, 7), Pharisees (xv. 5), and Greek-speaking Jews from the Diaspora (vi. 5), and that it was not rich. It disappeared completely, after Hadrian, on the conclusion of the war with Barcochba, had forbidden any circumcised person to so much as 4; c CÂ. set foot within the city.

â ow '" The new pagan city of lia Capitolina, founded on the site of Jerusalem, never rose to any great importance. Gentile

At the outbreak of the Jewish war Pella, like some other Hellenistic and pagan towns, was surprised by the Jewish revolutionaries, but it can hardly have been in the hands of the rebels when the Christians took shelter there. They sought refuge in a pagan town. This is all we can say with any show of probability. According to Renan Antichrist, p. 237), "no wiser choice could have been made." Scythopolis and Pella were the nearest neutral cities to Jerusalem. " But Pella, by its position across the Jordan, must have offered much greater quiet than Scythopolis, which had become one of the Roman strongholds. Besides, Pella was a free city, though apparently it had allied itself to Agrippa II. To take refuge here was to express open horror at the revolution."

- This is clearly brought out by Epiph., Hctr., xxix 7; also de Mens, et Pond., xiv. f., where we learn that there were only seven poor synagogues and one little church in Jerusalem when Hadrian visited the city prior to the revolt of Barcochba. The church was on Mount Zion, and the congregation is said to have been composed of those who had returned from Pella kox a-(p. tia. fnyaka eirftexovi). Eusebius Demonstr., III. v. 108), on the other hand, relates: ko! Ifftopla Se (cate'xei, is Kal fxiyi(TT7 ris v ikK T)Tia. XptcTOv iu to7s 'lepoffokvfiois iinh 'lousfttoiv (Tvykpotovxfvri fj-exp ' ' XP "" "' '""'J """"' 'ASptavb ' iro topkias (cp. Theophan., v. 45).

â Eusebius and Epiphanius (or their authorities) explicitly assert that all the Christians of Jerusalem withdrew to Pella. The statements of Acts (ii. 41, 47; iv. 4; vi. 7) upon the increase and size of the church at Jerusalem are unreliable. The " myriads" of Christians mentioned in xxi. 20 are not simply Jerusalemites, but also foreigners who had arrived for the feast. But even so, the number is exaggerated.

â Cp. the collection for Jerusalem, which Paul promoted so assiduously. Gal. ii. 10 is a passage which will always serve as a strong proof that the name " Ebionite " is not derived from a certain "Ebion," but was given to Jewish Christians on account of their poverty. (As against Hilgenfeld, and Dalman: Wertejesu, 1898. p. 42; Eng. trans., pp. 52, 53).

' Cp. Mommsen's Korn. Geschichte, v. p. 546 Eng. trans., ii. 225: " The new city of Hadrian continued to exist, but it did not prosper."

Christians, however, at once settled there, and the date at which the first Gentile Christian bishop (Marcus) entered on his duties is fixed by Eusebius, on reliable tradition, as the nineteenth year of Hadrian's reign, or one year after the war had ended. But before we put together the known facts regarding the church at Jerusalem, we must survey the spread of Jewish Christianity throughout Palestine.

"Churches in Judaea"" (where there were numerous villages, Tac, Hist. V. 8) are mentioned by Paul in Gal. i. 22 (cf. Acts xi. 29), and in 1 Thess. ii. 34 he writes: uxe"? juijujjtai iyeyi'jorjre Tuiv ekK t aiu)i Tov Qeov twv ov(jwv ev tij lovsala ei' piarco Itjcrov, oti Ta avra eiraoete Kai vfxeh viro tmp isiwi (TVju(pv â TU)v, caoctif Kcu avto viro twv 'lovsalcov. In Acts we hear of churches on the seaboard, in Galilee and in Samaria. The larger number of these were Hellenized during the following century and passed over into the main body of Christendom." When we

The Hellenizing forces were already in operation; in the independent Greek cities of Palestine and the neighbourhood lying over against the Jewish districts, the large municipal communities and even their rural surroundings were under Hellenistic influence. All that is known of their size, composition, and history will be found in Schiirer, II. pp. 72-175 (Eng. trans., div. II. vol. i. pp. 57 f.). The following are the 33 (29?) towns:â Raphia, Gaza, Anthedon, Ascalon, Azotus, Jamnia, Joppa, Apouonia, Straton's Tower (Cffisarea), Dora, and Ptolemais in the maritime districts; also the cities of the so-called Decapolis, i. e., Damascus Hippus, Gadara, Abila, Raphana, Kanata (?), Kanatha (= Kanawat), Scythopolis, Fella (= Butis), Dium, Gerasa, and Philadelphia (Arabia). Further, Sebaste (Samaria), built by Herod, Gaba (on Carmel), Esbon (= Heshbon), Antipatris, Phasselis, Caesarea Paneas, Julias (

= Bethsaida), Sepphoris (the leading city of Galilee, afterwards called Diocfesarea), Julias f = Livias), and Tiberias (rivalling Sepphoris in size and position; its population predominantly Jewish, despite its Greek constitution). In the case of some (., Antipatris, Phasselis, and Julias), it is doubtful whether they had a Greek constitution and independent position. In the post-Neronic age some other towns acquired the rank of independent communes; e. g., Neapolis (Sichem), Capitolias in the Decapolis, Diospolis (Lydda) Eleutheropolis, and Nicopolis (Emmaus), besides ALVia. Greeks also resided in other cities, e. g., in Jericho.

- Tilpthen the brothers and relatives of Jesus (who took part in the Christian mission; cp. i Cor. ix. 5) played a leading role also in these Christian communities outside Jerusalem; as may be inferred even from the epistle of Africanus to Aristides (Eus., .Â., i. 7), where we are told how the relatives of Jesus from Nazareth and Kochaba scattered over the country (tt?" onrr) yrj (â 7ri4oitr cravrfs), and how they bore the title of Sfcnroawoi (Â 14). The tradition of Hegesippus is quite clear. He begins by recounting that ol wphs yevovs Kara ffdpka tov Kvpiov (Eus., J7. E., iii. 11: "Those who were related to the Lord in the flesh") met 100 MISSION AND EXPANSION OF CHRISTIANITY ask what became of the Jewish Christians who could not agree to this transition, we are obhged to cast back for a moment

Xt' to the removal of the Christian community from Jerusalem.

yjfiy Eusebius writes as follows H. E. iii. 5): tov Xaov tj?? ev - lepoa-oxuiuoi eccxjo-Za? Kara Tiva xpwf ov toii? avtooi Sokifioig

Si' airoKaxvylrem ekdooevta irpo tov 7ro eui. ov jj-eravattTrivai r?

TToaeco? KUi Tiva T 9 TLepaia ttoxiv oiketv Kekexevcrjua'av, IlexXai' avr v ovoixci ovcriv, twv e9 Xpcrroi' TrewicrtevkOTOiv a-wo tj;9 'lepovaaxriij. mercpkicrpei'm', k. tx (" Thje people belonging to the church at Jerusalem had been ordered by an oracle revealed to approved men on the spot before the war broke out, to leave jlrr' "'the city and dwell in a town of Percea called Pella. Then after

V W thone xvjio believed in Christ had xvithdrawn thither,"'''' etc).

Epiphanius writes thus flwr., xxix. 7): ecrrt e avrri) avpecri?

after the death of James to elect his successor (" for the greater number of them were still alive," ir elovs yap cai tovtoiv nepnio'av ilaeti. rdre TCf 0tw). Then he tells of two grandsons of Jude, the brother of Jesus, who were brought before Domitian (iii. 19, 20). Finally, he states that, after being released by Domitian, they " ruled over the churches, inasmuch as they were both witnesses and also relations of the Lord" (iii. 20. 8: tovs airoxvoevras Tjyfjffacroai rwv (KKKT ai(iiv, uxtOLV 5 fidptvpas bjxov Ka dlirh ytvovs ouras tov Kvplov); cp. also iii. 32. 6: fpxovrai ovv Ka irpo-qyoiivrai. iracrris KKXrjcnas ojs jxaptvpes Koi airh yevovs rod Kvpiov ("So they come and assume the leadership in every church as witnesses and relatives of the Lord "). This statement about ruling is vague, but it is hardly possible to lake irpo-i yovvrai merely as denoting a general position of honour. Probably they too had the rank of "apostles " in the Christian churches; in I Cor. ix. 5, at any rate, Paul groups them with the latter as missionaries.

' A priori, it is likely that there were also Jewish Christians who spoke Greek (and Greek alone). And this follows from the fact that a Greek version of the gospel according to the Hebrews existed daring the second century. Outside Palestine and the neighbouring provinces (including Egypt), Jewish Christians who held aloof from the main body of the church were, in all likelihood, so few during the second century that we need take no account of them in this connection. Jerome (. ffi. ad Aug. 112, c. 13) does assert that Nazarenes were to be found in every Jewish synagogue throughout the East. "What am I to say about the Ebionites who allege themselves to be Christians? To this day the sect exists in all the synagogues of the Jews, under the title of ' the Minim'; the Pharisees still curse it, and the people dub its adherents ' Nazarenes,'" etc. (" Quid dicam de Hebionitis, qui Christianos esse se simulant? usque hodie per totas orientis synagogas inter Judaeos heresis est, quae dicitur Minaeorum et a Pharisaeis nunc usque damnatur, quos vulgo Nazaraeos nuncupant"). But this statement is to be accepted with great caution, and it must be qualified. Jewish Christianity also got the length of India (= South Arabia or perhaps the Axumite kingdom, Eus., H. E., X. 3; Socrat., i. 19; Philostorgius, ii. 6), as well as Rome. But the circles which it formed there were quite insignificant.

rj Na copacof ev t Bepoiaicov irepl tjv KoXÂ; i livpiav, Kai ev rrj AecatToxei ire pi ra t) ' liewtjg neptj, Kai ev rrj Ba(Tawtt(5i rrj Xeyojut-evrj Kookcl ii, Xoopd tj Se 'ESpaicrti Xeyoxev' CKeioev yap yj apxh yeyoie mera t v airo 'lepova-oxvim. coi' fxetaa-racrii iravraiv Toov ulaotjtwv ev lie AX (fikrikOTWV, Xpicrrou cprja-avtog Katoxei at TO. 'lepoa-oxvjuia koi avax' pw' i- t' W Vjw-ewe iracrx i-v iroxiopkiav, KOI ec Tij9 Toiavtt 9 VTrooea-ew Tip Ylepalav oiki'icravte? ekeicre to? e0i'; Sierpi ov ("Now this sect of the Nazarenes exists iii. Beroea m Coele-Syria, and in Decapohs' in the district of Pella, d in Kochaba of Basanitisâ called Khoraba in Hebrew. For thence it originated after the migration from Jerusalem of all the disciples who resided at Pella, Christ having instructed them to leave Jerusalem and retire from it on account of the impending siege. It was owing to this counsel that they went away, as I have said, to reside for a while at Pella'"'). Also Hwr., xviii. 1: ' a apaioi 'lovsatol eicri to yevo?, airo ryj? Takdastrisos koi BaaavlTi6os koi tcov eirekeiva tou lopsai ov 6pij. wij. evol (so that they were a pre-Christian sect!); and Hoer. XXX. 2: ctreisr yap Trafre? oi ej'? l picrrov Tretriarrevkoreii rrjv TLepalav kqt ekeivo Kaipov KatWKr aav, to irxeicrtOV ev IlexXj; Tivl TToxet KaxovULevt rij? Aecavroxeco? rj?? ev ro) evuyyextcp yeypajuLjuevi, Trxtja-iov r? Baraj aa? koi l acravitiso x P ' Trjuikauta ece? jetavactTavtOOv Km ekeccre SiatpiSovtOOv avtUv, yiyovev ec tovtov Trpofpaai tco 'Kpnovi. Kai apx TUi fxev Trjv KatOikrjcriu ex tv ev l wka n tlv Kwur eiri to. jueprj Ttji l apvaifx, 'Apvem. Ka 'ActTapcoo, ev t; l acravitisi X' P h? ' Oova-a et? i juLag yvoocriq Trepiexet meaning that the Nazarenes also were to be looked for there. VSij Se fxoi Kai ev axXoi? Xoyoi?. irepc tj?? TOTTooecria J cokajsoov koi t? 'ApaSla'? Sia irxatoug e'ipt Tai J. (" For wjien all who believed in Christ had settled down about v that time in Peraea, the majority of the emigrants taking up their abode at Pella, a town belonging to the Decapolis mentioned in the gospel, near Batanea and the district of Basanitis, Ebion got his excuse and opportunity. At first their abode was at Kochaba, a village in the district of Carnaim, Arnem, and Astaroth, in the region of Basanitis, according to the information which we have received. But I have spoken, in other connections and with regard to other heresies, of the locality of Kochaba and Arabia"). Al. so Epiph., (76' Mens, et Pond., XV.: rjvlKa yup ejuexXev t) Tro'Xi? uxia-Kequi inro tow Pwulaicof Kui ept ixovardul 7rpoexp ui-UTit0 Tav utto ayyexcw iruvtC' ol maoijtUi ixetarrtrjvai airo t;9 Troxeto? u. exKov(Tt i apsrjv UTToxXucroai, o' rivei JLeravaartai yevojuLevot WKtjcrai' ev JlexXr TH Trpoyeypaululei' iroxet itepav tov 'lopsavov')) Se Troxt? â k Aecavro'Xeft)? Xeyerai exval ("For when the city was about to be captured and sacked by the Romans, all the disciples were warned beforehand by an angel to remove from the city, doomed as it was to utter destruction. On migrating from it they. settled at Pella, the town already indicated, across the Jordan. It is said to belong to Decapolis"). Cp. lastly Epiph., jfitttr., XXX. 18: The Ebionites "spring for the most part from Batanea so apparently we must read, and not l a(3atta? and Paneas, as well as from Moabitis and Kochaba in Basanitis on the other side of Adraa to.? pi ag exovaiv airo re rr i Baraiea? Koi llavedsvi to irxelctTOv, McoaSrijo? re kui Kft)XÂ 3wv r s" ev Til aaruvlTisL ytj eirekeiva 'ASpam').

These passages and their sources (or source), together with the whole geographical and political situation, afford a wide field for discussion and a still wider for conjecture.- The above-mentioned Kochaba is hardly to be identified with the Kochaba of Julius Africanus. But their importance for our present purpose lies in the fact that they attest the scattering of most of the Jewish Christians resident in Palestine, west of

The Christian inscriptions found in Batanea include some from the pre Con-stantine period; cp. Le Bas, No. 2145.

- P'or examples of these, see Zahn's Forschiinge)i, vi. p. 270, and Kenan's Les Evangiles, pp. 39 f.

Thgreis a Koka b el Hawa S. E. of Tabor (cp. Baedeker's Palestiiic ' p. 252), but Kakab is still Tess distant (only jjioiits. north) frob Nazareth; it is natural, therefore, to take this as the village mentioned by Africanus (in Eus., H. E., i. 7) along with Nazareth. We can hardly think of the Kokaba of Epiphauius, which lay east of the Jordan, as Africanus mentions Nazareth and the other village in the same breath as the home of the relatives of Jesus, who were Galileans. It must therefore be regarded as accidental that the home of the relatives of Jesus and also a place east of the Jordan, where many Christians afterwards resided, were called by almost the same name.â Note, as a curious detail, that Conon, whose martyrdom is put by legend under Decius, and who lived and died as a gardener at Magydus in Pamphilia, declared at his trial that he came from Nazareth and was a relative of Jesus (cp. von (iebhardt's Ada Marl. Sdecta, p. 130).

the Jordan as well as at Jerusalem, in connection with and in consequence of the great war, and also their establishment, especially at Pella in Perea (or Decapolis), at Kochaba in Basanitis, and in Berea and its surroundings (Coele-Syria). Epiphanius, it is true, adds Batanea, Paneas, and Moabitis, but we cannot be sure that the dispersed Jewish Christians reached these districts at the same early period. Flying from '
From Pella came the Aristo who composed, in the first half of the second century, the dialogue between the Hebrew Christian Jason and the Alexandrian Jew Papiscus. Only a few fragments of it are extant, unfortunately. Perhaps Aristo himself was a Jew by birth who had gone over to Gentile Christianity. This dialogue ends with the triumph of Jason.

Kochaba (or Kochabe, a favourite place-name) is not the Kokab situated about twenty kilometres i2h miles. W. of Damascus (cp. Baedeker, pp. 295, 348, and the map), where Paul's conversion was located during the Middle Ages, for this spot disagrees with the detailed statements of Epiphanius, and, besides, Eusebius writes as follows in his Onomasticon: Xco d, 7 evrij ev apia-Tepa Aafji. a(TKOV. effri 5e koi Xw a Kdofiri ev tojs avrols fxfpiffiv iv 77 eicrli 'E paiol ol (Is XptftThv TTKnixxtavtis 'E iuvatoi Kaxovfiivoi (" Khoba, which is on the left of Damascus, There is also a village of Khoba in the same district where Hebrews are to be found, who believe in Christ; their name is Ebionites." So Jerome). This Khoba, as Fiirrer kindly informs me, is the modern Kabun, north of Damascus. With this all the statements of Epiphanius agree (see further, Har., xl. I: ev t 'Apa ia iv Kwxi JI, eu6a at tuv 'ESioicat'coj' re Koi Na ctipaiaiv (ti ai fvijp avto = In Arabia at Kochaba, where the origins of the Ebionites and Nazarenes lay). The locality, however, has not been re-discovered. Its site awaits future research, very possibly westward of Adraa (Der'at; cp. Baedeker, p. 186) and in the vicinity of Tell-el-Asch'ari, which lies not far N. N W. from Der'at, and may be identified with Karnaim-Astaroth (Baedeker, p. 183). Basanitis, or Batansea, belonged to Arabia in the days of Epiphanius. Zahn Fofsch., i. pp. 330 f.) is inclined to look for Kochaba much farther south; but in order to make such a site probable, he has to cast doubts upon the precise language of Epiphanius. For this there is no obvious reason, especially as Epiphanius Hcer., xxx. 2) observes that elsewhere he has given an explicit topographical account of Kochaba. Fiirrer kindly informs me that "Kochaba,,., or Chorabe in Hebrew, may be identified with Kharaba about 8 kilometres N. W, of Bostra. Kharaba, indeed, lies pretty far from Astaroth (Tel Astura) and Karnaim (Dschuren in Ledscha), E. and S. of these places. The name favours the identification. The form Kochaba has disappeared in the course of time." Cp. Renan, 43 f.

It is doubtful if this migration took place at so early a period. It may have occurred later. Jerome found Jewish Christians in Bercea de Vir. III. 3).

â â Moabitis owes its mention perhaps to the impression produced by the fact that the Elkesaites (Sampsaeans) were mainly to be found there; cp. Hcer., liii. I: Sauijatot T(V6S iv T7? rigpaia. iripav ttjj 'AAhctjs riroi Nikpas Ka ovfx. evtjs daxacrarts, iv ttj Mojajsivist xcopa, irtpl rhv x P-' PP' vv 'Apvuv koi iirekeiva 4v ry Irovpala koi Naysaritist ("Certain Sampsaeans in Peraea beyond the Dead Sea in Moabitis, in the vicinity of the Arnon torrent and across the borders in Ituraea hatred and persecution at the hands of the Palestinian Jews, they rightly supposed that they would fare, not comfortably indeed, but at least better in the Greek towns of the East and in the country. This migration, which had been carried out once before in the dispersion of the Jerusalem church after the outburst against Stephen, was i-epeated in a later age, when a number of Christian heretics during the fourth and fifth centuries fled from the state chmxh into the eastern districts across the Jordan. All these movements of flight presuppose, a group of people comparatively small in numbers, with little to lose in the shape of property. They lead us to form a moderate estimate of the numbers of these " Ebionites." The latter, broken up more than once and subsequently exposed in part to foreign influences, survived in these districts along the Jordan and the Dead Sea as late as the fourth century, and even later. Persecuted by the Jews, treated by the Gentile Christians as semi-Jews (and Jews indeed they were, by nationality and language Aramaic), they probably dragged out a wretched existence. The Gentile Christian bishops (even those of Palestine) and teachers rarely noticed them. It is remarkable how little Eusebius, for example, knows about them, while even Justin and Jerome after him evince but a slender acquaintance with their ways of life. Origen and Epiphanius knew most about them. The former gives an account of their numbers, which is more important than the statement of Justin in his Apology (I. liii.: irxelovm rovg e eovwv twv utto 'lovsaicop Kai am. upecoi' pictTiavov;, see above, p. 4), He remarks Tom. I, 1 in Joh. ed. Brooke, i. pp. 2 f.), in connection with the 144,000 sealed saints of the Apocalypse, that this could not mean Jews by birth or Jewish Christians, since one might quite well hazard the coitjectiire that there zvas not that number of Jexvish Christians in existence. Now this remark furnishes us with a rough idea of the number of Jewish and Nabatitis"). Whether the sect of the " Peratre," first mentioned by Clem. Alex. Slrom., VII. xvii. io8) has anything to do with Pera a, as Hort and Mayor suppose Coninent. on Strovi., VII. p. 354, 1902), is uncertain. Clement himself thinks that the name arose from some locality.

I need not raise the vexed question as to the relationship between Nazarenes and Ebionites.

Christians during the first half of the third century. Origen knew the districts where Jewish Christians chiefly resided, as is proved by his travels from Ca sarea to Bostra. He also knew the extent of the Jewish Christian synagogues in Alexandria and Lower Egypt. And these were their headquarters. Besides, we can appeal to yet another estimate of their numbers in this connection. Justin, himself a Samaritan by birth, observes in his Ajiology (I. xxvi.) that "almost all the Samaritans, with only a few foreigners, hail Simon Magus as their chief god." A hundred years later, Origen writes thus (c. Cels. i. Ivii): " At present the number of Simon's disciples all over the world does not amount, in my opinion, to thirty. Perhaps that is even putting it too high. There are extremely few in Palestine, and in the other parts of the world, where he would fain have exalted his name, they are totally unknown."

We now come back to lia-Jerusalem and to the Gentile Christian communities of Palestine which replaced the Jewish Christians. Marcus (135136 a. d.) was the first Gentile Christian president in Elia. Like the town, the church of Elia iiâ ver attained any importance, as is abundantly plain from the negative evidence of Eusebius's Church-History, even when we take into account the fact that Eusebius was bishop of Caesarea, the natural rival of yelia. The latter was called ". Elia" even in ecclesiastical terminology (cp., e. g., Eus., H. E., ii. 12. 3; Dionys. Alex., ibid., vii. 5; Mah. Pal., xi., though " Jerusalem" also occurs); which shows that even the church

Cp. with this TertulliajlS. notice de Ajiima, 7)â though it is not, of course, equally important â of the ssci, of. Menander, which must be also sought in Palestine (Samaria) especially. He calls Menander's adherents " paucissimi," and adds: " Suspectam faciara tantam raritatem securissimi et tutissimi sacramenti i. e., Menander's baptismal rite. cum contra omnes iam nationes adscendant in montem domini" ("I think it is suspicious when a rite of such protective and saving efficacy is so seldom observed. when, on the contrary, all nations are going up to the mountain of the Lord ").

The episcopal list (cp. my Chronologic i. pp. 220 f.) up to 250 A. D. shows nothingbut Greco-Roman names: Cassianus, Publius, Maximus, Julianus, Gaius, Symmachus, Gaius, Julianus, Capito, Maximus, Antoninus, Valens, Dolichianus, Narcissus, Dius, Germanion, Gordius, Alexander. Then come four namesâ Mazabanes, Hymenajus, Zabdas, and Hermonâ two of which, of course, are Syrian.

at first held that the old tradition had been broken. Nevertheless, as is well known, the sacred Christian sites were sought out during the second and third centuries; some of them were actually found and visited. A certain amount of theological activity is attested by the existence of a library which bishop Alexander established in Elia at the opening of the third r century (Eus., H. E., vi. 20).= j Once the metropolitan system came to be organized, the Wshop-A of Caesarea was metropolitan of Syria-Palestina; but it is quite lj-, AA " clear, from the history of Eusebius, that the bishop of JElia not C r Uierely stood next to him, but somehow shared with him the

By 300 A. D. the name "Jerusalem" had become wholly unfamiliar in wide circles. A good example of this is afforded by Mart. Pal., xi. 10, which tells how a confessor described himself to the Roman governor as a citizen of Jerusalem (meaning the heavenly Jerusalem). "The magistrate, however, thought it was an earthly city, and sought carefully to discover what city it could be, and wherever it could be situated." Even were the anecdote proved to be fictitious, it is still conclusive.

' Eusebius H. E., vi. 2, apropos of Alexander of Cappadocia) gives an early instance of this, in the year 212213. In consequence, the repute of the Jeriisalem church must have gradually revived or arisen during the course of the third century. The first serious evidence of it occurs in the case of Firmilian of Cassarea (Cyprian's Ep., Ixxv. 6), who upbraids the Roman church with failing to observe the exact methods followed by the church of Jerusalem. But even this yj evidence must not be overrated. Prominent Cappadocian Christians had been for "â long in close touch with Palestine. The real revival of the Jerusalem church belongs to the age just before Constantine, when the worship of heroes, martyrs, and sacred relics Ijecame part and parcel of the faith. Constantine then did his utmost to exalt Jerusalem.

We have only one important early trace of this library, and even it is enigmatic. It is to be found in the abrupt and paradoxical statement of Cod. Ambros. H. 150. Inf. Ssec. IX.: "In commentariis Victorini inter plurima haec etiam scripta reperimus: invenimus in membranis Alexandri episcopi qui fuit in Hierusalem quod transcripsit manu sua de exemplaribus apostolorum " (whereupon a perverse chronology of the life of Jesus follows); cp. von Dobschtitz in Texte u. Unters., xi. I,

TliÂ Â restige of Csesarea dates from the days of Herod the Great, who rebuilt the city on an imposing scale. It was the headquarters of the Roman procurators, and consequently became the ecclesiastical capital. Tacitus (Hisf., ii. 78) calls it " Judsek caput"; while after Severus Alexander it was the capital of the OW province Syria-Palestina. The ty was-aiways predominantly Greek, not Jewish; vf " Lhence it was possible to master and massacre the local Jews at the outbreak of the- Jewish war. Acts relates how the first real Gentile Christian was converted at Caesarea, and that his conversion became the basis of the Gentile mission (Acts x.).

e was the military captain of the place! The troops under command of the procurator were stationed at Ca; sarea.

management of the synod. And as time went on, he gradually eclipsed his rival. Under Origen, Caesarea became a second Alexandria in point of theological learning and activity. Paniphilus, who founded the great local library there for the purpose of biblical interpretation and in order to preserve the works of Origen, has the credit of having adhered firmly to the traditions of his great master, and of having made the work of Eusebius possible. We know nothing about the size of the Jerusalem church or the percentage of Christians in the city. But until the intervention of Constantine they were unable to secure possession of the holy sepulchre (or what they both took to be its site; the pagans had erected a temple to Venus on it; cp. Eus., Vit. Const., iii. 26), which shows their lack of power within the city.

The metropolitan nexus cannot be traced earlier than c. 190 a. d. (the Paschal controversy). Eusebius (v. 23) tells how Theophilus of C3esarea and Narcissus of Jerusalem were then at the head of the Palestinian churches and synod. In noticing the synodal communication (v. 23), he puts Narcissus first, while he distinguishes the bishops of Tyre and Ptolemais, who attended the synod, from the Palestinian bishops. The communication is interesting, as it incidentally mentions a constant official intercourse between the provincial churches of Palestine and the church of Alexandria. The leading bishops of Palestine were favourable to Origen. When he was in Cresarea, in 215216, he preached in church, though a layman, "at the request of the bishops" (of the local synod in session). Alexander, bishop of Jerusalem, and Theoktistus, bishop of Csesarea (mentioned in this order), defended this permission against the complaints of Demetrius, the bishop of Alexandria, in a joint letter (Eus., H. E., vi. 19. 16 f.) The consecration of Origen to the office of presbyter seems also to have taken place at a synod in Caesarea (Eus., vi. 23). Eusebius, however, puts the matter very strangely: tv 5ia naxaia-Tij'Tjs irp crfivtepiov x 'P"" Oecriav iv Kaiaapda nphs riov Tjjse iiricfk6-njov ava aj. fiayfi. We have also to assume a Palestinian synod about the year 231232, which refused to recognize the condemnation of Origen by Demetrius (cp. Jerome's Epp., xxxiii. 4). In his epistle to Steplianus (Eus., H. E,, vii. 5. i), Dionysius of Alexandria puts Theoktistus, bishop of Caesarea, before Mazabanes, bishop of lia. But in the synodal document of the great Eastern synod of Antioch in 268 (Eus., vii. 30. 2), the bishop of Jerusalem precedes the bishop of Caesarea, while at the synod of Nicaea Macarius of Jerusalem voted before Eusebius of Caesarea. Eusebius only gives the episcopal list of Caesarea as far back as I go a. d., and that of Jerusalem as far back as James. But did Eusebius know of bishops at Csesarea before 190? I pass over, as untrustworthy, the statement of Eutychius (cp. my Chronol., i. p. 222) that Demetrius of Alexandria addressed a circular letter to Victor of Rome, Maxim(in)us of Antioch, and " Gabius " (Gaius?) of Jerusalem.

"The Christian community in Caesarea seems to have been more influential. According to Socrates (iii. 23), who depends upon Eusebius, the later Neoplatonist Porphyry was beaten by Christians in Cassarea.

108 MISSION AND EXPANSION OF CHRISTIANITY

In Acts we hear of Christians, outside Jerusalem, at Samaria (and in Samaritan villages; cp. viii. 25), Lydda (Diospolis), Saron, Joppa, and Caesarea. Codex D of the New Testament locates Mnason, the old disciple (Acts xxi. 16), at an unnamed village between Caesarea and Jerusalem.

At Nicaga there were present the bishops of Jerusalem, Neapolis (Sichem), Sebaste (Samaria), Caesarea, Gadara, Ascalon, Nicopolis, Jamnia, Eleutheropolis, Maxinianopolis, Jericho. Sebulon, Lydda, Azotus, Scjthopolis, Gaza, Aila, and Capitolias Elsewhere we have direct or inferential evidence for the presence of Christians (though in very small numbers at particular spots) at Sichar ('Asker), Bethlehem, Anea near Eleutheropolis in the district of Beth Gubrin, Batanea near Caesarea (Aulana), Anim, Jattir, and Phasno. Eusebius (H. E., vi. 11. 3) mentions bishops of churches which were situated round (irepi) Jerusalem, even in the year 212213; but we do not know who are meant. Similarly, in Maii. Pal., i. 3, he mentions apxovtef twv e-jtixoopidov ekKX) cnu)i', "rulers of the country churches" (i. e., of churches in the neighbourhood of Caesarea), who were martyred at Caesarea under Diocletian, But unfortunately he does not specify the localities. Nor do we know anything about the 1 Acts ix. 35 seems to take Saron as a group of places.

- The birthplace of Justin the apologist. Epiphanius Hcer., lxxviii. 24) describes a peculiar local cult: Ovaias ol firixiptoi nxodffiy els 6voxa rris KSpris, Srjdev efrrpocpacrtws rris Ovyarphs 'lecpoae., koi tols â r)TTa""f)iji.4vois rovro yeyovsv tls likdfiriy elsa) o atpeias koi Ktvoxarpiias. He can also report a remarkable statement about Sichem (Hccr., lxxx. l): aaA. a kui npocnvxvs t6xos ev 2iciuotj, Â V rfi vvv Ka ovfxevti Neairoaej e co rris irsKews, ev tjj' ttssicisi, as anh ffr xiiwv Svo, Ofarpoeisris, ovtcos iv aepi kol alopicf tstcj) iffrl Karaakevaardfls I'inh rwv 'S. ap. apensiv iriivta TO rciv 'lovsaiwu fjn ovfuepoi.

3 The signatures to the Nicene council (Gelzer, Hilgenfeld, and Cunitz, 1898, p. Ix.) give a double entry: Map? f os ' efiaffttivis and Taiavhs l, e0a(XTrjs. Schwartz (Zur Gesch. des Athanas., VI. p. 286) thinks that the town and the district formed two churchesâ which is quite likely.

The presence of bishops or Christians in several of these towns is attested also by Alexander of Alexandria (in Athanas., de Synod. 17, and Epiph., Hcer., lxix. 4), and Eusebius Mart. Pal.).

I leave out the pseudo-Clementines.

Â " Batanea near Cresarea maybe identified with Khirbet Bethan (Ibthan); it is the one ruin S. of Zeita, and W. of Attil, in the district of Saron, about 4 hours E. S. E. from Csesarea. But this identification seems to me problematical. I would have rather discovered the holy springs of Betasenea (Batanea)"; so Flirrer writes. On the Guthe-Fischer map Batanea is put due E. of Caesarea.

church of Asclepius, the Marcionite bishop who was martyred in the persecution of Daza (Eus., Mart. Pal., x. 1), or about the place to which the bishop mentioned by Epiphanius in Hfrr., lxiii. 2 (ev TToxei juikpa t? Haxaia-Tivr â in a small town of Palestine), belonged. The latter outlived the era of the great persecution, as he is expressly termed a confessor.

The large majority of the localities in Palestine where bishops or Christians can be traced are Greek cities. It was among the Greek population that Palestinian Christianity from Hadrian onwards won most adherents. If we further assume that in general, until Constantine mastered Palestine, there were no Christians- at all in Tiberias,â which, with Jabne (Jamnia) and Lydda (Diospolis) formed the headquarters of rabbinic learning, â in Uiocassarea (Sepphoris), in Nazareth, and in Capernaum " (for the local Christians in primitive times had been driven out by the fanatical Jews); assuming also that

This can hardly mean the persecution under Julian, as the bishop in question was dead by 370 a. d., after a long tenure of the episcopate.

This does not follow from Epiph., Hcer., xxx. 4, for the permission granted by Constantine to Joseph to build churches there, might per contra suggest the presence of local Christians. But in xxx. 11 we read that Joseph merely secured one favour, viz., permission to build churches in those Jewish towns and villages throughout Palestine "where no one had ever been able to erect churches, owing to the absence of Greeks, Samaritans, or Christians. Especially was this the case with Tiberias, Diocsesarea, Sepphoris, Nazareth, and Capernaum, where members of all other nations were carefully excluded " vqa. ris oiisetrore tffxvcyfv olkusoxtJa-at 6cÂ Xr)(7Â ax, Sia rh fi'fite "E r va, ixijti 2a, uapâ it7ji, jx ts Xpiatiavhi fiicrop ahrsiv eivai â TOVTO 5e fiakictTa ev TiSepiast Kal ev ALOKaiffapiia, tjj koi '2, eir(povpiv, Kol ev Ka ipvaohj. (pvxaffcretat irap' avrols rov fir) elvai riva Wov edvovs). This is not contradicted by the statement of Epiphanius himself (xxx. 4) regarding a " bishop whose district adjoined that of Tiberias " iiriakowos ir ri(TL6xapos rrjs Tt eplcui' iii), in the pre-Constantine period; for this bishop was not exactly bishop of Tiberias.â There must have been numerous purely Jewish localities in Palestine; thus Origen in Aatt., xvi. 17. i) describes Bethphage as a village of Jewish priests. In Mart, Pal., p. 61 (ed. Violet) we read that "in Palestine there is one populous city whose inhabitants are entirely Jewish, called Lud in Aramaic and Diocksarea in Greek."â It may be purely accidental that rabbi Elieser met on the upper street of Sepphoris a disciple of Jesus called Jacob of Kephar Sechania (cp. Aboda Sara, 161, 1 a, and Midrasch rabba on Koh. i. 8; cp. Hennecke's NTliche Apocryphen, I. pp. 68 f).

On the Jewish schools at Lydda and Jabne ("une sorte de petite Jerusalem resuscitee "), cp. Kenan's Les Evatigiles, pp. 19 f.

' But apriori it is likely that originally there was a Jewish Christian community at Capernaum, and a passage in the Jerusalem Talmud confirms this supposition.

they were extremely scanty in the territory stretching away to the south of Jerusalem, then it is impossible to speak of Palestine being Christianized before the time of Constantine. Save for a few exceptions, the lowlands were Jewish, while in Jewish towns and localities Christians were only tolerated against the will of the inhabitants, if they were tolerated at all. In Diocaesarea, e. g. even under Constantine, the Jews were still so numerous that they essayed a rising (Socrat., H. E. ii. 33); and Theodoret H. E., iv. 19) relates how in the reign of Valens the town was inhabited by Jews who murdered Christians. In the Hellenistic towns Christians were to be met with, but even thereâ with the exception of Caesarea, perhapsâ they were not very numerous, while several important pagan towns with ancient shrinesâ especially those on the seaboard of Philistiaâ offered them a sharp resistance, and refused to harbour them at all. Thus in Gaza itself no Christian bishop was in residence, as may be certainly inferred from Eus., H. E., vm. 13, where Silvanus is described as bishop of "the churches round Gaza" (cp. Afart. Pal, xiii. 4: ec r? Ta alwv eiriarkoiro opjuLMfxevo? 2tx3., "Silvanus, a bishop from Gaza") at the time of the great persecution. Not until after 325 a. d. was the church organized strongly by Constantine amid the obstinate paganism of these towns (cp. Vit. Const., iv 38); thus even Asclepas, who was present at the council of Nicea (cp. Epiph., Hcer., Ixix. 4), was no more than the bishop of the churches round Gaza, although a rather small (and secret?) Christian conventicle is to be assumed for Gaza itself as early as the age of the persecution (see Eus., Mart. Pal, viii. 4, iii. 1).-

On some exceptions to this (Anim and Jattir), see below.â For idolatry in Mamre, see Vit. Const., iii. 51-53. Constantine had a church built at Mamre. Sozomen H. E., ii. 4) describes the summer festival attended by Christians, pagans, and Jews there.

- The seaport of Gaza, Majuma, undoubtedly belonged to this group of churches. But other towns and townships in the vicinity were still pagan entirely. Thus Sozomtn H. E., v. 15) declares that his grandfather and his grandfather's family were the first converts in Bethelia: (ccojuj? Ta aio â Kokvavgpdirrtf re ovar) koi Itpk e-xovcrr opx'"' ''''''''' "" Karaffkevri trefiva rois Karotkotxn, Koi ixakiara rh Uavdfov. Incidentally, we learn that Jews as well as pagans resided there.

A Christian woman " from the country of Gaza " rrjs Ta aloiv xÂ pao is mentioned in Eus., Alart. Pal., viii. 8.

Palestinian Greek Christianity and its bishops gravitated southwards to Alexandria more readily than to Antioch and the north (see above, on Eus, HE., v. 25); even in spiritual things it depended upon Alexandria throughout our period. This was the natural outcome of the purely Greek, or almost purely Greek, character of Christianity in Palestine, which is brought out very forcibly by the names of the martyrs recounted by Eusebius (in his Mart. Pal.). In that catalogue Jewish or Syrian names are quite infrequent (vet cp. Zebinas of Eleutheropolis, and Ennathas, a woman from Scythopolis, Mart. Pal, ix. 5-6V

Unfortunately, this treatise of Eusebius furnishes far less illustrative or statistical material for the church of Palestine than one would expect. We can only make out, from its contents, that it corroborates our conclusion that even in the Hellenistic towns of Palestineâ which Eusebius has alone in viewâ during the great persecution there cannot have been very many Christians. This conclusion is ratified by all we can ascertan regarding the history of Christianity in Palestine during the fourth century, especially along the Philistine seaboard. The attempt made by Constantine and his successors to definitely acclimatize Christianity in Palestine did not ' Eus., Marl. Pal., iii. 3, supports the view that in the seacoast towns of Palestine Christianity was to be found among the floating population rather than among the old indigenous inhabitants. Six Christians voluntarily reported themselves to the governor for the fight with wild beasts. "One of them, born in Pontus, was called Timolaos; Dionysius, another, came from Tripolis in Phoenicia; the third was a subdeacon of the church in Diospolis, called Romulus: besides these there were two Egyptians, Paesis and Alexander, and another Alexander from Gaza." Hardly any of the martyrs at C sarea were citizens of the town.â The relations between Palestine (Caesarea) and Alexandria were drawn still closer by Origen and his learning. We also know that Africanus went from Emmaus to Alexandria in order to hear Heraclas, and so forth.

- Old Testament namesâ after the end of the third century, at leastâ do not prove the Jewish origin of their bearers; cp. Mart. Pal., xi. 7 f.: "The governor got by way of answer the name of a prophet instead of the man's proper name. P'or instead of the names derived from idolatry, which had been given them by their parents, they had assumed names such as Elijah, or Jeremiah, or Isaiah, or Samuel, or Daniel."

â See some data upon this in V. Schultze's Gesch. des Untergangs des griechisch-r'dmischen Heideiitiims (1892), ii. pp. 240 f., and especially the " Peregrinatio Silvise " (ed. Gamurini, 1887).

succeed. Numberless churches, no doubt, were built on the sacred sites of antiquity as well as at spots which were alleged to mark past deeds and events or martyrs' graves. Hordes of monks settled down there. Pilgrims came in their thousands. But there was no real Christianizing of the country as an outcome of all this, least of all in the proud cities on the south-west coast. As late as 400 a. d. Gaza and Raphia remained essentially pagan. Look at Sozom., vii. 15, and the Vita Porphyri'i of Marcus (ed. Teubner, 1895). Here we are told that but a very few Christiansâ 127 in all'-â were to be found in Gaza, before Porphyry entered on his duties (394 a. d.), while the very villages near the city were still entirely pagan. For our purpose that number (127) is most valuable. It teaches us the necessity of confining within a very small limit any estimate we may choose to form of the Christianity which prevailed on the Philistine seaboard during the previous century. There is also significance in the fact that the name of " the old church" (p. 18. 6) was given to the church which Asclepas, who was bishop of Gaza during the great persecution and under Constantine, had erected shortly after 325. This means that previous to 325 there were no Christian edifices in the place. Ascalon, too, had a strongly pagan population as late as the fourth centurv, just as Dioca? sarea (see above) was inhabited by a preponderating number of Jews. The seaport

Cp. the important passage in Mart. Pal., p. 162 (ed. Violet).

- Vita Porphyr., p. 12. I: o T n ovth Xpirtiavoi, oxlyoi koi evapldfirjrot Tvyxiivovris (cp. p. 74. 15), "The Christians of that day were few and easily counted." It is also noted (p. 20. 2) that Porphyry added 105 Christians in one year to the original nucleus of 127. Compare the following numbers: on p. 29. 10 there are sixty named, on p. 52. i thirty-nine, then on p. 61. 16 we have one year with three hundred converts, koi 6 eveivou Ka6' fkaffrov eras av rjcriv ttresexf'o TO. Xpictiavwv ("And thenceforward every year saw an increase to the strength of local Christianity ").

Vit. Porphyr., p. 16. 7: â K t a'iov Fa rjy Kajfiai ruyxa-i'ovffi irapa Tr v dsby ahives VTrdpxovffiu rrjs ilsuaofiavias ("Near Gaza there are wayside villages which are given over to idolatry").

â Sozomen .Â., v. 15) does mention Christians at Ascalon who venerated his grandfather, but this refers to the second half of the fourth century.

Cp. Socrates. H. E., ii. 33: ol iv Aiokaiaapiia ttjs TlaxakTTivqs 'lov5a7ot, Kara 'Puj. aia)!" '6ir a a. vtfjpav koi TTtp tout Ttjirouj (Kiivovs Katfrpexof' aa. Xa tovtovs fxfu Tdwoi 6 Ka Kivvatdvttos, '6v Kalirapa Kataa-rrirras 6 Sacriasus fis rijv k(fav e anfftfthey, Svfauip a. Tro(rtei as KatT ya)yiaatO Kal tv Tt Aiv avrcei' Atokattapfiav of Anthedon remained entirely pagan as late as Julian's reign.

I now proceed to give a list of towns and localities in which Christians can be traced prior to 325, adding very brief annotations.

Jerusalem, represented by bishop Macarius at Nica? a; " churckes round Jerusalem " in the year 212213 are noted in Eus., H. E. vi. 11. 3. For the episcopal list, see above, p. 105.

Nazareth (Julius Africanus: relatives of Jesus here, but afterwards no Christians at all).

Caesarea. the best harbour on the coast, and perhaps the largest Greek city in Palestine, though with a number of Jewish residents (Acts x.). Bisliops are to be traced from 190 a. d., viz., Theophilus circa 190, Eus., H. E., v. 22. 25); Theoktistus (at the crisis over Origen in Alexandria, also at the time of the Antiochene synod upon Novatian and bishop Stephanus of Rome, Eus.,., vi. 19. 17; vi. 46. 3 where he is called "bishop in Palestine," as a metropolitan; we do not know if he was the immediate successor of Theophilus); Di)mnus (who only ruled for a short period, according to Eus., H. E., vii. 14; he succeeded Theoktistus in the reign of Gallienus); Theoteknus (who succeeded Domnus in the same reign, and took part in the synods against Paul of Antioch, Eus., vii. 14. 28, 30; vii. 32.

6(s esa os Kareuix nvai ekixivffiv ("The Jews who inhabited Diocksarea took up arms against the Romans, and began to lay waste the neighbourhood. Galhis, however, who was also called Constanlius, whom the emperor had sent to the East after creating him Caesar, despatched an armed force against them and routed them; whereupon, by his orders, their city, Diocsesarea, was razed to the ground ").

Cp. Sozom., V. 9: irapair r crioiis (as at Gaza) TTjuikavta Tif "E. riviafj. f Xalpoutra Kot irepl Tr; j' Bepaireiav twv oavoov eino-t nevr).

"During the second century in particular, these Gentile Christian churches were certainly to some extent infinitesimal. They were exposed to the double fire of local Jews and pagans, and they had no relations with the Jewish Christians. The following decision of the so-called Egyptian Church-Constitution is scarcely to be referred to Egypt. It rather applies to Palestine or Syria. 'Eav 6 tyavspi, a virdpx Kol ij. r)nov irxrjdos rvyxo-vr Toiiv Swafieuaiv prillraffdai irepl itri(TK6. wov fvrhs j)3' avspciv, eh ras ir ri(riov ekK 7 crias, oirov tvx"- " Treinjyvta, ypacpetwcrav, k. t. A. ("Should there be a dearth of men, and should it be impossible to secure the requisite number of twelve capable of taking part in the election of a bishop, let a message be sent to churches in the neighbourhood"); Texie ti. Unlers., ii. 5. 71 f.

YOt, It, 21, 24), and Agapius (Eus., vii. 32, 24). Ambrosius, Origen's friend, was a deacon, Proteknus a presbyter of Ca; sarea (cp. Orig., Exhort, ad Mati.). Romanus was a deacon and an exorcist in a neighbouring village (Violet, Mart. Pal., p. 11). Catholic Christians and a Marcionite woman, from the country near Caesarea, were martyred under Valerian (cp. Eus., H. E., vii. 12). Counc. Nic. (bishop Eusebius). Legend makes the tax-gatherer Zacchaeus the first bishop of Caesarea. For " churches at Caesarea," see Mart. Pal., i. 3. Christianity in Palestine had its headquarters at Caesarea. Even the pagan population circa 300 a. d. seems to have been inclined that way. In the fourth century the house of the chief captain Cornelius was shown, built into the church, " et Philippi aediculas et cubicula quattuor virginum prophetarum"" (Jerome, Ep. cviii. 8).

Samaria-Sebaste (Acts viii., Counc, Nic, bishop Marinus; here John the Baptist was buried, ace. to Theod,, H. E., iii. 3),

Lydda-Diospolis (Acjts ix,; Theod., i. 4; Counc, Nic, bishop Antius. Close by was Arimathaea, a place visited by pilgrims, etc., Jerome).

Joppa (Acts ix.).

Localities on the plain of Saron (Acts ix.),

Emmaus-Nicopolis (Julius Africanus; Counc, Nic, bishop Petrus, The local church in the fourth century was held to be built out of the house of Cleopas, according to Jerome, loc. cit.).

Sichem-Neapolis (Counc, Nic, bishop Germanus).

Scythopolis Mah. Pal., vi, p, 4, 7, 110, cp. longer form of Mart. Pal., ed, Violet in Texte u. Inters., xiv, 4; Alex, of Alex, in Athanas., de Synod. 17; cp. Epiph,, Hoer., xxx, 5; Counc, Nic, bishop Patrophilus),

Eusebius (Violet'sed., p. 42) tells how the miracle of the corpse of Appianus the martyr took place before the eyes of the whole city, "and the whole city (young men and old, women of all ages, and virgins) gave with one accord the glory to God alone, and confessed with loud voice the name of Christ," Cp. also pp. 69 f.

Simon Magus came from, Q tta, asajaaritan village, and Menander from the village of Capparetasa.

The biblical Beth-san (Baischan, Besan),

E leutheropo lis Mart. Pal, ix. 5, cp. Violet, p. 73; Epiph., Hcer., lxviii. 3, lxvi. 1; Counc. Nic, bishop Maxiiniis).

Maximianopolis (Counc. Nic, bishop Paulus).-

Jericho (Counc. Nic, bishop Januarius; cp. also Euseb., vi. 16).

Sabulon (Counc. Nic, bishop Heliodorus).

Ia, ninia Mart. Pal., xi. 5; Alex, of Alex, in Epiph., Hcer., lxix. 4; Counc. Nic, bishop Macrinus).

Azojhus (Counc. Nic, bishop Silvanus).

Ascalon Mart. Pal., x. 1; Alex, of Alex, in Epiph., Hier., lxix. 4; Counc. Nic, bishop Longinus).

Gazaj(for a small local conventicle with no bishop and the " churches round Gaza," under bishop Asclepas," see above; Epiph., Hcer., lxviii. 3; Counc. Nic Among the churches round Gaza, the seaport of Majuma was noted for its large number of Christians).

Aila (a seaport on the north-east corner of the Red Sea, included in Palestine at that period; Counc. Nic, bishop Petrus).

Gadara (Zacchasus a local deacon, Violet, p. 8; Counc. Nic, bishop Sabinus).

Capitolias (perhaps = Beter-Ras; Counc. Nic, bishop Anti-ochus).

Clermont-Ganneau, Conpt. rend, de VAcad. des Iiiscr. et Bell. Lettr., 1904, Jan.-Feb., pp. 54 f.; recently discovered inscriptions have laid bare the opening of this city's era (199 A. 1;.), when, as we now know, Septiinius Severus was in Egypt and Palestine and conferred autonomy on the city.â Epiphanius was born tbe sand uke,- a place near Eleutheropolis, c. 320 A. D. (accordingtotHe 'Cife"l, probably of Christian parents, but possibly of Jewish.

It may be the town between Ceesarea (Straton's Tower) and Scythopolis. Probably it is. But we may also think of the town N. of Bostra in the S. Hauran (now es-Suweda, cp. Baedeker, p. 191).

' Sabulon." says Fiirrer, "I take to be the Zabulon of Josephus, which is the same as his Chabolo, the modern Kabfll, on the border of the plain xaf Ptolemais."' â St Hilarion was burn (about 250 A. D. J aftTabalha, "a village lying about 5000 paces from Gaza," but his parents were pagan. Commodian calls him " Gasseus," but this has nothing whatever to do with Gaza.

" On account of its Christianity, Julian took away its civic rights and attached theni ICLGaza. Eusebius Vita Coz. f., iv. 37-38, and after him Sozomen, ii. 5, V. 3) tells how the local pagans suddenly were converted to Christianity under Constantine, and how the town received from the emperor its civic rights and the name of Constantia. Naturally, being a seaport, it contained a number of Christians before it openly professed the Christian faith. Constantine made it independent, in order to injure the pagan Gaza,

Bethlehem (the existence of local Christians is deducible from Orig., r. Cels., I. li.).

Anea, jvillage in the territory of Eleutheropolis twv opoov 'FixeooepotToxecoi, Mart. Pal., x, 2. Petrus Balsamus, the martyr, came from the district of Eleutheropolis; see Ruinart, p. 525).

Anim and Jether, two villages south of Hebron (on Jether or Jethira or Jattir, see Baedeker, p. 209; Anim = Ghuwin = Ruwen, as Seybold kindly informs me (so Guerin); cp. Buhfs Geogr. Pal., p. 164), which Eusebius, in his Onomasticon, declares were exclusively inhabited by Christians. This is a striking statement, as we are not prepared for Christians in these of all districts." We must not, however, measure the density of the Christian population on the soil of Palestine by this standard. These two villages must have formed an exception. to the general rule, although it remains a notable fact that there were villages already which were completely Christian.

Teptullian adv. Jiid. xiii.) writes: " Animadvertimus autem nunc neminem de genere Israel in Bethlehem remansisse, et exinde quod interdictum est ne in confinio ipsius regionis demoretur quisquam ludaeorum " ("We notice now that none of the race of Israel has remained in Bethlehem; such has always been the case since all Jews were prohibited from lingering even in the confines of the district"). Constantine had a church built on the grotto of the birth (Vita, iii. 41).

- Ftirrer, however, calls attention to the fact that many famous rabbis had also fled south.

â Eusebius (vii. 12) tells of three Palestinian martyrs (Priscus, Malchus, and Alexander) in the reign of Valerian, stating expressly that they lived on the land, and that they were reproached for thus enjoying an unmolested life whilst their brethren in the city were exposed to suffering. Hence they voluntarily betook themselves also to Caesarea, etc. Unfortunately, Eusebius has not specified their original home.

Fi'irrer writes to me as follows: "There is a slight confusion about Anim, Anea, and Anab. In the Onomasticon we read that Anab was in the district of Eleutheropolis, d Xa kox 'hva a evrj Kiiifxri 'lovsaiwf neyiarr) coxoujuevr; (ev tcj?) Aapcoj- Trphs v6tov Xebpwv a-rrh ctr iji. eiaiv 9'. Then, on Anim: (pv ris 'lovsa. AAr; 'Avaia Trarjcrioc ttjs irpoTepas, vvv oatj 'Kpiariavsiv rvyx' vei, oixra dvaroaiCTj ttjs irpotfpas. Anim has for long been identified with Ghuwin in the south of Hebron. There are an upper and a lower Ghuwin. The former is north-east of the latter, and would be the Christian

Anim. (In Anab, about six hours south of Eleutheropolis, there are ruins of a church which seem to date from the Roman period.) They were distinguished by their sites on two hills separated by a small valley; the aforesaid ruins lie on the eastern hill. I would be disposed to look for the two Aneas here. In the west, Jews resided; in the east, Christians. On the western hill there are also ruins of a shrine, which afterwards served as a mosque; the traces

Sichar-'Asker (as Eusebius observes in his Onomastkon that a church was alremy built there, it follows that there must have been some local Christians at an earlier date).

Batanaea, ajvillage beside Caesarea Mart. Pal., xi. 29; where we are not to read Mangansea, Baganaea, Balanea, or Banea; see Mercati's " I Martiri di Palestina nel Codice Sinaitico,""" Estr. dai Rendiconti del R. Instit. Lombard, di sc. e lett., Serie II., vol. 30, 1897).

Phaeno (according to Mart. Pal., vii. 2, and Epiph., Ha r., Ixviii. 3, Christians laboured in the mines at Phaeno in South Palestine cp. Mart. Pal., viii. 1, and the Onomasticon; according to Mart., xiii. 1, they built houses into churches, and were consequently dispersed by force into settlements throughout the various districts of Palestine." The Apology of Pamphilus for Origen is directed " To the confessors sentenced to the mines of Palestine'"' " ad confessores ad metalla Palestiniae danniatos"" ; cp. Routh s Reliq. Sacra; IV."-' p. 341).= of its Christian origin are still distinct,"â In the Onoviasticon (p. 58. 18) Eusebius writes thus: B7)6aa3apa, "" o-kov i v 'lojaijrjs atTTt 'oii'," " Trepai toc 'lopstii'oi'," kq. Si'ikiVTUL 6 tjttos, iv (f) Kal irkeiovs raty a. Se puy els ert vvv rh Kovrphv (ptaorixovvtai aixfidyiiy. This notice does not permit us to infer the existence of any spot; on the contrary, it suggests the absence of any such spot (cp. Orig., Conm. in Joh., vi. 50, and Preuschen in D. Berliner Philol. IVochenschrift, 1903, col. 1358.

In the larger recension of the Mart. Pal. (Violet, pp. 105 f.) we are told that the Coptic prisoners of Ph no were for a time together at Zoara (= Zoar). " Much people were with them, some who had come from elsewhere to see them, and many others who provided them with what they required, sought them out affectionately, and ministered to their wants. The whole day they spent in prayer, worship, teaching, and reading. they lived all the while as if it were a festival and convocation. But God's enemy could not bear this. Forthwith a governor was sent to them. His first act was to separate them," etc.

"Phffino has been again discovered; it lay in Eastern Edom, at a place where two valleys meet. The ruins are now called " Phenan " (Fiirrer).

In one town, Au. lqna,-Petrus Balsamus is said to have been martyred. He came from the district of Eleutheropolis (according to the longer Syriac recension of the Mart. Pal., he was born " in the district of Beth Gubrin "). The name of the place is perhaps misspelt, and we may identify it with Anea (see above). Fiirrer tells me, however, that there isa Beth-'AIam S. E. of Eleutheropolis, which reminds one of Aulona; so that Aulona perhaps should be distinguished from Anea. Nor was he martyred there. It was, on the contrary, the place of his birth. No chor-episcopi from Palestine took part in the council of Nicsea. Was it because there were none at all, or very few, in Palestine? If so, it is a fresh corroboration of the fact that Christianity had penetrated but slightly into the (Jewish) population of the country. One can hardly refute this by appealing to

To sum up, we may say that, judged from a purely statistical standpoint, the policy of Maximinus Daza, which aimed at the utter eradication of Christianity, was by no means so insensate a venture in the case of Palestine as it was in that of Syria. Christianity won but a slender footing amid the Jewish population of the Holy Land; such Jewish Chri fti aii s-a s-there-vyiere; had for the most part withdrawn across the Jordan. Amid the Greek population, again, Christianity had not as yet any numerical preponderance; evidently it drew its adherents from the fluctuating, poorer classes, rather than from the ranks of stable and propertied people.- It is perfectly obvious, to judge from the treatise on the Palestinian martyrs (see above), that the latter section was hardly represented at all in local â bristianity, and that so far as it did exist, it knew how to evade persecution. Thus it formed an unreliable asset for the church. The lengthy communication of Constantine to the the bishop " of the churches round Gaza " (see above), for probably in Gaza itself there could not be any bishop. Still, there were churches in the country districts of Palestine, as we have seen, and in all likelihood they had bishops.

1 We must not, indeed, underestimate their numbers, for Eusebius would never have been able to say that " Christians are nowadays, of all nations, the richest in numbers" H. E., i. 4. 2), unless this factor had been both noticeable and superior to the religious associations of the country. The historian could not have pronounced such a verdict, if Christianity had been an insigniticant factor in his own surroundings at Csesarea. From Eus., H. E., ix. 18 (fxeyas n Kal fx6yos ax-norts 6 Xpiffrlavhv di6s: "The Christians' God is great, and the only true God "), it follows also that public feeling, in Csesarea at any rate, was not absolutely unfavourable to Christians; cp. also the passage quoted above (p. 114), with ix. I. II (cos Kol Tuiis Trporepov Kad' rifiuiv (poviovras, rh 6avj. a Trapa iraaav opoovrts ikwisa, ffvyxaip i" ors yiyevrjixevois: "So that even those who formerly had raged against us, on seeing the utterly unexpected come to pass, congratulated us on what had occurred"), and especially ix. 8. 14 6e6v re toov XpittTiaviiiv 5o o eir, evaefiets Tf Koi f Sfovs Qeocti els rovrovs da.7j0wj trphs clvthiv ikiyx vt"- Twi irpayixclTuiv 6fj. o oyf7v: " Glorify the Christians' God, and acknowledge, under the demonstration of the facts themselves, that Christians were truly pious and the only reverent folk ").

"It would be important to know the nationality of the inhabitants of the villages which Eusebius describes as entirely Christian, i. e., the villages in which any Christians resided. They were Catholic Christians, not Jewish Christiansâ otherwise Eusebius would have noticed the point. They might be Greeks, but more probably they were Aramaic or Arabic speaking pagans who had been converted.

The excavations in Palestine, so far as I am aware, have as yet yielded extremely little for the history of local Christianity during the pre-Constantine age

Palestinian cities (Eus., Vita Const., ii. 23-42), issued shortly after the defeat of Licinius, also gives one the impression that local Chustjans wei.-e. X. uite an inferior minority.

Christians in Palestine used Greek as the language of their worship; but, as we might a priori conjecture, several churches were bilingual (Greek and Aramaic),

Direct proof of this is forthcoming in the case of Jerusalem and Scythopolis Mah. Pal., longer edition, pp, 4, 7, 110, ed. Violet), Procopius,, we are told, himself a native of ielia, did the congregation V v.

of Scythopolis the service of translating from Greek into .

Aramaic (Syriac), a statement which also proves that the service- "J books were still c. 300 a, d.) untranslated into the vernacular. 04 a. JI Translated they were, but orally. This statement also shows h hhflt fvip npprl n frnnslfltinn was nnf vpf nvpscino" H Ttincln " f"

that the need of translation was not yet pressing. Transla tions of the Scriptures into the Palestinian Aramaic dialect (I pass over what is said in Epiph,, Hoer., xxx. 3, 12) were (cp. Kaufmann, Handbuch d. christl. Archdol., pp. 103 f.), but a thorough investigation of the country has hardly begun. Some Christian graves can be shown to be ancient, but we do not know how far they go back.

1 We have already (cp. p. 105) called attention to the fact that the Gentile Christian bishops of Jerusalem down to the middle of the third century were wholly (ireekâ to judge from their names; two of them, however, had Syriac names after that period. The names of the nineteen Palestinian bishops at Nicsea are almost entirely Greek (the Roman name of "Longinus" occurs, at Ascalon). Two bishops indeed (Nicopolis and Aila) were called Petrus and Paulus, but this is no clue to their origin. Thus in 325 A. D. the Palestinian bishops were wholly or almost wholly Greek. At the same time, Semites, it must be recollected, took Greeic names. At any rate, they were within the range of Greek civilization. For the names of the martyrs, etc., cp. above, pp. Ill f.

In Gaza a boy of the lower classes, about 400 a. d., only spoke Syriac. His mother affirmed that neither she nor her son knew Greek (rjse avt v fj, r Se rh avrris tskvov elsevai 'EWrjiitrtt, cp. Marci diac. vita Porphyr. episc. Gaz., Ixvi. f., ed. Teubner, 1895).

Cp. here Silvia Peregrinatio, xlvii.: " Et quoniam in ea provincia Palestina pars populi et graece et siriste novit, pars etiam alia per se graece, aliqua etiara pars tantum siriste, itaque, quoniam episcopus, licet siriste noverit, tamen semper graece loquitur et numquam siriste, itaque ergo stat semper presbyter, qui, episcopo graece dicente, siriste interpretatur, et omnes audiant quae exponuntur. lectiones etiam, quaecumque in ecclesia leguntur, quia necesse est graece legi, semper stat, qui siriste interjiretatur propter populum, ut semper discant. sane quicumque hie sc, in Jerusalem latini sunt, i. e., qui nee siriste nee graece noverunt, ne contris-tentur, et ipsis exponit episcopus, quia sunt alii fratres et sorores graeci-latini, qui latine exponunt eis" (" And as in the province of Palestine one section of the population knows both Greek and Syriac, whilst another is purely Greek, and a third not made, so far as we have yet ascertained, until a later age. Fresh fragments of these versions have been recently made accessible, and we mav expect still more of them. But it is unlikely that their originals will be pushed back into the third century.

The inner development of the Palestinian Greek churches during our period showsâ though our materials are scantyâ no special features of any kind. The connection with Alex-iindria and the tenacious reverence for Origen, to which we have called attention, are the outstanding traits. In the history of the origin and growth of monasticism Palestine also runs parallel to Egypt, Furthermore, the veneration of heroes and martyrs (cp. the erection of martyr-chapels) can be proved for Palestine as well as for the rest of the East during the pre-Constantine age.

Â 2. Ph(enicia

As we learn from Acts, Christianity reached the cities of Phoenicia at a very early period. When Paul was converted, there were already Christians Damascus (Acts x. 2, 12 f., 19); knows only Syriac, therefore, since the bishop, though he knows Syriac, always speaks in Greek and never in Syriac, a presbjter always stands beside him to interpret his Greek into Syriac, so that all the congregation may know what is being said. Also, as the readings from Scripture in the church have to be in Greek, a Syriac interpreter is always present for the benefit of the people, that they may miss nothing of the lessons. Indeed, in case Latins here in Jerusalem, i. e. people who know neither Greek nor Syriac, should be put out, the bishop expounds to them by themselves, since there are other brethren and sisters, Graeco-Latins, who expound to them in Latin").

' Cp. Lewis and Gibson, 7'he Palestinian Syriac Lectionary of the Gospels (1899), and Violet's discovery in Damascus (see the Lexicon of Schulthess, 1903).

- Cp., e. g. Mart, Pal., p. 102 (Violet): tos â Ko. va."yia ffiiiaara tuv tov fleog fxaprlipdov irapesdoT Tafprj vauv oikoii irepikawfcri awoteoevta, ev lipols re irpo(revk-rrjpiots fls r)(TTov fxy-qj.-riu rcj rod deov a(fi Tifiaffdai rrapaseso. ueva.

Phoenicia, as a special province, separated from Syria by Septimius Severus, was equivalent to Phoenicia proper with the adjoining interior eastward, but without Auranitis, Batanea, and Trachonitis, which Diocletian added to the province of Arabia (cp. signatures of Nicka, and Marquardt's Staatsvenvalt., i. pp. 264 f.). That an ecclesiastical province of this name existed in 231-232 A. D. is proved by Jerome, Ep. xxx. 4: " Damnatur Origenes a Demetrio episcopo exceptis Palaestinae et Arabiae et Phoenicis atque Achaiae sacerdotibus."â Cp. Maps in., IV.

for Christians in Tyi e see xxi. 4, for Ptolemais see xxi. 7, for Sidon. xxvii. 3, and in general xi. 19.

The met ropolitan posi tion of Tyre, which was the leading -,, city in the East for manufactures and trade, made it the "- cm ecclesiastical capital of the province; but it is questionable if JZ ' Tyj; e eiijoyed. jthis pj e- minence as early as the second century,. for at the Palestinian synod on the Easter controversy Cassius, the bishop of Tyre, and Clarus, the bishop of Ptolemais, took counsel with the bishops of MWs, and of Caesarea (Eus., H. E., V. 25), to whom they seem to have been subordinate. L On the other hand, Marinus of Tyre is mentioned in a letter of Dionysius of Alexandria tbid. vii. 5. 1) in such a way as to make his metropolitan dignity extremely probable. Martyrs in orj'from Tyre, during the great persecution, are noted by Eusebius, viii. 7. 1 (viii. 8), viii. 13. 3 (bishop Tyrannion), Mart. Pal., v. 1 (Ulpian: a common name in Tyre; the famous jurist and this martyr were not the only Tyrians who bore this name), vii. 1 (Theodosia, the woman martyr). Origen died at Tyre and was buried there. It is curious also to note that the learned Antiochene priest Dorotheus, the teacher of Euse-bius. was appointed by the emperor (Diocletian, or one of his immediate predecessors) to be the director of the purple-dying trade in Tyre (Eus., H. E., vii, 32). A particularly libellous edict issued by the emperor Daza against the Christians, is preserved by Eusebius (ix. 7), who copied it from the pillar in Tyre on which it was cut, and the historian"'s work reaches its climax in the great speech upon the reconstrulc tion of the church at Tyre, "by far the most beautiful in all Phoenicia" (x. 4). This speech is dedicated to Paulinus, bishop of Tyre, in whose honour indeed the whole of the tenth book of its ' In the pseudo-Clementine Homilies, the island of Aradus (xii. 12), Orthosia (xii. l), and Paltus (xiii. i), the frontier-town between Syria and Phoenicia, are all mentioned. Whether Christians existed there at that early date is uncertain.

- Phoenicia,. was then. attached to Syria; it was not a separate province of the empire. We should expect the local bishops to associate with those of Syria daring the second century, but this was not so. Were they specially invited to the Palestinian synod, or did they take part in its proceedings as regular members? In the matter of Origen, they were at one with the bishops of Palestine (cp. p. 120, note 3), while the Syrian bishops seem to have condemned Origen.- history is written. Unfortunately we get no information whatever, in this long address, upon the Christian community at Tyre. We can only infer the size of the community from the size of the church building (which may have stood where the ruins of the large crusading church now astonish the traveller; cp. Baedeker's Palestine, pp. 300 f.). Tyre as a Christian city was to Phoenicia what Ca? sarea was to Palestine. It seems to have blossomed out as a manufqxrturing and trading centre during: the imperial age, especially in the third century. A number of passages in Jerome give characteristic estimates of its size and importance.

In-Sidon, Origen stayedfor some time (Hom. xiv, 2, in Josumn), while it was there that the presbyter Zenobius (Eus., HE., viii. 13. 3) died during the great persecution, as did some Christians at Damascus (ix 5).

Eleven bishops, but no chor-episcopi, were present at the council of Nicaia from Phoenicia; namely, the bishops of Tyre, Ptolemais, Damascus, Sidon, Tripolis, Paneas, Berytus, Palmyra, Xi ', Alassus, Emesa, and Antaradiis.2 v UW CLa. S' fr Already (under Palestine) I have noted that Jewish Christians also resided in Paneas (on which town see, too, Eus., H. E., vii. 17. 18).=

Tripolis is mentioned even before the council of Nicaea (in Mali. Pal. iii., where a Christian named Dionysius comes from Tripolis); the Apostolic Constitutions (vii. 46) declare that Marthones was bishop of this town as early as the apostolic age; while, previous to the council of Nicaea, Hellenicus, the l Where is this town to be sought for? Perhaps the name is misspelt. Perhaps we are to think of Alalis on the Euphrates (N. E. of Palmyra), for the province of Syro-Phcenicia reached thus far, probably, in the third century.

2 The last-named is not quite certain (see Gelzer, op. cit., pp. Ixv. f.). Perhaps a twelfth still falls to be added, if the e â T of some MSS. is genuine, and if we may identify it with " Thelsea,"' or " Thelsese," near Damascus tin. Aiit., 196. 2). So far as I am aware, we cannot tell where to look for the Phoenician locality mentioned by Eusebius in Vit. Cons., iv, 39: ravrov Se Ka erfpai irxiiovs Sie-TTpatTOVTO x P"' ' V f""! Tov otvikwy idovs ai'Tov Qacrixeios eircdvvixos, i)S oi iroxlral 5v(Te apiour Ta odvaiv ISpvfiata trupl-rrapasSvtis rhv ffcotTipiov a. vttkatr- afavtO ysfxov. What was it called? Constantinople? Constantine?

"' This passage at any rate leads us to infer that Christians existed there, whether the well-known statue (see above, vol. i. p. 119, and Philostorg., .Â., vii. 3) really was a statue of Christ, or was merely taken to represent him.

local bishop, opposed Arius (Theodoret, H. E., i. 4), though Gregory, bishop of Berjtus, sided with him loc. c'lt.; for Berytus, see also Mart. Pal. iv. The local church was burnt under Julian; cp. Theod., H. E., iv. 22).

JEiusebiu (viii. 13) jcalls ilvanus, at the period of the great persecution, bishop, not of Eniesa but of " the churches round Eniesa"" (tcov ax i t) v Yiixiaav â kk i (ti(Ji)l' etrictKOTro'i).-Emfesa "thus resenibled Gaza; owing to the fanaticism of the inhabitants. Christians were unable to reside within the town itself, they had to quarter themselves in the adjoining villages. Anatolius, the successor of Silvanus, was the first to take up his abode within the town. Theodoret H. E., iii. 7), writing of the age of Julian, says that the church there was veosfj. ijtO'i. With regard to Heliopolis we have this definite information, that the town acquired its first church and bishop, thanks to Constantine, after. 325 a. d. (cp. Vita Constant., iii. 58, and Socrat., i. 18)."- The Mati. Syriacum mentions one martyr, Lucian, at Heliopolis. Christians also were deported Mart. Pal., xiii. 2) by Daza to Lebanon for penal servitude.

One martyrdom makes it plain that there were Christians at Byblus.â Further, and finally, we must recall an interesting inscription, dated in the year 318-319 a. d. (630 of the Seleucid era), which was discovered at Deir Ali (Lebaba), about three

In ix, 6 he is simply called bishop, and he is said to have been martyred by Daza after an episcopate of forty years.

Eusebius emphasizes the unprecedented fact of a church being founded and a bishop being appointed even at Heliopolis. Then he proceeds: "In his zealous care to have as many as possible won over to the doctrine of the gospel, the emperor gave generous donations for the support of the poor at this place also, so as even thus to stir them up to receive the truths of salvation. He, too, might almost have said with the apostle, ' Whether in pretence or in truth, let Christ anyhow be proclaimed." " How tenaciously paganism maintained itself, however, in Heliopolis (which was still predominantly pagan in the sixth century) is shown by Schultze, op. cit., ii. pp. 250 f. On the local situation towards the close of the fourth century, note the remark of Peter of Alexandria (Theod., H. E., iv. 19): "In Heliopolis no inhabitant will so much as listen to the name of Christ, for they are all idolaters The devil's ways of pleasure are in full vogue there The governor of the city himself is one of the leading idolaters"

(cp. Sozom., V. 10, vii. 15). As late as 579 the pagans were still in the majority at Heliopolis, but shortly before the irruption of Islam the local church had got the upper hand.

miles south of Damascus, by Le Bas and Waddington. It runs as follows:â vvayoiyr M. apktuivicrt(j)v KWfx rjs)

Ac a ojv Tov K(vpio)v Kat o-to(T7)p(os) l7;(crov) Xpr (rtOv 7rpovoia(i) Ilavaoi; 7rpeal3 vtepov) â tov Xx tous-

"The meeting-house of the Marcionists, in the village of
Lebaba, of the Lord and Saviour Jesus Christ.
Erected by the forethought of Paul a presbyterâ In the year 630."

Thus there was a Marcionite community near Damascus in the year 318 (319) a. d. (Already, p. 109, we have found a Marcionite bishop in Palestine about the same period.)

At Choba (Kabun), north of Damascus, there were also numerous Jewish Christians in the days of Eusebius (cp. above, p. 103).

We have no information in detail' upon the diflpusion and density of the Christian population throughout Phoenicia. Rather general and satisfactory information is available for Syria, a province with which Phoenicia was at that time very closely bound up; even., the Pkoenician tongue had long ago been dislodged by Syriac. From the letters of Chrysostom and the state of matters which still obtained in the second half of the sixth century, however, it is quite clear that Christianity got a firm footing only on the seaboard, while the inland districts of Phoenicia remained entirely pagan in the main. Yet it was but recently, not earlier than the third century, that these Phoenician-Hellenic cults had experienced a powerful revival.

The situation is quite clear; wherever Christianity went, it implied Hellenizing, and vice versa. Christianity, in the first instance, only secured a firm footing where there were Greeks. The majority of the Phoenician towns where Christian bishops ' nsc. Grec. et Lalines, iii. 1S70, No. 2558, p. 5S2; cp. Harnack in Zeitschr. f. wiss. Theol. (1876), pp. 103 f.

- On Constanline's destruction of the temple of Aphrodite at Aphaka, in the Lebanon, see Vita Const., iii. 55; Sozom., ii. 5.

They show (especially those dating from 406-407 A. D.) that missionary operations were carried out in the interior of Phoenicia then, as they are to-day in purely heathen lands. There must have been populous towns and districts where Christianity was as yet entirely unknown, or where the local inhabitants would not tolerate it.

can be traced, lay on the coast; i. e., they were towns with a strong Greek population. In the large pagan cities, Emesa and Heliopolis, on the other hand. Christians were not tolerated. Once we leave out inland localities where " heretics," viz., Marcionites and Jewish Christians, resided, the only places in the interior where Christians can be found are Damascus, Paneas, and Palmyra. Damascus, the great trading city, was Greek (cp. Momnisen's Nam. Gesch., v. p. 473; Eng. trans., ii. 146); so was J't

Paneas. In Palmyra, the headquarters of the desert-trade, a strong Greek element also existed (Mommsen, pp. 425 f.; Eng. trans., ii. 96 f.). The national royal house in Palmyra, with its Greek infusion, was well disposed not towards the Greek- but towards the scanty indigenous Christians of Syria, as may be inferred from the relations between Paul of Samosata and Zenobia, no less than from the policy adopted by Rome against him. The overthrow of this metropolitan bishop meant a victory for Hellenism.-'- y Â 3. C(ele-Syeia3 '- Vr "" a–

In accordance with its tendency towards universal dominion,

Christianity streamed from Jerusalem as far as Antioch (Acts, y. xi.), the greatest city of the East and the third city in the,-w

Roman empire, ere a few years had passed over its head. It was J in Antioch that it got its name, which in all probability was originally a nickname; for Antioch was a city of nicknames 1 The names of the Phoenician bishops and Christians known to us are Greco-Roman, with two exceptions. Bishops Zeno, Eneas, Magnus, Theodorus,

Hellenicus, Philocalus, Gregory, Marinus, Anatolius attended the council of Nicaea; the bishop of Alassus alone has a Semitic name, "Thadoneus" (not given in Pape-Benseler), while "Zenobius" may be the Greek form of a Semitic name. It was in Phoenicia as in Palestine; Christianity appears as a Greek religion.

For the great catholic federation of churches must at that time have been felt to be a Greco-Rnman institution, and consequently a menace to Palmyra.

Cpv. Map IV.â Marquardt., op. at. i. pp. 324 f.; Mommsen, v. pp. 446 f. (Eng. trans., ii. 120 f).

So, from Josephus to the author of the Chroii. Paschale. We need only allude to the incomparable position of Antioch in the East.

â " According to Theophilus, ad Auiol., i. 12, the pagans in Antioch even as late as 180 A. D. took the name "Christian" as a term of ridicule irepl rod (tÂ Kanyexav jlOV, Kaxovyra fie Xpiffttav6i', ovk olsas t Aeyeis).

and of low-class literature. Here the first Gentile Christian community grew up; for it was adherents of Jesus drawn from paganism who were called "Christians" (cp. vol. i. pp. 411 f). Here Barnabas laboured. Here the great apostle Paul found his sphere of action for some years, and ere long the Christian community became so important, endowed with such a vigorous self-consciousness and such independent activity, that its repute rivalled that of the Jerusalem church itself.- Between the churches of Jerusalem and Antioch the cardinal question of the Gentile Christians was debated; it wg, s the church of Antiochâ mentioned along with Syria and Cilicia in Acts xv. 23, and the only city noted in this connectionâ which took the most decided step forward in the history of the gospel; and as early as the second century it gave further expression to its church-consciousness by designating the apostle Peter as its first bishop â although, to judge from Gal. ii. 11 f., it was no glorious role that he had played in Antioch. One of its churches was traced back to the apostolic age (see above, p. 85).

We know next to nothing of the history of Christianity in Coele-Syria during the first three centuries, but a succession of data is available for Antioch itself. We possess, for example, the list of the Antiochene episcopate, and the very names

We hear of this in the reign of Julian.

In this connection special moment attaches to Acts xi. 27 f. (where the wealthier church of Antioch supports the brethren in Judaea), and further, to Acts xiii. I f: 'Hctoj' v 'Avrtoxfif Kara TT y ovcrav (KK riaiav irpofpritai koi Sisdffkakot '6 re Bapvdfias Koi 2t; Uecbi' 6 KakovfjLfvos Niyep. Koi Aovkios 6 Kvprjvatos, Mava' v rt Hp(f)Sov tov Tftpdxov avvrpocpos Kai 'Savkos. Xfitovpyovftoiu Se avtwv fif Kvplw Kol vr)mv6vr(jov tlirtv rh TrvtvLia rh ayiov â apopl(Tati 5r) oi rhv Bapva av Kal Savaor fls rb epyoy, k. t. At the very outset a certain Nicolaus,-rrpuarjkvtos Avtioxtvs (a proselyte from Antioch), appears as a guardian of the poor in Jerusalem.

As also by the device of placing a great apostolic synod at Antioch (see the Excursus, in the first edition of this work, to Chap. V. Book I.). The great importance of Antioch is well brought out by Knopf in his Nachaposi. Zeitalter, pp. 50 f.â We have frequent evidence that church music spread from Antioch throughout the whole church. Socrates (vi. f) notices the legend that Ignatius the local bishop learned responsive chanting from the angels.

â â We know that a seat, or the seat, of the sect of the Elkesaites was at Apamea, whence the Elkesaite Alcibiades travelled to Rome (Hipp. Philos., ix. 13). The Elkesaites, however, belong to the history of Jewish Christianity. They were not a sect of the Catholic church.

'â ' Cp. my Chro7iologie, i. pp. 208 f. and elsewhere.
are instructive. Euodius, Ignatius, Heron, Cornelius, Eros, Theophilus, Maximinus, Serapion, Asclepiades, Philetus, Zebinus, Babylas, Fabius, Demetrianus, Paulus, Doninus, Tiniaeus, Cyrillus, Tyrannusâ the large majority of these names are
Greek, and Greek was the language of the church. Its fame fj is established by Igaaiius, after Paul. Several features (though - J y.

they are not many)itr the contemporary situation of the church at Antioch can be made out from the epistles of Ignatius, who proudly terms it "the church of Syria."' In Smyrn. xi. 2, he says that after the persecution it had regained its proper size ij iov fxlysofi). The claim which he advances, under cover of an exaggerated modesty, to instruct foreign churches probably sprang, not simply from his personal attainments as a confessor, but also from the ecclesiastical and commanding position of the city of which he was bishop. The central position of the church is indicated by the fact that jdl the Asiatic churches sent envoys to congratulate the church of Antioch upon its recovery. It now occupied the place once held by Jerusalem.

In later times it was given out that Euodius, the predecessor of Ignatius, had also been an author. This is erroneous. The bishops Theophilus, Serapion, and Paulus, however, were authors (writing, like Ignatius, in Greek), as was the Antiochene ' presbyter Geminus (Jerome, de Vir. III., Ixiv.). There were also letters from Fabius. Famous schools of learning were held by the presbyter Malchion (Eus., H. E., vii. 29), the presbyter Dorotheus (vii. 23), and above all by Lucian. The church of, u,6vt.

1 The Apology oi pseudo-Melito (Otto's Corp. Apol. ix.), composed about the beginning of the third century, was probably written in Syriac originally (and in Coele-Syria), but it is the only Syriac writing which can be named in this connection (cp. my Chronologie, i, pp. 522 f., ii. pp. 129 f.). Investigations into the Acts of Thomas have not yet advanced far enough to enable us to arrive at any certain decision upon the question whether they belong to the province of Edessa or to that of Western Syria. The great probability is, however, that they were composed in Syriac, and that they belong (cp. my Litt. Gesck,, i. pp. 545 f., ii. 2. pp. 175 f.) to Edessaâ in fact, to the circle of that great Eastern missionary and teacher, Bardesanes; cp. Noideke in Lipsius' Apokr. Apostelgeschichten, ii. 2. pp. 423 f., and Burkitt in hq Journal of Theological Studies, i. pp. 280 f The Syriac version of the gospels also belongs to Edessa, rather than to Western Syria. The gnostic Saturninus (Satornil) also belonged to Antioch (cp. Iren., I. xxiv. i), and other gnostic sects and schools (Ophites, etc.) originated in Syria. Their language was Greek, but interspersed with many Semitic loan-words.

Antioch also took part in the great general controversies, the Mohtanist, the Origenist (siding against Origen), the Novatian, the baptismal, and the Christological, and it maintained a vital intercourse with other churches. It mediated between the church at large, which was substantially Greek, and the Svriac East, just as the Roman church did between the former and the Latin-speaking West. Further, unless the evidence is deceptive, it was the ihurch of. Antioch which introduced into the cultus of Greek Christendom its strongly rhetorical element â an element of display and fantasy. Once more, it was in this church that the dynamic Christology received its most powerful statement; here Arianism arose; and here the ablest school of exegesis flourished. Thanks to the biblical scholarship of Lucian, the teacher of Arius, Antioch acquired a widespread importance for the development of exegesis and theology in the East (Arianism, the Antiochene school of exegesis, Nestorianism). The central position of the church is reflected in the great synods held at Antioch from the middle of the third century onwards, Dionysius of Alexandria (Eus., H. E. vi. 46) wrote to Cornelius of Rome that he had been invited to a synod at Antioch (251 a. d.) upon the baptism of heretics, by Helenus of Tyre and the other bishops of the country, as well as by Firmilian of Cappadocia and Theoktistus, a Palestinian bishop (of Caesarea). The outcome of the synod is described by him in a letter to Stephen of Rome ibid., vii. 5): " Know that all the churches of the East, and even beyond it, which previously were divided, have once more become united. All over, the bishops are harmonious and unanimous, greatly delighted at the unexpected restoration of peace among the churches." He then proceeds to enumerate the bishops of Antioch, Caesarea, Elia, Tyre, Laodicea, Tarsus, " and all the churches of Cilicia, besides Firmilian and all Cappadociaâ for, to avoid making my letter too long, I have merely named the most prominent bishops. Add all Syria and Arabia,. with Mesopotamia, Pontus, and Bithynia." Setting aside the two last-named provinces, we may

It is instructive to note how Cornelius of Rome plumes himself upon the greatness of Rome, in writing to Fabius of Antioch (Eus., If. E., vi. 43). He had reason to do so, in face of Antioch's prestige.

say that this forms a list of the provinces over which the influence of Antioch normally extended. To the last great synod at Antioch against Paulus, the Antiochene bishop, no fewer than seventy or eighty bishops gathered from all the provinces,

This also serves to explain the well-known passage in the sixth canon of Nicxa. dfji. oiois Se Kal Kara 'Avrisxeiav Kal ev rats ats iirapxiais to. irpiafi la (rd)Ce(T0at Ta7s fkKXfiffiais (" Likewise with regard to Antioch and throughout the other provinces, the churches are to have their due prerogatives secured to them "). This certainly refers to a kind of super-metropolitan authority, not simply to the metropolitan constitution (in Rome, Alexandria, and Antioch). The first sign of the metropolitan constitution emerges at Antioch, in relation to Syria (cp. Llibeck's Reichseiiiteihing nnd kirchliche Hierarchic, pp. 42 f.), and it is there also that we come upon the l eginnings of the super-metropolitan authority (prior to Diocletian). This is established by one fact after another. The bibhops of the "East" were conscious of forming, within the catholic church, a powerful group by themselves, with a unity of their own, centring in Antioch. There was a diocese of " the East" within the church long before the political division arose, (l) The great synods of Antioch were attended by bishops from many provinces, "TTe., of the "East" in general (excluding proconsular Asia and Egypt: bishops did come from the later diocese of Pontus, but the Alexandrian bishop Dionysius only seems to have been invited out of regard for his high personal reputation). Even when there was reason to make common cause against the bishop of Antioch at a synod, Antioch was chosen as the meeting-place; cp. the cases of Fabius and Paul of Samosata. (2) When Antioch had to be passed over, and another city selected as the place of meeting, the bishop of Antioch still presided over the Synod, as at Ancyra and Neo-Caesarea in the beginning of the fourth century. (Llibeck's contention, pp. 104 f., that the pre-eminence of Antioch grew up gradually out of the synodal custom, seems to me to confuse cause and effect. The starting-point of it certainly lay in the prestige of the city as the capital of what was an exceptionally large province at the beginning of the imperial period, as well as in the primitive importance of the local church. It is surprising that Antioch does not come forward at the Paschal controversy of 190 a. d., when the separate Eastern provinces act quite independently.) (3) According to reliable tradition, the firÂ t catholic bishop of Edessa was ordained by Serapion, the bishop â of. Antioch. ((4))yhe bishop of Antioch exercised supervision over Rhossus in Cilicia at thespening of the third century, though Cilicia had been an independent province since Hadrian (Eus., H. E., vi. 12). (5)-4ie had also certain rights in connection with the mission and the episcopate in mission-districts like Persia, Armenia, and Georgia. â The actual prerogatives irpiff ila) of the Antiochene bishop were distinct from those of the bishops of Alexandria and Rome. The facts of the case prove this. While the latter had the right of episcopal ordination in several provinces, all that can be shown to have been possessed by the Antiochene bishop was the right of ordaining the metropolitans of the Eastern provmces (and even this is not quite certain), the privilege of summoning Eastern synods, and the exercise of a certain control over them, together with the supervision of the propaganda (as missionary archbishop). For a true account of these functions, cp, Ll'ibeck, pp. 134 f. The distinctive and superior privileges of the Antiochene bishop, over against the metropolitans, must have consisted in practice

VOL. II. 9 from Pontus to Egypt; for, it must be remembered, the Christ-ological crisis, in which their metropohtan was the " heretic " of the hour, was of supreme moment to the church. Unfortunately, we know nothing of the seats of these bishops."

Although the information which we possess about Paul at Antioch in the role of bishop comes from a hostile pen, it throws liffht on the size and " secularism " of the local Christian com-munity in the second half of the third century (Eus., H. E., Â vii. 30). " At an earlier period he was poor and a beggar.

He neither inherited any means from his parents, nor did he make any money by any craft or trade whatever; yet he is now in possession of extravagant wealth, thanks to his iniquitous transactions, his acts of sacrilege, and his extortionate demands upon the brethren. For he officiously recommends himself to people who are wronged, promising to help them for a consideration. Yet all he does is to cheat them, making a profit for himself, without any service in return, out of litigants who are quite ready to pay money in order to get quit of a troublesome and custom rather than in definite, prescribed functions; in this respect he differed from the bishops of Rome and Alexandria. Hence, in the sixth canon of Nicsea Rome is bracketed with Alexandria, not with Antioch; it is with reference to Antioch that the general term irpe(rpt7a is employed.

Eusebius H. E., vii. 28) speaks of γtνpιoι ("thousands"), Athanasius gives seventy de Synod. 43), and Ililarius de Synod. 86), eighty bishops. Basilius Diaconus (fifth century) reckons a hundred and eighty.

The document issued by the Antiochene synod to the bishops of Rome and Alexandria as well as to the whole church (Eus., H. E., vii. 30) mentions, in its address, the names of Helenus (Tarsus), Hymenseus (Jerusalem), Theophilus (? perhaps Tyre), Theoteknus (Csesarea), Maximus (Bostra), Proclus (?), Nicomas (?),.(Elianus (?), Paulus (?), Bolanus (?), Protogenes (?), Hierax (?), Eutychius (?), Theodorus (?), Malchion (presbyter of Antioch), and Lucius (probably also a presbyter of Antioch). Unfortunately, the bishoprics of most are unknown, nor do we know why these alone are mentioned. Did the Eastern metropolitans, with some presbyters of Antioch, name themselves alone as the senders of the document? Photius thinks these were only a few prelates who ratified the deposition; he mentions twelve.

According to later Oriental sources (cp. Westphal, Unters. iiher die Qtiellen und die Glatibwih'digkeit der Pati-iarchalchi-oniken des Mdri ibn Sulaitndn, etc., r 1901, pp. 62 f.), Demetrianus, Paul's predecessor in the see of Antioch, was exiled to Persia. This tradition, which answers to the general situation (the city was sacked by the Persians in 260 a. d.) and has nothing against it, proves that about 260 A. D. both the church of Antioch and its bishop possessed some political weight. Labourt, however, questions its authenticity Le Christianisme dans rempire Perse, 1904, p. 19).

business. Thus he treats piety as a means of makibgâ some. profit. He is haughty and puffed up; he is invested with secular dignities; he would rather be called ' ducenarius' an imperial procurator of the second rank than ' bishop'; he strides ostentatiously up and down the public squares, reading or dictating letters publicly in the middle of his walk, and having a numerous retinue who escort him in front and behind. Thus, owing to his arrogance and insolence, our faith wins ill will and hatred from the public. In the assemblies of the church his inordinate ambition and vainglorious pride make him behave in an inexplicable fashion, and thus he captivates the minds of simple folks till they actually admire him. He has a platform and a high throne erected for himself, imlike a disciple of Christ. Also, like secular officials, he has his private cabinet secretnm). He strikes his hand upon his thigh, stamps with his feet upon the platform, and inveighs with insolent insults against those who, instead of breaking out in applause of himself, or waving their handkerchiefs like the audience in a theatre, or shouting aloud and jumping like the men and women of his own company who behave in this indecent fashion, prefer to listen to him reverently and quietly as befits the house of God. Dead expositors of the word of God are assailed in public with coarse and vulgar taunts, while the speaker exalts himself in swelling terms as if he were a sophist or juggler and not a bishop. Hymns in praise of our Lord Jesus Christ he puts a stop to, as too recently composed by modern men; whereas he has songs sung to his own praise and glory by women in the public congregation on the opening day of the paschal feast, songs which might well make any audience shudder. Similar courses are advocated, at his instigation, by the bishops of neighbouring localities and towns who fawn upon him, as well as by the priests in their addresses to the people. Thus he will not acknowledge, with us, that the Son of God has come down from heaven

Jesus, he says, is from below. Whereas those who sing hymns in his own honour and publicly praise him, assert that he himself has come down as an angel from heaven; and instead of checking such outbursts, the arrogant fellow listens when rv they ai"e uttered. Furthermore, he has ' virgines subintroductae' of his own, ' lady companions,"' as the people of Antioch call them. So have the priests and deacons in his company. Of this, as of all the rest of their pernicious errors, he is perfectly cognisant. But he connives at them, in order to attach the men to himself and prevent them, through fear of personal consequences, from daring to challenge his own unrighteous words and deeds Even if he should have committed no act of immorality with regard to the ' virgines', still he ought to have eschewed the suspicion of it He has indeed dismissed one such woman, but he still retains two in the bloom and beauty of their sex, takes them with him on his travels, and lives meanwhile in sumptuous and luxurious fashion. Such practices make everyone groan and lament in private. But no one dares to bring him to task, such is their dread of his authority and tyranny. Yet for such practices one would call him to account i. e., not condemning him outright, nor conniving at his actions, if he still were a catholic and belonged to our own number."'

I have quoted this passage in extenso, as I consider it is extremely important evidence for the spread and the position of the church in Antioch at that period. The best-established feature in the whole description (for a large number of the malicious charges, which are a proof of Antiochene journalism, may be brushed aside) is that the bishop had by this time assumed, perhaps had had to assume, the customs and bearing of a high state-official. This feature brings out vei y clearly the development and importance of the local Christian community. Besides, the relations between Paul and the royal house of Palmyra (Syrian by race), so far as these are known or may be conjectured,- show that Christianity already played a political role in Antioch. Furthermore, the authentic document pre- ' One of Paul's successors, Philogonius, was "caught up from the forum" fk xefft? rrjs ayopas aptrairdiis, Chrys., t. i. p. 495) and made a bishop, at the beginning of the fourth century. He was evidently a jurist.

â Paul's entrance on his episcopate at Antioch fell at the very period, and probably in the very year, when the Persians captured Antioch. As soon as the Persians retreated, Gallienus appointed Odsenathus to a position of practically independent authority over Palmyra and the East. Paul must have understood admirably how to curry favour with this ruler and his queen Zenobia, for, in spite of his episcopal position, he was imperial pr ocurator in A ntioch.

served by Eusebius tells us that Paul refused to admit his condemnation, nor would he evacuate his episcopal residence.

Whereuponâ Zenobia meanwhile having been conquered by
Rome, and the collateral rule of the house of Palmyra having been overthrown in Egypt and throughout the East â the matiter was laid before the emperor Aurelian, who ordered- j j i- (a. d. 272) the residence to be handed over to th0 bishop with ' 'â whom the Christian bishops of Italy and Rome were in epistolary communion. This forms one conspicuous proof of the political significance attaching to the church of Antioch.

The Antipchenejjishop was to be a support of Roman power in the chief city of the East; such was the meaning of

Aurelian's decision. It throws light on Constantin e's policy of making bishops the pillars of his rule.

It is impossible to draw up any statistical calculations with regard to the church about 320 a. d., but at any rate there were several chu rches in the c ity (Theoj., H. E. i. 2), and if the locar Christians really were in the majority in Julian's reign, their number must have been very large as early as the, year 320. I iodoriis. and Chrysostom preached in what was (j- substantially a Christian city, as the latter explicitly attests in) several passages. He gives the number of the inhabitants Z-vw'Cs ri, (excluding slaves and children) at 200,000 Horn, in Ignat. 4), v-Â- the total of members belonoino; to the chief church being; 100,000 Horn. 85 86, c. 4)." Antioch in early days was "; y always the strong hold of E asterxi-Cbristianity, and the local " f church was perfectly conscious of its vocation as the church of,4 I the metropolis. The horizon and effective power of the Uv (T

Antiochene bishop extended as far as Mes opotam ia and Persia,. Armenia and Georgia. He felt himself in duty bound to superintend the missions and the consolidation of the church

He writes as follows: when the peace began Vitalius was bishop, " who built the church ev T17 Xioxaia which the tyrants had destroyed. Philogonius, his successor, completed the buildings" os kox y) v iv rp Ua ai Karaxvoilffav virh ruv rvpavvwv (pkosiXTjcnv ikK riffiai'. LXoysvios Se fiera tovtov rriv irpoespiav Aa aiv ta t6 Kiiiroixiva T-p oikosoixio. irpoctTedeiki). The words may also be understood to mean, of course, that 7; ikKK-riaia iv tÂ Ylaxaia was the only local church.

Cp. Schultze op, cil, ii. p. 263); Gibbon The Decline and Fall, Germ, trans, by Sporschil, ii. p. 219) takes the 100,000 to represent the total of the Christians in Antioch itself.

throughout these countries. The execution of this task led to the steady jrowth of certain rights, which were never formally defined, but which were exercised by the Antiochene bishop throughout the East. Similarly, he recognized his duties with regard to the defence of the church against heretics, who were fond of resorting to the East. It was from Antioch that the missionary impulse of Chrysostom proceeded, as well as the vigorous campaign against the heretics waged by the great exegetes, by Dio doru s and Theodoret, and by Chrjsqstom and Nestorius.

Outide the gato o of An tioch, that " fair city of the Greeks (see Isaac of Antioch's Carmen 15, ed. Bickell, i, 294), Syr iac was tlie language of the people; in fact it was spoken by the lower classes in Antioch itself (Noldeke), and only in the upper classes of the Greek towns was it displaced by Greek. The Syriac spirit was wedded to Greek, however, even here, and remained the predominant factor in religious and in social life," although at first and indeed for long it did not look as if it would. Yet in this Syrian world, Christianity operated from

This was the case with the Marcionites and several gnostic sects, as is shown by the works of Theodoret, who boasts (e. g., in Â p. cxiii.) that over a thousand Marcionites had been converted in his diocese alone, and also by the writings of later authors (even in Arabic).

Even ill the Greek cities there were bishops who spoke Greek with a Syrian accent; cp. Socrates, vi. ii, on Severianus, bishop of Gabbala: 'S. ffi-qpiavhs Sokhv wiiratsfvcroai, ou irdvv Trj (paivrj ttjv â rivikr)V i erpdvov yaoocrffav, dwa kcli f 7 vi(TT (pdeyyofjlivos ' vpos? iv tv (puvijv ("Though Severianus was reputed to be a cultured man, he was very defective in his pronunciation of Greek, since he spoke Greek with a Syrian accent ").

â ' Mommsen, o. at., p. 451: "The relations between the Greeks and the older population of Syria may be inferred clearly from the local terminology. The majority of the towns and districts bore Greek names, mainly derived, as we have seen, from Macedoniaâ e. g., Pieria, Anthemusias, Arethusa, Bercea, Chalcis, Edessa, Europos, Cyrrhus, Larissa, Pella. Others were called after Alexander or some member of the Seleucid houseâ e. g., Alexandria, Antioch, Seleucis and Seleucia, Apameia, Laodicea, Epiphaneia. Th. e old native names kept their place indeed, as in the case of Beroea (formerly Chalep in Aramaic, or Chalybon), Edessa or Hierapolis (previously Mabug or Bambyce), and Epiphania (previously Hamath or Amathe); but the newer names mostly displaced the old, and only a few districts e. g., Commagene, Samosata, etc.) did without new Greek names."

â â It was in alliance with Greek that Syriac literature first arose; cp. Wright,.â 1 Short History of Syriac Literature (1894), and Duval, La LAtth-ature Syriaque (1899).

Edessa (see below) rather than from Antioch, unless we are r ') wholly mistaken. T he wide t-erritory lying between these cities.

was consequently evangelized from two centres during the third 1 VX century; from Antioch in the West by means of a Greek 'O vfi

Christian propaganda, and from Edessa in the East by means of one which was Syro-Christian. The inference is that the larger towns practically adopted the former, while the country towns and villages went over to the latter. At the same time there was also a Western Syrian movement of Christianity, though it did not amount to much, both in and after the days of Paul of Samosata and Zenobia.

The work of conversion, so it would appear, made greater headway in Ccele-Syria, however, than in Phoenicia. No fewer than twenty-two bishops from Coele-Syria attended Nicaea (two chor-episcopi, observe!), including several who had un-Hellenic-j names. Hence we may infer the existence of no inconsiderable number of national Syrian Christians. By about 325 the districts round Antioch seem to have contained a very large number of Christians, and one dated (331) Christian inscription from a suburban village runs as follows: " Christ, have mercy; there is but one God." In Cbrysostom's day these Syrian villages appear to have been practically Chi'istian. Lucian, the priest of Antioch, declares in his speech before the magistrate in Nicomedia (311 a. d.) that "almost the greater part of the world now adheres to this Truth, yea whole cities; even if any of this evidence seems suspect, there is no doubt regarding multitudes of country-folk, who are innocent of guile " (" pars

The peculiarity of the Antiochene (upper) bishop in early days was that his interest in missions, extending as far as Mesopotamia, was confined to the spread of a Greek Christianity; he did little for the establishment of a national Syrian church. This was where Edessa came in. But I think it too much to say, with Burkitt Early Eastern Christianity, p. lo), that "the church of Antioch was, so far as we know, wholly Greek.

The country districts, where there was a Semitic-speaking population, seem to have remained unevangelized. Where the Jews had settled, the new Jewish heresy followed, but the country-side remained pagan."

Eustathius, Zenobius, Theodotus, Alphius, Basanius, Philoxenus, Salamanes, Piperius, Archelaus, Euphrantion, Phaladus, Zoilus, Bassus, Gerontius, Manicius, Eustathius, Paulus, Siricius, Selencus, Petrus, Pegasius, Bassones.

In a fragment from a debate with Paul of Samosata, which Pitra Anal., III. p. 600 f.) has edited, Malchion is called Trpio-fivtipos 'A xeuv. Is this the name of some unknown place near Antioch?

136 MISSION AND EXPANSION OF CHRISTIANITY paeiie mundi iani maioi-huic veritati adstipulatur, urbes integrae, aut si in his aliquid suspectum videtur, contestatur de his etiam agrestis manus, ignara figmenti"); and although this may reflect impressions which he had just received in Bithynia, there was substantial ground for the statement in the local circumstances of Sjria. The numbers of the clergy in 303 throughout Syria are evident from Eus., H. E., viii. 6: " An enormous number were put in prison at every place. The prisons, hitherto reserved for murderers and riflers of graves, were now packed everywhere with bishops, priests, deacons, lectors, and exorcists."" The data at our command are as, follows:â, LV (1)-A ct s (xv.) already mentions churches in Syria besides Antioch.

(2) Ignatius, apropos of Antioch ad Philad. 10), mentions "churches in the neighbourhood" eyyiarta ekKKijaiai) which had already bighpps of their own. These certainly included Seleucia, the seaport of Antioch mentioned in Acts xiii. 4.

(3) Apamea was a centre of the Elkesaites (cp. above, vol. i. p. 62).

(4) Dionys. Alex, (in Eus., H. E., vii. 5) observes that the Roman church frequently sent contributions to the Syrian churches.

(5) The document of the Antiochene synod of 268 (Eus., vii. 30) mentions, in connection with Antioch, "Jbishops of the 1 If the Qidascalia Apost., of which Achelis has just pubhshed a scholarly edition Texie u. Unters., xxv. 2), belongs to Western Syria, it would supply a large amount of information on the ecclesiastical situation and the spread of local Christianity during the third century. But I think it more likely (though I am not sure) that it belongs to the province of Arabia (see below).

Some scholars, however, place these iyyicna ekK r Tiat in Asia Minor.

Unfortunately, we know no particulars. Were they town churches or country churches, Greek or Syrian? Had the Persian invasion reduced churches in Syria to the need of begging? Did the Roman bishop intervene of his own accord? In any case, we can understand Aurelian's edict still better when we put it beside this remark of Dionysius: al 2upia '6Kai (.?., not merely Coele-Syria) koi r; Apa ia, oils iirapke'ite (you, Romans) kkO-aron koi ols vvv etrso-rejaare. It appears from this that the Roman church regularly intervened there in cases of distress. This is very significant. If Antioch had already secured a certain authority over the churches of the Eastern provinces, the Roman bishop had also gained an informal influence by means of help in local cases of need, for a generous benefactor always acquires influence and power.

neighbouring country and cities " (exo-co7roi tcoj ojuopcov aypcov re Kai Troxecou). The towns in the vicinity of Antioch, far and near, must ah'eady have had bishops, in all or nearly all cases, if country bishops were in existence. From Eus,, vi. 12, we learn that by about 200 a. d. there was a Christian community (and a bishop?) at Rhossus which was gravitating towards Antioch.

(Q JCwo chor-episcopi from Coele-Syria attended the council of Nicaea. In Marty vol. Hkron. (Achelis, Mah. Hieron., p. 168), a martyrdom is noted as having occurred "in Syria vico Margaritato," as well as another (p. 177 f) "in Syria provincia regione Apameae vico Aprocavictu," but both these places are unknown.

(7) The number of bishops from Coele-Syria who were at Nicaea was as follows: Antioch, Seleucia, Laodicea, Apa-mea, Raphanete, Hierapolis (= Mabug, Bambyce), Germanicia (= Marasch; Theodoret, ij.Â., ii. 25: xo'Ai? â jt v ev imeoopm Tiji; Ktxtcctij Kat upwi kui J airtrasokOOv KCinei'tj), Samosata, Doliche, Balaueae (cp. Horn. Clem., xiii. 1)," Gabula, Zeugma, Larisa, Epiphania, Arethusa, Neocassarea (Theodoret, H. E., i. 7: cjypovpiov TOVTO twv tou v pdrov Trapakeip-evov bxqaii)-, Cyrrhus, Gindaron, Arbokadama (Harba Q'dam, unidentified; cp. Schwartz. Zur Gesch. der Athan., vi. p. 285), and Gabbala. These towns lay in the most diverse districts of this wide countxyv-on- the seaboard, in the valley of the Orontes, in the Euphrates valley, between the Orontes and the Euphrates, and in the north. Their distribution shows that Christianity was fairly uniform and fairly strong in Syria about 325, as is strikingly shown by the rescript of Daza to Sabinus (Eus., ' It is, of course, the Laodicea on the sea-coast that is meant, not that on the Lebanon (S. W. of Emesa).

' For the names, cp. Cuntz (" Stadiasmus Maris Magni") in Texle it. Unters., xxix. I. p. 9.

For the local events in Julian's reign, cp. Theodoret, H. E., iii. 7.

â The opposition offered to Christianity varied considerably in the various towns. In Apamea it would seem to have been particularly keen. Even for the period c. 400 A. D., Sozomen (vii. 15) observes: 'S.-uptav 5e fxakicrta ol tov vaov 'Airafj.(tas â ovs invdofxrjv 4ir (pvaakTi tuv irap avtols vawv crvpif. ax a-is XP' ' "-' "-'- " owakis Ta t aici v auspuv Ka rwv Trepi rhv Aifiavov KUifiuy, rh Se Texevtcuov eirl ToffovtOV irpoexdflv tjAutjx ws Mdpktwov rhy ttjsc ivlffkonov av(i'iy (" I have been told H. E. ix. 9)â for we must understand the experiences undergone by the churches of Syrian Antioch and Asia Minor, when we read the emperor's words about crxedov atruvrag avopdotTovg Katoxeicpoeicnji t? tow Oewv Oprjakcia? rw eovei rwv jlpi(TTiavo)v eavtOu (rv, ajuLâ iuiixota' (" almost all men abandoning the worship of the gods and attaching themselves to the Christian people "). This remark is not to be taken simply as a rhetorical flourish. For after speaking in one place about the first edict of Diocletian, Eusebius proceeds as follows: ovk et? fiakpov 8e erepwv KUTa Trjv M. e itrivi v outco Kaxoufxevrjv X(p(" ct' (iraxiv axXcov ajuLtpi Tt-jv vpcav eirkJivrival rrj acrixeia Tretreipajmevociv, rovg iravtaxocre tow ekK criwu TTaoecrtcora? elpkTUcg Kai Secriu-ol eveipai Trpocrtayula ecpoitU (aaikLKov ("Not long afterwards, as some people in the district called Melitene and in other districts throughout Syria attempted to usurp the kingdom, a royal decree went forth to the effect that the head officials of the churches everywhere should be put in prison and chains," viii. 6. 8). Eusebius does not say it in so many words, but the context makes it quite clear that the emperor held the j ' Christians responsible for both of these outbreaks (that in Melitene being unknown to history). This proves that the

Christians in Melitene and Syria must have been extremely numerous, otherwise the emperor would never have met revolutionary outbursts (which in Syria, and, one may conjecture, in Melitene also, originated with the army) with edicts against the Christian clergy.

All that we know about the earlier history of Christianity in the towns is confined to some facts about Laodicea (where bishop Thelymidres was pi'ominent about 250 a. d.; cp. Eus., vi. 46; he was followed by Heliodorus, vii. 5, and subsequentlv by Eusebius of Alexandria, and the famous Anatolius, vii. 32), Arethusa (cp. Sozom., v. 10; VH. Const., n. 62), and Samosata (the birthplace of Paul of Antioch, though we do not know if that the Syrian inhabitants ol Apamea often employed the men of Gahlee and the Lebanon villages to aid them in a military defence of their temple, and that at last they actually went so far as to slay the local bishop") who had had the temple demolished.

The spelling of this name as " Thelymitres" occurs in Pape-Benseler (in inscriptions) and in one manuscript of Eusebius.

he was of Christian birth). The bishop of Rhossus was not at Nicaea (Rhossus, however, may also be assigned to Cihcia). But, as we have seen above, Rhossus did possess a Christian church about 200 a. d., which came under the supervision of the church at Antioch. There was a Jewish Christian church at Beroea (Aleppo) in the fourth century (cp. p. 101). The local Gentile Christian church cannot have been important; cp. the experiences of Julian there Ep. xxvii., p. 516, ed. Hertlein).

Finally, we have to consider the pseudo-Clementine epistle de Virginitate, which probably dates from the beginning of the third century, either in Palestine or in Southern Syria. It contains directions for itinerant ascetics, and five kinds of places are enumerated where such people stayed and passed the night (ii. 1-6), viz.: (1) places with a number of married brethren and ascetics; (2) places with married brethren but without ascetics; (3) places where there were only Christian wives and girls; (4) places where there was only one Christian woman; and (5) places where there were no Christians at all. The third and fourth classes are of special interest. They corroborate what is otherwise well known, viz., that women formed the majority within the Christian communities (cp. above, p. 83). We also get an instructive picture of the state of morals and manners, in the directions given for the behaviour of an itinerant ascetic in places where no Christians were to be found at all. This account for which see vol. i. pp. 355 f. relates to small country churches. And their number must have been considerable. Theodoret (Ep. cxiii.) observes that

One bishop in Syria irpoeatcis ns ttjs eccarcn'os), Hippolytus relates in Daniel, p. 230, ed. Bonwetsch; see above, p. 79), by his enthusiastic fanaticism seduced his fellow-members into the wilderness with their wives and children in order to meet Christ. The local governor had them arrested, and they were almost condemned as robbers, had not the governor's wife, who was a believer (yutra iriati), interceded on their behalf. Unfortunately, Hippolytus does not name the locality. â There were also Novatian churches in Syria (cp. the polemical treatise by Eusebius of Emesa, in the fourth century; Fabius of Antioch had sided with the Novatians). But we do not know where to look for them.

Cp. my study of it in the Sitzungsberichte d. k. Pr, Akad. IViss., 1891, pp. 361 f., and Chro7iologie, ii. 133 f The epistle is only complete in the Syriac version, but we have large fragments of the Greek original.

140 MISSION AND EXPANSION OF CHRISTIANITY his diocese of Cyrrhus contained 800 parishes. By that time, of course, over a century had passed since the days of Constan-tine; still, a number of these parishes were certainly earlier than the emperor's reign.

The role of the Syrians in the empire, alongside of the Jews, is well known, especially from the Antonines onwards, rian traders (" The Syrians are merchants and the most greedy of men," Jerome, Ep. cxxx. 7) made their way into every province; they even went beyond the bounds of the empire. But Syrian settlers were also to be found engaged everywhere in trade. In their train the missionaries of the Syrian deities, with " mathematici " and sages, pushed westward and northward. Each, as a rule, preached one exclusive god; the relig ion was a kind of monotheism. The Syrian Greeks were also enamoured of this itinerant and commercial life, as philosophers, orators, litterateurs, and jurists. When one recollects that Antioch was the mother-church of Gentile Christianity, the spread of Christianity can be illustrated even from the standpoint of Syrian trade activity. The Romans and the Greeks did not esteem the Syrians very highly. Cicero reckons them among the nations which were born to be slaves. " Yet even this characteristic guaranteed to them the future," says Renan (Les Apotres, Germ, ed., p. 308), "for the future belonged then to slaves."

Â 4. Cypeus

AL-Salainis (= Constantia) and Paphos Barnabas the Cypriote and Paul had once done mission-work (Acts xiii.), while Barnabas and Mark returned to the island later on as missionaries (Acts XV.). Jews abounded in Cyprus, so that the way lay operr tor the Christian propaganda. It was Cypriote Jewish Christians who brought the gospel to Antioch (Acts xi. 20). The heretic Yalentinus is said ultimately to have laboured in Cyprus, and during the great persecution Christians from the mainland were banished to the mines of Cyprus Mali. Pal., xiii. 2). Three Cypriote bishopsâ Gelasius from Salamis,

Cyril from Paphos, and Spyridon from Trimithusâ were present at the comicil of Nicasa. and three bishoprics for an island of no great size meant a strong church. Nor were these all; for in the history of Spyridon we hear of "bishops of Cyprus,""

amongst whom was Triphyllius, bishop of Ledrae (Sozom., i. 11, cp. Jer., de Vir. III. xcii.). Besides, Sozomen (vii. 19) relates that there were bishops in Cyprus even in the villages, while at the synod of Sardica the signatures show that there were no fewer than twelve Cypriote bishops in attendance.

We do not know to what lengths the claim of Cyprus went,,: which insisted on autocephaly i. e., the right of self-ordination) '"

as against the jurisdiction of Antioch. The Cypriote bishops at Ephesus (431 a. d.) declared they had exercised this right j since the apostolic age. But bighop Alexander of Antioch explained (in his letter to Innocent I.) that the Cypriotes had not broken off from Antioch until the Arian controversy (cp.

Liibeck's Reichseint. imd Mrchl. Hierarehie, pp. 165 f.). Rufinus,-,

Socrates (i. 12), and Sozomen all tell us about the facetious and ' i ti- breezy Spyridon. He was a wealthy yeoman and herdsman, Ci r ' and remained so even after he was elected a bishopâ which, uwi throws light upon the classes of the population to which (j

Christianity had penetrated. Triphyll i us, his colleague, again, was a man of high culture who had studied jurisprudence at

Berytus. Sozomen relates a good story about the relations between the two men. At a provincial synod in Cyprus,

Triphyllius was preaching, and in describing the story of the paralytic man he used the word a-KijulTrovg (" bed ") instead of the popular term Kpa arrov (" pallet"). Kai 6 'ETrupiscou ayavuk-

Trjcra?, ov rru ye, eÂ , aulelvcoi tov KpappatOv eiprjkOTog, on Tai avrov Xe ea- iv etraicrxiivi Kexpn' Oai (" Whereupon Spyridon wrathfully exclaimed, ' Art thou greater than he who spake the word " bed," that thou art ashamed to use the very words which he used?"" "). The story illustrates a phase of the history of culture. Luke had already deleted the " vulgarisms" in ' 'Aurip ws T6 ewSyiJ-os Kol 5ia v6j. oiv affkriaiv iroxvv xp fov v rrj Brjpvtlaiv Tr6Ket Siatpifpas ("An eloquent and learned man who had spent many years at Berytus in studying law"). Cp. the Life of Gregory Thaumaturgus.â Ledrse = Leucontheon.

Athanas., Apol c. Arian. 50.

Mark and Matthew, but a number of terms in the gospels were still offensive to cultured Greeks.

Â 5. Edessa (Osehoene) and the East (Mesopotamia, Persia, Parthia, and India)

One of the most remarkable facts in the history of the spread of Christianity is the rapid and firm footing which it secured in Edessa (Urhrd).- The tradition about the correspondence between Jesus and king Abgar " the Black,"' and about the; local labours of Thomas or Thaddaeus (Eus., H. E. i. 13), is of course entirely legendary, while Eusebius is wrong in asserting (ii. 1. 7) that the entire city had been Christian from the apostolic age to his own time. But the statement must hold true of the age at which he wrote. In part, also, it has an earlier reference. For there is no doubt that even before 190 a. d, Christianity had spread vigorously within Edessa and its surroundings, and that (shortly after 201 or even earlier."') the 1 Cp. Map. IV.â Mommsen's Geschiche, v. pp. 339 f. (Eng. trans., ii. pp. 30 f.); Burkitt's Early Christianity outside the Roman EÂ ipire (1899), and his Early Eastern Christianity (1904; the best work on the subject which we possess); Duval's ZTw. cfj desse (isgz); Labourt's Le Christianismedanspewf ire Perse sous la dynastie Sassattide, 224-632 (1904); and Chabot on " Synodicon Orientale " in Reciuil des actes synodaux de Pt'glise de Perse, Notices et extraits des MSS., tome 37, with Hallier's Untersuch. iiber die edess. Chronik. (in the Texte u. Unters.," yi. i, 1892), and E. Meyer's article on "Edessa" in Pauly-Wissowa's Lexicon. Labourt also gives a map of the western provinces of the Persian empire (Mesopotamia).

' An earlier parallel is the conversion of the royal house of Adiabene to Judaism in the reign of the emperor Claudius (see above, vol. i., p. 2).

It still finds defenders, however.â At a comparatively early date the tomb of the apostolic missionary was also shown at Edessa, but there was great diversity of opinion upon his identity (Judas Jacobi, Thomas, or Thaddaeus?).

â â The strong local Judaism undoubtedly formed a basis for the spread of Christianity both here and still farther eastward to the bounds of Persia (cp. Schiirer, III. pp. 5 f., Eng. trans. II. ii. pp. 222 f.; Acts ii. 9 f.; Joseph., Aiitiq., xi. 5. 2, XV. 2. 2, xv. 3. i). Schiirer thinks the Jews in these provinces numbered millions, not thousands; their headquarters were Nehardea (Noapsa) and Nisibis.â The Aramaic element always predominated in the population of Edessa; only a thin Greek stratum overlaid it (cp. Chrysostom's remark on Edessa,-Kowthv aypoikorepa, eucrfSeorepa 5e, ii. p. 641). Caracalla put an end to the semi-regal native dynasty of the Abgars (semi-Syrian, semi-Arabian) in 216 A. D.; but Edessa had already been for long under the suzerainty of Rome, while Mesopotamia remained as it was till Septimius Severus, After 216, Edessa and (A v-VV-el-

CHRISTIANITY DOWN TO 325 A. D. 143 rojal house joined the church3a that Christianity became the AjulCt state-religion; while even during the Easter controversy c.–.

190 A. D.) "the churches in Osrhoene and the local towns" (implying that there were several bishoprics) addressed a communication to Rome. Christianity in Edessa, which was originally distinct from Catholicism, starts with two persons, Tatian "the Assyrian "and Bardesanes (born 154 a. d.). The former compiled his volume of the gospels (or " Diatessaron ") for the Syrian church, while the latter established and acclimatized Christianity by dint of his keenness in teaching, his fanciful theology, and his sacred songs. (Bardesanes was closely r" connected with the school of Valentinus. His party in Edessa 1 was called the Valentinian party; cp. Julian's Ep. xliii.). " " Neither was a "catholic" Christian. Measured by the doctrinal standards of the catholic confederation, both were

Osrhoene were a Roman 5rovince till the Persian conquest in the seventh century. The names of the bishops from Edessa and Mesopotamia who attended the council of Niceea show a mixture of Aramaic and Greek: Eithilas (Edessa), Jacobus, Antiochus, Mareas (Macedonopolis), and Johannes.

' On the "Ada Edessena" see Tixeront's Les origines de F glise d"Edessa (i888), Carriere's La h'gende d'Abgar (1895), von Dobschiitz's " Christusbilder" in the Texle u. Unters., N. F. iii., a. nd my Lttt.-Gesciichte, i. pp. 53: f. ii. 2. pp. 161 f. The great church-buildings were not erected till 313 (cp. the chronicle of Edessa in Texie 71. Uners., ix. i. p. 93), but there was a Christian church as early as 201 (cp. ibid., p. 86). The same chronicle contains some other interesting items on the church and the church-buildings. Julius Africanus had already claimed the Christian king Abgar as his friend (cp. Eus., Chroii., 2234-2235) while the Liber Potttific. preserves an ancient tradition (which was misunderstood and applied to Britain) to the effect that this Abgar corresponded with bishop Eleutherus of Rome (cp. my essay in the Sitztmgsberichte d. Preuss. Akademie, 1904, pp. 909 f.).

- According to the Liber Synod., there were eighteen of them.

In the Doctrina Addcti (p. 50; Phillips) Serapion of Antioch (192-209) is said to have consecrated Palut as bishop of Edessa. This may be, but Palut can hardly have been the first teacher and president in the see; he was simply the first catholic bishop. Tlie beginnings of the Christianizing of Edessa may still be made out in vague outline from this native "Doctrina Addaei" (legendary material of the fourth century), the Acts of Scharbel, and the martyrdom of Barsamya, together with the chronicle of Edessa (cp. Burkitt's Eastern Christianity, lecture i.). First we have an apostolic missionary, subsequently identified with a well-known apostolic personality; then a native teacher and leader, Aggai â then bishop Palut. Catholicism now comes upon the scene, for Palut was ordained by Serapion, it is said, and Serapion was ordained by Zephyrinus of Rome. Palut was succeeded by bishop Abschalama, and he by bishop Barsamya. The last-named conveited the great pagan priest Scharbel, was a contemporary of heretics. But they were " mild" heretics, And from the beginning of the third century onwards, the Edessene church came more and more into hne, at least partially, with the church at large; henceforward, catholics (Palutians) and Bardesanists opposed each other in Edessa. Rome, in ending the royal house of Edessa, ended the state-religion also; but the number of local Christians was not diminished.

Tatian's Diatessaron was retained by the catholic party in Edessa, although it was not entirely orthodox. The " Gospel of the Separated (ones)," which lies before us in the Syrus Sinaiticus and the Syrus Curetonianus, most likely originated within Edessa also. It came not long after the Diatessaron. Finally,

Fabian the bishop of Rome (this is emphasized), and lived to see the Decian persecution. This emphasis on dates, when taken together with the statements that Eleutherus wrote to Abgar and that Palut was contemporaneous with Zephyrinus, and with the fact of Osrhoenic bishops sending a letter to Victor of Rome, is a sure proof that there was an ecclesiastical connection now between Rome and Edessa. Zephyrinus was insignificant (it is erroneous, of course, to allege that he ordained Serapion), and he would never have been mentioned had he not played some role in the life of Abgar and the origins of the church at Edessa. At the time of Diocletian's persecution, Qona was bishop of Edessa, and Schamona and Guria (cp. Noldeke, "Uber einige Edess. Martyrakten," Sii-assburger Festschrift, 1901) were martyred then; under Licinius, the deacon Habbib was martyred (cp. the old Syrian Kalendariiim of 411 a. d.). Qona was succeeded by Sa'ad (died 324).â The mission to Eleutheropolis in Palestine, under Tiberius, with which the Abgar-Addjeus-Aggai legend commences, may be historical, but it belongs to the reign of Septimius Severus (so Burkitt, rightly), as is plain from the mention of Eleutheropolis and the name of Serapion of Antioch. As the legend puts only one teacher and missionary before Palut, the Christianizing of Edessa cannot have begun much before the middle of the second century. The legend antedates itself by far more than a century; as a result, it puts under Trajan what happened under Decius. In the chronicle of Michael the Syrian (died 1199) two bishops are mentioned before Palut in connection with Bardesanes, viz. Hystaspcs, who is said to have converted Bardesanes and his predecessor izani (Yaznai), besides another bishop who excommunicated Bardesanes, viz. Aquai, the successor of Hystaspes. The first two may have actually been Christian (though not catholic) leaders prior to Palut. In Aquai we may perhaps recognize Aggai; only, in that case, he is put too far down, and the account of him is unauthentic. Burkitt (pp. 34 f.) takes a somewhat different view.

1 " As heresies were increasing in Mesopotamia, Bardesanes wrote against the Marcionites and other heretics." This remark of Eusebius (iv. 30) displays astonishing ignorance. In the Philosoph. (vii. 31) of Hippolytus, Bardesanes is called "The Armenian." A distinguished pupil of Marcion, Prepon, is also mentioned and described as an "Assyrian"; he wrote against Bardesanes.â See above, p. 127, for the probable connection of the Ada Thovia: with the circle of Bardesanes.

Burkitt has recently shown almost to a certainty that the Peshitta (of the gospels) also arose in Edessa, and was issued by bishop Rabbula about 420 a. d. It was Edessa, and not i Antioch or any town in Coele-Syria, which became the head- ' C quartei's and missionary centre of national Syrian Christianity during the third century. From Edessa issued the Syriac versions of early Christian literature, and thus Syriac, which had been checked by the progress of Greek, became a civilized and. literary tongue, owing to Christianity.

The Christian city of Edessa, which probably had a larger percentage of Christians among its population than any of the larger towns during the period previous to Constantine, was certainly an oasis and nothing more. Round it swarmed the heathen. A few Christians were indeed to be found at Carrhae (= Haran), a town which was the seat of Dea Luna and contained numerous temples. This we know from the martyrdoms. But in the Peregrinatio Silvicc, c. 20 (circa 385 a. d.) we read: " In ipsa civitate extra paucos clericos et sanctos monachos, si AlMr'V qui tamen in civitate commorantur in the country districts they -v were numerous, penitus nullum Christianum inveni, sed totum gentes sunt" (" In the city itself, apart from a few clerics and holy monks, who, however, stay inside its walls, I found not a single Christian; all were pagans"). Cp. also Theodoret (H. E., iv. 15), who describes Carrhae, in the reign of Valens, as (Kexepo-wiuei') a barbarous place full of the thorns of paganism

Cp. Nestle's article on "Translations of the Bible" in Pro. Real-Encykl iii. pp. 167 f.; and Merx, Die vier kanonischen Evangelien nach ihrem dltesten bekannten Texte, ii. I (1902), pp. x. f. Burkitt (in his second lecture) shows that, prior to Tatian, Edessa probably had no version of the gospels at all (though the Peshitta of the Old Testament was probably earlier than Tatian), that the translation of "The Separated (ones)," Acts, and the Pauline epistles goes back to Palut or to his age (the version of "The Separated (ones)" is extant in Syr. Cur. and Syr. Sin.), and that the Peshitta is the revision completed by Rabbula. The differences in Syr. Cur. and Syr. Sin. show plainly how necessary a revision and adaptation of the current Greek text had come to be, but the Diatessaron was still the most widely circulated text of the gospels about 400 A. D. Syr. Sin. and Syr. Cur. have no liturgical traces; they were not liturgical texts at all.

"Its influence was only remote and vague.

No bishop, however, was permitted there. The name of the first bishop occurs under Constantius.

VOL. II.

(cp. V. 4, iii. 26, and similar statements in Ephraem). The existence of Christian churches, previous to 325 a. d., can be verified accurately for Nisibis, Resaina, Macedonopolis (on the Euphrates, west of Edessa), and Persa (= Perra), as the bishops of these towns, together with their colleagues from Edessa, attended the Nicene councils. (For other evidence regarding Nisibis, see Theodoret, H. E., i. 7.)

As regards the spread of Christianity in 3 esopuqÂ amia and Persia, no store whatever can be set by the statement (Assemani, Bthl. Orient. iii. 1. p. 611) that there were about 360 churches in Persia by the second century. There is no doubt, however, ' Haran was predominantly pagan even as late as Justinian's age (Procop., de Bella Pers., ii. 13). Christianity could never get a firm foothold there (cp. Chwolson, Die Ssabier U7td der Ssabismns, 1856).

- (=Antiochia Mygdonia) where Ephraem, the famous Syrian author, was born of Christian parents at the beginning of the fourth century. A Christian school can be shown to have existed at Nisibis not long afterwards. By the middle of the fourth century the city was for the most part Christian. Sozomen (v. 3) writes: 'Ntaifi'fjvois iis iravrtkus xp """Â-"(Cov(ri Kal U re rovs vaovs avoiyovfft ft-'fin eh ta Upa. poitW(Tiv 7Trrei 7 (Tâ (sc. the emperor Julian) fx.)) fio-r df7v, k. t. X. ("He threatened that he would not help the people of Nisibis, since they were entirely Christian and neither opened their temples nor frequented the sacred places ").

' Reference may also be made to Acts ii. 9 ("Parthians and Medes and Elamites and the dwellers in Mesopotamia "), but the results among those who were born Jews cannot have been large, here any more than elsewhere. A passage from the Jerusalem Talmud (cp. Graetz's Hist, des Juifs, III. p. 51, quoted by Labourt, p. 16) seems to corroborate this. Hananias, a nephew of rabbi Joshua, is said to have attached himself to the Christian church in Capernaum, and, in order to withdraw hin from Ckiistian influences his uncle sent him to Babylon. No reliable data can be got from the history of the Mandseans (cp. Brandt, Die fnanddische Religion, etc., 1889) bearing on the history of early Christianity in Persia. All we learn is that this pagan sect was influenced by Christianity. But it is not necessary to assume that this took place in the second or the third century. Sozomen H. E., ii. 8) puts it cautiously: kox X. iptwv 5t xp""""""Â Â """"aÂ T v apxh r yovu. at '6Toi rfj Trpocpdaet ttjs 'Offpotivuiy Kal 'Apjuevicsf ljr(i ias, ws (ik6s, Tois avrsdi Bdots avspdinv uifiikriffav Kal ttjs avrsiv apetrjs iirâ ipd6r cray ("I think the introduction of Christianity among the Persians was due to their intercourse with the people of Osrhoene and Armenia, in all probability; associating with these godly men they were incited to imitate their virtues also "). It is natural to suppose that after the conquest of Western Syria by the Persians, many Christians of the district (together with bishop Demetrianus of Antioch, cp. above, p. 130) were deported to Mesopotamia and Persia. For the " Mes-salians " in Mesopotamia, see the confused accounts in Epiph., ffter. Ixxx. (which include, perhaps, Mandsean traits).

â The Nestorian patriarch Timotheus I. (died 823 a. d.) writes to the monks of St Maron (cp. Pognon, Une version Syriaqut des aphorismes d'Hippocrate ., that Epiphauius Hwr., Ixii. 1) speaks of mjji J calSabellians,- ' ' i or that Dionjsius of-Alexandria (chra 250 a. d.) not only knew churches in Mesopotamia, but mentioned their intercourse and ' relations with other churches (Eus., vii. 5; they took part in the controversy over the baptism of heretics); while the dialogue of Philip, a pupil of Bardesanes (" On the Laws of Countries "â circa 220), presupposes a considerable extension of Christianity, even among the natives, as far as the eastern districts of

Persia t (cp. Eus., Prccp. Evang., vi. 10. 46), and Eusebius himself v–)r viii. 12) mentions martyrs in Mesopotamia after the rise and jtj CTC-l conquests of the Sassanidas, and during the persecution of Diocletian. Furthermore, the great Persian persecution during the fourth century points to a serious spread of Christianity in the course of the third century (cp. also the origin of Mani chaeism and the history of Mani in the Acta Archelai, which are of some use, though of course they are partly fictitiousâ T ' f

Archelaus himself being described by Jerome in the Vir. Illustr. (M A Ixxii. as bishop of Kaschkar Mesopotamia), Coiastantiue i- W- writes thus to king Sapur: " I am delighted to learn that the y finest districts in Persia also are adorned with the presence of

Leipzig, 1903, p. xxviii., in Syriac and French; German by Nestle in Zeilsch. J. k. Gesch., xxvi. 95): " No one will believe that Nestorius converted or baptized all the districts and peoples under this patriarchate. We had our Christianity about 500 years (!) before Nestorius was born, and about twenty years after the ascension of our Lord." Which is absurd.

Gyre ol iv Hapdla XpictTiavol iroxvyaixovai, Tldpdoi Tvyx vovres, ovd' ol ev M7)5ia Kval irpotioeacri Toiis ytkpovs, ovx ol iv Hipffisi yanovai ras Ovyarepas avtcov, Hepcrai ovTes, ov irapa Bacrpois Koi Tri ois (pdiipovcri rous ydxovs, (c. t. A. (" Nor are the Parthian Christians polygamists, nor do Christians in Media expose their dead to dogs, nor do Persian Christians marry their daughters, nor are those in Bactria and among the Gelse debauched," etc.).

"The Persians are referred to in Constantine's remark (77. Const., ii. 53) that the kardan'ans nowadays boasted of having taken in the refugees from the Roman empire during the Diocletian persecution, and of having detained them in an extremely mild form of captivity, permitting them the unrestricted practice of their religion and all that pertained thereto.

According to Sozom., ii. 13 (cp. Marutha), the chor-episcopus Mareabdes was taken captive and killed by the Persians, in the persecution under Sapur, together with his bishop Dausas of Bethzabde and about 250 clerics.

â â Manichseism showed a decidedly anti-Christian and anti-catholic front from the very first, though some time afterwards it modified its anti-Christian tendency. Hence Christianity must have been already an important factor in Persian life.

M: Christians." Finally, reference must be made to Aphraatea. r His homilies,- convposed between 337 and 345, reflect a Chris- 4- tianity which is substantially unaffected by the course of Greek

Christianity, and which therefoi'e occupied the same position before 325 as after. They also reflect, at the same time, a vigorous and far-reaching ecclesiastical system confronted by a large Jewish population and dependent on Jewish exegetical tradition. The number of organized churches in Mesopotamia

"X, j kj t- Const., iv. 13; cp. iv. 8: â irv96jxevos ye rot irapa rcji Tlepawv fdvfi-V JO j itxriqiveiv ras tov Oeov ikK T fflas aovs re xvpiavspovs rats Xpiffrov irolxvais ' â " ' ' 'ivayexdcecroai, k. t. ("On learning that churches of God abounded among the Persians, and that thousands of people were gathered into the fold of Christ," etc.).

"The place of their composition (in Mesopotamia, within the Persian realm) is uncertain; possibly it was the monastery of Mar Mattai, about four hours north from the ruins of ancient Ninive (cp. Texe u. Unters., iii. 3. 4. pp. xvii. f.).

â His fifth homily shows plainly, as indeed we can easily understand, how the sympathies of the Syrian Christians in the territory of Sapur were entirely with the Romans in the Persian war. The characteristics and idiosyncrasies of the ancient Syrian church have been excellently described by Burkitt (in his third and fourth lectures; cp. also Labourt, pp. 31 f.), who has discovered fresh items (in the works of Ephraem and Aphraates) bearing upon the theology of the church, especially upon the doctrine of marriage and the sacraments. The prirnitive Jewish Chxislian substratum of Syrian Christianity comes out even in Aphraates; it confirms the opinion that during the brief initial epoch of Christianity in Eastern Syria (of which we know nothing), the converts were principally drawn from

V v converted fe: ws. One very remarkable trait is that of sexual asceticism (derived from Tatian, of course, not from Judaism). Baptized persons are not to marry; any one who desires to marry is to abstain from baptism, for baptism is a spiritual marriage with Christ. Burkitt (p. 126) rightly speaks of "' a deliberate reservation of baptism for the spiritual aristocracy of Christendom " (cp. also his conclusions upon the b'nai Q'yama). This standpoint goes far beyond that of the Novatians, but it is quite in keeping witlttha't of Eustathius of Sebaste; it denotes a common Oriental type of primitive Christianity, which probably was focussed at Edessa (cp., however, the account of the preaching of repentance at Csesarea Cappadocia in Socrates, v. 22). A doctrinal and practical position of this kind must have made it difficult to oppose the Marcionites, who were numerous in Eastern Syria, for they too refused to baptize any except unmarried persons. From the works of Ephraem and the heresy-catalogue of Maruta of Maipherkat (Texte ti. Unlers., xix. I, 1899) we can judge how heresies swarmed in Eastern Syria and Persia even in the third century.â Monastjcism t'ntered Mesopotamia at the latest under Constantine, thanks to Mar Awgin Eugenius; cp. Butler's Laiisiac History of Palladiiis (1S98), p. 218, and Budge's Book of the Governors, p. xliv. Mar Awgin came from Egypt; he was a pupil of Pachomius and subsequently a friend of Jacob of Nisibis. He founded a monastery in the mountains near Nisibis. He died in 363, after living for more than thirty years in this monastery, which possibly was founded, as later Syrian witnesses assert, before 325 A. D.

before 250 a. d. must have been small. In one or two localities we can definitely assume the presence of Christians before 325, as, e. g., at Amida (= Diarbekir; cp. the Abgar legend, Acta Thadd. 5; the retrospective inferences are certain),"- and above all at Gjundeschabur (Beth Lapath), whither the captive Western Syrians were chiefly deported (Labourt, pp. 19 f.), and Seleucia-Ctesiphon (as may certainly be inferred from Aphraates, the history of bishop Papa, and the episcopal lists, which are not wholly useless). The Persian bishop at Nicasa, however, did o not come from Seleucia. The existence of Christians at Batana, â ' 1 Labourt, however, seems to me to go too far when he denies that there were any organized churches in Persia before the Sassanid dynasty ("Tout nous porte a croire qu'avant I'avenement de la dynastie Sassanide, I'empire perse ne contenait pas des cominunautes chretiennes organisees," p. 17).

According to Ebed Jesu, both the bishop of Amida and the bishop of Gustra (= Ostra? cp. Bratke's Religiotisgespriich am Hof der Sassaniden, 1S99, p. 264) were at Nicaea.

According to Greg. Barhebr., Chroit., iii. 22 f., and other legendary writers, Seleucia had three successive bishops who were relatives of Jesus (!). They were called Abres, Abraham, and Jacob. Which shows us what to make of them! On Mari, the founder of the patriarchate of Seleucia-Ctesiphon, cp. Raabe's Die Geschichte des Dom. Mari (1893), and Westphal's Unters. iiber die Quelleji u. die Glaiibiviirdigkeil der Patriarchenchroniken (1901), pp. 30 f.; and on an alleged correspondence of the catholicus Papa of Seleucia (died 326), see Braun in Zeitschr. f. kathol. Tkeol., xviii. (1894), pp. 167 f. On Papa, see Westphal, op. cit., pp. 60f., and Labourt, 20 f. The personality of this energetic and therefore sorely persecuted bishop, who died full of years, and perhaps the historicity of the synod which he convened (in 313-314 A. D.?), may be regarded as indubitable. His successor was Simeon bar Sabta'e, the martyr. Eusebius describes how at the consecration of the church in Jerusalem there was present one of the Persian bishops, who was a master of the divine oracles (Trap v koi Xlipahiv itriffkOTraii hphi xpVJ-a, to. 0(ia 6yia e r Kpi cckws avijp, Vit. Const., iv. 43). Hence there must have been several of them.â The aforesaid Mari may have been (so Labourt, p. 15) some actual bishop and missionary on the Tigris, but legend has treated him as if he were one of the twelve apostles, making him the founder of Christianity throughout the entire Eastern Orient. While the legends, which are connected with the central seat of Seleucia-Ctesiphon, and which endeavour to throw a special halo round the episcopate as well as to claim apostolic origin (Thomas) for the Nestorian church, are exceptionally full of tendency and quite audacious, they are nevertheless transparent enough and mutually contradictory; their numerous discrepancies indicate every possible variety of ecclesiastical interests (connection by delegation with Antioch, with Jerusalem, with Jesus himself; complete independence; and so forth). Labourt has recently criticized these legends (pp. 13 f.). Even from falsified sources and unreliable traditions, however, we can still see, as I have pointed out, that the Persian church of Mesopotamia must have been loosely organized before the great persecution of the fourth century. Thus there were previous to Constantine, may be deduced from the Silvias Pereg?: 19; and we may infer from the Acts of the Persian martyrs (edited by Hofmann) that there were also Christians at Harbath Glal, Kerkuk (= Karkha dh Bheth Slokh), Arbela Shargerd, Dara, and Lasom. This holds true perhaps (to judge from the Acta Jrchelai) of the village of Diodoris in Mesopotamia as well, and of Sibaptxiis (where there was a martyrdom). A Christian church may also be assumed to have existed at Kaschkar (Carchar) before 325.

"Your investigation into the Christian names," Noldeke now two bishops in Gundeschabur about the year 340, both of whom were martyred together; and this is not the only instance of the kind. Bishop Papa was probably the first to organize the Persian church.

i Jdi. z. Kxuide des Morgettlands, vii. 3., pp. 9 f., 46 f., 52, 268 (also Noldeke in Gdtf. Gel. Anz. 1880, p. 873, who opines that the first organized Christian church arose on the lower Tigris about 170 a. d.).

- The bishop who attended Nicsea probably came from one or other of the two last-named towns (cp. Westphal, p. 66).

3 In regard to the spread of Christianity throughout the East, Noldeke has been kind enough to write me as follows (Sept. 27, 1901): "It is a bold venture to attempt to exhibit the spread of Christianity in close detail, but you have certainly fixed a large number of points. Scarcely any serious aid is to be got from the East as the few reliable sources which are older than the fourth century yield very little in this connection beyond what is generally known. Aphraates and the early Acts of the martyrs certainly suggest that in the districts of the Tigris Christianity was widely diffused, with an organization of bishops and clergy, about the middle of the fourth century; but it is a sheer fable to assert that these Persian Christians constituted at that period a definite church under some catholicus. Simeon bar Sabta'e was merely bishop of Seleucia and Ctesiphon. The erection of churches, which subsequently became Nestorian, did not take place until the beginning of the fifth century, and at a still later period the Christian church of Persia (whose origin is unfortunately obscure) declined to submit to the catholicus. The stubborn adhesion of the people of Haran to paganism was partly due, perhaps, to a feeling of local jealousy of Edessa, which had early been won over to Christianity. It is a pity that none of the original Syriac writings of the pagans in Haran ('Sabians'), dating from the Islamic period, have been preserved." Mesopotamia was ihe birthplace of the monk Audius, who started a religious movement of his own in the days of Arius (cp. Epiph., Hcsr., lxx. i).â The figures relatint to the martyrs during the persecution of Sapur are quite useless, but it is remarkable to find that here the Jews are still described as the chief instigators of the persecution.

Cp. Westphal, p. 34; Labourt, p. 20. Kaschkar lay on the great canal between the Euphrates and the Tigris in the district 'Ziraaivov Xdpa, and the discussions between Manichreans and Christians about 270 a. d. are said to have taken place there. In the Arta Archelai a village called Diodoris in the region of Kaschkar is also mentioned. One account of a martyrdom mentions a martyr in Sibapolis. Does this mean India (the god Siva?).

writes to me, "has moved me to examine the only large and ancient list of Christian Oriental names which is known to me, viz., that of the martyrs during Sapur's persecution (in Wright's Mahyrologium, from the famous manuscript of 411 a. d.). It deals with clerics alone. There are over ninety persons mentioned. Aramaic names preponderate by far. It is not always possible to distinguish them accurately from the Persian names, especially as frequent conformations occur which admit of more than one interpretation. Several of the Aramaic names are palpably pagan, like those compounded with "B61" (so even in Palmyra), etc.; others are specifically Christian (according to the standard of the age), e. g. " 'Abdiso," " servant of Jesus," which occurs five times. The Persian names include Hormuzd and Narse; perhaps their pagan meaning was no longer felt. "Only a feware Greco-Roman: Longinus, Sabinus, and Menophilus (none of which I can find in the lists of Jewish teachers in the Mishna or the Talmud, where several other Greek and Roman names occur). I do not include among these Greco-Roman names " Andrew"" (twice), which occurs alongside of Paul (thrice) and Peter (once); it was certainly chosen as an apostolic name. Similarly with John (six times), though it was a favourite local name of the Jews. Simon (thrice) is doubtful; the name does occur often among the pagans of Palmyra, as well as among Jews and Christians. Silas (twice) need as little be derived from the New Testament, since it was common among Jews and pagans alike, either in its fuller form x'Plnt ' (2e ixa?, Palmyra) or abbreviated into vh (Gk. Seixa?, 2Xa?). It is remarkable that Abraham, which the Jews of that age still refrained from using as a common name, occurs five times here, with Isaac (five times) and Jacob (twice). The two latter were common among the Jews. The occurrence of an Ithamar, which is from the Old Testament but was not used by the Jews, is very remarkable. We cannot make much of the list with regard to the Jewish environment. I must admit I had expected more from it."

The Syro-Persian church deserves our unqualified sympathy. " It was tlie only large church which never enjoyed the official protection of the state. It maintained the traditions of Anti- ochene exegesis, it translated the works of Christian antiquity into Syriac with great assiduity, and it could pride itself on knowing Justin, Hippolytus, Methodius, Athanasius, Basil, the three Gregorys, Chrysostom, Diodorus, Aniphilochius,

Ambrose, and Theodore as well as the Greeks did themselves (cp. the evidence of the Nestorian patriarch Timotheus I., who died in 823). It also assimilated Greek philosophy and science, which it transmitted to the Arabians. At the present day it is crushed, impoverished, and down-trodden, but it can face its downfall with the consciousness that it has not lived in vain, but upon the contrary that it has filled a real place in the history of civilization.

Ij 'n In the third book of his commentary on Genesis, Origen alludes to a tradition that Thomas the apostle took Parthia as qi yam his missionary sphere, while Andrew's was Scythia (cp. Eus., ' H. E., iii. 1). From this it may be inferred that Christians were

I l known to exist there by the first half of the third century.

y; The same holds true of India. Of course the India to which

L. ysmJPantaenus journeyed from Alexandria (Eus., v. 10) may be South j " Arabia (or even the Axumitic kingdom). But the India where the early (third century) Acts of Thomas locate that apostle"s work is the N. W. territory of our modern India (for it is only

Cod. Pani, 1617, of the Martyrdom of Thomas, that drags in

Axum; cp. Bonnet, p. 87). Andrapolis is mentioned in Acta

Thorn. 3 as the scene of the apostle's labours; for other localities mentioned there, see Lipsius, Apotir. Apostelgesch., i. p. 280 (after Gutschmid). I pass over the traditions about Andrew, which mention various localities, as well as the traditions about

Simon and Judas (cp. my Chronologie, i. pp. 543 f.). They are all posterior to Constantine. It cannot be shown that the

"Thomas-Christians," discovered in Tndia in the sixteenth century, go back to the third century. I ' Compare, however, the passage from Origen aheady quoted on p. 13: "Nee apud Seras nee apud Ariacin audierunt Christianitatis sermonem."â Note that the first Protestant history of missions, published in Germany, was devoted to India, viz.,

M. V. La Croze, Is. dti Christ, des Indes, 1724 (cp. Wiegand in the Beitrdge z. Ford, chrisll. Theol., vi. 3. pp. 270 f.). La Croze, however, hardly touches the primitive age, as he regards the legends about Thomas as unauthentic.

6. Arabia

The large regions south of Palestine, Damascus, and Mesopotamia which bear the name of " Arabia " were never civilizedâ they were not even subduedâ by the Romans, with the exception of the country lying east of the Jordan and several positions south of the Dead Sea (cp. Mommsen's Rom. Gesch., V. pp. 471 f.; Eng. trans., ii. pp. 143 f). Consequently we can look for Christians during our epoch' only in the districts just mentioned, where Arabian, Greek, and Roman cities were inhabited by people of superior civilization. Immediately after his conversion Paul betook himself to "Ai-abia" (Gal. i. 17), i. e., hardly to the desert, but rather to the province south of Damascus. Arabians are also mentioned in Acts ii. 11.

We have already seen how the Palestinian Jewish Christians settled at Pella and Kochaba. Possibly this led the later Christians of the country to feel they were heirs of the primitive church,

Hippolytus Piilos., viii. 12) knew a Christian heretic whom he calls " the Arabian Monoimus,"" and whom he refutes. In the, days f Ori en there were numerous bishoprics in the towns

Cp. Map III. â For the changes in the political terminology and the metropolitan organization in Arabia, cp. Llibeck, o. cit., pp. 42 f., 75, 86 f., 91, 101, 161.

There ar e no Arab ic versions of the Bible previous to Islam, a fact which proves irrefragably that in its primitive period Christianity had secured no footing at all among the Arabs. Indeed it never secured such a footing, for the Arabic versions were not made for Arabs at all, but for Copls and Syrians who had become Arabians.

â " Mommsen, p. 485 (Eng. trans., ii. 158): "At this eastern border of the empire there was thus secured for Hellenic civilization a frontier domain which may be compared to the Romanized region of the Rhine; the arched and domed buildings of eastern Syria compare admirably with the castles and tombs of the great mea and merchants of Belgica." Bostra flourished greatly after the downfall of Palmyra. The emperor Philip (the Arab) made his birthplace, a small town, into a city called Philippopolis, which rapidly increased in size. We do not know whether this emperor's friendly attitude towards Christians was due to memories and impressions of his childhood, but his correspondence with Origen makes this probable.

What drove Paul to Arabia, and what he did there, we simply do not know. 1 retract my former conjecture that he retired to a region in which he might hope to avoid Jews. 154 MISSION AND EXPANSION OF CHRISTIANITY lying south of the Hauran and the Dead Sea, all of which were grouped together in a single synod. Bishop Beryllus of Bostra, well known (according to Eusebius, H. E., vi. 20) for his letters and writings, caused a great sensation, about 240 a. d., by propounding a Christological thesis to the effect that y'pergoaahiypostasis belonged to the Redeemer befoi'e he appeared irj time. The doctrine may have been designed to repudiate current conceptions of pre-existence as being Hellenic, and thus to give expression to a national Christian spirit (cp. Paul of Samosata"s doctrine). But this is uncertain. What is certain (for Eusebius, HE., vi. 33, reports it) is that "a large number of bishops'" carried on discussions and debates with him, and for these combatants we must look to Arabia especially, although Palestinian bishops may have also taken part in the controversy. Eusebius further relates that a synod was held at Bostra, to which Origen was invited, and of which he was the intellectual leader. Shortly afterwards a second synod was held at the same place, at which the rather untrustworthy Liber Synodicus declares that fourteen bishops were present. Origen again was invited, and again attended. The topic of discussion was a doctrine put forward by one section of the Arabian bishops, who held that the soul expired and decayed along with the body, and was revived along with it at the resurrection (Eus., H. E., vi. 37). The Semitic cast of mind in those who held this view, as well as their aversion to Hellenic speculation (with its essential immortality of the soul), are unmistakable. Christianity seems therefore to have penetrated such strata of the Arabian population as might be called nationalâ i. e., it spread among people who, while they rejected the Christianity of Alexandrian theology, were not barbarians, but worked out a theology of their own.

Horn, in Luc. xii. 0pp. v. p. 128, Lomm.): "Quia plerique de. Aegyptiis et Idumaeis proselyti accipiebant fidem Christi," etc. (" Since most of the proselytes among the Arabians and Idumreans accepted the faith of Christ").

- Some years earlier a provincial synod of Arabia had been held in connection with the proceedings against Origen; it decided in the latter's favour (cp. Jerome's Ep. xxxiii. 4). Qrigen was known personally by that time to the Arabian bishops, fqr about 215 a. d. he had travelled as far as Arabia at the request of the Roman governor, before whom he laid his views (Eus., H. E., vi. 19).

Whatever we may think of those two characteristic doctrinal views put forward in Bostra and "Arabia," in opposition to the Alexandrian theology, they furnish

The Arabian churches were connected with the church of Rome; and they required assistance from it, as we are fortunate enough to learn from an alkision which Dionysius of Alexandria happens to make in Eus., H. E viii. 5. The same passage also declares that Arabian bishops took part in the great Synod of Antioch (as to the question of the baptism of heretics).

Both the Onomasticon of Eusebius and the Acts of the Council of Nicaea show that Christians existed, during the days of Eusebius, in the towns lying east and north-east of the J3ead Sea. On Cariathaim (Kerioth, Kurejat, Kariatha; cp. Baedeker, p. 176) the Onomasticon observes, Yiapiaoaeiij. vvv ictTiv oxr X. ptcrtLav(iov Kwmt, irapu MrjsaBav ttoxlv Trj; 'ApaSla?, XeyojuLei Kapaidoa (on Madaba, cp. Baedeker, pp. 173 f.). There were present at Nicasa bishops from Philadelphia, Esbus (= Hesbon, Isbunda), and Sodom (whose site, so far as I know, has not been discovered; Usdum, south of the Dead Sea?). From the north there were the l shops of Bostra, the most important and finely situated city of the whole country, and a strong proof, at any rate, of independence and mental activity among the 4 '

"Arabian" Greeks. We may rank them with the pecuhar buildings whose ruins are to be found in Bostra, as evidence of a distinctive civilization. We do not know whether the idea, which was widely current in Arabia during the fourth century (Epiph., ffcer., lxxviii.), that Mary became the real wife of Joseph after the birth of Jesus, goes back to Jewish-Christian traditions. For Mariolatry in

Arabia, cp. under Thrace.â Photius (Cod. 48) calls Caius eiriffkoiros tuv eovwv, which is a twofold confusion: Caius = Hippolytus, and Hippolytus = Beryllus of Bostra. The latter must have been described in some contemporary source as iiria-KOTTos rav idvaiv (bishop of the Gentiles), which perhaps refers to widely scattered pagan tribes (cp. below, p. 156, note 3).

' From Optatus (ii. 12) we learn, casually, that there was intercourse also between Arabia and North Africa: "Quid Arabia provincia, unde probamus venientes a vobis sc. Donatistisj esse rebaptizatos? " ("What of the province of 1,1 '1 i Arabia, emigrants from which, we aver, have been re-baptized by you? ") In the "-O t t' burial-ground of the Great Oasis (Kaufmann, Â zu altchrisil. Pompeii in der libyschen IViiste, 1902, p. 22) this inscription has been found: Avdni vihs Md pko u Mco-yaSeo anh Koiifi-qs voi,,. fir Tp6iro is r) B6atpa. e TiYj s rs) yp a avri koi t(J) a. va'yiv(ii (T Kovti.

' " Cariathaim is now an entirely Christian village close to the Arabian city of Madaba, and called Karaitha."

Epiphanius Hcer. Ixxxv., and Epitome) observes that in Bakatha Bakathus firit-pokccfiia ttjs 'Apa ias ttjj iaase pias or ev Bakcioots rrjs i a5e pr yrjs Xitipas TTfpav Tov 'lopsdvov, the sect of the Valesians resided.

â It was the capital; cp. Lubeck, pp. 43 f., 86 f., 91. In a petition to the emperor Julian bishop Titus observes, apropos of Bostra, ifafiiwov ehai rw -'t- rv ionysias. The Nicene lists further contain, under Arabia, the name of a bishop called Sopater Beretaneus. Where this place (Beritana?) lay we do not know, for it cannot be identified with Bereitan (equivalent to Berothai? Baedeker, p. 358), which was situated in Lebanon. One tradition, which is not of course entirely trustworthy, makes an Arabian bishop from Zanaatha (? =Thana, south-east of the Dead Sea) attend Nicaea, but nothing is known of such a place. Finally, we may conclude, although the conclusion is not certain, from Epiph. li. 30 that there were Christians at Gerasa. It is impossible to prove that Christians lived in the Nabatean city of Petra earlier than Constantine;- but Sozomen (vii. 19) says there were bishops even in the villages of Arabia.

The efibrts made to introduce Christianity among the nomad . tribes, efforts that were both rare and rather fruitless, fall t outside our period, and consequently must be passed over here.

X y" Perhaps we should recall, in this connection, the fact that fpt Paiitaenus travelled from Alexandria to India, i. e., to Southern

"Arabia, about 180 a. d., and that many Jewish colonists and Â A many more proselytes were living in the latter district (Eus., - H. E., V. 10. 3). " He is said to have found there, among some of the inhabitants who were acquainted with Christ, the gospel of Matthew, which had reached that country before him.

'EWrifikcf Trki)6ei rh Xpi(Triavik6v (Christians equal in numbers to the Greek populace). This is an important statistical notice.

' The names of the bishops (Nicomachus, Cyrion, Gennadius, Severus, Sopater, another Severus, and Maron) are all Greek or Latin.

"According to Sozomen (vii. 5) the inhabitants of Petra and Areopolis (= Rabba, east of the middle of the Dead Sea) offered a vigorous resistance to Christianity even as late as 400 A. D. As for Petra, Epiphanius Hc k, li. c. 22; in Oehler, Appendix, t.

ii. p. 631), after describing the festival of the Virgin who had given birth to the ". on," proceeds as follows: rovro koi ev Ufrpa t ir6 ei fj.7jtp6iro LS Se iffti rrjs 'Apajsi'os) fv rcfi ike7(Ti flsai 'i(f) ovtcus ylifrai Kal 'Apa,3iki7 StaafkTCf i vxvovo-i t v U. ap9evoy, Kaxovvres avtr v 'Apa Lffrl Xaa ov, TOvtâ (niv K6priv yow T ap64yov, koi rhv e avrris yeyivvrjxfuov Aovffdpriv Tovtffftiv Movoytvrj tov Sea-Trrfrou (" The same thing goes on at the city of Petra, the metropolis of Arabia, in the local temple, where they sing hymns in Arabic to the Virgin, calling her by the Arabic name of Chaabos, i. e., Maiden or Virgin, and her son Dusares, i. e., the only-begotten of the Lord ").

3 Cp., e. g., Rufin., ii. 6 (= Socrat., iv. 36; Theodoret, iv. 20); Cyrillus Scythopolit, J ia Euthyinii iirlffkoiros rwv irapeul3o av); and see Duchesne's Les Missions chrstiennes au sud de Vempire Romain (1896), pp. 112 f.

For Bartholomew is said to have preached to these people and to have left with them a Hebrew version of Matthew's gospel, which they had kept until the time of which I speak.""

The extant Didascalia Apostolorum (cp. Achelis in Texte w. Unters., xxv. 2, 1904, and my Chronolog'ie ii. pp. 488 f.) is a unique and invaluable source of information upon the organization and life of an Arabic or Syrian (Greek-speaking) church during the first half or about the middle of the third century, ni Achelis (pp. 266-317) has drawn the picture for us. It portrays, not a village community, but a large church in an important city (Bostra.?), lying far from the main current of developing Christianity. We see its seductions, temptations, and complicated relationships. Jews and Jewish Christians lived in its environment, and a slight Jewish-Christian element is discernible within the church itself. The latter was so large in numbers that the bishop could no longer keep himself personally acquainted with all those who were in distress, or master each individual case. Still, there was only one church, and two deacons sufficed for the administration of poor-relief. The members seem for the most part to have belonged to the middle classes; few wealthy people were members, but the church was not wholly composed of poor and destitute persons. Worship was attended sometimes by distinguished men and women. Despite the lofty position already attained by the local clergy, brotherly feeling was still active. The love–feasts (which were distinct from the services of worship) were banquets to which the wealthier Christians invited their poorer fellow-members; the bishop seems to have been usually present at them. Hospitality towards travelling brethren was still a feature of the church's life, and the duty of looking after all its poor members was also recognized. The execution of the latter task devolved on the bishop, who administered the love-gifts of the church. The spirit of generous self-sacrifice was apparently strong. Several widows were so well provided for

Judaism' carried on a vigorous mission in Southern Arabia and Abyssinia (the Abyssinian Jews were Hamites, not Semites), and for a time managed to secure local control. It is inherently probable that Christians also reached this region at an early date, but we know nothing of the presence of primitive Jewish Christians.

that they could over and again realize their capital and loan it to usurers! Impure gifts were not to be received, but the writer knew some bishops who did take them. The list of those from whom no gift was to be taken (c. 18, p. 89, Achelis) is instructive; it shows the sort of people who either belonged to the churches or gave them money. They included people who were imprisoned for debt, masters who were tyrannical to their slaves, public prostitutes (even of the male sex), dishonest traders, criminal advocates, unjust prosecutors, factious lawyers, painters and bronze-workers and jewellers who worshipped idols or swindled, unjust revenue-officials, fortune-tellers, licensed victuallers who diluted their wines, rascally soldiers, murderers, executioners, " any official of the Roman empire who had been defiled in war or had shed innocent blood without due trial," usurers, etc. " If the churches are so poor that they need the contributions of such people to maintain their charitable work, then it were better to perish of hunger than to live by such means."

The solution of the difficulty always was to keep aloof from the heathen as far as possible in every relation of life. Emphasis repeatedly falls on the broad gulf between Christians and pagans. This church, however, does not feel it is oppressed by its pagan neighbours; on the contrary, it is living in peace and quiet, and it does not appear to be unpopular at all. Its aim is to make the best impression on the world by its manner of life (by simple living, decorum, diligence, etc.), and thereby to distinguish itself from the common ways of the world. Apparently it was still successful in this endeavour.

Â 7. Egypt and the Thebais, Libya and Pentapolis

The worst gap in our knowledge of early church history is our almost total ignorance of the history of Christianity in Alexandria and Egypt (in the wider as well as in the narrower

Cp. Map V.â Politically, Pentapolis (Cyrenaica) belonged to Crete; but I group it as above, since ecclesiastically, so far back as we can see, it gravitated to Alexandria and was added by Diocletian to Egypt. Apart from several sea- sense of the term) up till 180 a. d. (the episcopate of Demetrius), when for the first time the Alexandrian church appears in the daylight of history. It is then a stately church with a powerful bisho aiii a school of higher learning attached to it by means of which its influence was to be diffused and its fame borne far and wide. Eusebius found nothing in his. soui'ees- bearing on the primitive history of Christianity at Alexandria; and although we may conjecture, with regard to one or two very ancient Christian writings e. g. the epistle of Barnabas, y the Didache, the Preaching of Peter, the Apostolic Constitutions,. i cuui ' U etc.), that "their origin is Egyptian or Alexandrian, this can 3 I hardly be proved in the case of any one of them with clearness. rc. r

The following items sum up all our knowledge of the

Alexandrian or Egyptian church previous to Demetrius. lah I ports, it was a dismal region; cp. Dionys. Alex, in Eus., H. E., vii. il. 14, b Aluixiai'hs els Tpax repovs fiei ws esJ ei, Kal Atfiukcottpovs rifias tottovs fjilra-(TTTjaai ipov. T 6ri. The independence of Egypt within the empire (from Augustus to Diocletian), as well as its secluded position, can be made out from ecclesiastical as well as from civil history. Hence one must take care to avoid postulating for) Egypt the general ecclesiastical condition which prevailed throughout the empire. The characteristic division into nomes, the primacy of Alexandria, and the lack of towns,. vvere also of great significance for the development of local Christianity., ' Renan Les Apotres, Germ, ed., pp. 297 f.; cp. Les vangiles, p. 158) thinks that Christianity must have at first been slow to take any hold of Egypt, and refers for proof of this to the scanty intercourse maintained by the Alexandrian and the Palestinian Jews (!), as well as to the fact that the Judaism of Egypt " developed to a certain extent along its own lines: it had Philo and the Thera-peutse, and that was all its Christianity." He also believes that the Egyptian religion, as it then existed, afforded no favourable basis for Christianity (!), But it is very doubtful whether the scanty notices of Christianity in Egypt prior to 180 A. D. justify us in holding that Christianity was really weak and scanty. Even supposing that a long interval elapsed during which it was comparatively small, we would not be in a position, I think, to offer any explanation of the fact.

So that we also lymW next to nothing of the relations between the powerful Judaism of Egypt and of Alexandria and the development of the church. It is more than a conjecture, however, that a larger number of Jews were converted to JU

Christianity in the Nile valley than anywhere else; for (i) the inner development of Judaism never approximated so closely to a universal religion as it did in Alexandria, and (ii) we know that the gospel according to the Hebrews circulated in a Greek version in Egypt during the second centuryâ which implies the existence ' '; of an original Jewish Christianity (details below). We cannot, of course, appeal j to Jerome de Vir. 111. viii.: " Alexandriae prima ecclesia adhuc iudaizans").-

Cp. also the recently discovered " Sayings of Jesus " among the papyri.

â â Reference may be made to Apouos of Alexandria (Acts xviii. 24), who appears to have oined the Baptist's followers in Alexandria (though this is not (i) There was ajocal gospel, described by Clemeiit of Alexandria and others as " the gospel according to the Egyptians " (evayyexiov Kar AiyutTTiovg), but orthodox Christians had already dropped it from use by the end of the second century. The heretical asceticism and Modalism which characterize it throw a peculiar light upon the idiosyncrasies of early Egyptian Christianity. Originally it was not used merely by actually heretical parties, who retained it ever afterwards, but also by Egyptian Christians in general, as is plain from Clement's position, and still more so from its very title. For the latter either implies that the book was originally used by the Geutilfijchristians of Egypt as distinguished from the local Jewish Christians who read the evayyexiou Kao' 'Yibpalov? in an Aramaic or Greek version, or else it implies a contrast between KQT AiyutTTcov and kut 'AXe avspetav. In this event, the gospel would be the book of the provincials in contradistinction to the Alexandrians.- (ii) The heretic Basilides laboured in Egypt. Of him Epiphanius writes as follows (Tar., xxiv. 1): certain). We should possess an important account (though one which would have to be used with caution) of early Christianity in Alexandria, were Hadrian epistle to Servianus authentic. This is controverted, however, and consequently cannot be employed except for the third century. The passage in question runs as follows I'ita Saturn. 8): " Aegyptum, quam mihi laudabas, totam didici levem pendulam et ad omnia famae momenta volitantem. illic qui Serapidem colunt Christiani sunt et devoti sunt Serapidi qui se Christi episcopos dicunt; nemo illic archisynagogus Judaeorum, nemo Samarites, nemo Christianorum presbyter, non mathematicus, non haruspex, non aliptes. ipse ille patriarcha cum Aegyptum venerit, ab aliis Serapidem adorare, ab aliis cogitur Christum unus illis deus nummus est; hunc Christiani, hunc Judaei, hunc omnes venerantur et gentes" (" Tl; e gypt which you praised tome, I have found altogether fickle, flighty, and blown about by every gust of rumour. There people who worship Serapis are Christians, while those who call themselves bishops of Christ are adherents of Serapis. There no chief of a Jewish synagogue, no Samaritan, no Christian presbyter, but is an astrologer, a soothsayer, a vile wretch. When the patriarch himself visits Egypt, he is forced by some to worship Serapis, and by others to worship Christ Christians, Jews, and all nations worship this one thingâ money"; cp. vol. i. p. 275).

1 Clement still used both side by side, but he sharply distinguishes them from the canonical.

- Such is the opinion advocated by Bardenhewer, Gesch. der alikirchl. Litt., i. p. 387; but I do not think it probable. It is incredible that the provincial Christians of Egypt had any independent position at so early an age, over against the Alexandrian Christians. Preuschen Zur Vorgeschichte aes Evangelienkanons, Programm des Ludwig Georg Gymnasiums in Darmstadt, 1905) adheres to my iv Tfj Tcov AiyutTTicov X' P' ' f Siatpiai etroieitO, elra epx rai â 19 ra juepr rod UpoarwirttOV koi 'AOpi itOU, ov iui v awa Koi. irepi Tov a'ltijv Kot 'AXe avspeiav koi 'AXe avspeioTVoxitrjv

XjhpoV rjtOL VOjuLOV ' VOHOV yap 01 Aiyu-TTTlol (pacTL Trjv eka(TTr 9

TToaecof irepioikisa Vjtoi Treplxaopov (" After spending some time in Egypt, he went to the districts of Prosopitis and A thribisj not but that he also visited the district or nome of Sais and Alexandria and Alexandreiopolis. For the Egyptians give the name of ' nome to the environments or suburbs of a city ").

((iii) Another Egyptian, who probably began his work in Egypt, was Valentinus. Epiphanius (xxxi. 2), who declares that none of the early heretics mentioned his birthplace, writes that only one piece of information, and that of doubtful weight, was extant regarding this Egyptian: ecpaaav avrov rive yeyeurjcroai pe(3(t)VLTr)v ap aiditrjv rrjg AiyvtTTOv-Trapaxiwrrji, ev 'AXe-avspela Se Treiraiseucroai Tfjv twv ' XXi'jvoiv iraiseiav ("Some y said he was born at Phrebonitis or Pharbaethus in Egypt, Jrj and educated after the Greek fashion in Alexandria'"'); cp. 'J i also xxxi. 7: eiroirjo-atO Se ovrog to Krfpvyixa ko.) ev Alyinrrip t fe obev Sr KOi ft)? Xelxlraia ex Surj? oa-rewu en ev AiyvirtW irepi- Vp-v fv. Xeitrerai tovtov rj cnropa, ev re tw 'Adpi irr ko.) Jlpocrcotritu rtv(e

Kai 'Apcnvoitii Kai Qt a'isr Kai Toh kutoo nepecriv t? Trapaxla? Kai 'AX-eiavspeiotToxitij ("He also preached in Egypt. And one result is that his brood still survives in that country, like the remains of a viper's bones, in Athribis and Prosopitis, and Arsinoites, and Thebais, and the lower regions of the coast, and Alexandreiopolis "'"').2 This is confirmed by the author of the Muratorian Canon, who says that Valentinus was born at

Arsinoe; but the meaning of the phrase is not quite certain. l J

V. (iv) Justin Apol, I. xxix.) relates how an Alexandrian Chris-H T-tian had recently applied to the proconsul Felix for per- ' la- t' mission to be castrated, in order to refute the bitter calumnies 'JLL La levelled against Christians; he was refused. The popular fury y view, and tries boldly to develop it. In the sources, "Egyptians," as distinct-from Greeks, mean the old inhabitants, i. e., the Copts. But we can hardly "'P interpret the title of the gospel car' Alyvirriovs in the light of this. h ly.

I do not understand this expression.

Apelles, the son of Marcion, stayed for some time at Alexandria, as we ' know. VOL. II.

had evidently been whetted against Christians in Egypt also by means of calumnies. (v) From the Palestinian document of 190 A. D., mentioned by Eusebius (II. E,, v. 25), we learn that the Palestinian church had exchanged letters, for a larger or shorter period, with the church of Alexandria in reference to the celebration of Easter on the same date. (vi) According to the extant fragments of an Armenian epistle, Irenaeus wrote once to an Alexandrian Christian (Harvey's Opp. Iren. ii. 456). (vii) Eusebius introduces with a (paariv ("they say") the statement (which may be referred back to the opening of the third century) that Mark the disciple of the apostles preached the gospel in Egypt and founded "churches first of all at Alexandria itself" ekK cr a; re irpwtOv e-Tr' avr'ni 'AXe nispeiag, H. E., ii. 16). We have no means of checking this statement. But the expression "churches" (so all MSS.) is very singular. Alexandria was evidently a sort of province. (viii) An Alexandrian list (originally extant, so far as we know, in the Chronicle of Africanus, and therefore dating at the latest from the reign of Elagabalus) gives the bishops of Alexandria from Mark downwards; but unluckily it is quite fictitious, and hardly anything is to be learned from its contents (cp. my Chronol, i. pp. 124 f., 202 f.). Such is the sum total of our knowledge regarding the history of early Christianity in Egypt!

Matters become clearer with the entrance of Clement of Alexandria and of the long-lived Demetrius (bishop from 188189 to 231) upon the scene. But unfortunately the

The same passage mentions local work on the part of Barnabas, ' The names are partly Greek and partly Roman: Arrianus, Abilius, Cerdo, Primus, Justus, Eumenes, Marcus, Celadion, Agrippinus, Julianus, and Demetrius. The predecessor of Demetrius is quite unknown to us.

The importance of Alexandria throughout the church at large begins also at. J!., A this period. We do not know how old was the custom, attested by Dionysius of Alexandria, of the local bishop fixing the date of Easter for the whole church, but perhaps it began with Demetrius (cp. the Coptic-Arabic Synaxarium on the loth Hatur). Origen made the school of Alexandria a standard for the East, and it held this position even after he left the city. We learn incidentally, for example, that Julius Africanus (Eus., H. E., vi. 31) hurried thither to hear Heraclas. The church "-" and the school, which hitherto had not always co-operated, were closely united

J by Dionysius, who also succeeded by means of his personal influence, his learning, Avc ' wisdom, and discretion, in acquiring an authoritative position throughout Chris- former yields us very little concrete evidence regarding either the former philosopher, who lived on ideal heights, or the church. We learn that the church and its school already had by no means an insignificant role in Alexandria, that the school was frequented by p; gans asjvell as by Christians, that presbyters, deacons, and " widows" were to be found in the church, that it counted members from all classes and ranks, that it was partly secularized (cp. the Pcedagogtis) and that many Christian heretics disquieted the Alexandrian church. But this is about all, though Clement does remark (in Strom., vi. 18. 167) that Christianity had spread "to every nation and village and town" Kara eqvoi koi Kooulrjv koi ttoxiv iraa-av), gaining whole households and families, and including even philosophers in its membership. As regards the local organization, so much is certain, viz., that throughout the province (including the Thebais and Libyas) the Christian churches in each nome were at first, and for a long while, ruled simply by presbyters and deacons, or by presbyters and teachers (cp. Dion. Alex, in Eus., H. E., vii. 24), under the supervision, we may assume, of the Christian church in Alexandria. How old the monarchical episcopate is here, we cannot tell, for no certain conclusions, unfortunately, can be drawn from the relevant statements in Clement. Possibly it was instituted by, or shortly before, Demetrius. But once it was set up, all the powers of use and wont hitherto exercised by the Alexandrian tendom which was challenged only by the Roman bishop. This lofty position the see of Alexandria managed to retain under Petrus, while it was secured for quite a century by the powerful authority of Athanasius. The subordination of Egypt to the diocese of the "East" i. e., under Antioch) could not upset the authority and independent position of the patriarch; on the contrary, the latter could attempt to gain control over the entire political diocese of the " East," and thus to add a fresh chapter to the perennial conflict between Syria and Egypt. When the victory was wellnigh over, the Chalcedon catastrophe occurred. During the fourth and the first half of the fifth century, Egypt was a semi-sovereign ecclesiastical state.

The Marcionites and the Montanists both made their way to Egypt. Clement mentions the Valentinians, the followers of Basilides and Marcion, the Peratse, the Encratites, the Docetists, the Haimatites. the Cainites, the Ophites, the Simonians, and the Eutychites. Eusebius, in describing the youth of Origen, tells an interesting story about an Antiochene heretic called Paul in Alexandria I. E., vi. 2).

church were transferred to it. The course of affairs seems to have been as follows. Alexandria at first and alone had a monarchical bishop, who very soon came to rank himself and to act as the counterpart of " the chief priest of Alexandria and all Egypt." This bishop then began to consecrate other bishops for the chief towns in the various nomes. " Like the towns, the nomes also became the basis of the episcopal dioceses, in the Christian epoch" (Mommsen, p. 546; Eng. trans., ii. p. 235). According to one account (Eutychius, I. 332), which is not to be despised, Demetrius only consecrated three such bishops at first, while Heraclas, his successor, created as many as twenty. During the third century, perhaps all the leading towns in the nomes came to have bishops of their own (see below), under the autocratic supervision of the metropolitan, who was also the head metropolitan during the third century (as the sixth Nicene canon proves) of Egypt (including the Thebais), Libyae, and Pentapolis. He had the powerzol ordaining all bishops, of issuing general disciplinary regulations, and of presiding over all judicial proceedings of the church. The late rise of the episcopate in Egypt explains how he possessed this power. Towards the close of his life Demetrius

1 The rights of the Alexandrian bishop were not affected by the political division into provinces; on the contrary, he laid claim to authority over them all. We learn, e. g., that Heraclas, the successor of Demetrius, deposed the bishop of Thniuis.

2 "The pagan high priest himself had a far-reaching influence, even in respect of learning, over the entire country; he was i-mcnd. Ti s rod Movrnlov" (Marquardt, I."2) p. 505). Here we get the complete prototype of the Alexandrian bishop and his school.

See Mommsen's Jioi. Geschichte, v. 558 f., 568 (Eng. trans., ii. 238 f., 249), Liibeck pp. cif., pp. 106 f.). Reference may also be made to the position of the Jewish ethnarch over all Egypt, as a prototype.

â Schwartz (Athanasiana, V. pp. 182 f., in the second number of the Nachr. d. K. Geselsch. d. IV., Gottingen, 1905) rightly calls attention to the fact that the decision of Demetrius to ordain bishops for the x' P"- of Alexandria, i. e., for Egypt, is to be connected with Septimius Severus' gift (in 202 a. d.) of a nominal civic autonomy to prominent "villages" (improperly called capitals). But Demetrius was very prudent. He only ordained three bishops. Hence we must conclude that he only wanted to do what was absolutely essential. Heraclas was the first who really tackled the new situation and the needs of the growing Christian population outside the capital.

Into the origin and development of the organization in Alexandria and Egypt we cannot enter any further (cp. Liibeck, op. cit., 102 f., 105 f., iiof., held synods (against Origen); cp. Photius, Cod. 118: tvvo6o9 eiria-KOTrciov Kat rivoov TrpecrSurepcop (followed at once by the words, axV o ye A. fji-VTpiof cima tictlv eiria-KOTroi? AiyutTTLOi) a synod of bishops and certain presbyters. Demetrius too, along with certain Egyptian bishops.

As Eusebius (H. E., vi. i.) informs us that by 202 a. d. Christians were dragged to Alexandria " from Egypt and all the Thebais" (ax' Aiyvtrrov koi Ge3ai(5o? awdcrt?) and martyred, there must have been Christians in all parts, of the qountry. He says juvpioi (vi. 2. 3)â which is an exaggeration.

From the writings and history of Origen, a man to whom, far more than to Clement, the whole Eastern church was indebted for its fusion with intellectual culture, ample information (see above, pp. 10 f.) can be gained regarding the external and m V"

internal expansion of Christianity even beyond the confines of 7 V

Alexandria and Egypt. No doubt, as he concedes to Celsus i that the nui pber of Ch ristians,. was, still " extremely scanty," j relatively to the Roman empire, we cannot form any extravagant estimates of their number in Origen's native land down to the year 240 (cp. also his statement that Christian martyrs were rare and easily counted); but, on the other hand, as he finds the steady extension of Christendom (even-in-tbe upper circles of society) to be so marked that he can already contemplate its triumph, it follows that the number of Christians must have been qii ite considerable., 114 f.). I do not know what to make of the statement in Epiph., Hcer., lxviii. 7, iifo that Alexandria, unlike other cities, never had two bishops. With regard to the (' metropolitan powers of the bishop of Alexandria, one gets the impression that A they were not only as despotic as those of the apxiepevs irdcr-ns Alyvirrov, but as those of the emperor in the sphere of politics. Cp., e.:, Epiph., Har., lxviii. I: j

Tovto edos itrri, rhv ev Trj 'A i avspeia apxtitriffkOirov irdcrris re Alyinrtov Koi Â Tjjsai'Soy, Mapeu'TOv re Kal At vrjs, 'Aj, fj. vviakris, MapidrisSs re Kal niftatrsAeus ex "' TT)! ikKK7 (na(Trik-qv Sioikticrtv ("The custom is for the archbishop of all Egypt, the Thebais, Mareotis and Libya, Ammoniace, ivIareotis and Pentapolis, to have his ecclesiastical headquarters at Alexandria "). This confirms the evidence of the sixth canon of Nicsea. Schwartz (p. 185) deletes Mareotis twice; its mention is certainly remarkable in this connection. Seybold would read MapfiapikTis. 1

It is difficult to believe the statement of Suidas that Julius Africanus was a 1, A

Libyan by birth.

"Accurate statistics of the inhabitants of Alexandria were drawn up in connection with the relief of the poor, as is proved by the remarks of Dionysius Alex.

The number of nomes or cities in which we can prove that there were Christians previous to Meletius, to the Nicene council, and to the accounts furnished by Athanasius i. e., earher than Diocletian), is extremely small, although the fault lies solely with our sources of information. They are as follows:â

The districts of Prosopitis, Athribis, Sais Pharbaethus, and

Arsinoe (see above). On the last named, cp. Dionys. Alex, in

Eus., H. E., vii. 24, where we are told that the chiliastic move- r- ' ment was particularly popular in that district. Its bishop was r n M probably Nepos, whose bishopric he. cit.) is not named; and

"Dionysius also mentions " presbyters and teachers" of the brethren in the villages of the Arsinoe nome. Christianity had thus penetrated into the low country.

The Thebais (see above).

Antinoe: where, about 200 a. u., there was a Christian community (cp. Alex. Jerus. in Eus., H. E., vi. 11).

Thmuis: from the " Historia Origenis" in Photius (cp. my Litt. Gesch., i. p. 332), it follows that when Origen was exiled afresh by Heraclas from Alexandria, there was a bishop (in Eus., . E., vii. 21) upon the great plague of 260 A. D.: "Yet people are astonished. at our great city no longer containing such a multitude of inhabitantsâ even if one now includes little children and very old people in the censusâ as formerly it could number of those who were merely in the prime of life, so called. In those days people between forty and seventy constituted so large a majority of the inhabitants that their number cannot be made up nowadays s even by the inclusion of people between fourteen and eighty in the list compiled for the purposes of public charityâ those who, to appearance, are quite young, being now, as it were, coeval with those who formerly were full of years so that the dispensing of food was extended to such persons. Yet, although they see how the human race continues to diminish and waste away, they tremble not at the destruction of mankind which is ever advancing upon themselves." We must accordingly assume that a very serious diminution took place in the popula- tion of Alexandria about the middle of the third century.

'Ev fxev ozv TCf! 'Apcrevoe'itTi yev6fj.(vos, eyoa irph ttovov tovto firfiro a i rh SSyxa chiliasm, iis col crxiciato coi airo(Traffias '6 (iiv (KK 7icnwv so that there were several, or many, local churches even before 250 A. D, crvyka eaas tovs irpefffivtepovs Ka StsactKaxovs ran iv ra7s Ktiifj-ais a, Si paiv, izapdvtwv kox tuv ovkofxevoov a5(poov, Sjxotria r y f eraffiy iroffitraffbai tov 6yov â 7rpoâ Tpe 'aju'7Â ' ("When I was at Arsinoe, where this view had been current for a long while, so that there had been schisms and apostasies of whole churches, I summoned the presbyters and teachers of the brethren in the villages, and when those who were willing had gathered, I exhorted them to examine the doctrine openly").

(Ammonius) in Thmuis, whom Heraclas deposed. He was succeeded by Philip. Cp. also Eus., H. E., viii. 9.

Philadelphia in Arsinoe: from the libellus libellatici published by Wessely Anzeiger der phil-hist. Klasse der Wiener Jkad., 1894, Jan. 3), it follows that there were Christians here in the reign of Decius.

Alexander-Insula, a village on an island of the Fajjum lake (libellus libellatici, published by Krebs in the Sitzungsber. d. Pr. Akad. d. Wiss., 1893, Nov. 30).

Hermopolis magna; not the parvaâ near Alexandriaâ in Mareotis (so Feltoe); for a trustworthy statement (see note below) proves that there was no bishop in Mareotis: Dionys. Alex, wrote to Colon, the bishop of the local church (Eus., vi. 46).

Nilus Nilopolis: Chaeremon, the local bishop, is mentioned by Dionys. Alex, in Eus., H. E. vi. 42.

Ptolemais in Pentapolis: Christians lived here, according to Dionysius (in Eus., vii. 6).

There was an estate of Rostoces at Thmuis Marly7: Hieron.).

2 According to Dionys. Alex. (Eus., vi. 40), there seem to have been Christians at Taposiris (a small town about twenty-five miles south-west of Alexandria, at the end ot af long arm of the Mareotic lake) as well. In the village of Cephro (otherwiseunknown) "near the desert " (ra lepij ttjs AiSutjs), the exiled Dionysius first spread abroad the word of God successfully, according to his own account. ('Â; Tjj Kikppo'i Kal irowy ffwfdiifirjaev r tmv ikK r cria, rcov lev UTrh ttjs 'ir6 ews ase (piiov kirofj-ivuv, tuv 5e crvv6vt(tiv ixtt' Alyvirrov note the contrast ' kolku dvpav ilixiv 6 dehs ave(f e tov 6yov). In the Mareotic district, where the village of Colluthion (the fresh place of exile appointed for him) was situated (otherwise unknown), there were no Christians, or practically none, about the middle of the third century, although the district lay close to Alexandria (cp. Dionys. in Eus., H. E. vii. 11). There, too, it was he who planted Christianity. Mareotis (for Mareotic Christians, see Dionys., Eus., H. E., vii. 11) is mentioned in a document of the Jerusalem Synod (Athanas., Apol. c. Arzan, 85): "Mareotis is a district of Egypt. There never was a bishop there, nor a territorial bishop; the churches throughout the entire district were under the bishop of Alexandria. The separate presbyters had charge of the larger villages, to about the number of ten and upwards"; cp, Socrates, i. 27: MopswtTjs X' P" " V 'AAi avspiias iari' KUfiai 5e elffiv fv aiiry irowal crp65pa Kal iroavdiOpunrot, Kal ev avro'is ekKXriaiai TTowal Kal afj. Trpai. rartovtai 5e ai) al ikK 7 cnai inrh rcji rrjs 'AAi avspiias e'lritr-k6ttcji Kal ilmv virh Tr); auxtjc ttokiv oos vapoikiai (" M. is a district of Alexandria. It contains a very large number of populous villages, in which there are many splendid churches. These churches are under the jurisdiction of the bishop of Alexandria, and are subject to his city as parishes"). On the Christians in Mareotis, see also Athanas., op. cit., lxxiv., and Epiph., Hzr., lxviii. 7 (a number of local churches as early as 300 A. D.).

Berenice in Cyrenaica: a local bishop, called Ammon (Dionysius, ibid., vii. 26).

According to Eusebius (H. E., vii. 13), Gallienus wrote to Dionysius, Pinnas, Demetrius, and the rest of the Egyptian bishops. Where the sees of the two latter lay, we do not know; but it is natural to suppose (cp. the sixth canon of Nicaea) that they were the metropolitans of Libyae and Pentapolis, who were subject to the chief metropolitan of Alexandria.

Oxyrhynchus: History of Peter of Alexandria, cp. K. Schmidt in the Texte u. (Inters., N. F. v. 4, and Achelis, Alartyr., pp. 173 f., the latter of whom infers, from the Passio employed in the " Martyr. Hieros.," that the Christians in Oxyrhynchus j during the great persecution were still extremely few. Only seventeen are said to have been resident there. From the letter of Peter, published by Schmidt, one gets a different idea of the situation (the town having a bishop, and the presbyters being partly drawn from the better class of the citizens). But as the letter is unauthentic, its descriptions count for nothing.

According to the prelude of the festal epistles of Athanasius (ed. Larsow, p. 26) there were Christians in the small and in the large oasis by 329 a. d. We now know, as of course one might conjecture a priori (since the oases served as places of exile), that as early as the days of the persecutions, in Diocletian's reign or even previously, Christians and Christian presbyters (one called Psenosiris) were to be found at Kysis in the southern part of the great oasis, and possibly also in other quarters of the same district. Perhaps there were Christians also in Syene (Deissmann, p. 18) then. A very large number languished in the dye-factories of the Thebais during the persecution of Maximinus Daza' (Eus., H. E., viii. 9; Alaji Pal., viii. 1, ix. 1), while crowds were deported from Egypt to the mines ' Deissmann, Â in OriginaldÂ kument aus der dioklet. Verfolgung (1902), pp. 12 f. Eng. trans.

2 Cp. Violet, Mart. Pal., pp. 60 f. Texte n. Unters., xiv. 4): " Down to the sixth year of the persecution the storm blew hard, which had risen against us, and many companies of the faithful were in the mines called the ' Porphyritis," in the district of Egyptian Thebes. Those who broke the temple marble were also called Porphyrites. Such were the names borne by the large companies of the faithful who were condemned, all over Egypt; there were ninety-seven local martyrs."

in Palestine and Cilicia Mah. Pal, viii. 13: 130 Egyptian martyrs).

According to one papyrus (Amherst), dating from the days of Maximus, the bishop of Alexandria (264265-281282), there was a bishop called Apollonius then resident in the district of Arsinoe; cp. Harnack in Sitzmigsber. d. k. Pr. Akad. d. Wiss., 1890, Nov. 15. For other Christian Egyptian fragments of papyri, dating from the third or the beginning of the fourth century, cp. my Chronologie, ii. pp. 179 f.

In Esueh = I. atopolis (Thebais), Pachomius, when still a pagan, found Christians (cp. Vita Pack.).

The fragments of the correspondence of Dionys. Alex., and the record of the persecutions, give one the impression that the number of Christians in Alexandria was large, and that the spread of Christianity throughout the country, in towns and villages alike (Eus., vi. 42. 1), was considerable. Quite incidentally, for example, we find (in Eus., H. E., vii. 11. 17) that " special meetings" were regularly held " in the more remote suburbs" of Alexandria (ej Tryooacrreot? iroppcetepoo Keijuevoi Kara fxepo? a-vvaywyal). Egypt (Lower Egypt), after the middle of the third century, certainly belonged to those territories in which Christians were particularly plentiful, although Dionysius (Eus., H. E., vii. 7) was aware that there were provinces in Asia Minor where the churches were still more numerous.

By the time of the Decian persecution, Christians were already occupying public, positions in Alexandria, and many were to be found among the rich (Eus., vi. 41, vii.

11). Libelli, o certifiqates olexfiiupti9n. granted to apostates, saixyive from towns of no gteat size; but this proves at most the large number of local Christians. Dionysius, in his account of the Alexandrian victims in the persecution (Eus., H. E., vi. 41), distinguishes between Greeks and Egyptians (details below), but Christians were to be found among both classes of the population.

'â Practically no information upon ecclesiastical geography is furnished by the history of Egyptian monasticism previous to 325 a. d. The monastic settlements of Pachomius in Tabennisi (not Tabenne Nesus; cp. v. Schubert's Lehrb. d. k. Gesck., i. pp. 405 f.) and Pbow, however, are to be fixed within that period (not later than c. 320 A. D.), and we are also told how Pachomius was converted at Schenesit. X.= Chenoboscium) on the Nile in the Thebais district. It lay near the town of Diospolis parva in. Southern Thebais (cp. Griitzmacher, Pachomius und das dltesle Kloslerleben, 1S96).â I hesitate to infer from the Coptic-Arabic Synaxarium the localities which it connects with the stories of the Diocletian martyrs, 170 MISSION AND EXPANSION OF CHRISTIANITY

As regards the Egyptian episcopal hierarchy at the opening, of the fourth, century, we find ourselves in a particularly fortunate position. The episcopal lists certainly give a most imperfect idea of the spread of Christianity in Egypt, as each nome had at first only one bishop, while many large churches, in town and country alike, were governed by presbyters, and small villages had not even so much as a presbyter. But, on the other hand, we have to take account (i) of the statement of Alexander (of Alex.) in his encyclical letter, that he had gathered, c. 320 a. d., a synod of almost 100 bishops (Socrat., H. E., i. 6). Then (ii) there is the corroborative statement of Athanasius, for the age of the synods of Sardica (and especially for the earlier synod of Alexandria in 339), that " there are close upon 100 bishops in Egypt, the Thebais, Libyae, and Pentapolis."" See Apol. c. Arian, 1 and 71. Thus there were no bishoprics founded between 320 and 340. This is important evidence. Had not the episcopal organization been fully organized in Egypt by the opening of the fourth century, we J ' should have expected a number of bishoprics to be establishea just between 320 and 340. At the synod of Sardica 94 Egyptian bishops were actually present, or subsequently signed the resolutions (so Apol. c. Ar., 50, where their names but not their dioceses are given). Athanasius had all his bishops summoned to that council, (iii) There is also the fragmentary record, compiled by Meletius, of his adherents among the Egyptian hierarchy, which was laid by him before the council of Nicaea (325). This list includes twenty-nine or thirty bishops (cp. Athan., op. cit., 71); viz., in

Lycopolis (Meletius the archbishop), as legend (connected with graves and relics) may have invented a good deal. For example (Wtistenfeld, Syiiaxariiim, i. pp. 18-19), on 8 and 9 Tut it is noted: "The presbyter Timotheos from Uirschaba, belonging to the see of Dantu, martyred in the town of Atripe"; "The bishop Basura in the town of Masil." For the date of the rise of monasticism, cp., as against Weingarten's untenable hypothesis, especially Butler The Lausiac History of Palladius, 1898, pp. 215 f.). Antony, the father of all monks, began his significant work c 305, after twenty years' sojourn in the wilderness. Thus the monastery of Antonius i. e., the colony of monks) near the Red Sea, in the latitude of Heracleopolis, was founded at the beginning of the fourth century. The monastic settlements in the Nitrian and Scetic deserts belong to c. 330 A. D.

r-jijl j -Kip i-

Antiiioe (cp. also Palladius, Hist. Laus., 7; bishop Lucius),

Herniopolis magna (whither Joseph and the child Jesus are said to have fled; cp. Soz. v. 21, Hist. Laus., 8; bishop Phasileus, perhaps succeeded by Dius who attended Nicaea),

Cusag (= Cos; Achilles),

Diospolis (Ammonius),

Tentyras (upper Thebais, in the department of Ptolemais; Pachymes),

Coptus (east of the Nile, in the department of Maximian-opolis; Theodorus),

Hermethes (= Hermonthis above Thebes, Arab. = Erment, Ermont Cales),-Cynos super. (Colluthus),

Oxyrhynchus (Pelagius; in the days of Rufinus, it had twelve churches; " nuuus ibi invenitur haereticus aut paganus, sed omnes cives Christiani "),

Heracleopolis (Petrus),

Nilopolis (Theon),

Letopolis (Isaak),

Niciopolis (Heraclides),

Cleopatris (Isaak),

Arsinoites (Melas),

Leontopolis in the department of Heliopolis (Amos; cp. the history of Heraclas, who lived here, in Epiph., Hcer. lxvii.), ' Perhaps Diospolis parva (not D. magna = Thebes), as it is mentioned between Cusje and Tentyra.

' It is remarkable that no bishopric within our period i. e., pre-Nicene) is ever assigned to Ptolemais, though it was the second city in Egypt. This omission cannot be a mere accident. The city perhaps for long sharply excluded Christianity. Meletius, bishop of Lycopolis, discharged the duties of metropolitan in the Thebais, under Diocletian. As the town was not the political capital of the Thebais, Schwartz (p. 185) conjectures that Petrus delegated his metropolitan functions to him.

Quentin Anal. Boll., xxiv. 1905, pp. 321 f.) has recently discovered and edited the Passio Dioscuri. The scene is in Cynos (Anacipolis in Mart. Hietoti.), " praeside Culciano " (305-306), apparently in upper Cynos (p. 331). The father of D. was reader there, and he himself " debitor fisci" in virtue of his position as " curialis" (pp. 327, 329).

"No heretic or pagan is to be found there: all the citizens are Christians." The continued existence of pagan conventicles at Oxyrhynchus, assumed by Wilcken Archiv f. Papyriisforschung, i. 3. pp. 407 f.), rests, in my opinion, upon a misinterpretation of ira'ya. vika). avvtfxeiat, an expression which occurs in a document of 426 A. D.

Athribis (Ision),

Bubastus in Pharbethus (Harpocration),

Phakusa (Moses),

Pelusium (Callinicus),

Tanis (Eudaemon, who, with Cauinicus of Pelusium and Ision of Athribis, is mentioned in the fourth festal epistle of Athanasius),

Thmuis (Ephraim), Cynos infer, and Busiris (in the nome of Sais) (Hermaeon),
Sebennytus (Soterichus),
Phthenegys (Piminuthes), Metelis (Cronius),
Memphis (Johannes);
Also Agathammon and Dracontius ev 'AXe avspewv x P'? i. e., in the large territory of the capital, in which Hermopolis parva was the most important but not the only bishopric, Athanasius, in his fourth festal letter, mentions the Meletian bishop, Gelous Hieracammon, but his bishopric is unknown.

We also have the list of bishops from Egypt, the Thebais and both Libyas, who were present at Nicaea. These came from
Alexandria (Alexander),
Alpokranon (Harpocration),
Cynopolis (Adamantius),
Pharba thus (Arbetion),
Panephysis (Philippus),
Heracleopolis parva = Sethron in nome Sethroitis (Potam-mon), ' I do not know what authority Larsow has for putting Phthenegys in the extreme north of Egypt, south of Paralos, on the map in his edition of the festal epistles of Athanasius 1852). I have tried in vain to find the place in any source outside Athanasius.

In the notices of martyrdom during the great persecution, as well as in Eusebius (Dionys. Alex.), some further Egyptian episcopal names are preserved, but the localities are unknown; cp., e. g., the names in Eus., H. E., viii. 13. The presbyters who followed Meletius in Alexandria were Apollonius, Irenseus, Dios-curus, Tyrannus (and Macarius from Parembole); the deacons, Timotheus, Antonius, and Hephaestion.

"The site of the town is not known; the memory of it seems to have perished by the beginning of the Middle Ages. Two Coptic-Arabic writings note Alpho-cranon among the suppressed sees (cp. Amelineau, La giographie de ragypte a C poque Copie, Paris, 1893, pp. 572, 576, and 4639)," Gelzer, Cone. Nic, p.

Heracleopolis magna (Petrus; St Antony came from a small village (Soz., i. 13) called Coma, near this city; as his parents were Christian, there must have been Christians in Coma about 270 A. D. He afterwards stayed a, t Pispir; cp. Hist. Laus. 25, Jer., Vita Hilarion. 30), A- j j
Ptolemais (in Pentapolis: Secundus), i X VJ
Pelusium (Dorotheus),
Tijmuis (Tiberius),
Memphis (Antiochus),"
Panopolis (Gaius),
Schedia (Atthas),
Antinoe (Tyrannus),-
Lycopolis (Plusianus), erenice (Daces),
Barce (Zopyrus),
Antipyrgos (Serapion),
Tauche = Arsinoe (Secundus),
Paraetonium (Titus),
Marmarika (Theonas),

It is surprising that Ptolemais, the capital of Pentapolis, occurs here, and not in its proper place before Berenice. We must not think of Ptolemais Hermia, as at first we might be inclined to do; for the bishop's name (Secundus) is definitely fixed as that of the metropolitan of Pentapolis at that date (cp. above, p. 171).

For Memphis, see Constantine's speech to the holy synod (c. 16): roiydproi Kapirhv ijpavto rhv irpocr Kovta tjj roiavrr Opijffkfia Me icplS Ka Ba u civ, iprjfio)-di7(rai Kol a.(TikT)Toi KataaT)p6e7(Tal fuTo, twv varpificov dtcjiiv. kox ravra ovk e akoris Xe-yco, daA." avt6s tâ Trapuv Koi larop'tiffas evotrrrjs re yevsfieyos ttjs oikTpas rwv Tr6Xe(ev tvxi s. Mej.(pis iprjixos. The heretic Marcus came from Memphis; he went to Spain and there gained a noble lady. Agape, and an orator, Helpidius, who thereupon won over Priscillian (cp. Sulp. Sev., Ctron., ii. 46).

I follow here the Coptic recension.

â An inscription was found here in 1902, which shows that a Jewish community, modelled on Greek lines, existed here as early as Ptolemy Euergetes (247-222 B. C.). It had a synagogue of its own, "in honour of the king, the queen, and their children."

Antseopolis (cp. the Coptic list) is uncertain; it is only attested by a single witness.

Â The latter six are from Libya superior and inferior. â The names of the bishops are obviously not Egyptian, but almost entirely Greco-Latin. Paphnutius, bishop of an unknown town in Upper Thebais, was also at Nicasa.â Very likely there were Christians, and a Christian bishop also, at Darnis (Dardanis) before 325 A. D., as it was the metropolitan's headquarters for Libya II. during the days of Athanasius (cp. the 39th 367 festal letter of Athanasius, published by Schmidt in the Nachr. d. Gesells. d. Wiss. zu Giitt., 1901, 3. p. 5).â Immediately after)k Down to 325 a. d., therefore, we may assume Christians to ' have existed in about fifty towns (or nomes) of these provinces, more than forty of which were episcopal sees. In Alexandria there was quite a number of churches (cp. also Eusebius, as above, p. 162, on Mark's work at Alexandria), and we have actual knowledge of those in which Arius preached, besides those of Dionysius and those of Pierius, called after the famous head of the local school (cp. my Litf.-Gesch., i. p. 439), and several others." The Novatians also had several churches in Alexandria, which Cyril had ultimately closed (Socrat., vii. 7). The number of the Alexandrian clergy (including the Mareotic) at the opening of the fourth century may be calculated with fair precision. Epiphanius Hccr. Ixix. 3) declares that Arius won over in Alexandria not only 700 consecrated virgins but 7 presbyters and 12 deacons. The epist. encycl. of Alexander of Alexandria was signed by 17 presbyters and 24 deacons. In Mareotis 19 presbyters and 20 deacons also sided with Alexander. This gives us 24 presbyters and 36 deacons for 325 we get evidence for Christian churches (cp. Athan., Apol. Ixiv.) at the following Egyptian localities (none of which, in spite of great efforts, can be identified; so far as I know, they are never mentioned elsewhere; they were in the vicinity of Alexandria, viz., in Mareotis), viz., Dikella, Phasko, Chenebri, Myrsine, and Bomotheus. da Taposiris (see above). Hypselis, where Arsenius, the opponent of Alhanasius, was a bishop, may also be added to the places which possessed a church previous to 325.

Philostorgius H. E., vii. 13) mentions a bishop of Thebes, Heron by name, who fell away in the reign of Julian. In the 12th (19th) festal letter of Athanasius the following bishoprics, hitherto unmentioned, occur (it is true that we cannot be sure if they existed prior to 325 a. D., but (he great likelihood is that they did, as the notices of them 7-efer to successors of dead occupants of the respective sees): Paralus (at the extreme north of Egypt), Bucolia (not far east of Alexandria, on the coast, but deserted), Thebes, Apollonopolis inferior (where?), Aphroditon (east of Memphis, north of Nilopolis), Rhinocorura (on the Philistine border), Stathma (where? near Rhinocorura?), Garyatis orient, and merid. (both in Mar-niarika, but, so far as I know, unidentified), Syene, Latopolis, Hypselis, Prosopitis (cp. above, p. 161), Diosphacus ("which is on the sea-border," Athanasius adds: the place was evidently unfamiliar, and seems still to be unidentified), Saites (cp. above, p. 161), Xois (north of Sais), and Clysma (to the north of the Red Sea). These seventeen names bring up the number of bishoprics in Egypt, prior to the Nicene council, to about sixty.

- Epiph., Hcer., Ixix. 2: ejvl Traeious â r'bv aptofxhv iv rri 'A; ai5piia ikK rjalai. Atovvffiov Kaxovfxevt) fkK y)ria, kox 7 rov Â eoovs koi 7; XXupiov kox epavioivos Kol rj TTJs Uepcralas Kal t tov Ai v koi t) tov Mevsisiov nai 7 hwiavov koi t ttjj Bavkakeus Kal Wai " ev fiiq 5e tovtoiv 6 ov66s tis uirrjpxfv, ev kr4pa the city of Alexandria, while, if the Mareotic clergy are included, we get no fewer than 43 presbyters and 56 deacons, Evidently we are handling large numbers here. From the activity and position of Anatolius in Alexandria (cp. above, p. 39), we may conclude that Christians then formed a strong and influential party in the city. A further proof of the wide spread of Christianity in Egypt is furnished by the fact that it continued to be a power in Upper Egypt at the opening of the fourth century (compare the description of the Diocletian persecution which raged so fiercely in the Thebais itself), and also by the outburst and the propaganda of monasticism during the last thirty years of the third century. In Alexandria, more than in any other city and province, the church understood how to present Christianity in forms which were suited to the varied grades of human culture, and this feature undoubtedly proved an extraordinary aid to the propaganda of the religion, although at a subsequent period, of course, the multitude of uneducated Christians overmastered alike the educated members of the church and the bishop of Alexandria himself.

The uneducated were more strongly represented in the original population of Egypt (afterwards called Copts). But Christianity, as has been remarked, soon pushed its propaganda

Kapiriivris, ev ti 5e 'Zapfia-ras koi 'Apetos ovros, k. t. ("The churches in Alexandria are more numerous. There are the churches of Dionysius also mentioned by Philostorg., H. E., ii. ii; Athanasius was consecrated bishop in it, of Theonas cp. Theod., H. E., iv. 22, of Pierius and Serapion, of Persaia, of Dizus, of Mendidius, of Annianus, of Baucalis, etc.; in one there was a certain Colluthus, in another Carpones, in another Sarmatas and Arius," etc.). Har., Ixviii. 4: i v yap 6 "Apeios iv Boicoae(tt? ikKhricria ovtw Kaxovfievrj 'AAf arspeioj irpicr-fivtepos â Ka6' ekatrtTjc yap ds irpea VTipos icrriv airotitayxfuos â? irav yap iroxKax ekK-r (Tiai, vvv Se irkiiovs (" For Arius was presbyter in Baucalis, the church so named in Alexandria; for one presbyter is appointed to each church. There were nany churches then, but there are more ttow"). The statement of the Coptic-Arabic Synaxarmui (Wtistenfeld, II. pp. 210) that the believers had to meet in private houses and holes (??) till the era of bishop Theonas i. e., the reign of Diocletian), and that Theonas built the first church in Alexandria (in the name of the Virgin), may be untrustworthy, but it deserves notice. Theonas may have built a church to Mary, and it may have been the first large building. For the Alexandrian churches in the fourth century, cp. Schwartz Athanas., I. 336).

Cp. Snellmann, Der Anfang des arianischen Streits ()Oi), p. 49.

among them also. Bishop Dionysius distinguishes Greeks and Egyptians among the Decian martyrs (Eiis., H. E., vi. 41); the latter bear purely Coptic names. Aiyutrrioi, as Feltoe proves from the papyri (The Letters and other Remains of Dionysnis of Alexandria, 1904, p. 13), even elsewhere at that period denoted natives as opposed to Greeks. In one place Dionysius also calls a (Coptic) martyr 6 Ai u? (Eus., H. E., vi. 41). The present state of our knowledge regarding the origin and early development of national Egyptian Christianity has been recently sketched by Leipoldt Die Entstehung der Jcoptischen Kirche, 1905).

The first Christian who, to our knowledge, published his biblical studies in the Egyptian (Coptic) language was the ascetic H ieracas (Epiph., Hcer., Ixvii.), an older contemporary of Arius, who was suspected as a semi-heretic. jpachomius also belongs to the pre-Constantine age; his monasteries were assigned to Coptic yr-' Christians. Antony, who lived as an ascetic after 270 a. d., was a Coptic Christian. The three versions of the Bible, the

T Sahidic (Thebaic), the Akhmimic, and the Fayyumic (erroneously called the Bashmuric or Middle Egyptian), were extant by 350 A. D. (although the whole Bible perhaps had not yet been completely issued in these dialects; the Bohairic version is not earlier than the close of the fifth century). We may conjecture, though we cannot prove, that these versions partly go back to the third century. Christianity, in Egypt more than anywhere else perhaps, with the exception of Greece, adjusted itself to certain cardinal traits of the old national religion e. g., its conception of the dead, its vivid grasp of the future, its moral tone,

Even in Origen there are several passages which incidentally prove that Christianity was welcomed even by the native Egyptians; e. g., Horn. XII. iti Lucavi. 0pp. v. p. 128, Lomm.); cp. above, p. 154.

2 "The Berlin Sahidic MS. of the Apocalypse of John certainly belongs to the fourth century, and the Apocalypse was by no means the first scripture translated by the Copts into their vernacular. In fact, we know MSS. of the Psalter and the Wisdom of Solomon which may be very little later than that of the Apocalypse."

3 "This version was, even in the fifth century, the memorial of a decaying dialect, and was practically supplanted by the Sahidic." The Akhmimic version contains the oldest writings extant in any Coptic MS.

"I think it very likely that it is just as old as either the Akhmimic or the Sahidic."

its use of spells to safeguard life, etc.). Coptic Christianity lived amid these elements (cp. also its predilection for ardent apocalypses). It came forward as a transformed popular religion, without any philosophy or profound speculations or dogma. The peculiar affinity between Coptic Christianity and monasticism has not yet been adequately explained. But here too the leading role was that of beliefs about the dead and a passion for the world to come. If the Egyptians were for the most part Christians by the middle of the fourth century (what Leipoldt, pp. 5 f., adduces from Schenute regarding merciless pagan landowners about the beginning of the fifth century refers to Greeks), then they had created a sort of national religion for themselves out of the new religion by grafting on the latter to the cravings and remnants of the old. If the years between 350 and 450 are to be taken as the blossoming period of the Coptic church, then the number of Coptic Christians c. 300 A. D. must have been very considerable. Who can tell how many of all these millions were Christians (cp. Mommsen, p. 578, Eng. trans, ii. 259 f; Liibeck, p. 106) when the great persecution broke out? Certain it is, however, that the Christians had long ago outstripped the Jews numerically, and by the opening of the fourth century they were over a million strong. Their large numbers are also evident from the fact that during the fourth century there was a comparatively rapid decline of paganism, native and Hellenic, throughout Egyptâ apart, that is, from the cults at Philag and other outstanding temple-cities (cp. Wilcken, Archiv fi'ir Papyrusforschung, i. 3. pp. 396 f, who shows, however, that there were Christian churches even in Philas by the beginning of the fifth century). The outlying district of Bucolia, no doubt, is reported (Jerome, Vita Hilarion. xliii.) to have been still entirely pagan in the fourth century, while almost the whole of the city of Antinoe was still given up to idolatry in the reign of Valens. These, however, were the exceptions. And that was why inconvenient clerics were banished thither by the emperor (Theodoret, H. E., iv. 15). Other exiled clerics are said, about the same period, to have found nothing but pagans and an idolatrous temple on an island of the Nile (Socrat., iv. 24). But whatever value one VOL. II.

might attach to this disappears when one considers the question put by the pagans to the Christians when they landed, "Have you come hither also to drive us out?" (JX ere kui evravqa e exdcrai t ij. ai). The tale thus becomes a witness to the spread of Christianity. Judaism and Hellenism had plainly paved an open way for Christianity in Egypt, while the national religion, with all its peculiarities, which had long ago become quite meaningless, did not possess the same powers of attraction and resistance as certain of the Syro-Phoenician cults evinced.

We know nothing about the early history of Christianity in Pentapolis (Cyrenaica), where a very large numljer of local Jews had already created an atmosphere for the new faith. Irenaeus (i. 10) declares there were Christians in Libya. But the fact of Basilides being metropolitan (in Ptolemais) of Pentapolis in the days of Dionysius of Alexandria (Dionys., Ep. ad Basil.; Eus., H. E., vii. 20; Routh's Reliq. Sac, iii."' pp. 223 f.) shows

For the religion of Egypt, see Erman Die aegypt. Religion, 1905). Its final period, together with the social and political position of the natives from the third to the fifth century, may be seen most clearly in Leipoldt's Schemitc von Atripe Texle u. Unlers., xxv. i. 22 f., 26 f., 29 f.).â It is extremely remarkable how little notice is taken of Egyptian religionâ for all its deep influence on the Greco-Roman empireâ in early Christian literature. Even Christian Greek gnosticism, so powerfully influenced by the lore of Syrian and Asiatic rites, betrays few traces of the Egyptian cultus, apart from magical spells (yet cp. the Pistis Sophia). The latter must have been disintegrated during the second and third centuries, j'ielding place to Hellenism, and in part to rude household cults. Reitzenstein's Foimandres (" Studien zur griech.-agypt. u. frlihchristl. Lileratur," 1904) has certainly unearthed some lines of connection which had hitherto lain unobserved; but he goes too far, I think, with his bold speculative constructions

Cyrene is mentioned in the N. T. (Acts ii. 10), which proves, at any rate, that converted Jews from this district were known about 100 A. D.; cp. also the synagogue of the Cyrenians (Acts vi. 9) in Jerusalem, as well as the fact (noted in Acts xi. 20) that converted Jews from Cyrene and Cyprus were the first (in Antioch) to preach the gospel to pagans. Finally, Acts knows of a Christian teacher, Lucius of Cyrene, in Antioch (xiii. i); while the gospel mentions a Simon of Cyrene (Mark xv. 21 and parallels) who was obliged to carry the cross of Jesus. The Bible Christian Africans (like the negroes in America) nowadays honour this Simon as their hero. Jews and Greeks and Romans shared in the crucifixion of I Jesus, but an African carried his cross!

There is some likehood that Tertullian's story about the proconsul Pudens n ad Scapulam, iv.)had been enacted even in Cyrenaica previous to 166 a. d., which would prove the existence of Christians there at that period. But the transference of the tale is not quite assured. Crete also might be meant; cp. Neumann's Rom. Staat. u. allgem. Kirche, i. pp. 33 f.

that church life had been organized there, with a number of bishoprics e. g., Berenice, p. 168), by the middle of the third century. The modalistic Christology gained a specially large and resolute number of adherents in this district about the same time. Sabellius was a Libyan, and came from Pent polis. We have also evidence for martyrs in these provinces.

Not until the fourth century (Socrates, i. 19; Philost. iii. 4 f.) did Christianity penetrate the wide stretches of country south of Philas towards Abyssinia and Southern Arabia; cp. Duchesne's Les missions chretiennes au sud de Tempire Romain (1896). All tales relating to an earlier period are legendary. What we may call the " papal" power of Alexandria is further shown by the fact that the Abyssinian church rose and remained in a position of entire dependence on Alexandria.

We cannot tell how or when the Alexandrian bishop succeeded in bringing Pentapolis, which did not belong to Egypt politically, under his control. The local metropolitan, as such, was his colleague, but in one aspect was only his subordinate. We have no details about the demarcation of authority and jurisdiction between the metropolitans and the Alexandrian super-metropolitan for the fourth century, let alone for the third. Nor do we know how many metropolitans there were in the large territory over which the Alexandrian bishop presided. Perhaps during the third centuryâ apart from the metropolitan of Pentapolisâ there were no metropolitans there at all, in the strict sense of the term. But whether there was one or more, they were quite unsuccessful in their efforts to be independent metropolitans like their colleagues elsewhere in the empire. For the provinces and metropolitans in Egypt, cp. Schwartz, pp. l8o f., Liibeck, pp. 109 f., 116 f.

Catacombs are said to have been discovered in Cyrene, dating from the pre-Constantine period; cp. Smith and Porcher, History of the Recent Discoveries at Cyrene (London, 1864).â The coast of the Syrtes was as barren and barbarous then as it is to-day. "Vacua humano cultu omnia. ubi aversa quaedam a mari promuntoria ventis resistunt, terra aliquantulum solidior herbam raram atque hispidam gignit: ea ovibus pabulum est satis utile; incolae lacte vivunt " (Sulpic. Sev., Dial., i. 3 f.). There were no churches there, but perhaps one or two Christian settlers at the end of the fourth century.

Which does not exclude the possibility of Christianity having been preached ere this to certain " Ethiopians" on the borders. Origen seems to know of such cases having occurred. He writes: " Non fertur praedicatum esse evangelium apud omnes Aethiopas, maxime apud eos, qui sunt ultra flumen"("The gospel is not said to have been preached to all the Ethiopians, especially to such as live beyond the River"; in Alalth. Comment., Ser. 39, t. iv. pp. 269 f., ed. Lommatzsch).

Â 8. CilICIA

Ever since Antjoch had come to be a place of increasing importance, it had exercised a very strong and steady influence over Cilicia, the whole province gravitating more and more to Hellenic Syria. This feature comes out in its church history as well as elsewhere. Luke ranks Syria and Cilicia together as missionary spheres; Christian communities arose there contemporaneously with the earliest communities in Syria; Paul, a son of Tarsus, laboured in his native land; and the Cilician churches, together with those of Antioch and Syria, took part in the great Gentile Christian controversy (Acts-xv. 23, epistle from Jerusalem to the Gentile Christians in Antioch, Syria, and Cilicia; xv 41j churches in Syria and Cilicia; Paul himself groups together to. KXi-imara t. vpiai; k. Kixtca?, Gal. i. 21. Ignatius, cp. ad Philad. xi., was accompanied on his transportation by a deacon named Philo from Cilicia). At a later period, too, Cilician bishoprics were frequently filled up from Antioch. Ourjiiformation regarding the history of the Cilician church down to the council of Nicaea is extremely small. In the chronicle of Dionysius of Telmahar (ed. Siegfried and Gelzer, p. 67), a bishop of Alexandria parva Alexandretta is mentioned about the year 200. Dionysius of Alexandria once or twice mentions Heleuus, bishop of Tarsus, and from the mode of reference we may gather that he was metropolitan of Cilicia. This province must therefore have comprised a considerable number of bishoprics at that period (cp. Eus., H. E., vi. 46, vii. I 5: " Helenus, bishop of Tarsus in Cilicia, and the other bishops of that district," " Helenus of Tarsus and all the churches of r.

Cilicia"). Tarsus, distinguished as it w as for a flourishing jt- school of learning, formed at the same time the political capital of the province. L usus of Tarsus, Ampjiion the bishop-confessor - Under Domitian or Trajan even the Koivhv Kixikias, or Diet of Cilicia, met at Antioch.

There was a large number of Jews in Cilicia, and especially in Tarsus (cp. Acts vi. 9, and Epiph., IIi r. xxx.). The house of Paul was of course pointed out here (cp. Soz., vii. 19), â â For Rhossus, see above, p. 139.

of Epiphania, and Narcissus the bishop of Neronias (= Irenopolis) all took part in the synod of Ancyra (c. 314 a. d.); cp. also the synod of Neo-Cassarea, which immediately followed it. Many foreign Christians were deported to the mineji iu- Cilicia Mart. Pal., X. 1, xi. 6), and the presence of Christians in Pompeiopolis is implied in the martyrdom of Tarachus and his fellows (Ruinart, pp. 451 Â). The epistle of Alexander of Alexandria (Athan., de Syn. 17) and Philostorgius (iii, 15) vouch for a bishopr ic at A ngt axhus (Anazarba); and for a nameless episcopal seat in Cilicia, at the opening of the fourth century, see Epiph., Haer., xxx. 11.

No fewer than nine Cilician bishops attended the Nicene council, as well as one chor-episcopus; viz., the bishops of Tarsus, Epiphania, Neronias, Castabala, Flavias Adana, Mopsuestia, JEgae, and 5lexandria parva." Their numbers, and the fact of the chor-episcopate having already developed within Cilicia, would indicate that considerable progress had been made in the Christianizing of this province.

The bishop of Anazarbus, shortly after the Nicene council, was Athanasius, the pupil of Lucian (Philost., loc. cit.). For Borboriani in Cilicia, see the same passage.

According to Amm. Marcell. (xxii. ii. 3), Georgius, the bishop who opposed Athanasius, was born here. Bishop Amphion was a confessor at the time of the Nicene council (so Sozom., i. 10).

â Cp. the unauthentic Ignatian epistles.

â Alexander, subsequently bishop of Jerusalem (in the first half of the third century), is said by some authorities to have been bishop of Flavias at an earlier period. But this can hardly be correct.

The predecessor of the Macedonian in this see was Auxentius, of whom Philostorgius (in Suidas) has given an interesting account. He was originally a high officer under Licinius, and was obliged to resign. He was then made bishop of Mopsuestia.

Cp. the destruction of the local temple to Esculapius by Constantine; also the Acta Claudii et Asterii (Ruinart's Ada Mart., Ratisbon, 1859, pp. 309 f.). But is the gea of this martyrdom really the gse of Cilicia? The trial is conducted by Lysias, " praeses provinciae Lyciae." I have not, however, been able to find any. gea or. gse in Lycia.

" The register doubles Narcissus of Neronias as Narcissus of Irenopolis, but the two towns are identical. The names of the bishops are as follows: Theodorus, Amphion, Narcissus, Moses of Castabala evidently a Jew by birth Nicetas, Paulinus, Macedonius, Tarcodimantus of gse a Cilician by birth! Two Cilician kings of this name (Topcov5tvotos) and a prince (Tapcc(;'Srios) of upper Cilicia are known, and Hesychius. The chor-episcopus is called Eudsemon.

Â 9. Asia Minor (excluding Cilicia) Cappadocia, Armenia, Diospontus, Paphlagonia and Pontus

POLEMONIACUS, BitHYNIA, Asia, LydIA, MysIA, CarIA,
Phrygia, Galatia, Pisidia, Lycaonia, Lycia, Pam-
PHYLIA, IsaURIA.

Asia Minor, and indeed the majority of the above-named provinces, constituted A Christian country car' e oxw during the pre-Constantine era. This is a fact which is to be asserted with all confidence. Even the reasons for it can be discovered, although different considerations obtain with regard to the l various sections of Asia Minor as a whole. Here Hellenism had

IXa iv assumed a form which rendered it peculiarly susceptible to Christianity. Here again were other provinces which were barely touched by it, possessing but an imperfect civilization, and therefore forming virgin soil. Here, in many provinces, 5 a numeraus bpdy of â Jews were to be found, who, though personally hostile to Christianity, had nevertheless prepared its entrance into many a heart and head. Here singular mixtures of Judaism and paganism were to be met with, in the realm of ideas (cp. the worship of Oeos v' iaro) as well as in mythology; the population were open for a new syncretism. Here there were no powerful and unifying national religions to offer such a fanatical resistance to Christianity as in the case of the Syro-Phoenician religion, although there were strong local sanctuaries and several attractive cults throughout the country. The religious life of the land was cleft by as serious a fissure as was the provincial and nationalâ which must have been felt to be an anachronism in the new order of things, above

Cp. Map VI.â Mommsen's Rom. Gesch., v. pp. 295 f. (Eng. trans., i. pp. 320 f.), and the copious instructive article on " Asia Minor" by Joh. Weiss in the Prot. Reai.-Encykl wo. x. The collocation of districts so heterogeneous as the above can only be justified on the ground that the results of Christian propaganda were fairly uniform. The collocation is thus at best provisional.

- One must also notice at how late a period the whole eastern section of the province became really Romanized. Avowedly by 100 B. C., but actually not for two centuries later, did the Romans win practical and entire possession of Cilicia. Cappadocia was not secured till the reign of Tiberius; Western Pontus was added under Nero, Commagene and Armenia Minor under Vespasian, etc.

all, in the new order introduced by Augustus. The older national memories had almost died out everywhere. There was a total lack of any independent political life. Here the imperial cultus established itself, therefore, with success. But while the imperial cultus was an anticipation of universalism in religion, it was a totally unworthy expression of that universalism, nor could it permanently satisfy the religious natures of the age.- Besides, ambition, conceit, and servility clung to it. Civilization and manners differed widely throughout these provinces, where, in the West, trade, manufactures, and commerce flourished down to the beginning of the third century. But so far as there was any civilizationâ and in the West it was extremely highâ it was invariably Hellenic. Here, more than

Above all, in Asia proper, which had every reason to hail Augustus with real gratitude. Perhaps the most brilliant achievement of the imperial policy during the first century was the pacification and prosperity of Asia Minor; it was partly a renaissance, partly quite a new creation.

- Thanks to the newly discovered inscriptions, we now know better than ever the character, the consolidation, the provincial organization (with the 'Affidpxtjs, and an apxup is under him in every leading temple of the towns), the language, and the influence of the imperial cultus in Asia. How much we can gather from the history of the church, from inscriptions such as those of Priene Mitteil. d. Kais. Deutschen Archdol. Inst it., Athen, Abtetl, xxiii. 3. pp. 275 f., and my Reden ti. Atifs., i. pp. 301 f.), or from Hadrian's title of " 'OAujuttjos craitrjp Koi KTictTJis"! Liibeck (pp. 17 f., on the imperial cultus and the hierarchy of the church) rightly perceives that " in the end the Christian organization (in Asia) was obliged to resemble that of the imperial cultus in several, though not in many, respects: apparently it leant on the cultus, though it was quite unconscious of any such deliberate purpose?." Still, it cannot be proved that the seven churches addressed in John's Apocalypse were selected by John on account of their position and relation to the cultus of the ruling power and the emperor (so Liibeck, pp. 26 f.). Ramsay has put forward a fresh and independent view of this choice ("The Seven Churches of Asia," in Expositor, vol. ix. pp. 20 f.), and in his large work on The Letters to the Seven Churches of Asia, 1904, pp. 171 f.). He regards each church as the representative of a group of adjoining churches, as in jact a lort of metropolitan church. This was not the original grouping of John, however; these seven churches must have been already recognized as " the seven churches of Asia." "The gradual selection of seven representative churches in the province was in some way connected with the principal road-circiiit of the province They were the best points on that circuit to serve as centres of communication with seven districts: Pe gamum for the north (Troas, Adramyt-tium, probably Cyzicus, etc.); Thyatira Tor an inland district on the north-east and east; Philadelphia for Upper Lydia, to which it was the door (iii. 8); Laodicea for the Lycus valley and for central Phrygia; Ephesus for the Cayster and lower Maeander valleys and coasts; Smyrna for the lower Hermas valley and the North Ionian coast, perhaps with Mitylene and Chios."

in any other country, did Christianity amalgamate with Hellen- isin, and the result was that an actual transition and fusion took place, which, contrary to the development at Alexandria, affected, not merely religious philosophy, but all departments of life. This is evident from the Christian theology, the cultus, the mythology, and the local legends of the saints. The proof of it comes out in the fourth, and in fact at the end of the third century, in the way in which paganism was overcome. Here paganism was absorbed. There were no fierce struggles. Paganism simply disappeared, to emerge again, in proportion to the measure of its disappearance, within the Christian church. Nowhere else did the conquest and " extirpation " of paganism occasion so little trouble. The fact is, it was not extirpation at all. It was transformation. Asia Minor, in the fourth century, was the first pui'ely Christian country, apart from some outlying districts and one or two prominent sanctuaries which managed to survive. The Greek church of to-day is the church of Constantinople and Asia Minor, or rather of Asia Minor, Constantinople itself derived its power from Asia Minor in the first instance, and from Antioch only in the second. The apostle Paul was drawn to Asia Minor. Ephesus became the second fulcrum of Christianity, after Antioch. That great unknown figure, John, resided here, and here it was that the deepest things which could be said of Jesus were composed. Besides John, other apostles and personal disciples of Jesus, among them Philip the evangelist, and certainly his daughters (who were prophetesses), all came to Phrygia. Nearly all the great developments of the Christian religion during the second century originated in Asia, and it was in Asia that all the great controversies were mainly fought outâ the conflict between the itinerant and the local organizations (cp. 3 John, etc.), the gnostic struggle, the Christological controversy (Praxeas,

A good deal is to be learnt from Strzygowski's Kleinasien ein Neuland der Kunstgeschichte (1903) about the pre-Constantine church history of Asia.

'â Cp. Zahn's " Apostel u. Apostelschliler in der Provinz Asien" Forschungen, vi., 1900), which is not free from exaggerations and doubtful assertions. "The Asiatic presbyters who had seen the apostles " (so Papias, followed by Irenseus and the Muratorian canon) form a group which we can no longer make out clearly. Cp. my Chronoloi ie, i. 320-381.

Theodotus, and Epigonus all came from Asia), the Montanist controversy, which here and here alone assumed a popular form, etc. Here, too, the synodal and metropolitan constitution of the church was initiated. The worship of relics also received its initial impetus in Asia Minor.

Even before Trajan's reign we come across Christian communities at Perge (Pamphylia), Pisidian Antioch, lcorimm, j! L Derbe, and Ly tra (Acts xixlÂ â xiy-)? s well as at unnamed n localities in Galatia, Cappadocia, and Bithynia, at Ephesus, Colossag, Laqdicea, Phrygian Hierapolis (Paul's epistles), Sm na, Pergamum, Sardis, Philadelphia, Thyatira (Apoc. John), and 'Proas (Acts, Paul, and Ignat., ad Phil, xi.)." The churches at Magnesia on the Maeander and at Tralles are also earlier than Trajan's reign, undoubtedly (see Ignatius). Nor does this exhaust the number of towns where Christian communities were to be found at that period. The vigour and the variety of the forms already assumed by Christianity in these quarters are shown by the seyen eplg. t p. s to-Â he,. j; iiurches in the Johannine Apocalypse, by the whole tenor of the booic, and by

Plainly this organization had not yet become naturalized in Northern Africa, or at least only in the local Montanist church, when Tertullian wrote (in de Jejuiiio, xiii.): " Aguntur praeterea per Graecias under which we must include Asia ilia certis in locis concilia ex universis ecclesiis, per quae et altiora quaeque in commune tractantur, et ipsa representatio totius nominis Christiani magna veneratione celebratur"(" Besides, in definite localities throughout Greece there are held those councils of all the churches, by means of which deeper questions are treated for the church's common good, and the entire name of Christ is represented and celebrated with entire reverence"). In A5ia the synods were framed on the pattern of the local diets, which were a special feature of Asiatic life (cp. Clibeck, pp. 32 f.). Their significance for the growth and strength of the Christian cause is brought out by the Licinian legislation, which prohibited them Vita Constant., i. 51 â HV afirj j. ri5au. as a r ois itrikoivcovf7i tovs (TnttKOirovs fit S' iwisruxuv avroov i eivai rivi ry rov ireaas eccaTjcria, xrise ye avvosovs fir)Se fiovxcis Kol Siarrke lets Trtpl twv Xvanexoiv iroif7(T6ai= " Bishops were never to hold the slightest intercourse with one another, nor were they permitted to be absent on a visit to some neighbouring church, nor were synods, councils, or conferences on economic questions to be held ").

For the history of the founding of these churches, cp. especially the studies of Ramsay.

For the Apocalypse of John never mentions Tralles, Magnesia, or Colossae. Consequently, it must have also omitted other cities, even although these had churches of their own. Ignatius, too, merely gives a selection. Both he Tratt. xii., Polyc. viii.) and the address of i Peter poin t to the existence of other churches in Asia.

186 MISSION AND EXPANSION OF CHRISIlaNITY ; the Ignatian writings. The epistle to Laodicea (Apoc. iii. 17) ' sets before us a church which had ah'eady compromised with the world, and which felt itself to be rich and satisfied. For the John of the Apocalypse, for Ignatius, and for the unknown editor who called Paul's circular letter by the name of " Ephesians," Ephesus stood out pre-eminent among the churches of Asia. Ignatius mentions its populous character iroxvtrxrjdla, Ephes., i. 3). He only speaks of jrxtjoo? in connection with the others. S myrn a was originally a small church, oppressed by a powerful Jewish society, and so on. But by the time of Domitian the number of the Asiatic Christians was large. Thus the author of the

Apocalypse depicts an οχλος πολυς, ον αριθμησα-ας ουδεις εδυ'ατο (vii. 9) standing before the throne of the Lamb. A generation earlier, jlj Sl 0. â- Paul had written an epistle (the so-called " Ephesians"") to Asia, whose historical outlook implies the glorious experience of Christ's power to unify mankind, and of that peace among men which the Saviour came to bring. Christ, not Augustus, is our peace. He it is who made out of twain one, and hath broken down the wall of partition. The language of imperial adoration is applied here to the Redeemer (Ephes. ii. 14).

This sketch may be rounded off by a piece of non-Christian evidence which, however familiar, cannot be valued too highly. It refers to Bithynia and Pontus, two provinces of Asia Minor, where (as the opening words of 1 Peter already inform us) Christians were to be found at an early period, though no further details can be gathered on this point from the New Testament itself. Pliny's account of them, however (for it is Pliny to whom I allude), certainly relates to the provinces of 1 Paul did not found this church; it arose after several of the other Asiatic

Christian communities (Polyc, Ep. xi. 3).

Y,- This epistle shows unquestionably that Christianity had spread to some extent
A throughout these provinces. The counsels of the author definitely presuppose
f certain relations between the Christian and the non-Christian population. Not so
' the Pauline epistles. The local Christians have obviously excited a disagreeable interest in their affairs; they are exposed to the hostility of the provincials, although the authorities still refrain from any action. The epistle may belong to the earlier years of Domitian.

3 In an ancient preface to John's Gospel (cp. the old manuscript of Toledo) we hear of brethren from Pontus. The preface is not entirely valueless.â Ramsay is
Asia and Phrygia alike. He informs the emperor Trajan Ep. xcvi., c. 111-113 A. D.) that persons of all ages nd ranks (even including Roman citizens) are implicated in the proceedings taken against the Christians, while several apostates had explained they had been Christians for many years, but were no longer so. One of them affirmed that he had been converted over twenty years ago. Pliny then goes on to say: " Dilata cognitione ad consulendum te decucurri. Visa est enim mihi res digna consultatione, maxime propter pericli-tantium numerum. Multi enim omnis aetatis, omnis ordinis, utriusque sexus etiam, vocantur in periculum et vocabuntur. Neque civitates tantiim sed vicos etiam atque agi'os superstitionis istius contagio pervagata est; quae videtur sisti et corrigi posse. Certe satis constat prope iam desolata templa coepisse celehran et sacra sollemnia diu intermissa repeti pastumque venire victimarum, cuius adhuc rarissivms emptor inveniehatiir. Ex quo facile est opinari quae turba hominum emendari possit, si sit paenitentiae locus"" (cp aboyejj). 3).

There were reasons why Pliny should represent the spread of the movement in as strong terms as possible; but, even after allowance has been made for this, his testimony remains sufficjen remarkable. He cannot have invented the spread of the Christian religion in the lowlands, or the grip which it had taken of all classes in the population. But who the missionaries were by whose efforts this had been accomplished, we cannot tell. How well prepared, too, must have been the soil, if the Christian crop sprang up so luxuriantly! In short, we may claim this letter of Pliny as the most outstanding piece of evidence for the advance of Christian missions alonsr the whole of the western coast.

Pliny does not name any city or locality; evidently he would probably right in holding that Bithynia was hardly reached by Christianity by land. Similarly, the Pontic towns on the Black Sea had Christian communities at an early date, whilst the interior of Pontus still remained pagan throughout.

This letter to Trajan was probably written in the east of Bithynia-Pontus, i-as the letters near it in the collection are dated from this district (Amastris? Amasia?),

He wanted the e mperor to approve of his comparatively lenient treatment of the Christians.

188 MISSION AND EXPANSION OF CHRISTIANITY have had to mention too many. And the Christian writers are so reticent that these gaps in our knowledge remain unfilled, nisus in Pontus is the only place at which we can prove from Christian sources, with some show of probability, tliajLChristians existed about 100 a. d, (cp. Ramsay's The Church in the Roman Empire, 1893, pp. 211, 225). h (j U f f j

Between Trajan and the death of Marcus Aurqliii's, our sources supply fourteen fresh names of Asiatic towns containing Christian communities, in addition to the seventeen already notedâ an infinitesimally small number in view of the riumei'ous new churches which must have been planted throughout Asia Minor during these eighty years. Those named are Si nop e on the Black Sea (the home of Marcion, whose father is said to have been the local bishop; Hippol., in Epiph., Hivr., xlii. 1), Philomelium in Pisidia (cp. the epistle of the Smyrniote church upon Polycarp's death), Parium in Mysia (for in this connection we may trust the Acta Onesiphori)," Njcomedia (cp. the epistle of bishop Dionysius of Corinth to the local church in Eus., H. E., iv. 23), Amastris "and the other churches in Pontus" (the epistle of Dionysius to them, loc. cit.; here the metropolitan organization was in working order by the reign of M. Aurelius), and Hieropolis in Phrygia (however one may view the famous inscription of Abercius, we may infer from it that Christianity had by that time reached Hieropolis). The other eight towns are known to us from sources connected with the Montanist movement, viz., Ag gyra j u, Galatia (Eus., v. 16), Otrus, Pepuza, Tymion = Dumanli., (Ardabau) ep nj Kara. Ti v pvyiav Mi cra = Kardaba?," A gam ea (Kibotos), Cumane, anclEumenea, all in Phrygia (cp. Eus., H. E., v. 16. 18). So far as we know, the first synods in connection with the

In this connection one must also recall the rescript of Hadrian to Minucius Fundanus and the interpolated rescript of Pius to the diet of Asia Texte u, Unters., xiii. 4), both of which presuppose no inconsiderable extension of Christianity in Asia. The local diet has already to deal with Christians. On the other hand, no weight is to be attached to the story told by Lampridius in his Vita Alex. Severi, 43, about Hadrian and Christianity.

' Cp. also Acta SS. Fbr., H, p. 42.

The Acta Pauli probably testify also to the existence of a church at Myrrha in Lycia, during the second century.

â â Cp. Ramsay's Phrygia, p. 573.

Montanist controversy were held in Asia Minor, although they did not confine themselves strictly to one province.

Before entering into the evidence available for the several provinces of Asia Minor, I shall briefly put together some data which prove the wide diffusion of Christianity by the close of our epoch, chra 325 a. d.

(1) The edi. ctÂ, jof- Maxiininus, Da. ZÂ L against Christians, with tkeir declarations that "almost all men"" have gone over to Christianity (Eus., H. E., ix. 9), refer mainly to the situation in Asia Minor (and Syria). From the servile petitions of the cities, even of Nicomedia (loc. cit., and ix. 2 f.), asking the emperor to issue a command that no Christian should reside within their bounds or even in their surroundings, we must not conclude that the local Christians were, relatively speaking, a small body. As for Bithynia in particular, this edict of Daza implies the existence of a particularly large number of Christians. The petition sent up by the cities had simply the effect of prohibiting public worship within the city walls. Perhaps it was not meant to be serious at all; the idea of such petitions was to curry favour with the emperor.

(2) In the speech already quoted (p. 16), which was delivered in Nicomedia, Lueian of Antioch declares that " pars paene mundi iam maior huic veritati adstipulatur, urbesmlegrae; aut si in his aliquid suspectum videtur, contestatur de his etiam agrestis manus, ignara figmenti."'"' (3) The expression, "urbes integrae," is corroborated, so far as regards Phrygia, by Eus., H. E., viii. 11. 1, where we read how an entir e town (Ramsay, Letters to Seven CMiixhes of Asia, riv'ika avvelzov, crx ov Unavras avbpwirovs Kata eip9eiffris rris rsiv Qisiv Opriffkfias TCfj tdvii rs)u Xptartavoip eavrovs (TVfj. fj, efj. ixitas (cp. vol. i. pp. 271, 495 â)' so the edict in ix, y. 9: o-xes j dire'iv ta iravraxov rrjs olkovfiivris o(Vx' ''a! s evte e ("Christianity, it may almost be said, ciushed the whole world with its shame "). l"he designation of Christians as rh ebvos roiy Xpia-navoiv occurs pretty frequently in the imperial rescripts of that period.

Even if one assumes that the petitions were really meant to be taken seriously, with their demand for the formal ejection of all Christians, no light is yet thrown upon the number of Christians. We must remember, by way of comparison, how strong the Huguenots were in France, when the general policy was to root them out. One always reckons in such cases upon the majority abandoning their faith.) pp. 426 f., thinks of Eumenea) in this province, which was Christian, was burnt during Diocletian's persecution (' Stj yovv o y V pi(TTiavuv irokiv avtavspov afkpi t v pvytav ev kvkxo) 7repi3a ovtei OTrxcrai, irvp re v)a'yp-avte; Kate(j) e av avtOvq dfjia vrjtTcoii; KOI yvvai l, tov piarov e-Tri ooojuievovg). Even eighty years earlier (for so, I take it, we must understand the authority cited in Epiph., Hcer. li. 33), Thyatira was practically a Christian (i., a Montanist) city.

(4) From he Vitcl. Constantmi, II. 1-2, it follows that there were several churches at Amasia in Pontus during the reign of Licinius. If there were several in a town like this, which was not in the front rank, we may safely assume that many towns of Asia Minor already contained not one church but many.- (5) Dionysius of Alexandria (Eus., H. E. vii. 7) had already described the churchesqÂ J! hrygia.-aud the adjoining provinces as " the most populous churches." These districts had the largest number of bishoprics and the largest churches in the Eastâ a fact which is confirmed by the council of Nicaea. For although attendance at the council depended upon all sorts of

accidental circumstances, so that inferences fi'om it are not quite certain, still the local strength of Christianity in a province which was, comparatively speaking, so remote and wild as Isauria, is clearly shown by its representation at Nicaea of thirteen bishops and four chor-episcopi, drawn from all parts of the country.

' "A whole town of Christians, in Phrygia. was surrounded by soldiers when its citizens were inside. Fire was flung into it, and the troops burned it up, with men, women, and children, all calling upon Christ." The sequel is particularly instructive, as showing the extent to which Christianity had become naturalized in the country; even the authorities of the town were Christians '6ti 5 Trav-qixel iravtfs 01 Tr v Tr6 iv olkovvres, oyifftr s re avrhs Ka crtpatTfyhs avv rois iv rixei Tracri Kal b (fi Stjxij), Xpicrriavovs (Tpas dfioxoyovvtfs, ov5' viraxrrtovv to7s irpoardt-rovcnv flswaoxarpetv etrtiddpxovv, cp. p. 40). Lactantius also fistL, v. 11) mentions the incident: " Unus in Phrygia universum populum cum ipso pariter conventiculo concremavit" ("One burned up a whole town in Phrygia, with its assembly and all").

- Throughout the towns it is obvious that the churches generally were quite small; for Licinius (Fta Constaniiiii., I. liii.), pleading hygienic reasons, decreed that Christians were to conduct their worship in the open air. On his part, this was purely a pretext for either ridding the towns of their presence or throwing obstacles in the way of their worship.

(6) Besides the mere number of chor-episcopi attending NTcseatthe Christian inscriptions from the small townships of Phrygia, which were publicly erected and bore the name of Xpia-riavog, the story of Gregory Thaumaturgus (see below, the evidence ofjLucian, and other sources as well, show still more forcibly that Christianity during the third century had penetrated deeply into tjie population of the towns and country districts throughout Asia Minor, partially absorbmg into itself the native cults, a (T) Palpably, the reaction under Julian failed to get any k footing in Asia Minor, owing to the strong hold of the country , j already won by Christianity. This explains, among other " i jj things, why the names of the bishoprics, which we can verify for Asia Minor, determine the actual number of these bishoprics still less accurately than is the case with the other provinces. If a large number of the Eastern provinces generally fell under the verdictâ a verdict which cannot, of course, be strictly proved â that by about 325 a. d. the network of the episcopal hierarchy had been completed, leaving few meshes to be added at a later period, then Asia Minor comes pre-eminently within the sweep ' An admirably comprehensive work upon the Christian inscriptions of Asia Minor has been written by Cu mont: Les Ijiso, Chn't. de PAsie tninetire, Rome, 1895 Extr. des Melanges d'Archeologie et d'Histoire, t. xv.). True, we cannot verify more than nine dated inscriptions for the pre-Constantine period (besides the inscription of Arycanda, which refers to Christians), but Duchesne and Cumont have shown that internal evidence justifies us in clairning a considerable number of undated inscriptions as pre-Constantine (cp. Renan's Paul, Germ, ed., 323 f.). The dated inscriptions come from Hieropolis, Eumenea, Sebaste, Apamea, Pepuza, and Trajanopolis. On the position of Christians in Asia, Cumont rightly observes (pp. 26 f.): "La paix relative ou vecurent ces communautes, n'y laissa pas grandir comme ailleurs la haine contre l'Etat remain. On pouvait devenir Chretien et rester bon citoyen; on aimait a faire l'eloge de sa ville natale, on y exer9ait des fonctions publiques, on deposait aux archives la

copie de son testament, on stipulait contre les violateurs de son tombeau des amendes au profit de la caisse municipale ou du tresor publique Rien d'etonnant que dans un pareil milieu les idees et les coutumes antiques se soient plus qu'ailleurs melees aux convictions nouvelles, que dans la vie journaliere on ait cherche un compromis entre le passe et le present."

' Cp. above, p. 158, on Egypt. There are but few traces of new bishoprics having been founded in the East by Constantine or his sons. Most of the sees had evidently been created previously. The main concern of the first Christian emperor was the building of churches i. e., new buildings or the enlargement of old ones), and their equipment.

of such a judgment. Still, to avoid the introduction of uncertain data, I shall refrain from adducing, by way of evidence, the diocesan distribution of the Asiatic provinces, since our knowledge of this dates only from a later period. I shall merely add in this connection an allusion to such towns and localities as can be clearly proved to have had Christian communities up to 325A. D.1 '

A. Cappadocia

This province was no t Grecized tilljia te, and even then only slightly. It was neither densely populated nor rich in towns, and it was passed over by Paul. His steps turned westward.

But, as 1 Pet, i. 1 implies, there were already Christians in ryk Cappadocia. Seven Cappadocian bishops attended Nicaea, from â M i L-C aesar ea. Tyana, Colonia, Cybistra, Couiana, Spania (= Spalia?

' r where is it?), and Parnassus, besides no fewer than five chor- - episcopi. This proves how deeply Christianity had permeated the population of the country. By about 258 a. d. it must

Hilary, who wrote during his exile in Asia, declares (in de Sftiodts) that, "apart from Eleusius of Cyzicus and a few of his company, the ten Asiatic provinces in which I stayed had really no knowledge of God." If this was the state of matters, it is a melancholy testimony against the real Christianity of the Asiatic Christians, but the passage must not be connected with the problem of the spread of Christianity. Augustine Â p. xciii. 31 f.) properly brushed aside the Donatist Vincentius in Mauretania, who concluded from the passage that there were practically no Christians in these ten provinces, and thus tried to give it an anti-catholic bearing.

- Mommsen, v. p. 306 (Eng. trans., i. 332); "Cappadocia itself was hardly more Greek at the beginning of the imperial age than Brandenburg and Pomerania were French under Frederick the Great." But matters were entirely changed by the third and fourth centuries.

â The last-named town is doubtful, however. Still, there is no doubt that there were local Christians by the middle of the third century, for such were to be found in the village of Sadagolthina near Parnassus. Perhaps Camulia, near Csesarea, had also Christians about this time (cp. von Dobschiitz's Christusbilder, p. 40, 14).

â â Cappadocian chor-episcopi also attended the synod of Neo-Csesarea. The bishop of Caesarea was at Ancyra. The chor-episcopate was strongest in Cappadocia and Isauria.

Â The naiyes of the bishops show how entirely Greek Christianity had become, even here: Leontius, Eutychius, Erythrius, Timotheus, Elpidius, Paulus. The chor-episcopi were called Gorgonius, Stephanus, Eudromius, Rhodon, and Theophanes.

have comprised a large Christian population, for the Gothic invaders in that year dragged off Christians, and even some of the clergy, among their captives. These included the Greek parents of Uliilas, who were already Christians, and had resided in the village of Sadagolthina near the town of Parnassus (Philostorg., H. E., ii. 5). The story of the father of Gregory Naz. proves also that there was a Christian corninunity at Nazianzus (Dio-Caesarea) prior to Constantine.

After the second century we frequently come across Cappa-docian Christians in other provinces (cp., e. g., the Acta Justini 41, where Euelpistus comes of Christian parents in Cappadocia)." Tertullian, far off in Carthage, can even report a Cappadocian persecution (cp. Neumann, op. cit., i. p. 70) between 180 and 19 1 "Claudius Lucius. lierminianus- in Cappadocia, cum indiffne ferens uxorem suam ad hanc sectam transisse Christianos crudeliter tractasset solusque in praetorio suo vastatus peste convivis vermibus ebulisset, nemo sciat, aiebat, ne gaudeant Christiani aut sperent Christianae. postea cognito errore suo quod tormentis quosdam a proposito suo excidere fecisset, paene Christianus decessit (ad Scap. iii.: " Enraged at the conversion of his wife to this sect, Claudius Lucius Herminianus in Cappadocia treated the Christians cruelly. But afterwards, left alone in his palace and devoured by disease, he grew fevered with worms eating his vitals, and would cry out, ' Let none know of it, lest the Christian men rejoice and Christian wives take heart." Subsequently, he came to see his error in having forced some to give up their faith by means of torture. And he died almost a Christian himself").

The bishopric of Caesarea, which was the metropolis of Cappadocia and " the medium of the busy traffic between the seaports on the west coast and the region of the Euphrates," was widely known throughout the church on account of two

For evidence of Christians, during the reign of M. Aurelius, in the district of Melitene, west of the upper Euphrates, which may be grouped also along with Cappadocia, cp. below, under "Armenia."

"Also Afar(. Pal., p. 75 (ed. Violet). The martyrs of Caesarea (Palest.), Seleucus and Julianus, came from Cappadocia ibid., pp. 97, loi).

The bishopric was in close touch not only with Antioch and Palestine, but also with the West.

VOL. II.

MISSION AND EXPANSION OF CHRISTIANITY men, both friends of learning, viz., Ale ider and Firmilian. The former (cp. my Litt.-Gesch., i. pp. 505 f.; ii. 2, pp. 6 f., 92 f.) was bi. shop at Caesarea Avhen quite a youth (c. 200 a. d.); he was a friend of Clement and of Origen; and as bishop of Jerusalem he died full of years, after having founded a library in Jerusalem. Clement stayed with him, after leaving Alexandria, and took part in mission-work at Caesarea. Alexander distinctly says that he added to the local church (Eus., H. E., vi. II. 6). J'irmilian. who also was a man of Alexandrian culture and an ardent admirer of Origen (c. 230-268), was connected with the most prominent people in all the church, even with Cyprian of Carthage (cp. my Litt.-Gesch. i. pp. 407 f.; ii. 2. 102 f.). Thanks to his episcopal efforts Caesarea became a centre of theological culture; and it was here that the learned maiden Juliana resided, who harboured Origen for two years and received one or two books from Symmachus. A good deal of information upon the history of the Cappadocian church during the first half of the third century is yielded by Firmilian's letter to Cyprian (Ep. lxxv.), where we read of synods, persecutions, heretics, and fanatics. Special interest attaches to his account of a prophetess (c. 10) connected with the earlier prophetesses of Phrygia, who stirred up the whole Christian population during the reign of Maximinus Thrax, and even captured a presbyter and a deacon. In the controversy over the baptism of heretics, Firmilian sided with Cyprian. The most famous Cappadocian martyr was Mamas, a simple shepherd (in the days of Valerian?). But unfortunately we have no J eta at our disposal.

Alexander and (especially) Firnijlian were responsible for the theological importance of the Caesarean and Cappadocian

Eusebius did not know, at any rate he did not say, what place it was, but Gregory of Nyssa (Migne, xlvi. p. 905) mentions it.

Gregory of Nyssa calls him a " distinguished " Cappadocian. He lived to see the terrible invasion of Sapur and the siege of Caesarea. The raid of the Goths and the invasion of the province by the Persians were simultaneous.

Origen stayed at Caesarea (in the house of a certain Juliana), by the request of Firmilian, " for the good of the churches" (Eus., H. E., vi. 17; cp. Pallad., Hist. Laus. 64); cp. my Ckronologie, ii. p. 33.

â His body was deposited in the imperial estate of Macellum, near Csesarea (Soz. v. 2.).

church. As regards the fourth century, we can even speak of a distinctively Origenist Cappadocian theology, which proved of the utmost significance for the church at large, and in point of fact became an orthodox theology itself. Basil (6 t? oikovuevr (p(t)(Trr p, Theodor., iv. 19) and the two great Gregorys were c "2, sons of Cappadocia. Withal, a popular Christianity developed simultaneously in Cappadocia, which became fused with paganismâ as may be inferred from numberless statements and hints scattered through the works of Cappadocians (cp. also the cult of the " Hypsistarii,"' votaries of 6e6 v' ictto), and

With the high rank of these men and their successors we may perhaps compare the special position of the pagan high priest of Cappadocia in earlier days.â The Arian sophist Asterius also was a Cappadocian.

- It is remarkable and instructive to find how Eusebius Vi. Const., iv. 43), in describing the bishops who assembled for the dedication of the church at Jerusalem by their provincial origins, or in grouping them by one distinctive feature, speaks thus of the Cappadocians: kox Kaw-irasokciu 5' 01 Trpwroi Tratsevaa 6yci)t xeffoi Tols iracri Siiirpeirov (" And these were the chief of the Cappadocians, pre: eminent amongst the rest for learned eloquence "). They were the successors of Firmilian, and the predecessors of the Gregorys. Eunomius also came from Cappadocia (Philostorg., iii. 20).â According to Philostorgius (ix. 9), his grandfather Anysius was presbyter in the town of Borissus in Cappadocia secunda unidentified, so far as I know. Hence we may infer perhaps that Borissus had a Christian community by 325 a. d. Philostorgius himself was born c. 360 a. d. JI.Â., X. 6).

Cp. H. Gregoiie s recent stwdy, Sahifsjumeaux et dt'eux caz'ah'ers Pa. ns, 1905), in which the evidence of the recently discovered Greek Maprvpiov r. ay. rpiwv vr)iriiav lirivcf'nr-Kov, 'EXaa-iirnov, Ka Mfxearltnrov kui ttjs tovtcov fj.7jtpbs 'Neoviwas (MS. of Genoa, Saulianus 33)â the very divergent Latin text was published by Bougaud in Atude hist, et crit. siir la mission, les actes, et le cnlte de s. Bhiigne (Autun 1859)â is used to describe the transformation of a pagan cult into a Christian in Southern Cappadocia, which was famous for its horses. " A I'epoque de I'Empire," so Gregoire ends his study, "et sans doute plus anciennement, pres d'Andaval (Andabilis), dans la region de Tyane"â i. e., not far from the estate of Pasmasus Pasa, Paspasa = the villa Pompali of the Bordeaux Itinerary, 333 a. d., "unde veniunt equi curules"; cp, Ramsay's V. Geogr. of Asia Minor, p. 347, Gregoire pp. 55 f.â "une population d'eleveurs de chevaux rendait un culte aux Dioscures grecs, probablement associes a une vieille divinite du pays. Vers la fin du IIP stecle, le christianisme amena la transformation de ces divinites en une triade de saints jumeaux et cavaliers. Une legende relative a ces saints fut redigee vers la meme epoque" this does not seem to me to be made out. "Les saints representes comme des esclaves, furent mis en relation avec de grands proprie-taires de I'endroit, dont I'un Palmatus, qui vecut sous le regne de Valerien (253-260), avait laisse un souvenir tres vivace." An 'Opffdsoov Kcox fj also occurs in the legend, which Gregoire tries to identify with Olba in Cilician Isauria (Ramsay, p. 364), in the region of Cetis, near Seleucia, This Olba was also called especially in the letter of Basil to Glycerins Ep. clxix. ccccxii,). Following in the wake of Gregory Thaumaturgus, their teacher, these Cappadocians were skilled in adjusting Christianity to Hellenism in the interests of the cultured, Hellenism being viewed as a preparation for the gospel. They understood how to Christianize the cults. But above all, they knew how to plan everything so as to hei ghte n the power and sanctity of tlae catholic church, and how to enthrone it over every form and phase of contemporary syncretism; they knew how to put an end to the latter and at the same time to perpetuate them in the sense of subordinating them, as local and justifiable varieties of religion, to the authority of the one church and of her cultus. Such an achievement would have been impossible, had not Cappadocia been practically Christian by about 325 A. D., even though its Christianity was cleft in twain.

Finally, the church of Cappadocia is invested with still further importance as the mother of the Gothic and, in company with the Edessene church, of the Armenian chuj'ches as well.

B. Armenia, Diospontus, Paphlagonia,
AND PONTUS POLEMONIACUS.

The early history of the church in Armenia, Major and Minor, is wrapt in obscurity. Apart from the district of Melitene, it emerges first of all in the statement of Eusebius H. E., vi. 46), that Dionysius Alex, wrote " to the brethren in

Urba, Orba or Orbas, and Urbanopolis. Alternative forms like Thymbrias and Thymbriada, Thebasa and Tibassada, are preserved in these districts, as well as altered forms like Amblada and Ambladon, Nasada and Nasadon, Lausanda and Lausadon.

' Cp. Ramsay, TAe Church in the Roman Empire, pp. 443 f.
- See under the following section.

-jfulian (cp. Sozom., v. 4) is said to have "deleted Csesarea from the list of towns, taken its name from it, and persecuted the inhabitants with bitter hatred, because they were all Christians and had long ago destroyed the local temples " (ois TTovsTjiel ' pia-TlavicfivTas kox iraaaj Ka. Qi 6vtas rovs irip' avrols Viws). The last temple, that of Fortune, was not destroyed, however, till Julian's day, when the pagans were still tuopi'Oxtjtoi; uoaa in the city.

â Hippolytus (Philos., vii. 31) calls Bardesanes "the Armenian." But this is out of the question. Bardesanes was a Syrian (see above).

Armenia, whose bishop was Meruzanes." Mei; ui5aj). es was either bishop of Sebaste in Armenia Minor, a town which was the capital of the province at the time of the council of Nicaea, or bishop of some unknown town in South-East Armenia. From the mode of expression in Eusebius (Dionysius) it seems probable that Sebaste was, not-ihe only Christian church in Armenia about 200 a. d. As for the district of Melitene,, v which is to be assigned to the southern section of Armenia Z ' Minor, we can verify local Christians in the reign of M. Aurelius, since, as is clear from the story of the miracle of the rain, there were numerous Christians in the Thundering Legion quartered in that district (see above). We may rightly assume (Eus., V. 5) that the soldiers of this legion were recruited largely from the local population, and Eus. viii. 6 proves that Christianity there was very strong (see further the remarks on this passage on p. 138).

The period of the Licinian persecution furnishes us with an invaluable source of information for Armenia Minor, in the testament of the Forty Martyrs of Sebaste, which shows that â The name is Armenian; an Armenian satrap is so called in Faustus of Byzantium (iv. 23. p. 144).

Gelzer, in pp. 176 f. of the essay mentioned below, thinks of Armenia Major, on account of the Armenian name. But was there any bishop at all in that district at that period? Gelzer's idea is that Meruzanes was a scion of the princely house of Arzruni, and bishop of Vaspurakan in the S. E. (the district of Taron lies S. W.). The Armenian name of the bishop tells against Sebaste in Armenia Minor; for Christianity, so far as we know, was Greek in Armenia Minor.

I find, among my notes, Nicopolis (rj tov noMir-niov) in Armenia Minor described as a town where martyrdoms prove the existence of Christians before Constantine. But I am unable to give the reference.

Eusebius seems to regard the legion as composed practically of Christians.

The Christian soldier Polyeuctes, who was martyred under Decius or Valerian, also belonged to the Melitene legion (cp. the ancient Syrian Martyrologium for 7th Jan.; Conybeare's (j. and Acts of Apouonins and other Monuments of Early Christianity, 1894, London, pp. 123 f.; Aube's Polyeticle dans Fhistoire, Paris, 1882; and Acta SS., Febr. T. ii. pp. 650 f.). If we may trust a remark in what is, relatively speaking, the best recension of the Acta Polyeuctes, to the effect that he was the first martyr at Melitene, then Christianity must have been able to develop there uninterrupted till the reign of Decius. The statement of Eus., H. E., viii. 6. 8, that there were numerous clergy everywhere about 300 a. d., refers to Syria and Melitene.

Cp. Bonwetsch in Neue kirchl. Zeitschr., iii. (1892), pp. 705 f., and in the Stud. z. Gesch. d. Theol. u. Kirche (1897), pp. 73 f.; also von Gebhardt's Acta Martyr. Select a (1902), pp. 166 f.

Christianity was at that time as wi, dely-diffused throughout the smaller localities of the province as in Cappadocia. There were Christians in Sarin, Phydela, Chaduthi (not Chaduthb), Charisphone, and Ziniara (none of which, except Phydela jcan be identified, so far as I am aware), besides other villages which are not named. Even here the Christianity is Hellenic (cp. the numerous personal names). Presbyters rule the village-churches

The editors hitherto have followed the MS. in writing "Ximara," but Cumont Anal. Boll., xxiii,, 1904, p. 448) has shown that "Zimara" is the correct reading. " Zimara est une ' static' de la route militaire de Satala a M6litene, dans la petite Armenie, non loin de l'Euphrate (Itiner. Anton., 208, 5; cp. Ptolem., v. 7. 2, et la Table de Peutinger). Aujourd'hui encore le village qui lui a succede porte le nom de Zimarra. Un eveque de Satala assistait au concile de Nicee, et Melitene aussi avait une eglise des l'epoque des persecutions. Rien d'etonnant done que, vers la meme date, une communante chretienne ait existe dans une bourgade situee sur la grande voie qui reliait ces deux cites. Le testament des 40 martyrs nous fournit ainsi une indication interessante sur la diffusion du Christianisme le long de la frontiere orientale de l'empire."

- It is uncertain whether the town of Zela (Pontus) is really mentioned in the Acts, or whether the name has been corrupted. There seems to have been a Zela in Armenia also (cp. Pape-Benseler).

â Very few of the names of the forty martyrs are not Greek or Latin; viz., A770S, y ovvi. wv, 'laidvy-qs, and Nikolwos (?). Twice we get a very characteristic phrase of the period, in "6 Kai" Aeoirios 6 koi Â etjctJcrtos) (Bicparios o Kal Bi iavss).

As the following passage Tes. iii.) is almost unique, I shall cite it here: wpo(Tayopivofj. ei rhv Kvpiov rhv irpiff impov ikimrov koi HpnkXiavhv koi Atoytyrju ajxa Tp ayia 4KKKr aia. ' irpocrayopivofx. ti' Thv Kvpiov VlpokAiavhv iv t(j5 X' P V vsi a afjia T'p ayia ekKArjcrlcf, fiira twv isioiiv. irpoaayopivofxey Ma Lxov ixfra rrjs efcaTffoj, Mayvoy fiera rrs eccarjtri'ax. 7rpoffo. yopivoiji. ev A6fj. vov j-era rwv ISiwy, "l r v rhv irarepa r x(ty Kal Ova, 7 y yuera rrjs ekKAriaias. Trpoffayopevcd Kal iyw Mfaerios tovs ffvyyiyiis fiov Aovrdyioy Kpi'tnrof Kal T6pstoy fura rooy isiaiv. "Kpoffayoptvoixey Koi TOVS iv T(f x P V aptiv, rhv irpecr vtepoy; U6Ta Twy ISiwv, tovs Siakoyovs fieta twv isiwy, Md ifioy xetU twv isiaiv, 'Uffvx'ov xera rw;' ISitey, Kvpiakbv yuera tuv isicoy, trpoffayopivofifv tovs iv Xasovdl iravtas kut ovoia, Trpoffayopivoxiv Kal tovs iv Xapiff(pwv7i Travtas kut' ovofia. irpoffayopivoo Kal iyw Aetios tovs ffvyyevels fiov Mdpkhy Kal 'AKV ivav Kal rhv Trpefffivtepov K avsiov Kal tovs asek(povs fj. ov Mdpkov, Tpvipwra r6psiov Kal Kpiairov Kal tos ase pds fxov Kal t v avfj. i6v xov ASfxvav uero Tov iratsiov xov. irpoffayopevw koi iyw Kvtvxios tovs iv aifj-dpois, Tr v x-qtepa xov lovxiav Kal tovs a. St (poiis fiov Kvpiwov 'Povcpoy Kal 'Piykoy Kal KvpikXav Kal T y yvij. priv xov Baffiaeiav Kal tovs Siakovovs K avsiov, Kal "Poviplvov, Kal Ilpoirxov, Trpoffayopevoj. ev Kal tovs virr petas tov 6eov airpiktov tiv tov) 'Aj. fj. wyiov Kal Vfyefftov, Kal 'Zwffdvyav xeto, twv ISiwv (" We hail the presbyter Philip and Proclianus and Diogenes, with the holy church; Proclianus in the district of Phydela, with the holy church and his own people; Maximus with his church, Magnus with his church, Domnus with his own people; lies, our father, and Vales, with his church. I, Meletius, hail my kinsmen Latanius, Crispus, and Gordius, with their households. We hail also those in the district of Sarin, the presbyter and his people, the along with deacons, but there are also village-churches with bishops of their own.

The bishops (Eulalius and Euethius) of Sebaste and Satala (in the extreme northeast of Armenia Minor) attended Nicaea. Caesarius, the father of Eudoxius, bishop of Germanicia (and afterwards of Antioch), came from Arabissus, a town in the southwest. He died there as a martyr (cp. Philostorg., iv. 4, and Suidas, s. v. "Eudoxius'"). Philostorgius calls Eudoxius himself an Armenian (iv. 8). Meletius of Antioch came from Melitene (Philost., v. 5).

One of the most remarkable facts in all the history of the spread of Christianity is that Armenia Major was officially a Christian country by the end of the third century. " Deposuit pharetras Armenius," says Jerome Ep. cvii. 2). Eusebius calls the Armenians simply by the name of Christians, and deacons and their people, Maximus with his people, Hesychius with his people, and Cyriacus and his people. We further hail all in Caduthi by name, all in Carisphone by name. I, Etius, hail my kinsfolk Marcus and Aquilina and Claudius the presbyter, my brothers Marcus, Tryphon, Gordius, and Crispus, with my sisters and Domna my wife and my child. I, Eutychius, also hail those in Zimara, my mother Julia, and my brothers Cyril, Rufus, Riglos, and Cyrilla, my bride Basileia, and the deacons Claudius, Rufinus, and Proclus. We also hail and salute God's servants Sapricius (the son of?) Ammonius and Gencsius, and Susanna with her household").

The Testament of the Forty is inscribed: rols) cora iraffav tt6Kiv koi x PÂ '" = village, here ayiois itriakSwois. The chor- episcopus Anthogonius was martyred at Sebaste (cp. Achelis, I Iartyrol, Hieron., pp. 46 f., 163, 245).

'â Not to be confounded with the Pontic and Colchian Sebastopolis. The son and successor of Eulalius, bishop of Sebaste (in Armenia Major bishoprics were also hereditary as a rule), was Eustathius, the pupil of Arius, who founded monasticism in Armenia Minor and Paphlagonia and Pontus(Sozom., H. E., iii. 14. 31). He was born about 300 a. d. His dogmatic development and his relation to Basil of Caesarea are discussed by Loofs Eustathius von Sebaste, 1898). Socrates (ii. 48) and Sozomen (iv. 24) both make the mistake of assigning Csesarea Capp., instead of Sebaste, to the father of Eustathius.

Sozomen (ii. 8), apropos of the reign of Constantine, says that the emperor ascertained that the Armenians had been Christians long ago (ttoaij' Tvpsrepov). Judaism seems to have previously wrought here also among the Armenian aristocracy (cp. pp. 136 f. of Gelzer's essay undermentioned). But it still remains to be seen whether the strong Jewish influences were really pre-Christian and not of an Old Testament Christian nature. Certainly they cannot be put farther down than the fourth century.â Moses Choren. (cp. my Litt.-Geschichte, i. p. 188) relates that Bardesanes fought against the pagan cultus in Armenia, but he found no trace of it locally.

200 MISSION AND EXPANSION OF CHRISTIANITY describes the attack made by Maximinus Daza as a religious war (H. E., ix. 8. 2: " In addition to this the tyrant was obliged to make war upon the Armenians, men who had been old allies

and friends of Rome. Being Christians and earnest in their piety towards God, this foe of God tried to force them to offer sacrifice to idols and demons, thus turning friends into foes and allies into enemies"). When Constantine recognized and granted privileges to Christianity, he was only following in the footsteps of the Armenian king. Unfortunately the Greek sources for the Christianizing of Armenia are extremely reticent (yet see Sozom,, ii. 8), while no account need be taken of the late Byzantine or the romancing Armenian chroniclers. We merely learn (from the Nicene lists) that two bishops from Armenia Major took part in the Nicene council, their names alone (Aristakes, who is said to have been the son of Gregory the Illuminator, and Akrites) being mentioned, not their sees. Authentic statements by Armenian historians are not infrequent, and we can still make out the main facts. The headqiiarters of the Christian mission in Armenia during the third century, and (so far as the mission survived) during the fourth, were Caesarea in Cappadocia (with Sebaste in Armenia

Tovtots wpoaeiravia'Tatai Tij5 rvpavvw 6 wphs 'Apfxivlovs ir6 e)xos, vspas 6 apxaiov (p'lkovs re koi avjxfiaxovs 'Pooulaicov, ovs koi avrovs Xpiariavoiis ovras koi T7)v els rh Quov iixre fiav Sia cnrovsris iroiovjj. evovi 6 dio jlicrrjs flsu ots Oveiv koi haifiofftv itTavaykacrai ireirfipanevos ix P' " avrl pi cov koi troxefxiovs oliti o'li uax' "' KOT6(rt7j(rato.

Both names are Armenian, Grecized.

It is uncertain, and indeed unlikely, that Aschtischat was the permanent location of Gregory and his successor Aristakes.

' Cp. Gelzer in Prol J? ea-Â ncykJ- ii. pp. 74 f., and also his essay on "The Beginnings of the Armenian Church" Berichte d. k. Sachs. Gesellsch. d. IFissensck., 4th May 1895); Weber, Die kathol. Kirche in Armenien, ihr Begriindung u. Entiuicklung vor der Trenmins; (1903); Ter Mikelian, Die armenische Kirche in ihrer Beziehung zitr byzaniinischcn (1892); and Erwand Ter-Minassiantz on "The Armenian Church in its relations to the Syrian Churches, down to the end of the Thirteenth Century" (Texe u. Untersuch., xxvi. 4, 1904). Gutschmid Kleine Schrifteit, iii. pp. 339 f.) had already proved, in his study of Agathangeliis, that a considerable and coherent legend can be disentangled from the story of king Trdal and St Gregory, and that the incorporated story of the conversion of Armenia and of the succeeding period is trustworthy. The history of Faustus of Byzantium is a good source for the fourth century.

' How strong and far-spread Christianity must have been in Armenia Minor and Cappadocia and the neighbouring provinces at the close of the third century,

Minor) and Edessa (cp. the reception of Thaddaeus, and the Abgar legend), " nien Antioch and perhaps Nisibis as well (cp. Marquardt, Zeits. deutsch. morgenl. Geselkch., 1895, p. 651). As a result of this, the Armenians got both Greek and Syrian Christianity, as well as the literature of both these peoples (although all the literature that could come to them from Syria consisted in the main of translations from the Greek). In one or two districts of Armenia, Syriac even became for a time j the ecclesiastical language. The great missionary, or rather the ' ' great church-founder, of Armenia was Gregory the Illuminator, y-i who had fled before the Persians from his native land. He a may have been of high rank, even of royal descent. HeycA ' y adopted Christianity (i. e., Greek Christianity) in Caesarea. On r yjy the Persian yoke being flung oft' by the Armenians, Gregory 'tjr–stood by the king (Trdat, 261-317), who was only hostile to i 7X- Â Christianity at the outset; and Christianity, preached in the vernacular, was set up against the hateful and imported Persian when the Armenian monarch resolved to elevate it to the position of the state-religion in his country!

According to Faustus of Byzantium, Gregory the Illuminator was in Sebaste, and persuaded many of the brethren to accompany him to Armenia in order to preach the gospel. The local Christians were Greeks, not Syrians (cp. above).

â It baffles me to know how far individual Syrian-Edessene missionaries (cp. Bardesanes and perhaps Meruzanes) had laboured before Gregory in S. E. Armenia, and possibly founded bishoprics with native bishops. Gregory did not work exclusively with Greeks as missionaries. He employed Syrians as well. Daniel, the Syrian ascetic, must have been very prominent among them; he laboured in the district of Taron, and almost rivalled Gregory's fame and influence. Faustus of Byzantium calls him " the old, holy, and great chor-episcopus, Daniel." Probably he disseminated Christianity before Gregory, who then made common cause with him. The strong influence of the Syrian church on Armenia is shown partly by the translations from Syriac, partly by the fact that the Syrians afterwards secured high office in the church, and that their language for a while almost threatened to become the language of the church. But we know no particulars about the rivalry of the Greek and Syrian influences in the early period.

The Armenians afterwards identified him with the man (Gregory?) who wrote to Aphraates and received the latter's homilies by way of answer (the letter is printed in the introduction to the Homilies; cp. Texte u. Unters., iii. 3-4, pp. I f., xxi. f.); but chronological reasons alone make the identification impossible.

â Armenia was a feudal state, with a strong aristocracy and a wealthy priesthood.

) 02 MISSION AND EXPANSION OF CHRISTIANITY -wjorship of fire. As an exclusive religion it was far better adapted than the cults of Hellenism and the native Armenian faith to safeguard the Armenians against the Persians, By the help of the nobility against the priesthood, the country was systematically and vigorously Christianized. The temple-worship was overthrown. The temple property was made over to the churches. And, by desire of the king (so we are told), Gregory was escorted by a brilliant retinue of Armenian feudal lords on his journey to Caesarea, where Leontiusâ the bishop who attended the Nicene councilâ consecrated him as Catholicus of Armenia. Caesarea remained a soit of metropolis for Ai menia down to the last quarter of the fourth century. The most sacred sanctuary of the kingdom was destroyed at Aschtis chat, and the chief church of Armenia, the mother-ch ch of the country, was erected. Bagravan in Bagrevand then became a second, but inferior centre. Gregory himself, however, apparently did not reside at Aschtischat, which was the seat of Daniel. Perhaps the archbishop had at first no definite centre. Twelve bishoprics it is said, were instituted by Gregory, after the work of conversion had been forcibly carried

"This was intended to create a counterweight to the dominant power of the nobihty, which was crushing the royal power. Under Trdat and his son Chosrow this pohcy was attended with decided success" (Gelzer, p. 133). But there were pagan reactions and insurrections. The women of the upper classes were especially devoted to the old faith, e.Â:, Chosrow's own wife and also the mother of king Pap.

- The civil position and powers of Csesarea in relation to Armenia are obscure. They cannot have been strictly defined. Even Gregory's ordination by Leontius is not indisputable (cp., however, Gelzer, p. 165, against tlie scepticism of Gutschmid), while Aristakes was not consecrated catholicus in Caesarea. He was set apart by his father Gregory. The subsequent patriarchs, down to Narses, however, were all consecrated in Csesarea. Then came the rupture, under king Pap and the catholici of the house of Albianus. The political independence of the country must have prevented Csesarea from becoming metropolis of Armenia in the strict sense of the term.

Aschtischat was in the territory of Taron.â The tradition that Gregory was led by a vision of Christ to make Valarschapat, the old royal town (afterwards Etschmiadzin), the headquarters of the church, probably dates from a later age (in Agathangelus it occurs in a section which Gutschmid recognizes to be an apocalyptic fragment from the middle of the fifth century). It is a tendency-legend, designed to prove the autocephalous and independent character of the Armenian church of Csesarea. Aschtischat in the south was, according to Faustus, " the great original church, the mother of all the Armenian churches in through. An d all this was accomplished by the very begin-ningofjtha fourth century (Gregory's consecration took place c. 285-290), By the time the council of Nicaea met, Gregory had died, and (Aristakes) his son, previously an anchorite in Cappadocia, had succeeded him. For the distinctive character of the original Armenian Christianity, which was quite different from the later catholic Christianity of " the golden age" (founded by Narses), cp. below, under " Diospontus."

The wide spread of Christianit y in Fontus about the year 170 is attested by Lucian Alex. A bun., 25. 38), who writes that "the whole country is full of atheists and Christians." Here (including Paphlagonia as well) there were a number of churches, during the reigns of M. Aurelius and Commodus, which had a metropolitan resident in Ainastris. This follows from the letter of Dionysius of Corinth addressed to them (in Eus., H. E., iv. 23: t; ekKXrja-la rrj irapoikOvcnj ' Amacrtptv ajiia rai Kara lXovroi), and from the part taken by the Pontic church in the Easter controversy (ibid., v. 23: a writing Tcov Kata Hoi'Tov etTLakOTrwv, wv Ilax ca? w? apxaioTatO TrpovrerakTo). Of the local churches, we know Pompeiopolis and Ionopolis, whose bishops, together with the bishop of Amastris attended the Nicene council. There was certainly a district of Taron," " the first, the most eminent, and the chief seat of worship, since here a holy church was first of all built and an altar erected in the name of the Lord." Thus it is called "the chief altar, the princely throne of the patriarchs " with the local saints John the Baptist and Athenogenes, whose relics Gregory had brought from Cappadocian Csesarea. Here, in this southern town, the first provincial synods of Armenia were also held. The centre of gravity of the country then lay in the south, where king Tiran (326-337), the successor of Chosrow (317-326), was particularly fond of staying. It is possible, however, that Faustus has exaggerated the importance of Aschtischat, owing to his partiality for the town.

' Or were there not so much twelve bishoprics as twelve bishops who were constantly with the catholicus? The complete organization of the Armenian church does not go back to Gregory, but he certainly founded some bishoprics.

- The dignity of catholicus (as the Christian high-priest, who enjoyed royal honours) belonged to the family of Gregory. These high-priests were therefore married mea, though this was not always the case. The grandsons of Gregory succeeded to the throne when they were still boys. The Armenian bishoprics were frequently hereditary even in other cases.

The names are naturally Greek: Philadelphus, Petronius, and Eupsychius.

chui'ch at Gangra, too, about 325 a. d.; for, as the town had a metropolitan circa 350 a. d., it cannot have been entirely pagan some twenty-five years earher. Hippolytus (Comm. in Dan., p. 232 f., ed. Bonwetsch) has preserved for us one episode from the history of Christianity in Pontus, an episode which reminds us very strongly of the incident of the prophetess in Cappadocia and of the Montanist movement in Phrygia, and which proves at the same time how readily the Chiistian population of Asia Minor were disposed to take up with such fanatical movements. Unfortunately he does not name the town whose bishop enacted the movement in question. The Novatians were particularly numerous in Paphlagonia (see ' It was only by accident, therefore, that the bishop was absent from Nicaea. The synod held at Gangra in 343 a. d. (cp. Braun in His, airi. Gorres. Gesell., vol. xvi., 1895, pp. 5S6 f.) mentions, in its communication to the Armenian bishops, thirteen members of that synod, giving their names but unfortunately not their sees. Even the names have not been accurately transmitted to us. The monastic movement which the bishops censured was in opposition to the popular semi-pagan Christianity which had shot up to a rank growth especially in Pontus, Armenia Minor, and Armenia Major. The movement was also directed against the cult of the martyrs and the festivals of the martyrs (can. 20), which were particularly popular in these districts as a substitute for the pagan cultus.

"Erepos TLS dfxoiais iv rcji Tlsvrcf Koi alrhs irpotcrrccs ekK r (rias, evka rjs j-fv avijp Kal Tatrâ tv6((pciu, furi irpocrext i' 5e aacpaactis rats ypapa7s, awa to7s opdfiacriv ols avrhs kwpa fxawov iiriarevev. eirituxcor yap ip iv Ktxi Seutepcfj Kal Tpiro) ivvki'icfj, fjp atO onrhv irpoxeyeiv to7s ase (pots iis irpo(pt)rrjs ' Tose elsov Kal rsSe jlewei yivtadai, kou 8); irore irxav7)dels elirev ' yivciffkert, asexcpol, ori fxera iyiavthv r Kpiffis fiewei yiveaoai. ol Se akovcravres aiirov itpo (yovtos, ws '6ti iveffrrikev i) Tjfxepa rod Kvpiov, xera KXavdfjldiv Kal odvpficov iseovtO tov Kvpiov jvkrhs Koi T ji. epas irph (Xpdakfxsiv fx"'''''' '''V" etrfpxofj-evriv rrjs Kpicrecos rjfjapav. Kal eis TOffovtov yayev d6 os kox Sei ia roiis ahekcpovs, Surre eacrai aircov ras x' P"- 'f roxis aypovs ipi)fi. ovs, to. re KTr fxara avrwv ot Traei'ous Kateirwkriaav. 6 5e e rj avrols ' iav yuTj yfvrjrai Kadats iiirov, xtjceti xijse to? s ypacpals Trjtrtei fftjte, awa iroieltoi ikaaros vp. wv h fiovkerai. at Se ypapal ecpdvqffav axridevovaat, ol Se ase pol evpedriffav ffkavsaxt jxevot, Siffte Koiirhv Tas irapdevovs avrtov yrjjlai Kal Tovs 6. vdpas eirl r-qv ytoipyiav; a)p o'ai â ot Se etwp ra eavtwv KTrixara Troikiiffavtes evpfd-qaav vimpov iiraitovvtes ("Likewise was it with another one in Pontus, himself a leader of the church, who was pious and humble-minded but did not adhere close enough to the Scriptures, giving more credit to visions which he saw. For, chancing to have three dreams, one after another, he proceeded to address the brethren as a prophet, saying, 'I saw this," ' This will come to pass." Then on being proved wrong he said, ' Know, my brethren, that the judgment will take place after the space of one year." So, when they heard his address, how that 'the day of the Lord is at hand," with tears and cries they besought the Lord night and day, having before their eyes the imminent day of judgment. And to

Socrat., ii. 38), and they had regular churches. They were strongest in Mantinium.

Three bishops from Diospontus attended Nicaea, from Amasia and Comana and Zela. The last-named was also present at the synod of Ancyra in 314. Amasia even in the days of Gregory Thaumaturgus (circa 240 a. d.), was an episcopal see and the metropolis of Diospontus, while Comana had got a bishop from Gregory (cp. Gregory of Nyssa; Vita Gregorii, c. 19 f.). The church of Sinope in Diospontus was founded as early as the beginning of the second century. Marcion (cp. p. 188) came from there, and it is obvious from the account of the exceptionally keen persecution of Licinius (Vit. Const., ii. 1. 2; Il. E., X. 8. 15, "Amasia and the rest of the churches in Pontus") that there were several episcopal churches in Diospontus before 325 a. d. Two of these we know, Amisus (cp. above, p. 92) and Sebastopol. The Meletius mentioned by Eusebius at the end of the seventh book of his History with such praise, as a Pontic bishop, was bishop of Sebastopol, according to Philostorgius (i. 8). The latter is probably wrong, however, in declaring that Meletius was at Nicaea. The list of members does not mention him.

The life of Gregory Thaumaturgus, which has just been mentioned, is thrown by its author, Gregory of Nyssa, into the such a pitch were the brethren worked up by fear and terror, that they deserted their fields and lands being evidently a country church, most of them selling off their property. Then said he to them, 'If it does not happen as I have said, never trust the Scriptures again, but let each of you live as he likes." The year, however, passed without the prophesied event occurring. The proph. et. was proved to be a liar, but the Scriptures were shown to be true, and the brethren found themselves stumbling and scandalized. So that afterwards their maidens married and the men went back to their husbandry, while those who had sold off their goods in haste were ultimately found begging ").

This place, so far as I know, is unidentified.

- Eutychianus, Elpidius, and Heraclius.

â "All the citizens" of Comana are alleged to have besought Gregory to establish a church. He gave them Alexander, a philosopher and ascetic, for a bishop. An " episcopus Comanorum" is said by Palladius to have been martyred along with Lucian at Nicomedia (Ruinart, p. 529).

Sinope was a town with Roman civic rights.â Aquila, Paul's friend and coadjutor, was a Pontic Jew who had settled at Rome and been converted.

form of an oration; but it supplies us with some excellent information upon the Christianizing of the western part of Pontus Polemoniacus, and at the same time with an extremely instructive sketch of the way in which the mission was carried out, and of how paganism was "overcome"â i. e., absorbed.

Gregory, the Worker of Wonders, was born of pagan parents in Neo-C sarea, but was converted by Origen. Striking up a fast fr endÂ hip with Firmilian of Cappadocia, he returned to his native place and was consecrated bishop of Neo-Caesarea about 240 a. d. by Phaedimus, the bishop of Amasia. At that time there were said to be only seventeen Christians in the town and its environs. When he died (shortly before 270 a. d.) jjj only the same number of pagans are said to have been counted o," within the town.- Certainly the Chi'istianizing of the town and (f country was carried out most completely. Gregory himself (Epist. Canon. 7) uses YiqvtLKol Kat picmai'OL as a hendiadys, in contrast to the barbarian pagan Goths. This acute and energetic bishop succeeded because he set up Christian-miracles in opposition to those of paganism, because he had the courage to expose the cunning and trickery of the pagan priests, and because he let the rude multitude enjoy their festivals stilly in Christian guise. " The preaching of the gospel made its way in all directions, the doctrine of mysteries operated powerfully, and the aspiration for what was good increased, as the priesthood got introduced in every quarter." As was customary in the country, Gregory held assemblies in the open air. During the Decian persecution, " as that great man understood well the frailty of human nature, recognizing that the majority

Migne, vol. xlvi. pp. S93 f.; cp. also Rufinus' Church History (vii. 25), the Syriac "Narrative of Gregory's exploits," and Basil, de Spiritu, Ixxiv.

2 " Gregory carefully explored, not long before he died, the whole of the surrounding country, to find out if there were any who had not accepted the faith. On discovering that there were not more than seventeen, he thanked God that he had left his successor as many idolaters as he had found Christians when he himself began." Basil loc. cit.) says he converted the entire nation, not only in the cities but in the country.

Atheaodorus also took part in the work. He was Gregory's brother, and bishop of some unknown place in Pontus.

Mary and John appeared to him, and he turned such visions to good account. So far as I know, this is the first c sof a vision of the Virgin in the church.

CHRISTIANITY DOWN TO 325 A. D. 207 were incapable of contending for their religion unto death, his counsel was that the church might execute some kind of retreat 1(4 A before the Jierce persecution."' He fled himself. " After the- a persecution was over, when it was permissible to address oneself y-J' "

to Christian worship with unrestricted zeal, he a gain returned kjjj to the citj, and, by travelling over all the surrounding country, v increased the people's ardour for worship in all the churches by holding a solemn commemoration in honour of those who had contended for the faith. Here one brought corpses of the martyrs, there another. So much so, that the assemblies went on for the space of a whole year, the people rejoicing in the celebration of festivals in honour of the martyrs. This also was one proof of his great sagacity, viz., that while he completely altered the direction of everyone's life in his own day, turning them into a new course altogether, and harnessing them firmly to faith and to the hnoxvledge of God, he slightly lessened the strain upon those ivho had accepted the yoke of the faith, in order to let them enjoy good cheer in life. For, as he saw that the raw and ignorant multitiide adhered to idols on accotmt of bodily pie assures, he permitted the people â so as to secure the most vital matters, i. e., the direction of their hearts to God instead of to a vain worshipâ permitted them to enjoy themselves at the commemoration of the holy martyrs, to take their ease, and to amuse themselves, since life would become more serious and earnest naturally in process of time, as the Christian faith came to assume more control of it."'" Gregory is the sole missionary we know of, during these first three centuries, who employed such methods; and he was a highly educated Greek. If such things could occur in the

On the blending of religions in Asia, cp. also Texfe u. Unters., N.!"., iv. i (Marutas, pp. ii f.)â Gregory's exploits and testimony were subsequently extended by Theodoret to the church at large Grcec. affect, curat., viii. yfw., opp. ed. Schulze, iv. pp. 923 f.), but without any of Gregory's naivete and without his naive attitude towards the festivals: ra fx v yap fkeiucov iravtexws Siexvori rexevr, iis fj. T Se (rx'Â 7M"Ta)j' Staxelyat rh elsos, fxTise rwv Ujxwv rhv tvkov tovs vw avbpdirovs eiriataadat ' ai 5f tovtohv v ai Kaowirtcodriffav rots twp xaprvpccv CTjcois. roiis yap olkeiovs vekpoiis 6 Sâ (Tw6Tr s avrelarj e tois ifxerepois Oeots ' Kal tovs juec (ppovsovs aireprive, rovrois 8e rci ikilvuv aireveine yepa. avt yap 5 tuv Tlav ioov Kol Aiaaicev Ka Aiovvffwv koi tsv Wwv vjxwv hoprwv Vlerpov Kal Tlavxov Kal Â cu S Kal epyiov Kal Mapkewov Kal Aeovriov Kal UavteketJuouos Kal 'Aytaivivov koi Mavpikiov koi rsiv Wo3v fiaptvpcav eirireaovvrat S-qfiodoivlai, Kal avrl rrjs wdkai green tree, what must be expected from the dry? The cult of themartyrs, with its frenzied pagan joy in festivals, took the place of the old local cults, and the old fetishes were succeeded by the relics of the saints (cp. Lucius, Die Anfdnge d. christl. Heiligenkultiis 1904). Undoubtedly the method proved an extraordinary success. The country became Christian. A sphere which had been overlooked at the outset of the mission rapidly made up lost ground, and the country ranked along with the provinces of Asia Minor, which had been Christianized at an earlier period, as substantially Christian.

Gregory the Illuminator obviously copied, in the neighbouring regioiis'of Armenia Major, the missionary methods of Gregory Thaumaturgus and this new, wild growth of Pontic Christianity (the reaction against it, as we have seen, being due to Eustathius of Sebaste). What we know of the earliest Armeftiaxi Christianity tallies entirely with that of Neo-Caesarea. Asqhtischat and Bagravan possessed relics of Gregory; they had even a festival (Gelzer, p. 128) of their own. The great church of Christ in Aschtischat assumed the place and position of the ruined pagan shrine (cp. p. 156);

TTOfxTreias Koi alctXpovpyias Kol al(TXpopprifjLOTvvi s ffwcjipoves eoprd ovrai Travrfyvpets (" For the glebes of those idols were utterly destroyed, so that not even the very form of their statues remains, nor do people of this age know the shape of the altars. Their graves were also devoted to the sepulchres of the martyrs. For the proprietor substituted the corpses of his own family for your gods, showing plainly that the latter were gone, and conferring on the former the honours which had pertained to their predecessors. For instead of the Pandia, Diasia, Dionysia, and the rest of your festivals, the feasts of Peter, Paul, Thomas, Sergius, Marcellus, Leontius, Panteleemon, Antoninus, Mauricius, and the other martyrs are celebrated; and instead of the former ribaldry, obscenity, and foul language, orderly assemblies now keep feast"). Cp. also pp. 921 f., where the martyrs, in all emergencies (and Theodoret enumerates dozens of cases: unproductiveness, dangers in travel, etc.), appear as semi-divine helpers who are to be invoked. Perhaps, too, we should see the acceptance of a pagan custom in the statements oi Aca Archel. ii., where a Christian explains the following custom to the Christians of his own country, near Edessa: "Est nobis mos huiusmodi patrum nostrorum in nos traditione descendens, quique a nobis observatus est usque ad hunc diem: per annos singulos extra urbem egressi una cum conjugibus ac liberis supplicamus soli et invisibili deo, imbres ab eo satis nostris et frugibus obsecrantes" ("Our fathers had a custom of this kind, which has come down to us and which we still observe: every year we all go outside the city, with our wives and children, to pray to the one, invisible God, and to beseech him for enough rain for ourselves and our crops"). The sequel shows that they fasted'and spent the night there.

it became the sacred centre of " Christian" Armenia. The feast of the local saints, John the Baptist and Athenogenes, which Gregory had ordered to be kept on the 7th of Sahmi every year, was one of the greatest in Armenia. " Such was the custom of the archbishops of Armenia, in common with the kings, the magnates, the bishops, and the populace, to venerate the places which had previously harboured images of the idols and were now sanctified in the name of the Deity, having become a house of prayer and a place for vows. They assembled especially at this the main centre of the church, in memory of the saints who slept there, and offered sacrifice to them seven times a year'"" (Faustus of Byzantium, iii. 3. p. 7;

Gelzer, p. 130). "Pagan customs, especially the disorderly one of wailing for thi ead, which the clergy strenuously opposed they were even against the festivals of the martyrs, also prevailed in the succeeding age. Even about 378, the

Mamiconians deposited the body of their head, Muschel, on the top of a tower, with the words, ' Because he was a valiant man, the Arlads emerge and raise him'" (Faustus, v. 36.

p. 245; Gelzer, pp. 33 f.). Indeed, between 290 and 370, while

Christianity in Armeniar-Avas-the state-religion, the masses at bottom declined to know anything about " this deception of humanity"" (such was the language used even under king Tiran, 326-337). The northern mounted tribes declared, just like the

Kurds of the present day, "If we do not rob or plunder and seize other people's property, how are we to live, with all our innumerable hosts?" (Faustus, iii. 6; Gelzer, p. 135). By means of a latitudinarianism unexampled elsewhere in the primitive history of missions, an attemptwas made to adapt the new religion to their tastes. The attempt did not succeed.

Here, as elsewhere, it is evident that the mo nasti c, catholic

Christianity, as that deyelpped even in Armenia after the close of the fourth century, was the first thing to win the nation for the Lofi Câ In 315 (or thereabouts) a large synod was held

Cp. Routh, Reliq. Sacrce ", iv. pp. 179 f. The legislation restricting the powers of the chor-episcopi (and chor-priests), which had begun shortly before at Ancyra (see below), was carried forward at Neo-Csesarea (cp. the 13th canon). Some of the bishops who attended Ancyra (314 A. D.) were also at this synod, together with two Cappadocian chor-episcopi. Their names possess no interest.

VOL. ji, at Neo-Caesarea, the capital of Eastern Pontus, under the presidency of bishop Longinus. Its Acts are extant. It set itself the task of determining certain cardinal features of the cathohc discipline, in view of loose and disorderly practices. Christianity had also made its way into the Greek seaports of Eastern Pontus Polemoniacus by 325 a. d. Bishop Domnus of Trapezus, and even bishop Stratophilus from far-away Pityus, were at T icaea. As their names signify, they were Greeks. Christianity had also got the length of the North Armenians and the Iberians (Georgians and Albanians) by about 300 a. d., preceded by Judaism. It spread thither from the above-named cities, from Armenia, and finally, across Armenia from Syria (cp. Theodoret, H. E., i. 23). A graiidsoil of. Gregor y the Illuminator, himself called Gregory, became catholicus oÂ Â he Iberians and the Albaniansâ for in Iberia and Albania the holder of the supreme clerical office was also called the " catholicus."" He attained to this position at the age of fifteen, " because he was already mature and had the knowledge of God in him." I have before me a manuscript history, in German, of the Georgians (by Prince Dschawachoff, 1902), which shows that Christianity was established there by the beginning of the fourth century, and the country organized ecclesiastically not long afterwards. The rivalry, ov rather the enmity, between the Georgians and Armenians was always keen. Consecjuently the church of Georgia gravitated more and more to the Western church of Constantinople. Ere long it approximated more closely to the Greek than to the Armenian church.

C. BrihYNIA

After we pass the first epistle of Peter and the authentic and surprising testimony furnished by Plinj to the wide diffusion of Christianity in this province (see above), which was wholly Hellenized in the imperial age, we practically come upon no further traces of it till the age of Diocletian. All we know is

Socrates (i. 20) and Sozomen (ii. 7) furnish an account of the conversion of Iberia, which is pure legend. But the fact and the date of the conversion are correct.

that Dionysius of Corinth addressed a letter to the church of Nicomedia, evidently it was the capital) about 170 a. d., warning it against the heresy of Marcion (cp. Eus., H. E. iv. 24), and also that Origen s pent some time here Ep. Or'ig. ad Jul. Afric.) about the year 240 a. d. The outbreak of Diocletian's persecution, however, reveals Nicomedia as a semi-Christian city, the imperial court itself being full of Christians."- From the very numerous martyrdoms, as well as, above all, from the history of Nicomedia duringthe age of Constantine and his sons (the historical source here being quite trustworthy and ample), we are warranted in holding that this metropolis must have been a centre of the church. The calendar of the majority of churches goes back to"the festal calendar of the church of Nicomedia. And what holds true of the capital, holds true of the towns throughout the province; all were most vigorously Christianized. Constantine located his new capital at Constantinople, for the express reason that the opposite province was so rich in Christians, while the same consideration dictated without doubt the choice of Nicaea as the meeting-place of the famous council.

Cp. my Chronologie, ii. p. 34.

Maximinus Daza, in a rescript (Eus., H. E., ix. 9. 17), also testifies to the very large number of Christians in Nicomedia and the province of Bithynia: MstCt 5e Tacra, 8tâ to) irapfxQovti eviavrcfi ivT jx s iirefiriv fls t v HikOfx Sfiav. eyvqiv Trkiifftovs ttis out s dprja-Kelas vspas iv avrois tois fj-epecnv olkiiv (" Afterwards, when I went up last year to Nicomedia, I found that a large number of people belonging to this religion resided in these regions"). I may point out also that both of the contemporary writers who attacked Christianity appeared in Bithynia; cp. Lactantius, Inst., v. 2, "Ego cum in Bithynia oratorias litteras accitus docerem,. duo exstiterunt ibidem, qui jacenti et abjectae veritati insultarent" (" When I was teaching rhetoric in Bithynia, by invitation, two men were there, who trampled down the truth as it lay prostrate and low "). The one was Hierocles, but the other's name is not given.

â This has been demonstrated by Duchesne with regard to the ancient Syriac Martyrologium, which is the Martyrologium of the church of Nicomedia (in the days of Arius). It includes "ancient" Byzantine martyrs, i. e., from the pre-Diocletian period. Under Diocletian, Anthimus suffered martyrdom. He was bishop of Nicomedia (cp. Eus., H. E., viii. 6. 13, and Lucian's epistle to the Antiochenes in Chron. Pasch., p. 277). The large and important â fragment bearing his name, which Mercati has published Studi e Testi, v., 1901, pp. 87 f.), is not authentic (cp. my Chronologie, ii. pp. 158 f.). It is doubtful if Anthimus was an author at all. But in the martyr-Acts of Domna and Inda (Migne, Gr. Tom., 116. p. 1073, cp. 1076 A) a letter of his is mentioned, full of kindly encouragement, which he wrote during his concealment in a village.

212 MISSION AND EXPANSION OF CHRISTIANITY

At the same time, apart from Nicomedia, not a single Christian community in Bithjnia is heard of before the great persecution, i. e., before 325 a. d. No Christian writer mentions any. The reason for this, however, is that no prominent bishop or author was vouchsafed to that country before the days of Eusebius of Nicomedia. The council of Nicaea testifies to the existence of episcopal churches at the towns of Nicaea, Chalcedon, Kius, Prusa, Apollonia, Prusias, Adriani, and Caesarea, besides Nicomedia itself. In the country, also, there were episcopal churches, as is shown by the presence of two chor-episcopi (Theophanes and Eulalius) at Nicaea. The Novatians had numerous churches also in Bithynia (on the Hellespont), at Nicomedia (cp. Socrat,, i. 13, iv, 28) and Nicaea (ibid., iv. 28, vii. 12. 25), etc. (cp. v. 22); and a famous Novatian recluse, Eutychianus, stayed at Mount Olympus in the days of Con-stantine (Soz., i. 14).

D. Galatia, Phrygia, and Pisidia (with Lycaonia)

In their Christian capacity these central provinces of Asia Minor, whose boundaries or titles were frequently altered, had a common history, although S. W. Phrygia gravitated

If, however, as is highly probable, "Apamea" is to be read for " Aprima" in the Acfa Tryphonis et Respicii (Ruinart's Acta Mart., Ratisbon, 1859, pp. 208 f.), we must presuppose a Christian church at Apamea (Bithynia), a town with Roman civic rightsâ though these two saints came not from the town itself but "de Apameae finibus de Sansoro Campsade? vico" (from the borders of Apamea, from a village called Sansorus). There was also a Christian community at Drepana (= Helenopolis), which had a church of the martyrs Vii. Const., iv. 61).

Before he became bishop of Nicomedia, he had been bishop of Berytus in Phoenicia. He was a friend of Arius, and a pupil of Lucian. He was also distantly connected with the royal family (Amm. Marcell., xxii. 9).

â " Local martyrdoms are reported, as at Nicaea. Both Apollonia and Adriani are also assigned to Mysia.

Their names are: Eusebius, Theognius, Maris, Cyril, Hesychius, Gorgonius, Georgius, Euethius, and Rufus.â From the ita Const., iv. 43, it is plain that the number of the bishoprics was large.

The names of Phrygia and Galatia were often employed in a broader or a narrower sense, without any regard to the legal and current political divisions. I refrain here from entering into the question of what " Galatia" means in Paul and elsewhere. Renan, Hausrath, Ramsay, Zahn, J. Weiss, and many others hold that towards Asia. The Montanist movement, which arose in Phrygia proper, and, blending with the Novatian movement, forthwith became national, was particularly characteristic of these provinces. The Phrygian character shows a peculiar mixture of wild enthusiasm and serjQUsness. Thus So g gies, who was favourable to them, writes (H. E. y iv. 28): alveral Tu pvyoav eourj cruxppovecrtepa elvai tcou awcou eovoov' kui yap Sr Kat (nraviakK pvye ofxvuovcriu' etrikparei yap to fxev OujuLikOv irapa Kvoai Kai Opa i, rip Se etTioufxrjtikO) ol ttoo? avicrxovta i'fkiov Tt i o'lkfjcriv k'xpvre irxeov Sov euov(Ti' tu Se lla(pi ay6v(jou kui pvycou edvtj 7roo9 ovserepov tovtoov iirippetrcog e'xei' ovse yap LTnrospout. iai ovse Oeutpa (JTrovsa ovrai vvv Trap' aut0i9. (Of fxvcros e alariov irap avtol rj Tropve'ia vojui erai' Kai yap olacrsi'itrote axXr aipecrecog cr(af)povejTepov lovvra? pvya? Ka). Hacpxayovag ecrriv evpeiv ("The Phrygians appear to be more temperate than other nations. They swear but seldom. Whereas the Scythians and the Thracians are naturally of a passionate disposition, whilst the inhabitants of the East are prone by nature to sensuality. The Paphlagonians and Phrygians, on the other hand, are not inclined to either it included Pisidia, Lycaonia, and Isauria. This is denied, especially by Schiirer. But there are strong reasons for thinking that the former scholars are right. Galatia, in the narrower sense of the term, was ethnographically a province by itself, while Phrygia ethnographically embraced Pisidia and large sections of Lycaonia. Iconium was a Phrygian town, and the Lycaonian language which Paul heard at Lystra (Acts xiv. ii) was probably Phrygian.

The epistle of the churches at Lyons and Vienne (177178), which describes their sufferings, is addressed to the churches of Asia and Phrygia. We may perhaps assume that Phrygia here means simply the south-west section.

The inhabitants of Phrygia, even in the second century, were decried, together with the Carians, as barbarians. Cp. Justin's Â m, cxix.: ovk (UKata(pp6vntos Srjfiss efffiiv ov5i apfiapov 4v ov ovde onola. Kapwv pvyoiv edirj. So even Homer's Iliad, ii. 867 (Kapij' 77j(rato ap apop(ivuv) and the adage quoted by Cicero in Pro Flacco, 27: " Phrygem plagis fieri solere meliorem."

Wherever the movement spread throughout the empire, it was known as the "Pl rygian" or Cataphrygian movement. There was a Montanist-Novatian church intHrygia, with numerous branches, in the fourth century (Socrat., iv. 28, V. 22, etc.).

According to Theodoret, Hczr. Fab., iii. 6, Montanism was not accepted by Pontus Polemoniacus, Helenopontus, Armenia, Cappadocia, Lycaonia, Pisidia, Pamphylia, Lycia, and Caria. This means that there were no longer any Montanists there when Theodoret wrote, so that probably they must have been always few in numbers in these countries, with the exception of Pisidia, of these vices, nor are the circus and theatre in vogue with them at the present day. As for fornication, they reckon that a gross enormity'"). The Phrygians described here were already Christians. Their wild religious enthusiasm was restrained, but the seriousness remained. Before Mqiitanus was converted, ho had been a priest of Cybele. Movements such as that initiated by him had occurred, as we have seen, in Cappadocia and Pontus; but Montanus and his prophetesses knew how to make their movement both effective and permanent, supplying it at once with a firm organization. In these inland parts primitive Christianity survived longer than elsewhere. I W The third century still furnishes us with instances of (non-clerical) j teachers, as well as prophets, being drawn from the ranks of the "" y laity; and in a letter written cijra 218 by Alexander of Jeru-"" ' ' salem and Theoktistus of Caesarea, in connection with the case of Origen, we read that " Wherever people able to profit the brethren can be found, they are exhorted by the holy bishops to address the people; as, for example, Euelpis in Laranda (Isauria) by Neon, Paulinus in Iconium (Pisidia) by Celsus, and Theodorus by Atticus in Synnada (Phrygia), all of whom are our blessed brethren. Probably this has also been done in other places unknown to us ' brrov cupicrkovrai ol etritrjseioi 7rj0O9 TO wipexeiv roiv? dsekcpov, Kai rrapakoxowtai tw aui irpoaoixixelv viro to v aymv eirictKO'Troov, cocnrep ev Aapavsoi Eiea,7ri9 VTTO Ne'covo? koi iv 'Ikoviw Havxivos viro excrov Kat ev 2wja 0i9 Geo(56t)po9 viro Attikov tciov nakapicov asexcpwv. eikOs Se KOI ev axXoi tottoi? tovto yiveaoai, tjjuag Se fxt eisevai}. Lay-teachers like Euelpis, Paulinus, and Theodorus did not exist any longer in Palestine or Egypt;- as is plain from the Palestinian bishops having to go to the interior of Asia for examples of this practice.

Almost from the very hour of its rise, the Montanist movement indicates a very wide extension of Christianity throughout Phrygia and the neighbouring districts of Galatia;

The fanatical and wild Messalians emerged at a later period in Asia Minor.

2 But there were still SisattKaxoi in the Egyptian cantons, as Dionysius of Alexandria reports (Eus., . E., vii. 24).

â This passage cp. vol, i. p. 361 also is an excellent proof of how well known the chinches were to one another.

even in small localities Christians were to be met with. Our knowledge on this point has been enlarged during the last twenty years by Ramsay's thorough-going investigations of the whole country; thanks to his meritorious volumes, we are better acquainted with the extant inscriptions and the topography of Phrygia and Pisidia than with any other province in the interior of Asia Minor. We have learnt from them how widely Judaism and Christianity were diffused, locally, in the earliest periods, and we have been taught how to distinguish and make ourselves familiar (even inside Galatia and Phrygia) with those districts where Christianity found but a meagre access.

With great rapidity the Montanist movement flowed over into Galatia and Ancyra on the one side, and into Asia upon the other. The synods held by the church party, in order to defend themselves against the new prophets, were got up by churches belonging to the central provinces, and in fact were attended by representatives from the most distant quarters of the country (Eus., H. E., v. 19). A few decades afterwards, when these churches were agitated by the question of the validity of heretical baptism, large synods were held at Iconium and Synnada (between 230 and 235), attended by bishops from Phrygia, Galatia, Cilicia, and the rest of the neighbouring

The first village, known to us by name, which had a Christian community (by 170 A. D.) is Cumane in Phrygia. Pepuza and Tymion were also small centres.

2 Besides large volumes on The Historical Geography of Asia Minor, The Cities and Bishoprics of Phrygia, St Paid the Traveller and the Rotnan Citizen, and The Letters to the Seven Churches (1904), this scholar's recent works fall to be noticed, viz., Deux jours en Phrygie (reprinted from the Revue des itudes anciennes, 1902), Pisidia and the Lycaonian Frontier (reprinted from the Annual of the British School at Athens, No. 9, 1902-3), "'Lycs. onid " Jahreshefte d. osterreich. archdol. Instituts, vol. vii., 1904), Topography and Epigraphy of A ova Isaura (reprinted from ihe. Journal of Hellenic Studies, vol. xxv., 1905), and also Miss A. M. Ramsay's The Early Christian Art of Isaura Nova (reprinted from i ve Journal of Helle7iic Studies, xxiv., 1904). The sketch-maps appended to these volumes are particularly serviceable. What has elsewhere been achieved by the combined efforts and agencies of an academy, one man has achieved here single-handed.

Rafflsay, Phrygia, pp. 667 f.: " Akmonia, Sebaste, Eumeneia, Apameia, Dokimion, and Iconium are the cities where we can identify Jewish inscriptions, legends, and names."

The anti-Montanist (in Eus., v. if. 4) found the church of Ancyra quite carried away by Montanism.

5 Tliyatira fell entirely into their hanis (Epiph., Hir., li. 33).

provinces (Cappadocia). Firmilian and Dionys. Alex., who give some account of them, speak of numerous bishops, but they give no numbers. Aygus-tine, on the other hand, following some source which is unknown to us, declares that theie were fifty bishops at Iconium alone. Which is a remarkable number!

In the following pages I shall give a list of places in Galatia, Phrygia, and Pisidia where we know Christians were to be found.

Galatia:â

In this province, so poor in towns, Christianity was naturally as Hellenic in all essentials as in the neighbouring provinces, although the country lay " like a Celtic island in the flood of Eastern peoples." The internal political organization of the country remained Celtic for long (cp. the three divisions), but, from a religious point of view, the new inhabitants were first Phrygian and then Greek Christians. The Celtic names did not long survive the age of Tiberius, but the vernacular remained Celtic (cp. Pausanias, Lucian's Alecc. 51, and Jerome's Com. in Galat. ii. at the opening). Probably, however, a Celtic Christianity and a Celtic church never got beyond the embryonic stage. From Sozom. v. 16 (the epistle of Julian to Arsacius, the pagan high-priest of Galatia) we find that under Constantius there were many pagan priests in Galatia who had Christian wives, children, and slaves.

Ancyra, the metropolis and headquarters of the governor; cp. the anti-Montanist in Eus. v. 16, also the remark in Mart. Syr. "Ancyrae infantes qui de alvo matrum martyres

Cp. Firmilian (Cyp., Ep. Ixxv. 7, 19): " Quod totum nos iam pridem in Iconio, qui Phrygiac locus est, coueciti in unum convenientibus ex Galatia et Cilicia et ceteris proximis regionibus confirmavimus " ("All of which we have long since established in our common gathering at Iconium, a place in Phrygia, gathering from Galatia and Cilicia and the rest of the neighbouring provinces "); " Plurimi simul convenientes in Iconio diligentissime traclavimus" (" The majority of us have carefully handled this, gathering together in Iconium "). Dionys. Alex. (in Eus., vu. 7 â fj-ffj-adrika koi tovto, '6ti xt) vvv oi ev Afpp'ikrj fj.6vov rovro irapn-orriyayov, awa Koi irpo ttowov Kara tovs trph 7 ixuv ektffkOirovs ev Tors iroxvavopai-â jtOTarats ikK T criais koi tois (rw65ois rwv asekcpwi ev 'lkoui(f Kal vvydsois Kal TTOpa-irowo s tovto eso iv): "I also learnt that this was not a recent practice introduced by those in Africa alone, but that long ago, in the days of the bishops who were before us, it was resolved upon by the most populous churches, and by synods of the brethren at Iconium and Syrnada, and by many others."

facti sunt" (children at Ancyra who were martyred from their mother's womb). A large synod was held here in 314, whose Acts are still extant.

Malus (a village near Ancyra, t 9 Troxecog airwkLrrfxevov (TijfjLekiov fxikpov Trpo? Tectcrapakovta = " distant all but forty miles from the city," Acta Theod. x., etc.) seems to have been entirely Christian. Its small Christian community was managed by one pinesbyter, and remained unmolested during the persecution which raged in the metropolis. It is doubtful, however, whether the Acta can be trusted so far as to permit us to include this spot in our list (so with Medicones).

Medicones (a village near Ancyra, Acta Theod. x.; here also there seem to have been Christians).

Tavium (bishop Dicasius was at Nicaea).

Gadamaua Gdmaua==Ekdaumanaj (bishop Erechthius at Nicffia).

Kina? (bishop Gorgonius at Nicaea).

Cp. Routh, Reliq. Sacrp iv. pp. 113 f. Of the twenty-five canons of this synod, three bear specially on the history of the local expansion of Christianity, viz., the 13th, the 7th, and the 24th. The first contains regulations for the chor-episcopi, delimiting their powers (for the first time in their history), while the two latter prohibit pagan sacrificial feasts and all pagan superstitions (7: irepj Tojr (rvieffttaofjTwp iv eoptr iovikTj, iv T6ircji apuiptffij. fvcf tois 46viko7s, i5m 0pw-fiara iirikojuffafifvaiv Kal (paysvtooy evidently this was a protective custom!, e5o â Siitiau vtrotTeaovras Bf')(9r vai. 24: ol Kara i. a. i'TevsJ. ei'ot Kal tois trvvrjoiiais Tiiiv (dvsiv i ano ov6ovvres rj iiffdyovres rivas els rovs eavru'v oikovs ev) avivpecni (papixakeiwu f) koi Kaod-paei, k. t.). Eighteen or nineteen bishops signed these resolutions, viz., the bishops of Syrian Antioch, Ancyra, Cassarea (Cappad.), Tarsus, Amasia, Juliopolis (Gal.), Nicomedia, Zela (Pont.), Iconium, Laodicea (Phryg.), Antioch (Pisid.), Perga, Neronias, Epiphania, and Apamea (Syr.), though not all of these localities can be proved indubitably. Galatia, Syria, Cappa-docia, Cilicia, Diospontus, Bithynia, Pisidia, Phrygia, Paraphilia (perhaps Cyprus as well), were thus represented. The names are Greco-Latin: Vitalis, Marcellus, Agricolaus, Lupus, Basilius, Philadelphus, Eustolus, Heraclius, Petrus, Nunechius, Sergianus, Epidaurus, Narcissus, Leontius, Longinus, Amphion, Alphius, Selaus (?), and Germanus. The Marcellus of this list is the famous bishop of Ancyra, who made so effective an appearance at Nicaea. The picture of the church at Ancyra given by the Ac a Tieodoii ed. Franchi de Cavalieri, 1902, Rome) is instructive, though the Ac a themselves are unauthentic and quite legendary. They warn us against forming extravagant ideas of the size of the church. It was ruled by the huckster Theodotus. Apart from the local church or churches there were also two oratories, a fxaprvpiov tuv irarpiapx y and a fi. tsiv iratepoov (c. x6). Franchi has shown that the latter was probably a re-consecrated pagan shrine, and even the local saint Sosander (c. 19) may have been a re-consecrated hero.

Juliopolis (bishop Philadelphus was present at Ancyra in 314 A. D. and at Nicaea). Phrygia:â

Laodicea (the metropolis: cp, Paul's epistles, the martyrs, especially the famous bishop and martyr Sagaris cp. Poly-crates in Eus,, H. E. v. 24, the local controversy on the Paschal question, Melito in Eus., H. E., iv. 26. 3, and the council of Nicaea, where bishop Nunechius was present). Hierapolis (Paul; the evangelist Philip and his daughters; Papiast Apollinaris of Hierapohs; Eus., iii. 31, 36, 39, iv. 26, J V. 19, 24; bishop Flaccus at Nicaea). â fr Colossas (Paul).

(Otrus (Eus., H. E., v. 16).

w-;-â Hieropolis (inscriptions).

Pepuza (Eus., v. 18; a dated inscription of 260 A. n.; cp. Cumoht, op. cit., p. 36, No. 156; Philostorgius, iv. 8, mentions it as the place to which Aetius was banished). Its site is not absolutely certain; cp. Kiefert's latest map. Tymion = Dumanli? (Eus., v. 18). Ardabau (birthplace of Montanus; Eus., v. 16). Apamea Cibotus coins of the town with Noah's aric (Eus., V. 16; bishop Paulus at Nicaea).

It is surprising that the bishop of Pessinus (usually assigned to Galatia) is never mentioned at the synods of Ancyra or of Nicaea. Even otherwise the town is ignored in the early Christian literature. But it is clear from the epistle of the emperor Julian to Arsacius that the town was at that time extremely backward as regards the worship of the "Magna Mater"; i. e., it was substantially Christian (cp. Soz., V. 16). Hence it must have had both Christians and a bishop at an earlier date.

Duchesne Orig. dii ciilte, p. ii) rightly observes: "La Phrygie etait a peu pres chrelienne que la Gaule ne comptait encore qu'un tres petit nombre d'eglises organisees." Cp. Ramsay, as cited above (p. 95).â For Phrygian martyrs in Palestine (including a Thekla) under Diocletian, cp. Alari. Pal. (ed. Violet, pp. 18 f., 48). A Phrygian, Alexander, was martyred at Lyons (Eus., H. E., v. i) under Marcus Aurelius.

"The three churches at Laodicea, Hierapolis, and Colossse were closely connected in their origin (cp. Col. iv. 13). Paul did not found them himself; he was never there (Col. ii. i). It was his disciples who founded them; e. g., Epaphras the missionary in Colossse.â In the Mart. Sy?: for 27th June we read: "In Laodicea Phrygiae e numero. Kadapwv i. e., Novatians in persecutione secundum. uniti sunt et adnumerati ecclesiae, deinde confessi sunt Theophilus episcopus et Philippus et alii quinque."

â Hierapolis was the birthplace of Epictetus.

Cumane, a village (Eus., v, 16).

Eimieoea (Eus., v. 16, v. 24; Thraseas, a bishop and martyr of the second century, who was buried at Smyrna Polycrates in Eus., H. E., V. 24, in the cemetery ttjo t 'E ecriakrj (Baa-ixelag sc.-TTuxtji Vita Polyc. 22, where Polycarp's predecessor Bucolus is also said to have lain; two dated inscriptions from 249 or 250 A. D.; cp. Cumont, p. 36, Nos. 135, 136).

Sanaus (bishop Flaccus at Nica? a).

Synnada (Eus., vi. 19, vii. 7; " early " martyrs, etc., in Mart. Syr.; bishop Procopius was at Nicaea).

Trajanopolis (a dated inscription of 279 a. d.; cp. Cumont, p. 37, No. 172). This town is the same as Grimenothyrae; cp. Ramsay's Phiygia, p. 558.

Ezani (bishop Pisticus at Nicaea).

Dorylaeum (bishop Athenodorus at Nicaea).

Eucarpia (bishop Eugenius at Nicaea).

Cotijeum (a local Novatian bishop; Socrat., iv. 28).

Lampe and the Siblianoi district (inscriptions; cp. Ramsay's Phnjgia, pp. 222 f., 539 f.).

The Hyrgalic district, together with Lunda and Motella (inscriptions; cp. Ramsay, pp. 540 f.).

Sebaste or Dioskome (two dated inscriptions of 253 or 256 A. D.; cp. Ramsay, pp. 560 f., and Cumont, p. 36, Nos. 160, 161).

Stektorion (inscriptions; cp. Ramsay, pp. 719 f.).

Bruzus (inscriptions; cp. Ramsay, pp. 700 f.).

The Moxiane district (inscriptions; cp. Ramsay, pp. 717 f.).

' Bishop Agapetus of Synnada, who was inclined to Aiianism and was famous for his miracles, was perhaps the predecessor of Procopius. I'liilostorgius mentions him HE., ii. 8). He was originally a soldier, then a presbyter, and then a bishop. Cp. the fragment about him excerpted from Philostorgius by Suidas, s. v. a. yatrr T6s, where it is narrated how he almost fell a victim, as a soldier and a Christian, to the persecution of Daza.

Merus (between Cotiseum, Appia, and Amorium) must also have had a Christian church by 325 a. d. It cannot be identified with certainly (cp. Kiefert's map). What Socrates relates about the reign of Julian H. E., iii. 5; cp. Soz., V. 11) presupposes an old Christian community and the extinction of paganism in the town. Probably there was a Christian community at Pazus also (a village in Phrygia, ivqa. rov 'Sayyapiov Trotafji-ov flfflv at-rrriyai, i. e., north-west of Amorium; unidentified), since some of the Phrygian Novatians (or Montanists) met there for a synod about the middle of the fourth century (Socrates, H. E., iv. 28, v. 21).

Prymnessus (martyrdom of Ariadne; cp. Franchi de Cavalieri, Acta Theodoti., etc.).

Themisonion (inscriptions; cp. Ramsay, p. 556). Akmonia or Keramon Agora (inscriptions; cp. Ramsay, pp. 56 f., 621 f., 674; for the pagan reaction here in 314 a. d., cp. ibid., pp. 506 f., and Deux jours en Phrygie, pp. 8 f.). Tiberiopolis (martyr). Amorion (martyr).

Cheretapa (Socr., ii. 40; Philostorg., vii. 6; in Southern

Phrygia, on the Pisidian border) had a bishop in Juhan's day.

, It cannot be identified with certainty; perhaps = Dioc3esarea, yjjSfcp. Kieferfs map.

jv. J Pisidia and Lycaonia:â v it Iconium (the metropohsâ Paul, Acta Theclcc perhaps composed by a local presbyter. Acta Justini, Hierax of 1 In the late A(:a Acia ii Ru'mart, Acta Mart., Ratisbon, 1859, pp. 199 f.), which are said to belong to the reign of Decius, a distinction is drawn (in the fourth chapter) between " Cataphryges, homines religionis antiquae" and " Christiani catholicae legis." Is the Antioch mentioned in the first chapter, whose bishop was Achatius, Pisidian Antioch? Or was

Achatius chor-episcopus in the vicinity of the city? He is called " a shield and succour for the district of Antioch" ("scutum quoddam ac refugium Antiochae regionis"). Towards the close of the Acta a certain " Piso Traianorum (Trojanorum?) episcopus" is mentioned. Is not this town the Phrygian Trajanopolis, which lies not very far from Pisidian Antioch? We can hardly think of a bishop of Troas in Mysia Minor, who would be termed "episcopus Trojanus."â The parish of Alexander the Montanist is mentioned, but not defined, by Eusebius (v. 18. 9).

'â Cp. Ranosay, Pisidia and the Lycaonian Frontiei' 02-'), with an excellent map and numerous corrections of Histor. Geography. The large majority of Pisidian bishoprics lay 00 the Lycaonian border, i. e., S. E. and then N. W. Christianity thus lay along a broad diagonal line, stretching from S. E. to N. W. i. e., to Bruzus, Hieropolis, Otrus, etc.). Right and left of this (the eastern limit being somewhere between Laranda and Iconium, the western between Humanades and Apamea Cibotus), the country was for long Christianized only here and there. The direction of this line is towards Cilicia (Tarsus) as its base, and from the N. W. it was met half-way by the expansion of Christianity in Asia-Phrygia. The metropolitan arrangements (Lubeck, pp. 10, 94 f.) must have been uncertain in these provinces prior to Diocletian. Certainly the prominence of Iconium, Laranda, and Synnada in the epistle of the two Palestine bishops to Demetrius of Alexandria was not accidental. They represented three central points. Sagalassus was not yet the capital of Pisidia, any more than perhaps the political headquarters (against Marquardt, I.(-) p. 68). It never occurs in the pre-Nicene Christian literature, and it had no bishop at Nicaea. As for the separate towns, cp. for Antioch, Ramsay, p. 247 (really a Phrygian town); for Neapolis, p. 250; for Limense Limnae, p. 251; for Pappa, p. 254; for Baris and Seleucia, p. 256;

Iconium, born of Christian parents, Eus., H. E., vi. 19, vii. 7, vii. 28; Eulalius, the bishop of Iconium, council of Nicaea).

Antioch (Paul, Acta Theclce?).

Lystra (Paul).

Derbe (Paul). i

Philomelium (ep. Smyrniote church to the local church, circa 156 A. D.).

Hadrianopolis (bishop Telemachus at Nicaea).

Neapolis (bishop Hesychius at Nicaea).

Seleucia Sidera (bishop Eutychius at Nicaea).

Limense (bishop Aranius at Nicaea).

Amblada (bishop Patricius at Nicaea).

Metropolis (also assigned to Phrygia; bishop Polycarp at Nicaea).

Apamea (= Celaenae; close to Apamea Cibotus, also assigned to Phrygia; bishop Tarsicius at Nicsea; also an earlier dated inscription of 254 a. d.; cp. Cumont, p. 38, No. 209).

Pappa (bishop Academicus at Nicaea).

Baris (bishop Heraclius at Nicaea).

Usada = Vasada (bishop Theodorus at Nicaea).

Calytis = Canytis? in Pisidia (martyrs).

As with Bithynia, so with Pisidiaâ the number of bishops at Nicaea proves that the province i. e., its western division) was widely-Christianized. But as it produced no prominent bishops or writers, we learn nothing of its local church-history, apart from Iconium; although Ramsay tells me that, to judge from for Amblada, pp. 264 f.; for Vasada Isaur., p. 266; for Humanades Isaur., pp. 268 f. Further, cp. Ramsay's great study of Lycaonia (which discusses Isauria also). For Laranda, cp. pp. 70 f. ("the leading city of Southern Lycaonia, had the title of metropolis from the time of M. Aurelius and perhaps earlier "); for Derbe and Passala, pp. 73 f.; for Isauropolis, pp. 77 f.; for Barata, pp. 82 f.; for Gdmaua Gal., p. 97; for Coropassus, p. 100; and for Cybistra Capp., pp. 113 f.

Lystra and Derbe were the first Christian communities which were almost entirely composed of Christians who had been born pagans (cp. Kenan's Paitl, Germ, ed., p. 90).

Amblada was in bad repute. Constantine banished MWns thither (ekfl cakcd? airopp7) a(toi';8iof, Sia rh 0ap0apov Kal fjuffdvqptairov tsjv evoikOVvtoiv, avxJ-ov Se Kal Aoifiov ttjj x' P " X""' ' avviroiffrov). So still in the days of Philostorgius (v. 20), though at the beginning of the fourth century it had a bishop.

This bishop occurs aho in the Isaurian list of the Nicene council, and indeed with more right there than here.

222 MISSION AND EXPANSION OF CHRISTIANITY the inscriptions and ruins of the fourth century, it must have been more thoroughly Christianized than even Asia and Phrygia.

E. Asia (Lydia, Mysia, Hellespontus and Carta)

Thanks to Paul and the unknown John,- Asia became the leading Christian province throughout Asia Minor. It was rich in towns, and flourished by its trade and industries. As has been already noted, the churches of Ephesus, Sm yrna Pejji gamum, Sardes, Philadelphia, Thyatira, Troas, Magnesia on the Maeander, T ralles, and possibly Parium, were all founded in the primitive age. Speaking from the experience of his travels and all he had seen in Asia, Ignatius mentions p. 3 eiria-KOTToi Kara to. ireputa so. tov Kocrfxov opia-Oivteg â so widespread and numerous did the Asiatic bishops seem to him (ad Ephes. 3). fapylus (Maii. Carpi, ch. 32; see above, p. 5) tells the magistrate at Pergamum, ei 7racr; eirapxi-G fÂ ' Troaei elctLv juiot rekva Kara Oeov, referring primarily to Asia. Ir eneeus (iii. 3. 4) speaks of " all the churches in Asia," and the epistle of Polycrates, bishop of Ephesus, to Victor of Rome during the aster controversy (cp. Eus., H. E., v. 24) brings out very clearly the dignity and the self-consciousness of the church at Ephesus. Ephesus was the custodian of the reat memories of the churches of Asia-Phrygia, memories which secured to these churches a descent and origin at least equal to that of the church of Rome. " For in Asia, too, great luminaries have sunk to rest which shall rise again on the day of the Lord's coming; namely, Philip, one of the twelve apostles, who rests in Hierapolis, with his two daughters, who grew old as virgins, and his other 1 This provincial designation has been omitted by an early oversight from the Nicene list (before Asia), so that we now find, under Aaias, the bishop of Cyzicus before the bishop of Ephesus (cp. Llibeck, p. 77, and Schwartz, Ztr Gesch. des Athafias., vi. p. 267).

2 The traditions that "John" organized the church in Asia, and that he ruled over the churches as a mission-superintendent, are above suspicion. Eventually (cp. 3 John) he came into conflict with the local organization.

2 Cp. Clare, de Rebus Thyatirenorum, and Ramsay, Detix jours en Phrygie, pp. 9 f.

â Paul's epistle to the Ephesians (whose address is admittedly unauthentic, as we read it to-day) was sent to several Asiatic churches; perhaps it was the same letter as the Colossians (Col. iv. 16) were to expect from Laodicea and to read.

CHRISTIANITY DOWN TO 325 A. D. 223

daughter who hved in the Holy Spirit and lies buried at Ephesiis. Then, too, there is John, who reclined on the Lord's breast, and who was a priest wearing the sacerdotal plate, a martyr, and a teacher. He also rests at Ephesus. And Polycarp, too, in Smyrna, both bishop and martyr; and Thraseas, also a bishop and martyr, from Eumenea, who rests at Smyrna. Why need I further mention the bishop and martyr Sagaris, who rests at Laodicea, or the blessed Papirius, or Melito the eunuch, whose whole life was lived in the Holy Spirit, and who lies at Sardes? " Note also how Polycrates proceeds to add: " I, too, Polycrates, hold by the tradition, V of my relatives, some of whom I have closely followed; for s evt v- of rft jrdniive." rvere bishops, and I am the eighth. " We do not know where these seven bishoprics are to be looked for in Asia, and unfortunately we are just as ignorant about the members of that largely attended Asiatic synod, convoked during the Easter controversy, of which Polycrates writes thus: " I could name the bishops present, whom I had summoned at J J your desire i. e., of Victor, the bishop of Rome; were I to go over their names, they would amount to an extremely large number" (ttoxXo: ttxtOj?, i. e., perhaps one or two dozen).

Important sources relative to the church in Smyrna are available for us in the epistl of John, Ignatius (two), and Polycarp, as well as in the epistle of the church to Philomelium and in the Martyrdom of Pionius (in the reign of Decius); see also the acco ynts of Noetus th e modalistic Christian, at Smyrna. One outstanding feature is the local struggle between Â ,-i the Jews and the Christians, and also the high repute of o Polycarp (" the father of the Christians," as the pagans called y him; Ep. Smym. xii.). During Polycarp's lifetime, there were-' "v.-0 several Christian churches near Smyrna, for Irenasus tells Florinus that Polycarp addressed letters to them (Eus., v. 24), There was also a Marcionite church at Smyrna or in the neighbourhood during the days of Pionius, for the latter had a Marcionite presbyter called Metrodorus as his fellow-martyr.

The sharp emphasis laid on "the cathohc church" in the Martyrdom of Pionius indicates plainly that there were sectarian, especially Montanist, churches in Smyrna and Asia.

224 MISSION AND EXPANSION OF CHRISTIANITY

But unluckily nonqjof all thesjeâ sources furnish idea of the Smyrniote church's size. In the Vita Polycarpi of Pionius, and in the Apost. Corn-tit., vii. 46, there is a doubtful list of the first bishops of Smyrna.

Pergamunij where the first Asiatic martyr perished, is familiar to us in early church history from the martyrdo m of C arpus, Papylus, and Agathonike (apart from the Johann e letter to the church), as well as from the martyrdom of Attatus of Pergamum at Lyons (Eus., H. E., v. 1); Sarcjes is known to us through Melito, the local bishop, c. 170 a. d,, whose large ideas upon the relation of the church to the empire would not have been possible had not Christianity been already a power to reckon with at Sardes and in Asia. The authority employed by Epiphanius in Hcer. li. 33 declares that almost the whole of JTh BiaTSi was won for Christ by the opening of the third century; he also mentions churches which had arisen in the neighbourhood of Thyatira, but without giving any names. Papylus, who suffered martyrdom in Pergamum, was an itinerant preacher hailing from Thyatira. The martyr Appianus in C qesar ea Pal. came from Lydia (cp. Mart. Pal., pp. 24 f., Violet). For martyrs at Miletus, cp. Sozom., v. 20. The author of the Vita Pollcarpi (25) mentions the bishop of Teos (south-west of Smyrna), a certain Daphnus; and, whatever be thought of the date of this Vita, we can believe there was a bishop at Teos in the third century.

1 In the Aari. Pionii a village called Karina is mentioned as having a Christian presbyter.

2 The discussion of the Vita Polycarpi (per Pionium) has entered on a new phase, owing to the efforts of Corssen Zeits. f. NTlicke IViss., v. pp. 266 f.) and Schwartz De Pionio et Polycarpo, Gottinger Programm, 7th June 1905), both of whom regard Pionius, the Decian martyr, as the author of the treatise. According to the Vita, Bucolus was the predecessor of Folycarp (preceded by the disciple of Paul, Strataas a son of Lois, who had laboured as a teacher of the church. The list, according to the Apost. Constit., runs thus: Ariston, Strataas, the son of Lois, Ariston another?).â In the Vita, ch. xxi., bishops tsv irepi irikiwv are mentioned on the occasion of Polycarp's choice as bishop of Smyrna, as well as Christian yx " Tajv irikiniv kox Koofxuv Kal aypwv (cp. 27: Tj Kara tos Kcofias fkKX7)(Tisiv (ppovris). This is quite credible, for the third century. Against Corsscn's hypothesis, see Hilgenfeld in his Zeits. fiir Wiss. Theol. (1905), xlviii. pp. 444 f.

3 There were Christians in the town of Parethia on the Hellespont (Parium?), but it has not been identified. Cp. Achelis, Mart. Hier., p. 117.

The exceptionally wide diffusion of the Asiatic churches, and the zeal they displayed in the interests of the church at large, h come out in a passage from Lucian's tale of Proteus Peregrmus," ' where, after narrating Proteus' conversion and imprisonment (.â Ijlaa-in Syria, he goes on to say: " In fact, people actually came from 'Q v several Asiatic towns despatched by the local Christians, in J order to render aid, to conduct the defence, and to encourage the man. They become incredibly alert when anything of this kind occurs that affects their common interests. On such occasions no expense is grudged."

The writings of Iren aus, Hippolytus, and Tertullian furnish a good deal of material for our knowledge of the relations between the churches of Asia Minor and the West, and vice versa. Polycarp of Smyrna, when quite an old man, travelled to see Anicetus at Rome, in order to take counsel upon the Easter date and other matters. The relations between the churches of Asia and Rome must have been close and vivid. Any Asiatic controversy was transmitted to Rome. Asiatic Christians were found at Lyons during the reign of Marcus Aurelius. The churches of Lyons and Vienne describe their sufferings to their Asiatic brethren. Most probably the canon of the four gospels originated in Asia Minor (at Ephesus), where the ground was also prepared for the formation of the New Testament (cp. Melito). The Paschal controversy (c. 190 A. D.) seems to have alienated the Asiatic church from the general body of the church.

Thereafter it never had the same central position as before. What it lost, Rome gained. But the Asiatic church steadily increased in numbers. The purely fictitious Acta Pauli (c. 180 a. d.) came from an Asiatic presbyter; they are extremely important for our knowledge of popular Asiatic Christianity.

The subscriptions of the Nicene council furnish further evidence of Asiatic (Lydian and Mysiau) and Cariau towns with local churches; viz., Cyzikus (Theonas: where there was also a Novatian church; Socrat., ii. 38), Ilium (Orion), Ilium

Christianity in this town or its jurisdiction must have still been in a weak state, for under Julian a proposal was brought forward to restore the pagan temple (Sozom., V. 15).

VOL. II. 15 (another: =Dascylium? bishop Marinus), Hypaepa (Mithres), Anaea (Paulus), Bagis (Polhon), Tripolis (Agogius), Ancjra ferrea (Florentius), Aurelianopolis (Antiochus), Standus? Silandus? Blaundus? (bishop Marcus), Hierocaesarea (Antiochus). In Caria: Antioch (Eusebius), Aphrodisias (Atnmonius; martyrs Mart. Str. and Christian inscriptions), Apollonias (Eugenius), Cibyra (Laetodorus: inscriptions; cp. also Epiph., Hcer., li. 30), and Miletus (Eusebius). Martyr-Acts from the reign of Decius (Ruinart, p. 205) also prove the existence of a Christian church at Lampsacus, where Parthenius was bishop under Constantine (cp. Acta SS. Febr., II. pp. 38 f.). Sardes was the capital of Lydia, but we do not know whether Antioch or Aphrodisias was the capital then of Caria. For Novatian churches in Asia and Lydia, cp. Socrat., vi. 19. i '

F. Lycia, Pamphylia, and Isauria I v-

No fewer than, twenty-five bishops from these three southern provinces of Asia Minor were present at Nicaea (including four chor-episcopi from Isauria)â a sad contrast to the little we know of the churches in these districts. With regard to Lycia (Olympus and Patara), we are acquainted with the personality of Methodius, that influential teacher of the church who lived circa 300 a. d. His writings give us a picture of the ideas and intercourse of educated Christians iii iiycia. The newly discovered inscription of Arycanda (Maximinus Daza) also informs us that there were Christians in that locality, and that the town joined in presenting servile petitions against them." Finally, it is probable, from the Acta Pauli, that there were Chris ians in Myrrha, while similar evidence is perhaps afforded by Eusebius Mart. Pal. iv.-v.) with regard to Gagae, not far from Olympus. Nothing 4s 4ieard of the churches in Eam- '

The bishops of Ephesus (Menophantus), Smyrna (Eutychius), Sardes (Artemidorus), Thyatira (Saras), and Philadelphia (Hetoimasius) were also present at Nicsea.

Archaol.-epigraph. Mittheil. aus Oesterreich-Ungarti., ed. von Benndorf u. Bormann (1893), pp. 93 f., 108.

"Gagae" (not Pagse) is to be read; cp. Mercati's Martiri di Palestina del Codice Sinaitico (Estratto dai "Rendiconti" del R. Inst. Lomb., Serie ii., vol. XXX., 1897).

. ihjjja owever, from the allusion to Perge in Acts down to the council of Nicaea, apart from one martyrdom in Attalia; while all we know of Isauria is the notice in Eusebius (vi. 9) which has been already cited (cp. p, 214). The following is a list of the churches throughout the three provinces, known to us for the most part from the council of Nicaea:â

LyoM L-' Patara (Method., Martyr., Nic. bishop Eudemus), Olympus (Method.), Arycanda (inscr. from reign of Daza), Gagae (Euseb.), Myrrha Acta Pauli), Perdikia? (Nic, but doubtful).

Pam hylia: Perge (Acts, Nic. bishop Callicles), Termessus, Uarba = Syarba (where.?), Aspendus, Seleucia, Maximianopolis, Magydus (all six, with bishops Heuresius, Zeuxius, Domnus, Quintianus, Patricius and Aphrodisius, from Nic, though Magydus is also supported by the tradition of St Conon's martyrdom under Decius; cp. von Gebhardfs Acta Mart. Sel., pp. 129 f.), Side (since this town is mentioned shortly afterwards as the metropolis of Pamphylia, it probably had a church circa 325 A. D.),2 Attalia (Mart.).

Isaii7'iaj It is amazing that Christianity had spread so far J in this wild province that thirteen bishops and four chor-episcopi came from it to the council of Nicasa. For Ramsay's investigations, cp. above, pp. 215, 220. Laranda (Alex, of Jerus., in Eus., H. E., vi. 19, Nic. bishop Paulus), Barata, Koropissus, Claudi-opolis, Seleucia (Tracheia) Metropolis (?), Panemon Teichos, Antioch, Syedra, Humanades (= Umanada), Ilistra (the last signature runs, Eycre' fo? Sioikicreo)? rtj? irapoikia Icravplag). The Isaurian bishops are called Stephanus, Athenaeus, iedesius Agapius, Silvanus, Faustus, Antoninus, Nestor, Cyril, Theodorus, Tiberius, Eusebius. The chor-episcopi are called: Hesychius, Anatolius, Quintus, and Aquila. Obviously they are purely

Perhaps = Lyrbe, north-east of Side (cp. Ramsay's map of Pisidia).

"Side was also the birthplace of Euslathius, afterwards bishop of Bercea and Sebaste. As Athanasius calls him a confessor, he must have attested his Christi-anity in Side during the Diocletian persecution.

â Sej-euc a was. the starting-point of the Thekla-cultus. Thekla dispossessed the Athena and the Apollo of Seleucia.

â Here follows, in the Nicene list, Theodorus of Vasadaâ probably the same as Theodorus of Usada = Vasada in Pisidia (see above). The connection with Isauria is more probable than with Pisidia, however.

Greco-Roman names. The Christianizing of Isauria meant an increase of Hellenizing, as was always the case in Asia Minor. Perhaps the name of a (Lycian) locakty is also hidden in the surname of " Amasceunites"" borne by Sistelius (Method., de Kesu7T., i. 1. 2; Bonwetsch, p. xxxiii).

We cannot get any clear idea (cp. Lubeck, p. 96) of the political and ecclesiastical capitals of these provinces. The Nicene lists suggest Patara (Lycia: yet this was the only Lycian bishop at Nicaea), Perge (Pamphylia), and Barata (Isauria). Gelzer's map makes Seleucia the metropolis of Isauria, without any basis for this; it was probably the political capital. Lubeck calls attention to the fact that no city " Metropolis" occurs in Isauria; hence, it is argued, the bishop who signed from " Metropolis" was simply the bishop of the unnamed political capital of Isauria at that period (which perhaps was not the same as the ecclesiastical). But it is unexampled to find fxrirpoirokiq in the Nicene lists instead of the name of a town or city. The second difficulty lies in the last signature. Schwartz Zur Gesch. des Athan., vi. pp. 283 f.), who has recently discussed these problems in connection with the synodal document, which he discovered, of a synod at Antioch held shortly before the Nicene council (immediately after the death of Philogonius, bishop of Antioch), holds the Syrian reading 'Ewo-e fo? TrapoikLa? 'laavpoiroxeoo's to be original. With the aid of the 190th letter of Basil (to Amphilochius), which mentions small localities near Isaura which had bishops, he proves that while Eusebius was the bishop of the town of Isaura, his authority extended beyond the town, and his parish did not coincide with that of the municipal church, though he was not the metropolitan of the province. The latter was, in Schwartz''s judgment, the SXomio? Mytoo7roaeco? mentioned fifth in order. This position Schwartz thinks he can explain by the fact that the sees already mentioned, i. e., Barata, Coracesion (Coropissus), Claudiopolis, and Seleucia were autocephalous at the date of the Nicene council. " They did not lie in Isauria proper, and the ecclesiastical organization did not exactly follow the political at this point." This does not seem to me to solve the problem yet. For what town was the metropolis? Cp. Ramsay's Litcaonia (p. 77), and his Pisidia and the Lycaonian Frontier (pp. 266 f.), on this question. The latter scholar thinks that the two neighbouring cities of Isaura nova and Corna had bishops at an earlier period, " but were submerged in the great autocephalous bishoprics of Isaura palaea sometime after 381."' Â 10. Crete and the Islands (including the Ionian)

From the epistle to Titus it is clear that Christianity had reached Crete before the close of the apostolic age, and that Titus had a special connection as a missionary with the islandâ though Paul is also said to have visited it (Tit. i. 5). About 170 A. D. Dionysius of Corinth wrote an epistle "to the church of Gortyna and to the other churches of Crete " (Gortyna being evidently the metropolis), and a second epistle to the Cretan church of Cnossus, whose bishop, Pinytus by name, wrote him a reply (Eus., H. E. iv. 23). But nothing further is known of early Christianity in the island, and no bishop came from Crete to the Nicene council. For a considerable conversion of Jews in Crete, cp. the tragi-comic story of Socrates (H. E., vii. 38). It is clear that the Jews were scattered all over the island.

Achelis Zeitscjir. filr die mutest. Wissensch., i. pp. 87 f.), like some other scholars before him, has tried to prove, from the evidence of the inscriptions, that Christian churches existed on the smaller islands, particularly in Rhodes and Thera and

For Isaura nova = Dorla, cp. Ramsay, Topog7 and Epigr. of Nova Isaura (1905), and the above-mentioned essay of Miss Ramsay. In this extremely interesting essay the monument sketched and discussed on pp. 264 f. is of special importance. It belongs to a bishop b nakoiptos irdiras) called on the inscription 6 deov pi os. By a custom of the pagan priests, his name is not given. Or w as he called Theophilus? The monument must be pre-Constantine, as its general character and the ornaments prove. The inscription for rhv ivan (pikov iirlffkOTrov Maj-nay (pp. 269 f.) also seems to be pre-Constantine, possibly too that on bishop Sisamoas (p. 272). The other antique monuments which have been discovered and described belong also to the years 250-400 A. D. The rarity of Greek names on them is extremely striking; the Latin are more numerous. For that very reason, one must not go too far with them.

2 Cp. Map VII.

Evidently there were several local churches.

â Cp. the publications of Hiller von Gartringen with their interesting Christian inscriptions yye os).

Therasia, as early as circa 100 a. d.; but the proofs of this are unsatisfactory, both as regards the fact of Christianity and the age of the inscriptions. Thus, even in the third century, one may put a query opposite Thera and Therasia in connection with Christianity. But in Melos (Malus) Christians seem certainly to have existed in the third century." Patmos, with its great associations, they would hardly leave unclaimed till the fourth century; and martyrdoms are connected in tradition with Chios. Bishops from Rhodes (where early inscriptions have been also discovered), Cos (the seat of Asclepius!) Lemnos, and Corcyra (Euphrosynus, Meliphron, Strategius, and Aletodorus respectively) attended the Nicene council. Mytilene (Lesbos) had a bishop in the days of Julian (cp. Socrat., H. E., ii. 40).

Paul is reported (Const. App., vii. 46) to have installed Crispus as the first bishop of ginaâ a legend which denotes the existence of a church there at some early period. The presence of gnostic Christians at Same in Cephallenia may be inferred from Clem. Alex., Strom., iii. 2. 5.

Â 11. Thrace, Macedonia, Dardania, Epirus, Thessaly, Achaia

We have but a faint knowledge of Christianity in the Balkan peninsula Xth? diocese of Iuyria) during the first centuries. No

For Christian catacombs in the ravine of Ceima in Melus, cp. Ross, Reisen aiif d. griech. Inseln des agdischen Meers (1845, 3rd vol., pp. 145 f.).

"Among the signatures of Nicsea (cp. Gelzer, Ixiii.-Ixiv.) are (n. 167) STpat yios A yuj'oj; and (n. 214) ttpa. T'i-yios 'HpaitTilas â the one in the islands, the other in Achaia. They are identical, for Hephasstia lies in Lemnos.

Epiphanius the gnostic, whose father was Carpocrates, was connected with Cephallenia through his mother, koi 0ehs ev Sctxj? rrjs Kepoi. X rjvias Titifiritat, ivoa avtcf liphv pvtoiiu Xidaiv, oofioi, Texevrj, fxovcrelov cfkos6fj. ritai re Koi KaqUpunai, Koi ffvvi6vtts its rh liphv 01 Kij'awTJi'es Kara vovfirivlav yevioXiov atodetcaiv Qvovaiv Eiri(pdvei, cnrevSoucri tÂ koi fvooxovvrai Kal vfjivoi Kiyovrai (" He is honoured as a god in Same of Cephallenia, where a shrine of huge stones, with altars and precincts and a museum, has been erected for him, and consecrated. And the Cephallenians celebrate his birthday at new moon, assembling at his shrine, doing sacrifice, pouring forth libations, and feasting, with song of hymns to him"). But does not this story perhaps rest on a confusion of names?

Cp. Map VII.â These represent different provinces of the church with metropolitans of their own (cp. Optatus, ii. I: "Ecclesia in tribus Pannoniis, in Dacia, Moesia, Thracia, Achaia, Macedonia"). I group them together merely for the outstandibg Â giireil emerge, and Dienystas-uil-Corinth, who exhorted and counselled many churches East and West by his letters during the reign of M. Aurelius, and collected these letters into a volume (Eus., H. E., iv. 23), stands quite by ' himself. The extension of Christianity was far from being uniform. In "Europe," over against Bithynia, and Thrace, there must have been numerous churches previous to 325 (cp. also Vit. Const., iv. 43), as is evident from the church-history- irv of Thrace during the fourth century, Corinth and Thessalonica j?

had flourishing churches. In Carthage it was known about 220 j Ux y A. D. that councils were he d.(" quae per Graecias certis in locis ex universis ecclesiis â ") throughout Greece, " per quae et altiora quaeque in commune tractantur, et ipsa representatio nominis Christiani magna venei'atione celebratur."" But the larger part of the peninsula cannot have had more than a scanty population of Christians up till 325, so that we cannot speak of any common Christian character or type, of course, in this connection. I shall therefore proceed to set down a list of the yarjous places, not according to their provinces, but as far as possible in chronological order. First, those which are known to us from the earliest period.

Philippi, irpcorr irpurrr? nieplsog r. Makesovlag Troai? (Acts sake of unity, as we know little of th eir respective histories. Duchesne's study, Les anciens ivechds de la Grke (1896), and the earlier works of de Boor Zeits. f. K. Gesch., xii., 1891, pp. 520 f.) and Gelzer Zeits. f. IVtss. Theol., xxxii., 1892, pp. 419 f.), refer to a later period, but even the period previous to 300 may have some light cast on it by the list (Duchesne, p. 14), which assigns to Euboea three bishoprics (Chalcis, Carystus, Porthmus), to Attica one (Athens), to Northern Greece ten (Megara, Thebes, Tanagra, Platsea, Thespise, Coronia, Opus, Elataea, Scarphia, Naupactus), to the Peloponnese seven (Corinth, Argos, Lacedsemon, Messina, Megalopolis. Tegsea, Patras). Tertuuian de Virg. Vel. ii.) writes thus: " Per Graeciam et quasdam barbarias eius plures ecclesiae virgines suas abscond-unt." As he means by " Graecia " in ch. viii. Greece proper i. e., Corinth, etc.), we should probably locate these churches among the neighbouring barbarians in the northern half of the Balkan peninsula.â Could we avail ourselves of the episcopal list of Sardica, we should be able to verify a large number of bishoprics for Achaia, Macedonia, and the provinces farther north. But (cp. above, p. 90) we cannot use this list for the pre-Nicene age.

1 The tone of his letters, which can be felt even in the brief extracts of Eusebius, shows that he wrots, to-Athens and Laced mon as metropolitan, to Crete and Pontus as a colleague and equal, and to the bishop of Rome as a modest and admiring colleague (cp. vol. i. p. 468).

232 MISSION AND EXPANSION OF CHRISTIANITY xvi. 12; Paul, Epaphroditus, Euodias, Syntyche, Clement;! Polycarp 's epistle; pseudo-Dionysius is our only witness to aa i anotherâ unauthenticâ letter of his addressed to Athens). Xyi-i j ' Thessalonica (where there was a synagogue, or else the tj- synagogue of the province; Paul; Antoninus Pius wrote to yj this city, forbidding any rising against the Christians Melito, in Eus., H. E., iv. 26J; the metropolitan Alexander was present at Nicaea, and also at the dedication of the church of Jerusalem, Vit. Const., iv. 43). J Beroea (Paul).

thens (Paul). From the outset the church here was small and small it remained, for in this city of philosophers Christianity could find little room. According to Dionysius of Corinth,) Dionysius the Areopagite was the first bishop of Athens; Antoninus Pius forbade the city to rise against the Christians (see above); and after the persecution of M. Aurelius, Dionysius of Corinth wrote to the church (Eus., H. E., iv. 23), "accusing them almost of apostasy from the faith since the death of their martyred bishop Publius; and mentioning Quadratus who suc-y ceeded Publius in the episcopate, testifying that the church had 5 K been gathered together again by his zealous efforts and had gained new ardour for the faith." The apologist Aristides came from Athens (0taocro o? 'AOrjvaio). So did Clement of Alexandria, perhaps. Origen, who spent some time in Athens (Eus., vi. 23. 32), mentions the local church in c. Cels., III. xxx.: " Thqqi a- church of God at Athens is a peaceable and orderly body, as it desires to please Almighty God. Whereas the assembly of the Athenians is refractory, nor can it be compared in any respect to the local church or assembly of God." The bishop of Athens,

For " Macedonia," see J. Weiss's article in the Frot. Real-Encyk. vol. xii. Philippi gave Paul his first experience of a city which had a considerable Latin element in it.

U Jr 2 ggg tj g instructive article on "Greece in the Apostolic Age," by J. Weiss, ; ibid., vol. vii. Apart from Corinth, Greece was in a reduced position by the time â p' it came into contact with Christianity.

ILQjk Being raised perhaps to the episcopate from the position of an influential member, perhaps a leader of the local church. " Circa 230 A. D., and again between 238 and 244, "on pressing church ., JX,-r, business" and " for the conversion of heretics." On his journey to Rome he had O already touched at Athens (between 211 and 215216).

Pistus, attended Nicaea. For the pagan character of the city in the middle of the fourth century, see the remarks in Gregory of Naz.

CQnnth(the metropolis: Paul; the epistle of the Roman church to, Jthe-cliurch of Corintn c. a. d.; Hegesifipus, in Eus., H. E., iv. 22, eireinevev fj ekKKrjaia rj opivoiwp ev rw opoo) Aoyo) fj. expt ptjuLOU eiricTKOTrevovtO ev ls. opiv6(p' oh crwejui a Trxecov etv 'Ydoiutjv, kui crvvsietpi' a roh opivoioi rjucepa ikavag, ev ah a-vvavetrdtjuiev rw opoco Xoyw = "the Corinthian church remained by the true faith till Primus was bishop in Corinth. I conversed with them on my way to Rome, and spent some time with the Corinthians, during which we refreshed each other with orthodox teaching." Also the letter of Soter, the Roman bishop, to Corinth = 2 Clem. The Moscow MS., in the appendix to Polycarp's Mart., mentions a Socrates at Corinth, Dionysius of Corinth. BaÂ chyllusj bishop of Corinth, during the Paschal controversy. Tertullian, who knew the local practice with regard to the veiling of virgins de Virg. Vel. viii: hodie denique Corinthii virgines suas velant. Origen, who speaks of Corinth in the same term as of Athens, c. Cels. III. xxx. Martyrs in Corinth, according to Mart. Syr.)."

enchreae (Paul; the Apost. Constit. vii. 46 mentions the first bishop of this seaport, whom Paul is said to have appointedâ a remark which deserves no credence).

Laced3ej! iipn (Dionysius of Corinth wrote a letter to this church Eus., H. E., iv. 23 enjoining peace and unity; the fact of a Christian community existing in acountry town like Lacedaemon by the. year 170, proves that missionary work had been done from Corinth throughout the Peloponnese, although as we see from the subsequent period, Christianity only got a footing there 1 With unusually high praise of their virtues prior to the split (Clem. Rom. i.-ii.).

' The second recension, extant only in Syriac, of pseudo-Justin's " Address to the Greeks" (cp. Sitzungsber. der K. Preuss. Akad. d. W., 1896, pp. 627 f.) hails from Corinth perhaps, or at any rate from Greece. It is a third-century document, and opens with these words: " Memoirs which have been written by Ambrose, a senator of Greece, who became a Christian. All his fellow-senators cried out against him, so he fled away and wrote in order to show them all their mad frenzy." In any case the reference is to the conversion of a councillor in a Greek city.

with difficulty. The "bishop of Achaia" sided with Origen

Jr in his dispute with Demetrius (231 a. d.). â Philostorgius (iii. 2) iw relates how the emperor Constantius brought the remains of the apostle Andrew and of Luke from Achaia to Constantinople (cp. Jerome, rfg Vir. Inl. vii.). It isjiot impossible that Andrew and Luke really died in Achaia.â The allusion to " Arcadia " in the ninth similitude of Hei'mas (the angel of repentance conveys him thither) has no bearing on the history of the spread of Christianity; " Arcadia" here is simply an apocalyptic accessory borrowed from paganism.

i, arissa. iÂ-Thessaly (Melito in Eus., H. E. iv. 20 tells us that Antoninus Pius wrote to this town, forbidding it to rise against the Christians; the metropolis; its bishop was at Nicaea, for the " Claudian of Thessaly,"" as he is called in most of the lists, is the bishop of Larissa. The Greek recension actually describes him as such).

Debeltum in Thrace (Eus. v. 19 informs us that this town had a bishop towards the close of the second century. From the same passage we may perhaps infer that a Thracian provincial synod was held there over the Montanist controversy, but more probably the Thracian bishops in question went to Apollinaris at Hierapolis).

Anchialus in Thrace (which also had a bishop about the same time; loc. cit.). Philippopolis was the capital of Northern Thrace (cp. the semi-Arian synod there in 343), so that it certainly had a bishop also before 325.

ckicopolis in Jipi MS (according to Eus., H. E., vi. 16, Origen was there; so that there must have been local Christians at that time Paul wished to winter there, according to the epistle to Titus).

Byzantium in Europe (where the Christologist Theodotus

This edict, designed by Pius for Thessalonica, Athens, Larissa, and "the Greeks" (the scope of this address is unfortunately obscure), shows that the strength of Christianity in these cities must not be underrated. Of course, one has to bear in mind the intolerance of Greeks in all matters of religion.

He found a version of the Old Testament hitherto unknown to him.

According to Epiph., Hcer., liv. i, Theodotus abjured his faith during a persecution (hence there was one before 190 in Byzantium, i. e., perhaps under Marcus Aurelius).

was born about 190 a. d. Hippol., Philos., vii. 35; perhaps one may refer also to Tert., ad Scap. iii,; local martyrs, cp. Mart. Syr. and Eus., Vit. Const., iii. 48; on Alexander, the local bishop when Arius appeared, cp. Alex, of Alex, in Theodoret, H. E., i. 2; on 9. Qth Nov. 326 Constantinople was founded., and on Wth May it zaas dedicated)." x i:

Heraclea = Perinthus in Europe, the iiieti: opolis (numerous martyrs, according to Mart. Syr.; cp. also Erbes in Zeits. f. K. Gesch., XXV. 3; also a "primitive" martyr called Marcianus; J j- i Nicaea, bishop Paederus).

Stobi in Macedonia (bishop Budius at Nicaea). TDhebes in Thessaly (bishop Cleonicus at Nicaea). n Euboea (Bishop Marcus at Nicaea).

I Pele in Thessaly (bishop Ballachus at Nicaea; doubtful, how- ever).

Scupi = Uskub in Dardania (Nicaea. The entry runs as follows: Aapoaiza? " Aaco? Mafe(5ova?, alluding to this bishopric).

Trustworthy notices of the martyrs permit us finally to assume the existence of Christians in Adrianopolis Mart. Syr.,

Ruinart, p. 439; cp. Theod., H. E., ii. 15), Drizipara = Drusipara, - and Epibataju- nidentified) in Thrace, Buthrotum in Epirus, and
Pydna.3"

1 Cp. the pretty legend in Philoslorg., H. E., ii. 9: Koovfftavtlvov rhv vipifioxov dpt vevov, fidsriv re ireptieyai, rh Sopv rrj X 'P (pfpovra' etrel 5Â to7s iiroixtvois is6Kei xei oj i) irpoatike rh fietpov ekTiivew, wpo(Te 6i7y Tt alnif riua cot Siawv- Bdviffdai, ioos TTOv, diffitOTa â Thv 5e awokpivdj. tvoi' 5iappr 5T v (pdvai, kics i 6 fXTrpoaofv jxov (Try, iirisri oi' â jroiovvta, oij vvafits avTOv tis ovpavia irporiyolTO, Tov Trparrofjlevov Sisdffkakos (" Constantine, he says, went out on foot to mark the circuit of the city, carrying a spear in his hand. When his attendants thought he was measuring too much ground, one of them came up to him, and aslced him, How far, O prince? He replied, Until He who precedes me stops. By this answer he signified that some divine power was leading him on and instructing him what to do ").

' The presence of Christians at Chalcis in Euboea, under Decius or Valerian, may be inferred with some likelihood from Jerome de Vir. Inl. Ixxxiii.)â a passage in which Methodius of Olympus seems to be confused with a certain Methodius of Chalcis who was martyred under Decius or Valerian.

At Tricca in Thessaly, a certain Heliodorus was bishop (according to Socrates, H. E., V. 22). If he is to be identified, as Socrates declares he is, with the author of the romance, he must have lived at the close of the third century, for the romance dates from the reign of Aurelian, and was a youthful work. Rohde, however, doubts this identification.

â V-, Thracian Christianity was that of Bithynia. No distinctive Macedonian or Greek Christianity ever arose, hke the Christianity of Asia Minor, or of Syria, or of Pontus-Armenia, or of Egypt, vigorous as the missionary efforts of the Thessalonian church may have been. The martyr-Acts furnish one or two indications of Christianity as it developed at Thessalonica and elsewhere.

Â 12. M(Esia AND Pannonia, Noricum and Dalmatia"

On the soil of Moesia (and of Pannonia, in part), while the â Â Cc Romans and the Greeks competed for the task of ruling and , ru developing the land, the former gradually got the upper hand, 1e 6 Â- and the province must have been counted as Western in the e, Y main at an early period. Here, too, we find from Acts of y y't martyrs (under Diocletian) and the church's history in the fourth tft K century, that Christianity had secured a firm footing in the : diird century. Even by the time that Eusebius wrote, however, the local churches (like those of Pannonia) were still young. At r,1 the dedication of the church at Jerusalem, he writes Vita Con- stant. iv. 43), the Mcesians and Pannonians were represented by

"the fairest bloom of Godisyouthful stock among them " ra Trap' avtoh auoovvta KaxXrj r? tov Oeov ieoaaa?). All that we

V learn from the Nicene subscriptions is that in " Dacia "" (the country south of the Danube, modern Servia) at Sardica there was one bishopric (Protogenes, a Greek), with another (bishop

Pistus) at Marcianopolis in Moesia (near the shores of the Black

Sea), but the Acts of the martyrs attest the presence of Christians at Dorostorum = Dorostolum = Durostolum (Ruinart, p. 570, and Mati. Dasii)J Tomi (Mart. Sijr.

Axiupolis (Mart. Syr.)., and Noviodunum (in Moesia Inferior; Mart. Syr.) previous to the council of Nicasa. Perhaps there was also a bishopric at ' According to Epiphanius Har,, lxxviii. 23 and lxxix. i), the heretical worship of Mary arose in Thrace (and Scythia Superior) and was imported into Arabia (ftis fts uvofia. rris oanrapoevov Kowvplsa Tiva 4iritf elv sc. women Ka ffwayeffoai itrl TO avtO kox Â jj ovona ttjs aylas irapohyov inrep rh xetpof ri irfipaffdai a. dâ j. itf Kol P affl'finj ewixfipi i' irpayfiari Ka tls vvofxa avrris iepovpyelv 5ia yvfaikoiv).

- Cp. Map VII.

Leontius the bishop of Lydian Tripolis, cina 340 A. D., came from Moesia (cp. Philostorgius in Suidas, s. v. "Leontius").

Naissus (Moesia Superior) before 325 a. d.; the bishop was at the synod of Phihppopohs.

One Pannonian bishop (called Domnus) was present at Nica a (bishopric unknown). The Acts of the martyrs tell us of Christian communities at Sirmium Mart. Syr., Ruinart, p. 432), Cibalis (ibid., pp. 433 f.), Siscia (ibid., p. 521; cp. Jerome's Chron., ad ann. 2324), Singidunum (ibid., p. 435),- Scarabantia (ibid., p. 523), and Sabaria, the birthplace of Martin of Tours, whose parents, however, were pagans (ibid., p. 523). " Very many years" (plurimi anni) had elapsed in 304 a. d. since bishop Eusebius suffered martyrdom at Cibalis; and as he probably perished under Valerian, this is our earliest piece of evidence for the existence of a Christian community in these regions. The diocese of the notorious bishop Valens at Mursa would also be ante-Nicene (cp. Socrates, he. cit.). Even the distant Pettau (in modern Styria) had a bishop chxa 300 a. d., and in Victorinus j it had one who was famous as a theologian and author, well versed in Clraek Christian literature. Pannonia was Romanized, but the last offshoots of Hellenism may have penetrated to this province.

It is extremely surprising how few bishops from Moesia or Pannonia (even from the provinces mentioned under Â 11) were present at Nic a. Was the emperor indifferent to their presence? Or had they themselves no interest in the questions to be debated at the council? We cannot tell. Nevertheless, the fourth century saw a large part of the mental interchange between East and West realized in the church of one province, and that province was Moesia.

The likelihood is that the number of bishops (and consequently of churches also) was still small (see above).â It is intrinsically probable that Christianity also penetrated

In these regions military martyrs seem to have been particularly numerous.

Ursacius was the bishop of this place (cp. Socrat., H. E,, i. 27).

â Cp. Hauck, Kircheng. d. Deiitschla7tds, I. '- ' pp. 346 f.: "Noricum was a purely Latin province (cp. the Vila Severini, and Mommsen, v. 180). The neighbourhood of Italy, and the brisk trade (dating as far back as the Etruscan age) with this country, suggest an early invasion of Noricum by Christianity. From the East, too, several seeds of the faith would be borne to the Alpine regions, for Syrian traders visited the towns of Noricum as well as of Gaul."

Noricum, a country studded with towns and wholly Romanized by 300 A. D., with Pettau, too, lying close upon its boundary. But the only direct evidence we possess is a notice of the martyrdom of St Florian in Lorsch Martyrol. Jer.: " in Norico ripense loco Lauriaco," cp. Achelis, op. cit., p. 140). A saint called Maximilian was also honoured in Salzburg (Hauck's Kirchen-gesch, Deutschlands, i. p. 347), and Athanasius mentions bishops of Noricum about the year 343 (Apol. c. Avian i.; Hist, ad Mon. 28) who attended Sardica. But, apart from Lorsch, no church in Noricum and no bishopric can be certainly referred 'v I" to the pre-Constantine period. Next to Lorsch, Teurnia has the best claim to be assigned an early bishopric. There is no pre-Constantine evidence for Juvavum.

Paul seems to imply that he visited Illyrian territory (Rom. XV. 19), and we are told that Titus went to Dalmatia (2 Tim. iv. 10). The wealth of inscriptions which have been discovered reveal a considerable amomit of Christianity in Dalmatia, which may be held with great probability to go back to the pre-Constantine period, particularly as regards Salona (martyrdoms also; cp. Mart. (S r., and now C. I. L., vol. iii., Supplem., Pars Poster.), where a local churchyard is traced back as far as the beginning of the second century (Jelic, in the Rom. Qiiartalschrift, vol. v., 1891; cp. Bull, di archeol. et storia Dahnat., vol. xv., 1892, pp. 159 f.). The episcopal register of Salona can still be partially reconstructed. Domnio was bishop of Salona, and was martyred there under Diocletian. He was followed by Venantius (before 312 a. d.), and shortly afterwards by Primus, whose epitaph has been discovered by Bulic. He is called " nepos nephew? of Domnio the martyr. " Four Christian stonemasons worked in the mines of Fruschka Gora, whither Cyril, bishop of Antioch, was also banished (cp. Passio quattuor coronat., in Sitzungsherichte der K. Preiiss. Akad. d.

1 The " Martyrdom" which is extant is worthless.

â â Was this originally the Mauretanian, whose remains were brought to Rhsetia?

3 i. e., Lauriacum at the mouth of the Enns.

i. e., Tiburnia, in Carinthia, on the upper waters of the Drave.

Cp. Annal. Boll., xviii. (1899), pp. 369 f. ("Saints d'Istrie et de Dalmatie"), and Delehaye's essay on " L'hagiographie de Salone d'apres les dernieres d couvertes archeol." (a'., vol. xxiii., 1904, p. is).

Wissensch., 1896, pp. 1288 f.). No Christians, or at least extremely few, would be lodged in the Dalmatian islands, which were, as a rule, thinly populated (cp. Jerome's Ep. Ix. 10: " insularum Dalniatiae solitudines ").

Â 13. The North and North-West Coasts of THE Black Sea

Theophilus, bishop of " Gothia,"' ' and Cadmus, bishop of Bosporus, attended the Nicene council. Both bishoprics are indeed to be looked for on the Tauric peninsula, but it is possible that " Gothia " was the bishopric of Tomi. It does not follow that because there were Christians in those cities there were Christian Goths by that time, for the cities were Greek. But it is certain that the conversion of this German tribeâ though of individuals in it, onlyâ had commenced before the year 325. On a military raid through Asia Minor in 258, the Goths had captured and taken home with them a number of Cappadocian Christians, who maintained their Christian standing, continued to keep in touch with Cappadocia, and did mission-work among the Goths themselves (Philostorg., ii. 51. It was Ul filas, of co urse, who initiated the work of converting the Goths upon a large scale, but shortly before his day mission-work in the interior of Gothia (ev ra ea-dorara rrjg Torolag) was undertaken by the Mesopotamian monk Arnobius, who had been banished to Scythia (cp. Epiph., Hcer., Ixx. 14). Still,

Sozomen (viii. 19) notes as a striking fact, that the Scythians had only one bishop, although their country included 1 Cp. Map VII.

2 The version of the Bible by Ulfilas proves that Gothic then possessed a considerable number of Latin loan-words, but hardly any Christian ecclesiastical terms. There was also a later and smaller proportion of Greek loan-words (perhaps originally the creation in part of Ulfilas himself), which included many ecclesiastical technical terms.

This connection between the Gothic Christians and Cappadocia survived and revived in the fourlh century. The epistle of the Gothic church, recounting the martyrdom of St. Sabas (Ruinart, pp. 617, f., ed. Ratisbon), is addressed to a Cappadocian church towards the close of the fourth century. Cyril of Jerusalem Catech., x. 19) mentions martyrs about the middle of the fourth century, not only in Persia but among the Goths, meaning not Greek residents but Goths themselves.

a number of towns (in which, of course, there were Christians). Tradition tells us of some martyrdoms, which are not quite certain, at the Tauric town of Cherson (Sebastopol) during the reign of Diocletian. So far as I know, the inscriptions discovered in Southern Russia have not revealed any Christian item which can be referred with certainty to the first three centuries.

Â 14. Rome, Middle and Lower Italy, Sicily, AND Sardinia

For these and all subsequent regions in our discussion, the Nicene list ceases to be of any service; all it furnishes is the bare fact that deputies from the bishop of Rome, bishop Hosius of Cordova (as the commissioner of Constantine), bishop Marcus of Calabria (from Brindisi?), bishop Caecilian of Carthage, and bishop Niqasius of Duja in Gaul (= Die), were present at the council. In place of it we get the episcopal lists of the synods of Carthage (under Cyprian), Elvira (in Spain, c. 300), Rome (313 a. d.), and Aries (314). The beginnings of Christianity in the Western towns (including Rome) and in the provinces are obscure throughout. A priori, we should conjecture that Rome took some part in the Christianizing of these regions, but beyond this conjecture we cannot

The statement of Sozomen (ii. 5) does not seem unhistorical: iraai apfidpois he is thinking primarily of Goths and the allied races crxtshv TTp6ta(ns ffwefi-r) irpefiivfiv tj) S6yfia, ruiv Xpi(TTtavav oi ytvi juvoi koto. Kaiphv 'Pa)fj. aiots n Kal a o(pv ois iwl rrjs Fawfftvov fiytfiovias Kal twv (ht' avrhu fiaffikfcov ("Almost all the barbarians professed to honour Christianity, from the date of the wars between the Romans and the foreign tribes under Gallienus and his successors").

2 Cp. Map VIII.

The authoritative position of Rome among the Italian churches is exactly parallel to the metropolitan position of the provincial capital in the province. Italy was first divided into (17) provinces by Diocletian, so that there were not any ecclesiastical provinces. As the Italian communities were treated as part of the Roman community, so the Roman Christian community also held and exercised authority, practically and therefore legally, over the Christian churches of Italy. The Roman bishop became not so much the metropolitan of Italy as the regulative authority for all the Italian churches in virtue of his position as "episcopus Romanus." The alteration which took place towards the close of the fourth century lies outside our present purview. The supreme power of the Roman bishop included the right of ordination, as soon as ever that developed. What held true of the Roman community in relation to the Italian churches, applied alsoâ though less definitely and rigidlyâ to iis relations with the Christian go. The later legends which vouch for systematic missionary enterprise on the part of the Roman bishops are unauthentic one and all. Some basis for them may have been afforded by the famous passage in the epistle of Pope Innocent I. to bishop Decentius Ep. xxv. 2): " It is certain that throughout all Italy, Gaul, Spain, Africa, and Sicily, and the intervening islands, no one has founded any church except those appointed to the priesthood by the apostle Peter or his successors." But this passage itself is a product of tendency, and destitute of historical foundation.

In Rome and throughout Italy Christianity at first spread among Jiia Greek population and retained Greek as its language. E ven Hippolytus, who belonged to the Roman church and died circa 235 a. d., wrote exclusively in Greek; and the first jiuthor to employ the Latin tongue in letters, so far as I know, is the Roman bishop Victor (189-199). The episcopal list of the Roman church down to Victor contains only a couple of Latin names. When Polycarp of Smyrna reached Rome in 154 he conducted public worship there i. e., in Greek), and it was in Greek that the ancient Roman symbol was composed (about the middle of the second century, or, as communities of the Roman world at large. " Ecclesia Romana semper habuit primatum," i. e., it possessed it, as soon as the circumstances of the political organisation and authority began to be important and normative for the churches of the Roman empire, while at the same time a sort of politico-ecclesiastical unity began to prevail in all the churches.

1 One recollects Seneca's remarks upon the population of Rome: "Jubeistos omnes ad nomen citari et unde domo quisque sit quaere; videbis maiorem partem esse quae relictis sedibus suis venerit in maximam quidem et pulcherrimam urbem, non tamen suam" (" Have them all summoned by name, and ask each his birthplace. You will find the majority have left their homes and come to the greatest and fairest of citiesâ yet a city which is not their own"), adv. Helv. 6.

"I have discussed the origin of the first 48 (47) popes in the Sitzungsber. der K. Preuss. Akad. d. IVissensck. (1904), 14th July, pp. 1044 f. The fqllaffling;. 2? " Nicene bishops are described in the list as "Groeci," viz. (Anacletus), Euaristus, Telesphorus, Hyginus, Elcutherus, Anterus, Xystus II., and Eusebius; Anicetus is said to have been a Syrian, Victor and Miltiades Africans, Gaius a Dalmatian. The rest are " Romani" (Cletus, Clement, Alexander, Xystus I., Zephyrinus, Callistus, Urbanus, Pontianus, Fabianus, Cornelius, Lucius, Stephanus, Felix, Marcellinus, Marcellus, and Sylvester) or " Itali" (Linus and Pius) or " Campanus " (Soter) or "Tuscus" (Eutychianus). The origin of Dionysius is undefined. From Victor onwards (perhaps even earlier) the majority of the vol,. II.

some hold, later). The Roman clergy did not become predominantly Latin till the episcopate of Fabian (shortly before the middle of the third century), and then it was that the church acquired her first Latin writer of importance in the indefatigable presbyter Novatian. Long ere this, of course, there had been a considerable Latin element in the church. Since the middle of the second century, there must have been worship in Latin at Rome as well as in Greek, necessitating ere long translations of the Scriptures. But the origins of the Latin versions of the Bible are wrapt in mystery.

They may have commenced in Northern Africa earlier than in Rome itself. Very likely they were prior to 200 a. d.

The church of Rome was founded by some unknown missionaries at the beginning of the apostolic age. It was already of considerable importance when Paul wrote to it from Corinth; it comprised several small churches (ecclesiolae, Rom.

statements seem to me trustworthy. Anacletus and Telesphorus are said to have come from Athens, Euarislus from Antioch, and his Jewish father Judas from Bethlehem; Anicetus is reported to have journeyed from Emesa, Rufinus from Aquileia, Soter from Fundi, Eleutherus from Nicopohsâ all these items are worthless. But it is credible that Eutychianus (275-283) came from the town of Luna in Tuscany. The districts of five of the bishops born at Rome are given (possibly some local churches were connected with the memory of these popes).

Jordan Rhythtnische Prosa in der altchristl. lat. Lift., 1905) has recently attempted, on the ground of the rhythm, to prove that the Latin text is the original. But, apart from the fact that this involves a transposition in one passage, the rhythm affords no convincing evidence.

- Possibly there are some Roman writings among the pseudo-Cyprianic writings, which are earlier than Cyprian.

According to the "Shepherd" of Hermas, the church still seems entirely Greek; at least, the author never mentions bilingual worship, though he might have done so. Still, the Latin versions of his own book, of Clemens Romanus, and of the baptismal symbol, fall probably within the second century.

â It is very remarkable that the founders of the Roman church are never mentioned. The list of persons saluted in Rom. xvi. opens with Prisca and Aquila (and the church in their house). Though this indicates that they were the "most prominent" Christians in Rome, yet they are specially mentioned for their services not to the local church but to Paul (and with Paul). If the " church in their house" probably was the oldest circle within the Roman church (though this is not certain), Prisca and Aquila certainly were not the first Christians in Rome or the founders of the church as a whole. Then comes Epsenetus, " the first-fruits of Asia for Christ." Obviously there was a Christian elite; this description of Epzenetus (who was either a temporary or permanent resident) explains why he was put second. Then comes a woman who has deserved well of the church, Mary; then two " apostles," older in point of Christianity than Paul himxvi.); and " its faith was spoken of throughout all the world " (i. 8). By the time Paul himself reached Rome, there was even a small church " in Caesar s household" (ev alcrapo? oikia, Phil. iv. 22). Not long afterwards, when the Neronic persecution burst upon the church, an " ingens nmltitudo Christianorum" (Tacitus) or-kokv ttaj o? ecxecrwi (Clem. Rom. vi.) were resident in Rome. Allowing for the fact that "crowd" means one thing in the case of judicial murders and another thing in that of popular assemblies, we may still regard both of these calculations as sufficiently weighty. The members of the church of Rome must at that time have been already counted by hundreds.

Paul and Peter both fell in this persecution. But the church soon recovered itself. We meet it in the epistle of Clement (about 95 A. D.), consolidated, active, and alive to the duty of caring for all the church. The discipline of " our troops" presents itself to this church and the other churches as a pattern of conduct, uniting them together in the ranks and regulations of Christian love. The " rule of tradition " is to be maintained by the church. Order, discipline, and obedience are to prevail, not fanaticism and wilfulness; every element of excited fervour seems to be tabooed. The Christian church of Rome had in fact adopted even by this time the characteristics of the city, Greek though the church was in nature. It felt itself to be the church of the world's capital. And already it numbered among its members some of the emperor's most intimate circle.

self, Andronicus and Junias. These, however, cannot have been the founders of the Roman church. They only came to Rome later, after having once been in prison with Paul. The Roman church had really no proper founders; or else those who might have claimed this title were insignificant people who perhaps were already dead.

Many scholars, of course, refer this chapter to Ephesus, but I cannot perstiade myself that ol e'c ran 'Apifftopovxou and ol in tsov Hapxiffaov (lo-li) are to be looked for anywhere except at Rome.

The Roman Christians Claudiu s E 3hesus and Valerius Biton, mentioned in Clem. Rom., would also belong to this group. They are aged and honoured circa 95 A. D.

T. Flavius Clemens and Domitilla, cp. above, p. 46.â The first Chiijtian catacombs at Rome were already begun. It is impossible to discuss them here. Let me only say that the number, the size, and the extent of the Roman catacombs

This consciousness on the part of the Roman church, which was justified by the duties which it discharged, was recognized by other churches. Ignatius, the bishop of Antioch, extols it about 115 A. D. in extravagant language as being the "leading church in the region of the Romans" Trpokaoijrat ev to'ttod Xwpiov 'J Mulalwv) and " the leader of love" 'jrpokaorjixevr) rrii ayairt?, ad Rom., inscript.), whilst Dionysius- of Corinth writes to her, about 170 a. d. (Eus., H. E., iv. 13), in terms that have been already quoted (cp. vol. i. p. 184).

These and other passages imply that the church had ample means at her disposal, and this, again, suggests a large number of members, including many rich peopleâ an inference corroborated by the " Shepherd " of Hermas, a Roman document which opens our eyes to the state of the church in Hadrian''s reign. It reveals a very large number of Christians at Rome, and the presence among them of a considerable number of well- to-do and wealthy members, with whom the author is naturally wroth. The epistle jf-Igttatius also proves how the church had pushed its way into the most influential circles of the population. Why, the good bishop is actually afraid of being deprived of his martyrdom through the misguided intervention of the Roman Christians! It goes without saying that, under such circumstances, the needs of the Christian community at Rome could not be met by a single place of assembly. Justin Acta Justint) says so explicitly. When asked by the j udge, "Where do you meet?" he replies, "Where everyone chooses and wherever we can" which is evasive. " Think you we can all meet in one place? Not so" evoa â Ka(TTU) 7rpoaipecri9 Kai ovvafxii; ecrti. irai rm yÂ p vofxii eig eiri TO avtO cruvepx fyoai yua? Trajra?; ovx oitco? 8e). Still more which can be certainly referred to the pre-Constantine period is so great that even from them we may infer the sizc-of the Roman church, its steady growth, its adherents from distinguished families, its spread all over Rome, etc. Wilpert, in his monumental work on Dze Malereien der Katakomben Rows (1903), has established important data for the chronology. He carries on the work of de Rossi Roma Sotteranea and Inscript. Christiana: Urbis Romce Saculo VII. Antiijiiiores, 1861-1888), but the Christian inscriptions of Rome still await an editor who shall complete the labours of the latter distinguished scholar.

We know that Marcion brought her a present of 200,000 sesterces when he joined her membership (cp. above, vol. i. p. 156).

valuable is the evidence afforded soon after 166 a. d. by the Koman bishop Soter, the author of the so-called second epistle of n lement. He observes, in explaining a prophetic passage, (c. ii.), that Christians were already superior in numbers to the Jews; and although the statement is general, one must assume that, as it was written in Rome, it applied to Rome, and especially to middle and lower Italy. This statement occurs in a letter (i. e., in a homily) addressed by Soter to Corinth. The fact of Soter addressing a foreign church, and of the church in question accepting its superiors communication with such gratitude and respect as we find expressed in the reply of Dionysius of Corinth, is a further proof of the repute enjoyed by the Roman church far beyond the bounds of Italy. The Corinthians promise to read this communication on Sundays, as they had already done with the Roman encyclical forwarded by Clement.

Thanks to the large number of Christians from all provinces and sects who continued to flock to Rome, not merely did local Christianity go on increasing, but the church would have had the duty of caring for the interests of the church at large ' He is explaining Isa. liv. i, partly of the Jews, partly of the Christians; and in this connection he observes, eprj uos e56K(i dyai airh tov 6iov 6 ahs 7)fiwv, vvv Se TTicrrevcravtis irkiioves iyiv6fjl(0a rwy Sokouvrwy ex '-" (ce above, p. 4).

An almost complete survey is given by Caspari in his Quellen z, Gesch. des Taufsymbols, vol. iii. (1875)-

Cp. the fresh evidence for the size of the Roman church circa 180 A. D. in the Coptic Acta Palling. Schmidt, p. 83). But the most important testimony to the size and prestige of the Roman church is that of Irenigus (iii. 3): " Sed quoniam valde longum est, in hoc tali volumine omnium ecclesiarum enumerare successiones, maximae et antiquissimae et omnibus cognitae, a gloriosissimis duobus apostolis Petro et Paulo Romae fundataeet constitutae ecclesiae eam quam habetab apostolis Iraditonem et annuntiatam hominibus fidem per successiones episcoporum pervenientem usque ad nos indicantes confundimus omnes eos, qui quoquo modo. praeterquam oportet colligunt. ad hanc enim ecclesiampropterpoientiorem principalitatem necesse est otnnem cotivenire ecclesiam, hoc est eos qtii sunt tmdique Jideles, in qua semper ab his qui sunt undique consei-vata est ea quae est ab apostolis traditio" (" But since it would be very long in such a volume as this to enumerate the series of bishops in all the churches, we confound all who in any way. otherwise than they ought, meet for worship, by pointing out the tradition (which it holds from the apostles) of the most great and ancient and universally known church founded and established at Rome by the two most glorious apostles, Peter and Paul, and also the faith declared to men which comes down to our own day' through the episcopal successions. For to this chtirch, on account of its more thrust on her, even had she not spontaneously assumed it.

s pesides, her position in the city grew stron ger day by day. In i U ' ' connection the age of Commodus marked an epoch by itself.

' Eusebius relates (v. 21) how "our affairs then became more favourable, while the saving word led an uncommonly large i ic number of souls of every race to the devout worship of God.

In fact, a number of those who wei'e eminent at Rome for their ‚Â.0 "' wealth and birth, began to adopt the way of salvation, with their whole households and families." It is well known, e. g., how much influence the Christians (cp. above, pp. 47-48) had ",. with Marcia, the " devout concubine â " ((pixooeo i TraaAao) of the

I emperor. The growing size and prestige of the church soon j k vi showed themselves in the despotic attitude assumed by Victor, the Roman bishop, towards the controversy between the Asiatic church and the catholic church (c. 190 a. d.) over the Paschal question.- e The advance made by Christianity among the upper classes, VATt 'S-i d especially among women, in Rome, resulted in the edict of bishop Callistus, which gave an ecclesiastical imprimatur to

"sexual unions between Christian ladies and their slaves.

tlc yia Furthermore, the importance attaching to Christianity in Rome is proved by a number of passages from JTertullian, by the attitude of the Roman bishops after Victor, andhy the large number of sects which had churches in Rome at the beginning f A powerful lead, every church, i. e., the faithful everywhere, tiiust resort; since in it j I the apostolic tradition has been preserved by those who are from everywhere "). Cp. U t my essay in the Sitzungsber. d. K. Preuss. Akad. d. Wiss. (1893, 9th October).

Hippol., Philos,, ix. 12. Thg Rom an bishop Victor went to and from her freely. One gathers from this passage also that the Roman church kept a list of all'who languished in the mines of Sardinia. The archives of the Roman church certainly went far back; cp. my study of the origins of the popes (above, p. 241).

- The Coptic-Arabic Synaxaritun notes, on the loth Hatur (Wiistenfeld, I. p. no), that Victor then held a Roman synod (for which there is other evidence), attended by fourteen bishops and a number of presbyters. The statement may be correct, though the number is so low.

3 The statement of the papal catalogue about Callistus having built a church in Rome across the Tiber ("trans Tiberim ") may be quite authentic. It is quite authentic, at any rate, that under Zephyrinus he was put in charge of a Kotfit TTipiov at Rome, and that he ordained bishops for Italy (Hippol., Philos., ix. 12), â He writes, e. g., of the emperor Septimius: " Sed et clarissimas feminas at clarissimos viros, sciens huius sectae esse, non modo non laesit verum et testimonio exornavil" ad Scap. iv.; cp. above, p. 48).

of the third century. Besides the catholic churches, we know cl.

of a Montanist, a Theodotian (or Adoptian), a Modalist, a Â- jq Marcionite, and several gnostic churches besides the church of (Hippolytus.

After the reign of-Commodus and the episcopate of Victor, (f A the reign of Philip the Arabian and the episcopate of Fabian (236-250) form the next stage in the story (cp. Protest. Real-I EMcymop V. pp. 721 f.). Two phases of organization mark I the growing size of the church at Rome. One is the creation t.vw of the l ower cl ei:Â a. wijbh their five orders, the other is the jl t- division of the Roman church into seven districts (or 7 X 2),. corresponding to tke different quarters of the city (Catal. IC Liber.: " Fabianus regiones divisit diaconibus â '").2 Two items qfevidence throw light upon the extent and the importance of the church at this period (c. 250 a. d.): one is the saying of.

rdecius, that he would rather have a rival emperor in Rome than J a bishop; and the other is the statement of Cornelius, bishop of V Rome, in a letter (Eus., vi. 43), to the effect that " there were ; 46 presbyters, 7 deacons, 7 sub-deacons, 42 acolytes, 52 exor-! t cists, readers, and doorkeepers, and 1500 widows and persons I j in distress, all of whom the Master"'s grace and lovingkindness support'" tt peer But epovi Tecrcrepakovra e, SiakOfovg etrrd, VTTodiakovou evrra, ako ov6ovg Svo Km Tecraepakovra, e opkicTTo. j Se Ka avayvukTTa djixa Truxcopot? Svo koi irevtijkOVTa, XVp(9 crvv' OXi oULevoi? virep Ta? xixlag irevtakocrla, ov â Travta(i rj tov SemrotOV X P' ""â ixavopootrla Siatpe ei).

' Fabian had been a country-bishop in the neighbourhood of Rome, or even a farmer (Eus., H. E., vi. 29).

Cp. Duchesne's Le Liber Pontif,, i. p. 148; and Harnack in Texte u. Inters., ii. 5. The entry in the papal list runs thus: " Hie regiones dividit diaconibus et fecit vii subdiacones."â Apropos of Clement I., the papal list had noted: "Hie fecit vii regiones, dividit notariis fidelibus ecclesiae sic, qui gestas martyrum souicite et curiose unusquisque per regionem suam diligenter perquireret." The statement, of course, is valueless. See further under " Euarestus."

So we learn from Cyprian, Ep. Iv. 9. With this antithesis we may compare a remark of Aurelian, preserved by Flavius Vopiscus Aurelian, c. xx.): " Miror vos, patres sancti, tamdiu de aperiendis Sibyllinis dubitasse libris, proinde quasi in Christianorum ecclesia, non in templo deorum omnium tractaretis" ("I am astonished, holy father, that you have hesitated so long upon the question of opening the Sibylline books, just as if you were debating in the Christian assembly and not in the temple of all the gods").

So far as regards statistics, this passage is the most important in our possession for the church-history of the first three centuries. In 251 a. d. the Roman church had evidently 155 clergy (with their bishop), who were maintained and fed, together with over 1500 widows and needy persons. From this I should put the number of Christians belonging to the catholic church in Rome at not less than 30,000, The forty-six priests perhaps denote as many places of worship in the city; for, as we see from Optatus (ii. 4), there were over forty basilicas in Rome about the year 300 (" quadraginta et quod excurrit basilicas""), This large number indicates the great size of the church.

The great Novatian schism split the Roman church, but only a minority went over to the " Purists." From a letter of bishop Cornelius to Fabius, bishop of Antioch (Eus., H. E., vi. 43), we learn that Novatian was conseci-ated by three imported bishops from " a small and very limited district'"' of Italy paxv n nepoi? Koi. exdxkTTOv), whom Cornelius deposed, ordaining others in their place and sending them to the aforesaid dioceses. In ' So too Renan Marc-Aurele, p. 451). Probably this estimate is too low (Renan: 30,000-40,000). At Antioch, as Chrysostom narrates 0pp., vii. pp. 658, 810), the 3000 persons in receipt of relief were members of one church consisting of over 100,000 souls. In the case of Rome, then, we might put the total at about 50,000, which is the estimate of Gibbon, followed by Friedlander and Dollinger ' Hippolyt und Callist, p. 24). One may assume, however, that the readiness of Christians to make sacrifices was greater about 250 in Rome than it was about 380 in Antioch, so that I should exercise caution and calculate only 30,000, which would amountâ if one puts the population of Rome very roughly at 900,000â to about a thirtieth of the population. Friedljinder's Siltengesch., iii. p. 531) calculations bring out a twentieth (50,000 to a million). He may perhaps be right; at any rate, the total about 250 A. D. lies somewhere between a twentieth and a thirtieth (from 5 to 3 per cent.). But between 250 and 312 an extraordinary increase of Christianity certainly occurred everywhere, including Rome, which I doubt not is at least equivalent to a doubling of the previous total (from 10 to 7 per cent.).

For the reasons which led to an increase of presbyters in any town, cp. Schafer Parrkirche u. Stift, 1903). His work deals with the mediaeval situation, but it also throws light upon the early Christian church. He also discusses (pp. 85 f) the Kavwv of the council of Nicsea (can. 16, 17).

Athanasius Apol 2 adv. Artait) mentions the church of Biton the presbyter at Rome as one in which a synod was held.

â This proves (i) once more that the Roman bishop possessed and practised the right of ordination, in fact under certain circumstances the right of appointment, in Italy; (2) that he himself was ordained by Italian bishops, that any the same letter Cornelius tells of a Roman synod held in connection with the schism, attended by s'locty bishops and a larger number of presbyters and deacons, while he closes with a list (which is unfortunately lost) of those bishops who had appeared at Rome and condemned the folly of Novatian. " In this list he gives their names and also the diocese which each represented. He also gives the names of those who did not put in an appearance at Rome, but gave their assent in writing to the decision of those already mentionedâ together with the town from which each wrote." From this we may argue that in thg niiddle of t t the third centui ' Italy possessed at least nearly one hundred il W" bishops; for the absentees and the adherents of Novatian i I ' must be added to the sixty who were present at the Roman synod.) 0 0 '

Shortly after Fabian, Dionysius (259-268) apparently insti- Tv" tuted the class of parish churches in Rome, and at the same 'y-J time fixed the episcopal dioceses under the metropolitan see of n the caoital. the former task beinsr comoleted bv Marcellus v s the capital, the former task being completed by Marcellus V k (308309). Such is Duchesne's (op. cit. i. 157) correct reading of the statements in the papal list: " Hie presbiteris ecclesias dedit et cymiteria et parrocias diocesis constituit," and (p. 164) ' hie fecit cymiterium Novellae via Salaria et xxv titulos in urbe Roma constituit, quasi diocesis, propter baptismum et paenitentiam multorum qui convertebantur ex paganis et propter sepulturas martyrum." The parish churches of the city,

Italian bishop could be summoned to the ordination (for Cornelius did not demur to the abstract right of the imported bishops), but that as a rule bishops in the vicinity of Rome completed the ordination (Cornelius himself being consecrated with the help of sixteen Italian bishops; cp. Cypr., Ep. Iv. 24). According to the Liber diiinms, j). 24, the bishop of Ostia usually consummated the ordination, while the bishops of

Albano and Portus offered up the prayers. But we cannot decide whether this custom obtained as early as the third century. Incidentally, we find that bishop Ursinus was ordained by the bishop of Tibur in the middle of the fourth century.

' In the Coptic-Arabic Synaxariuin for the 12th of Kihak (Wustenfeld, II. pp. 172 f.) the number of presbyters, with the sixty bishops, is put at eighteen. The Roman synod at which Athanasius vindicated his character numbered " mpre than fifty bishops " (f . c. A-zan,.). The numerical agreement is remarkable, but perhaps it is no more than an accident. The two synods were almost a century apart.

- There is no occasion to go into details with regard to these churches, as we have no sources bearing upon their further statistics. But their large number is to the number of twenty-five, are the churches inside the city with their respective districts. The grayeyards are the churchyards connected with the churches round about Rome (there being no rural parishes in the Roman church, and chor-episcopi being unknown in Italy). The "parochiae diocesis" are the episcopal churches under the control of the metropolis; but unfortunately we know neither their number nor their names.

The depth to which Christianity had struck its roots, even in the soil of culture, and the extent to which its doctrines rivalled those of the philosophers, may be seen from the discussions upon the dogmas of the various Christian parties in which Plotinus found it necessary to engage (cp. Carl Schmidfs " Plotinus and his Attitude to Gnosticism and the Christianity of the Church," Texte u. Inters., xx. 4). The Syrian ladies of the royal house, Alexander Severus, Philip the Arabian, and the consort of Gallienus, had already directed their attention to Christianity, while (as we have seen above, p. 133) Aurelian used the church as a basis for his Eastern policy, and favoured that party in Antioch which held by the bishops of Rome and Italy. As for the brotherly feeling and wealth of the Roman Christians at this period, the best proof of these is to be found in their. J support of the churches in Syria, Arabia, and Cappadocia (cp.

above, pp. 136, 155). These contributions, which had become an old custom by the time of Soter (c. 170), were carried out by j(the latter bishop, and are again to be met with in the middle of j the third century; they show, better than all other evidence, -A ij how comprehensive was the care taken of the church at large by the church of Rome.

During the subsequent period we find the usurper Maxentius assuming the mask of friendliness towards Christianity at the beginning of his reign, " i7i order to cajole the people of Rome."" If this statement is reliable (Eus., H. E., viii. 14), it proves that itself significant. The papal catalogueâ erroneously, of courseâ makes Pope Cletus create twenty-four parishes each under a presbyter at Rome; then again we read of Euarestus, " hie titulos in urbe Roma dividit presbiteris."

Dollinger (jv und Callist, pp. io8 f.) is hardly right in arguing that the seven suburban bishops were not so closely connected with the Roman church till the eighth century. But we know no particulars.

Christians must have formed a very considerable percentage of the population. It is contradicted, however, by the fact that Maxentius ere long relied on Roman paganism, and persecuted the Christians. Furthermore, we gather from the measures taken by Constantine immediately after the rout of Maxentius, as well as from his donations, how much importance he attached to the Roman bishop. Finally, the sixth canon of Nicaea informs us that the Roman bishop exercised the unquestioned right of ordination, as metropolitan, over a number of provinces (Italy having been divided up into provinces by Diocletian). The precise delimitation of this large diocese (c. 325 a. d.) cannot now be ascertained, but there can be no doubt that Middle as well as Lower Italy (and Sicily?) was subject to his jurisdiction. Italy was not divided into ecclesiastical provinces by the time of the Nicene council. It is impossible here to discuss the nature

It deserves notice at least that, according to the Liber Pontif., "tempore Marcellini papae fuit persecutio magna, ut intra xxx dies 17,000 hominum pro-miscui it YM per diversas provincias martyrio coronarentur Christiani."

For the older controversies on this topic, see Hefele's Comiuen-Gesch."'- i. (Eng. trans., vol. i.). For the idea of the " urbica diocesis,"' see especially the essay of Mommsen on "The Italian Regions "in 'Cn. o. Kiepert-Festschrift (1898), although it hardly covers the ecclesiastical conception. " In Italy, during the republican period, there were no districts delimited by law, but only city territories." The subjection of the peninsula to Rome found expression in the dissolution of all local confederations (even the surviving Etruscan federation became merely sacro-legal). The names of the tribes survived, without any strict demarcation or administrative significance. This was not altered under the emperors. Previous to Diocletian there was only one division for Italy, viz., that of the eleven Regions (instituted by Augustus), which were simply numbered. These Regions, however, were not spheres of judicial administration (which were excluded by the Roman rule in Italy); they simply served as a basis for the census. The sharp contrast between Italy and the provinces thus remained unaltered. Special districts were only created ad hoc for definite administrative purposes. The "urbica diocesis" for chancery cases is an exception; during the second and third centuries it embraced Latium, Campania, and Samnium. Furthermore, the territory up to the looth milestone along the city-roads formed a special sphere for the " praefectus urbis." But neither this nor the "urbica diocesis," so far as we can judge, has any bearing" on the metropolitan position of the Roman bishop, who enjoyed from the very outset the advantages accruing to him from the lack of any Italian provincial divisions. He was the archbishop of all Italy. Here, too, the political organization is reflected in the history of the ecclesiastical. It was through the provincial redistribution of Italy under Diocletian that the position of the Roman bishop was first threatened indirectly; he now encountered rivals whom he had to subdue. Let me distinctly

Jtrl 252 MISSION AND EXPANSION OF CHRISTIANITY of the practical primacy enjoyed by the Roman bishop, as that comes out in his relations with Africa, Spain, Gaul, and the East, in the middle of the third century.

Such are perhaps the most weighty testimonies available for the increase, the extent, and the importance of the Roman â (uv church. At the same time it must not be overlooked thatj; he i majority of the aristocracy were still pagans (cp Aug., Confess. ' J " viii. 2, 3, etc.).

As for the other Italian cities, we have to bewail the silence of our sources, although the above-mentioned information, which we were able to cull from Cornelius"' account of his synod, is of some value. We saw that there were certainly about one hundred bishoprics in Middle and Lower Italy about 250 a. d.; possibly there were also some in Tipper Italy. Hence it follows that there must have been considerably more at the beginning of the fourth century, for the period 260-300 a. d. was in general a period of the greatest external advance in Christianity. A further inference is that, by the opening of the fourth century, almost every town of considerable size in Italy (perhaps with

I state that such terms as "metropolitan jurisdiction" or "higher metropolitan jurisdiction" cannot properly be used with reference to any of the Western provinces, for there was really no metropolitan class in the West before 325 a. d., as there was in the East. All that transpired was the accruing of certain powers to Rome (and Carthage) under the practical exigencies of the situation. We must think of these powers as in part less, in part greater, than those of the Oriental metropolitan centres, but in any case they were still indefiniteâ an indefiniteness which lasted down to the beginning of the fourth century, and which told in favour of Rome subsequently. The position of Rome as the higher metropolitan and superior church has been recently discussed by LUbeck, op. cit., pp. 92 f., 118, 125 f., 131 f., 208 f.â The acts of a Roman synod held under Sylvester describe its members as including 284 (Italian) bishops, 57 Egyptian bishops, 142 Roman priests, 6 deacons, 6 subdeacons, 45 acolytes, 22 exorcists, and 90 readers from Rome, with 14 notaries. But as the Acts are a forgery, these numbers are worthless.

A synod was held at Rome shortly before that of Cornelius, during the vacancy in the papacy. Novatian (Cypr., Ep. xxx. 8) says of it: "Nos. et quidem multi et quidem cum quibusdam episcopis vicinis nobis et adpropinquantibus et quos ex aliis provinciis longe positis persecutionis istius ardor eiecerat" (" We. in large numbers, and moreover with some neighbouring bishops so that there must have been some in the adjoining towns and some within reach, and some who had been driven away by the heat of that persecution from other provinces at a long distance'"). It is remarkable that bishops, when forced to flee, made their way to Rome.

the exception of the interior) would have Christians (or a bishop) within its walls. Churches can be traced in the following towns:â

Euteol4-.(Acts xxviii. 13 ly

JSaples (the catacombs render it likely that there were Christians here as early as the second century; see also Liber Pontif., s. v. " Sylvester." The local Jews must have been numerous from a very early period).

Antium (Hippol., Philos., ix. 12; the local cemetery above ground was probably very old, cp. Bullett. 1869, pp. 81 f.)."

Portus (Hipp.; synod of Aries in 314 a. d.: " Gregorius episcopus de loco qui est in Portu Romae ").

Dstia (synod of Rome in 313 a. d., '"â Maximus ab Ostia"; synod of Aries, the presbyters Leontius and Mercurius; Lib. Pontif., s. v. "Sylvester").

Ibanum Lib. Pontif., s. v. "Sylvester").

Fundi Lib. Pontif, s. v. " Anterus "). (

Amiternum, near Aquila Texte u. Unters., xi. 2. p. 46).

' The assertion of the papal list (s. v. " Sylvester"; cp. Duchesne, pp. cxxxv. f.), which recurs in other sources, to the effect that Sylvester held a synod of 275 bishops (not that mentioned above), after the council of Nicsea, may be correct. But I pass over this point.

Hermes Vis., ii. 4) unfortunately does not name the "outside cities" (e a) Trdkiis) to which a certain booklet was to be sent. They need not have been confined to Italy. One of the teachers of Clem. Alex, was a Syrian who, during the second half of the second century, stayed in Greater Greece St?-oi., i. 1; cp. Eus., V. 11). Another in the same country came from Egypt. Skily first came into the history of the church in connection with the "Sicilian bee," Pantsenus loc. cit.).

Nissen Italiscke Landeskunde, II. i. (1902), p. 122) ranks Puteoli in the first class of Italian towns, with regard to the number of inhabitants. Puteoli had a strong community of Jews, and the Acta Petri, vi. (Vercell.) presuppose the existence of local Christians. For Pompeii, cp. above, p. 93.

â â Jews (cp. Schol. on Juv., Satir., iv. 117 f.), but not Christians (despite the Acta Petri, vi.), are to be traced at Aricia.

For the signatures to the council of Aries, cp. Routh's Reliq. Sacr." iv. pp. 312 f.

"For the signatures to this synod (nineteen bishops), cp. Optat., I. 22 f.; Routh, pp. 280 f.

" If Ursimis was consecrated (see above) by the bishop of Tibur in the fourth century (middle of), Tibur must have had a bishopric by the date of the Nicene council.

Aureus Mons, or some other locality in Picenum ibid. pp. 47, 53).

Tres Tabernas (synod of Rome, 313 a. d., "Felix a Tribus Tabernis").

Sinna Cesena? Siena? Segni? (ibid. y "Florianus a Sinna").

Quintianum (ibid., "Zoticus a Quintiano"").-

Rimini ibid., "Stennius ab Arimino"").

Florence (ibid., "Felix a Florentia").

Piga (ibid., "Gaudentius a Pisis ").

Faenza (ibid., "Constantius a Faventia").

Forum Claudii Oriolo ibid., "Donatianus a Foro Claudii"").

Capua (ibid., "Proterius a Capua "; Aries, 314 a. d., "Proterius episc, Agrippa et Pinus Agrippinus? diacones diaconus "; Lib. Pontif., s. v. "Sylvester." There was also a local Jewish community).

Terracina (Rome, 313 a. d.; " Sabinus a Terracina"'; cp. Acta Petri et Pauli, 12, and Acta Ner. et A chill.).

Praeneste (ibid., "Secundus a Praeneste"").

Ursinum (ibid., "Evandrus ab Ursino""). â '

Beneventuin (i6id, "Theophilus a Benevento "'â ').

Brindisi (cp. above, p. 240).

Syracuse (Cyprian; Eus., H. E., x. 5, 21; Aries, 314 a. d., "Chrestus episcopus, Florus diaconus ").

The bishop stood between the bishops of Prreneste and Ostia; hence the Tres Tabernse in question is that on the Via Appia, not any of the other places of this name.

"Perhaps = Quintiana on the coast, north of Centumcellse.

It is looked for near Rome, but I know no place of this name. We cannot suppose any misspelling (Urbinum).

â â The earliest proof of any Christian churches in Sicily is furnished by Cyprian's thirtieth epistle, c. 5, although the sites of the Christian catacombs may actually go back as far as the second century. This epistle informs us that during the Decian persecution letters were sent by the Roman clergy to Sicily. As Syracuse is known to have been the capital of Sicily in the fourth century, there must have been a local church in existence about 250 A. D. Cp. Fiihrer's Forsch. zur Sicilia Sotteranea (1897), pp. 170 f. He shows that one catacomb-structure in Syracuse was made shortly after 260 a. d. "While the smallnumberof Christians in the town, during the first centuries of our era, contented themselves, to all appearance, with a series of small subterranean chambers or isolated catacombs of no great size as burial-places,â such as have been preserved near the erstwhile Capuchin monastery and southwards along the railway to Catania,â the need for larger cemeteries was first felt during the era of peace which followed the stormy persecution of Valerian

Civita Vecchia Centumcellae (Aries, 314 a. d., "Epictetus a Centumc").

Civitas Arpiensium in Apulia (Aries, 314 a. d., "Pardus episc, Crescens diaconus"). r iy'"

Cagliari ibid., "Quintasius episc, Ammonius presbyter"). i vis-"

Gseta (Acta Petri et Paidi, 12).

In the towns now to be mentioned, the existence of Christian churches (or bishoprics) is proved from martyrdoms and various notices. Such sources are not absolutely reliable in every case; but when one reflects that there were certainly about a hundred bishops in Italy circa 250 a. d., and still more circa 325 a. d., it becomes a priori probable, on this ground alone, that these towns had Christian churches in them. They are as follows:â

Ancona.

Aquila. p A j

Ascoli Asculum in Picenum. 'â. I fv–

Assisi.

s vellino Abellinum

Bassano (Baccanae in Etruria).

Bettona.

Camerino Camerinum?

Catania (. l.) and added a host of new adherents to the Christian faith. Thus it was after 260 A. D. that the oldest part of the cemetery of S. Maria di Gesu was founded, as well as the foundations of the elaborate catacombs of Vigna Cassia." Of all the other Sicilian catacombs which Fiihrer has enumerated and described (" and no province of the Roman Empire," says N. Muller, "is as rich as Sicily in sub–terranean graveyards, large and small'"), there is not one which I would venture to assign with any confidence to the pre-Constantine period, although Schultze Archao!. Siudien, 1880, pp. 123 f) believes that he can deduce from the evidence of the monuments the existence of a Christian community at Syracuse by the second century, and even by the opening of that century.

For Christians in the mines of Sardinia, cp. Hipp., Philos.,. 12; Catal. Liber,, s. v. " Pontian "; probably also, at an earlier date, Dionys. Cor., in Eus., H. E,, iv. 23. Catacombs in Cagliari.â Eusebius, who became bishop of Vercelli in 340, came from

Sardinia. Paganism long survived in this province. Pope Symmachus (498-514) was a Sardinian (cp. the Lib. Poftlif.). From his Apolog. adv. Anast. we learn that on reaching Rome ("veniensex paganitate") he was baptized.

According to the Acta Euplii. I no longer employ the Acta Felicis episc. Thibiuccb, from which I formerly took Girgenti and Taormina; Monceaux Rev. Arch ol., fourth series, v., 1905, May, June, pp. 335 f.) has shown that the second part of them is unauthentic, and that in the towns of Italy which are in

CumÂ. Â–)
Fano.
Ferentino.
Fermo.
Foligno?
Forli?
Forlimpopoli? (Brictinorium, Bertinoro).
Hybla maior.
Ijeontion.
(Lilybaeum.)
Lucca.
Messina (so Acta Petri et Pauli, 7).
Nepi (et Sutri)?
Nocera.
Nola (the martyr Felix).
(Palermo.)
Perugia.
Pesaro?
Salerno.
Sipontum.
Spoleto.
Teano.
Terni.
Todi.
Trani.

We can probably assume that a Christian church existed at Clusium (in Etruria), as the cemetery of St Catherine appears to belong to the third century (see Bormann in Co7-p. Inscr. Lat., xi. pp. 403 f.).

Lower Italy, as our survey shows, had unquestionably a question (also Messina and Catania) it was not Felix himself, but only his relics which were taken round. Still, there is a certain likelihood that both Girgenti and Taormina had bishops before 325 a. d. I have passed over the bishops (or bishoprics) mentioned in the Lzder Predest., but as it is probable that ch. xvi. rests upon a sound, though misunderstood, tradition, and as it mentions bishop Eustachius of Lilybreum and Theodorus of Panormus, there is some probability of bishoprics having existed in these places about the year 300, and of a Sicilian synod having been held about that time.â On the post-Constantine date of the Maltese catacombs in general, see Mayr, Rovt. Quartahchrift, XV. iii. pp. 216 f. But there were certainly Christians in Malta prior to Constantine.

CHRISTIANITY DOWN TO 325 A. D. 257 larger number of Christian churches than Middle Italy (apart from Rome); though we cannot prove this. The state of matters which prevailed in the interior of Middle Italy, and in fact not very far from the coast, even as late as the opening f of the sixth century, is revealed by the history of Benedict of Nursia. In spite of the prevailing uncertainty, a glance at the map shows that Christianity probably had three central settlements in Italy, viz., Rome, Puteoli-Naples, and Ariminum (Rimini). There seems 'to have also been a small nucleus on the upper waters of the Tiber.

Â 15. Upper Italy and the Romagna

Not merely from negative evidence, but from the history of the church in these districts (though they stood apart politically and in point of civilization) during the fourth and fifth centuries, it is certain that Christianity entered them late and slowly, and that it was still scanty about the year 325 a. d. As it passed from east to west in Upper Italy, Christianity must have fallen off and become more and more sparse. Before 325 we

The existence of numerous bishoprics in Lower Italy is proved by the rescript of Constantine (21st October 319) to Octavian, the viceroy of Lucania and Bruttium (Mommsen, Theodos. Codex, p. 835): "Qui divino cultui ministeria religionis impendunt, i. e., hi qui clerici appellantur, ab omnibus muneribus excusentur, ne sacrilego livore quorundam a divinis obsequiis avocentur."â There was a strong Jewish community (as the catacombs show) at Venosa, but it is uncertain whether there was any Christian church prior to Constantine (cp. N. Miiller, Prot. Real-Encyks x. p. 807).

As I have already (vol. i. pp. 445 f.) discussed it with some thoroughness I do not take up at this point the passage in Theodore of Mopsuestia's commentary on the Pauline epistles (Swete, vol. ii., 1882, pp. 121 f.). " In every province there were usually two, or at most three bishops, at firstâ a state of matters which prevailed till recently in most of the Western provinces, and which may be found still in one or two of them. As time went on, however, bishops were ordained not only in towns but also in small districts." The fourth canon of Nicaea presupposes that in none of the Eastern provinces were there fewer than four bishops. â For the rapid Christianizing which went on during the fourth century, a passage in the eighth sermon of Gaudentius, bishop of Brescia, is very instructive (Migne, Lat. XX. col. 892): "Constat populum gentium ex errore idololatriae, in quem fuerat olim devolutus, nunc ad christianae veritatis cultum celeritate rotae cuiusdam properare currentis."

258 MISSION AND EXPANSION OF CHRISTIANITY have no trustworthy account of any Christians in Piedmont and Liguria. The sole exception is Genoa, and even that is doubtful. The first bishopric in Piedmont was not established till after the middle of the fourth century (cp. Savio's Gli antkhi vescovi (TItalia. II Piemonte, 1898),

The eastern side of Upper Italy, however, can be shown to have possessed several bishoprics, from whose subsequent demeanour and position it is plain that their authority was derived (" auctoritas praesto erat â ") hardly from Rome (at least, not exclusively) but from the Balkan peninsula. Ecclesiastically, it was a longer road from Rome to Ravenna and Aquileia than from Sirmium, Sardica, and Thessalonica. And this state of matters did not originate in the fourth century; on the contrary, it was not till then that, owing to the new political conditions of the age, the Roman church exerted any preceptible 1 The statement of Sulpicius Severus (C raÂ., ii. 32) about the divine religion being received only at a late period on the other side of the Alps (" serius trans Alpes dei religione suscepta," see below) may also be referred to the Maritime Alps.

At the synod of Milan (355 A. D.), Dionysius, bishop of Alba (Pompeia), was present; and Socrates (ii. 36) describes Alba as rj 'Iraxuv j. ritp6iro is. In spite of this, however, we have no guarantee that Alba had a bishopric before 325 a. d. In fact there is the less reason to assume this, as Socrates is most probably wrong in making Dionysius bishop of Alba. He was bishop of Milan. Or, had he previously been bishop of Alba?â Vercelli ("olim potens, nunc raro est habitatore semiruta," Jer., Â p. i. 3) became an episcopal seat in 355 a. d., and Eusebius ("ex lectore urbis Romae," Jer., de Vir. III. xcvi.) was probably the first bishop. In his Kirchetrgeschichte Deiilschlafids, I. ' (p. 26), Hauck thinks he can prove from Ambrose, Epist. i. 63, that some of the bishoprics in Upper Italy had not been long in existence by the time of Ambrose. I do not doubt this. Only I would not rest on the passage in question. Ambrose is writing to the church of Vercelli: "I am consumed with grief, because the church of God in your midst has not a priest yet, it being the only one destitute of such an official in all Liguria or Emilia or Venetia or the rest of the lands bordering on Italy" ("Conficior dolore, quia ecclesia domini, quae est in vobis, sacerdotem adhuc non habet ac sola nunc ex omnibus Liguriae atque Aemiliae Venetiarumque vel ceteris finitimis partibus Italiae huiusmodi eget officio"). Hauck recalls, correctly enough, that the bishopric of Vercelli was several decades old when Ambrose wrote, so that "adhuc non habet" means simply a temporary vacancy; but he infers from "nunc ex omnibus" that the bishoprics of all the Upper Italian churches were of recent origin. Yet, if "adhuc non" merely denotes a temporary vacancy, one can hardly take what follows in a different sense. Indeed, one might infer from the passage that the Christians in all the larger communities of these districts had now bishops of their own.

influence over these towns and districts. The bishoprics were as follows:â

JR. avenna (twelfth bishop at Sardica, 343 a. d.).

Milan (synod of Rome, 313 a. d., bishop Merocles; seventh bishop, the said Merocles, with Severus the deacon, at Aries, 314 A.-D. y

Acjuileia (synod of Aries, bishop Theodorus and the deacon Agathonâ evidently a Greek).

Brescia (fifth bishop at Sardica).

Verona (sixth bishop at Sardica).

Bologna (Mart. Vitalis et Agricolce; see also Martyriol. Syriaciim).

Imola (Mart).

The evidence of martyrdoms and episcopal lists is uncertain upon the existence of churches at Padua (though this is probable on a priori grounds), Bergamo, Como, Piacenza, Modena, Cremona, and Genoa.

The insignificance of the churches even in the larger towns of Upper Italy about the year 300, seems to me to be proved by a passage from Paulinus Mediol. Vita Amhrosii, 14), where we read that " on the invitation of the Florentines, Ambrose travelled down as far as Tuscany. and erected a basilica in the city, where he placed the remains of the martyrs Vitalis and Agricola, whose bodies he had exhumed in Bologna. For the bodies of the martyrs had been buried arnongst the bodies of the Jews nor was their location known to the saints, had not the holy martyrs revealed it to the priest "'â ' (" Invitatus

Hilarius Pict., Liber c. Const, imper., c. ii: " Mediolanensis piissima plebs."

'â Constantine (in 317 A. D.) banished Csecilian, bishop of Carthage, for a time to Brescia. He would not have sent the bishop to a town which had no Christians in it.

St Martin of Tours, when a lad of ten i. e., circa 326-329 a. d.), stayed at Jay ia along with his father, who was an officer of high rank. As Sulpicius Severus (Vita Martini, 2) remarks that " he fled to the church against his parents' wishes, when a lad of ten, and demanded to be received as a catechumen " (" cum esset annorum decem, invitis parentibus, ad ecclesiam fugit seque catechumenum fieri postulavit"), it follows that there must have been a Christian church in those days at Pavia.â The first bishop of Padua of whom we possess reliable information lived in the reign of Constans. There is no trace of bishoprics at Como or Bergamo till the age of Theodosius 1.

Ambrosius a Florentinis ad Tusciam usque descendit. in eadem civitate basilicam constituit, in qua deposuit reliquias martyrum Vitalis et Agricolae, quorum corpora in Bononiensi civitate levaverat. posita enim erant corpora martyrum inter corpora Judaeorum, nee erat cognitum populo Christiano, nisi se sancti martyres sacerdoti ipsi revelarent"). The Christian community at Bologna would seem therefore at the time of the Diocletian persecution to have still been so small that it had no churchyard of its own.

Â 16. Gaul, Belgica, Germany, and Rh. etia

On the shores of the Mediterranean and in the Rhone valley, where the Greek population was in close touch with Asia, Rome, and even Syria, Christianity established itself not later than about the middle of the second century. While the 1 I must avoid entering into any details upon the previous history of the church in the three great centres Ravenna, Milan, and Aquileia. The legend of Ravenna assigns the eleventh and twelfth bishops a reign, between them, of 116 years, in order to run the twelve bishops (dating back from 348 A. D.) back to Peter. If the twelfth bishop of Ravenna attended the synod of Sardica, the local church may have been founded by the opening of the third century or the end of the second. In the early Byzantine period, Milan claimed to have been founded by the apostle Barnabas, and consequently to be the only directly apostolic church in the West, besides Rome. This claim, however, is untenable. The fact of seven bishops having ruled till 316 A. D. suggests that the bishopric (and the church) was founded during the first half of the third century.-The founding of the church at the large town of Aquileia came at a still later period, probably not until the Diocletian era, or shortly before it. Still, a reconstruction of the local church had to be undertaken in 336 a. d., as the older building was no longer adequate (Athanas., Apol. ad Const, imp., 15).

On Hellenism in Southern Gaul, cp. Mommsen's Rom. Gesch., v. pp. 100 f. (Eng. trans., i. no f.), Caspari's Quellen zur Gesch. des Taufsymbols, vol. iii. (1875), and Zahn's Gesch. des neuiest. Kanons, i. pp. 39 f., 44 f. At the opening of the fifth century, monasticism in the maritime districts of Southern Gaul was still in close touch with Eastern monasticism, which is the last clear proof of a vital connection between that seaboard and the East. Even in the third century, however, Greek must have been the language of educated people in'lsouthern Gaul far more than Latin.

For Christians in the valley of the Rhone, see Irenaeus (I. xiii. 7), who speaks of the vicious activity displayed by adherents of the gnostic Marcion: ev rots Ka6' rifxas Khifxaai ttjs 'Posavovcrlas irowas i rtirat-fikaffi yvvatKas ("In our own districts of the Rhone they have deluded many women ").

evidence as regards Marseilles, however, is only inferential (since the inscription which vouches for local Christianity cannot be assigned with absolute certainty to the second century), Vienne and Lyons are attested by the letter sent from the local Christians to the churches of Asia and Phrygia apropos of the persecution in 177 a. d. (Eus., H. E. v. 1 f.), while Lyons is visible during the last two decades of the second century through the works of Irenasus. From the former document we see that Lyons ha J a bishopric by 177 a. d. Vienne was not far from Lyons, although it was in a different province (Narbonensis), but the relationship disclosed by the epistle as subsisting between the two churches is obscure, and we may question, with Duchesne (Fastes episcopaux de Fancieime Gaule, vol. i., 1894), whether Vienne had a bishop of its own at that date. This is not the place, however, to go into such a problem (see above, vol. i. pp. 453 f.). Suffice it to say that it Jiad a Christian community. I cannot accept the opinion that Vienne was quite untouched by the persecution (Neumann, Der r'dmische Staat md die allgem. Kirche, i., 1890, p. 29, note).

All that can be ascertained with regard to the church-history of I yons down to the days of Constantine has been carefully put together by Hirschfeld (" Zur Geschichte des Christ, in Lugdunum vor Konstantin'" in the Sitzungsbeyichte d. K. Preuss. A had. d. Wiss., 1895, pp. 381 f.). I single out the following points.

1. The church must have been predominantly Greek in the days of Irenaeus. This follows from the Greek language of the

The church of Lyons could not have been Greek at all, unless Greek Christianity had existed at the estuary of the Rhone.

- On the peculiar political position of Lyons in Gaul, see Mommsen's A'om. Geschichte, v. pp. 79 f. (Eng. trans., i. p. 87 f.). The percentage of inhabitants who spoke Greek in Xryons cannot have been large, as "unlike any other in Northern Gaul, and unlike the large majority of the Southern, it was founded from Italy, and was a Roman city, not only as regards its rights but in origin and character." The local church, nevertheless, was still predominantly Greek circa 190 A. D.

We should have a much earlier witness, if the reading YakJia. v were correct in 2 Tim. iv. 10 (where Crescens, Paul's helper, goes ets P.), but probably Faaatiaj is the true reading (cp. above, p. 94). Renan allows himself to imagine that Paul visited a seaport of Gaul on his way to Spain Antichrist., Germ, ed., p. 85).

Cp. also Montet, La Ligende (flrhiie et fintrod. du Christianisme h Lyon (1880).

262 MISSION AND EXPANSION OF CHRISTIANITY letter and of the works of Irenaeus, as well as from the names of those who perished in the persecution. Still, as these names indicate, a Latin element was not awanting either. We look in vain for any Celtic names.

2. The church cannot have been large; for, although the persecution was extremely severe, and although it aifected the whole church, the number of the victims did not amount to more than forty-nine. Hirschfeld, who p-p. cit. pp. 385 f.) has made an accurate udy of the list of their names, so far as these have been handed down, throws out the conjecture, which is not unfounded, that the number was even smaller, inasmuch as in a number of cases the public name and the cognomen are probably separated, and thus individuals have been doubled. The paucity of the church members follows also from the fact that a list of the surviving adherents of the faith was in existence even as late as Eusebius (though he has not reproduced it). At this point we must also recollect the general evidence as to the beginnings of Christianity in Gaul, which we possess, e. g. in Sulpicius Severus, Chron., ii. 32: " Sub Aurelio deinde, Antonini filio, persecutio quinta agitata; ac tunc primum inter Gallias martyria visa, serius trans Alpes dei religione suscepta" (" Then under Aurelius the son of Antoninus, the fifth persecution broke out. Then at last martyrdoms were seen in Gaul, the divine religion having been late of being accepted across the Alps"'). In the Passio Satumini (of

Robinson's attempt Texfs and Studies, I. 2. pj). 97 f.) to prove, from the Biblical quotations in the letter, that worship was already conducted in Latin throughout Gaul, is abortive.

- The names are bishop Pothinus, Vettius Epagathus probably a Roman citizen; Gregory of Tours, Hist. Franc, i. 31, says that Lercadius, a senator of Bourges, was a descendant of his, Macarius, Alcibiades, Silvius, Primus or Silvius Primus, Ulpius, Vitalis or Ulpius Vitalis, Cominius, October or Comin. Oct., Philumenus, Geminus, Julia, Albina or Julia Albina, Grata Rogata?, â Emilia, Potamia or JExn. Pot, Rodana, Biblis, Quartia, Pontica, Materna, Helpis quae et Ammas, Sanctus diaconus (from Vienne), Attalus a Roman citizen, Alexander, Ponticus, Blandina, Aristaeus, Cornelius, Zosimus or Corn. Zosimus, Titus, Julius, Zoticus or Tit. Jul. Zot., Apollonius, Geminianus, Julia, Auxentia z'. i. Ausonia, perhaps = Jul. Aus., Emilia, Jamnica or. Emilia Jam, Pompeia, Donina or Pomp. D., Mamilia, Justa or Mam. Justa, Trophima, Antonia.

Cp. also Chron,, II. 33 (of Constantine's reign): "Hoc temporum tractu mirum est quantum invaluerit religio Christiana."

Toulouse) we also readâ ". after the sound of the gospel stole out gradually and by degrees into all the earth, and the preaching of the apostles shone throughout our country with but a slow progress, since only a few churches in some of the states, and these thinly filled with Christians, stood up together for the faith " (" Postquam sensim et gradatim in omnem terram evangeliorum sonus exivit tardoque progressu in regionibus nostris apostolorum praedicatio coruscavit, cum rarae in aliquibus civitatibus ecclesiae paucorum Christianorum devotione consurgerent"). We must reject, as totally untrustworthy, the statement made by Gregory of Tours Hist. Franc. i. 29: " Irenaeus. in modici temporis spatio praedicatione sua maxime in integrum civitatem reddidit Christianam"), to the effect that "in a short space of time Irenagus made the whole city Christian again by his preaching."

3. Among several other unreliable allusions to Christians ii Lyons during the third century, the epitaph of a " libellicus " falls to be noted i. e., of an official in charge

of the " libelli" during the reign of Decius? Hirschfeld, p. 397), as well as a certain bishop Helius of Lyons " tempore paganorum " (Gregory of Tours, Gloria Confess. 61). It is certain that during the age of Cyprian Ep. Ixviii. 1) Faustinus was bishop of Lyons, and that the synod of Aries (314 a. d.) was attended by a bishop, from Lyons called Voccius (Vocius.), with his deacon Petulinus. C "C

Irenaeus relates that he had to preach in Celtic, that there were churches ev Ke Arot? (I. x. 2), and that there were Christians J among the Celts, who possessed the orthodox faith " without ink or paper." The statement that his emissaries reached Valentia and Vesontio is perhaps trustworthy (see Hirschfeld, pp. 393 f),

Cp. in general Le Blant, Inscriptions chr tiennes de la Gaule (1856-65).

Contr. Har., pref.: ovk itrtcrjt crets â wap' rijisiv twv ev Kearois SiatpifiivtCDf Kal irepl fiip apov Sid ekTov rh TrxdctTOv atrxoxouuevoiv KSyaiy Te vri"-

III. iv. 1.: " Cui ordinationi assentiunt multae gentes barbarorum primarily Celts and Germans eorum qui in Christum credunt, sive charta vel atramento scriptam habentes per spiritum in cordibus suis salutem et veterem traditionem diligenter custodientes," etc. ("In agreement with which are many barbarian nations, who believe in Christ, having salvation written by the Spirit in their hearts, and not with ink or pen, who preserve, however, the ancient tradition with care"). Small store is to be set by the passage in Tertullian's adv. jfud. vii. ("Galliarum diversae nationes Christo subditae "=" different nations of Gaul, but we must certainly form a modest estimate of the results of the Celtic mission during the third century. The statements of the Historia Francorum (ix. 3) as to the Western district, where the origins of Christianity are not earlier than the fourth century, hold true of many other parts of the country. But it is otherwise with the larger towns. These, however, owing to the peculiar constitution of Gaul, were not numerous, and only developed by degrees.- As against Duchesne, I am unable to understand Eus., H. E., v. 23 (cp. above, vol. i. pp. 460 f.), except as meaning that when the Paschal controversy was raging, about the year 190, there were several bishoprics in Gaul toov kqtu TaxXlai irapoikioov, a? Yiiprjuaio etrecrcotret, "parishes in Gaul superintended by Irenaeus," cp. v. 24. 11), and that their occupants held a synod at that period under the presidency of Irena us. For these bishops we must look in the first instance to provincia Narbonensis, and the sixty-eighth epistle of Cyprian proves that about the year 255 a. d., at least, there was a bishopric at Arles. Rightly read, this epistle further proves that there was an episcopal synod held not only in the province of Narbonensis but also in that of Lyons, while ci7-ca 190 A. D. they stil seem to have formed a single synod. Hence it follows that several Gallic bishoprics, whose origin Duchesne would relegate to the second half of the third century, arose as early as the first half of that century, in fact even by the end of the second century. A priori, it is probable that at one time Lyons had the sole episcopal see in the provincia subjugated to Christ"). More weight attaches to Hippolytus, Philos., x. 34. From the passages in Irenseus one gets the impression that he must have spoken more Celtic than Greek.

' I pass by the legendsâ e. g., that of seven bishops being sent from Rome to Gaul during the days of Pope Xystus II., and their founding of the churches of Tours, Aries, Narbonne, Toulouse, Paris, Clermont, and Limoges.

'â The poem " Laudes Domini" (cp. my Chronologie, ii. pp. 449 f.) was written by a Gallic Christian orator of Autun, during the reign of Constantine. In Antun also bishop Reticius resided, who wrote against Novatian and composed a commentary on the Song of Solomon ibid., p. 433). Hence Latin Christian literature in Gaul must have begun about 300 A. D. The conflict with Novatianism (see below) shows that the Gallic church stood in the general current of ecclesiastical movements.

Bishop Marcianus of Aries was inclined to Novatianism, and this inclination had to be stamped out in Gaul generally.

Lugdunensis and Belgica, although this cannot have lasted for very long. It is utterly improbable, however, that Lyons was always the bishopric for the provincia Narbonensis.

Special evidence for the Gallic bishoprics is first furnished by the lists of the synods of Rome (313) and Aries (314), as well as by one or two martyrdoms. The following are indubitable:â

In Narbonensis:â Vienne (cp. the epistle; Mah. Aries, bishop Verus and the exorcist Bedas).

Aries (Marcian, the bishop in the days of Cyprian, was an adherent of Novatian; bishop Marinus attended the synod of Rome in 313, cp. Eus., H. E., x, 5. 19; at the synod of Aries in 314 there were forty-three churches represented, from most of the western provinces; besides Martinus, the presbyter Salamus, and the deacons Nicasius, Afer, Ursinus, and Petrus are mentioned at the synod of 314),

Marseilles (Aries, bishop Orosius and Nazarius the reader). Vaison (Aries, bishop Daphnus and Victor the exorcist). Nizza Portus Nicaenus (Aries, the deacon Innocentius and Agapius the exorcist). Orange (Aries, the presbyter Faustinus). Apta Julia (Aries, the presbyter Romanus and the exorcist Victor). Toulouse Ma7i., also trustworthy inferences from later periods). In Lugdunensis:â Lyons (cp. the epistle, Iren., Faustinus, who was bishop in the days of Cyprian; Aries, bishop Voccius and Petulinus the exorcist).

Autun (Flavia Eduorum; Eus., H. E., x. 5. 19; bishop Reticius at Rome, 313, also at Aries with Amandus the presbyter). Rouen (Aries, bishop Avitianus Ausonius, Avidanus?

with Nicetius the deacon). Die (council of Nicaea, 325, bishop Nicasius). Paris Mart., also trustworthy inferences from a later age). Sens Mart., also trustworthy inferences from a later age). In Aquitania:â Bordeaux (Aries, bishop Orientalis and Flavins the deacon).

Eauze (Aries, bishop Mamertinus and

Leontius the deacon). Mende (Aries, Genialis the deacon). Bourges (Aries, bishop Mamertinus and Leontius the deacon). In Belgica:â Treves (Aries, bishop Agroetius and Felix the exorcist). Rheims (Aries, bishop Imbetausius Ambitausus.? a Celt at any rate and Primigenius the deacon). The investigations of Duchesne render it likely that there were Christians, but scarcely bishoprics in the majority of cases, during the pre-Constantine period at Angers, Auxerre, Beauvais, Chalons, Chartres, Clermont, Digne, Embrun, Gi'enoble, Langres, Limoges, Metz, Nantes (martyrs), Narbonne, Noyon, Orleans, Senlis, Soissons, Toul, Troyes, Verdun, and Viviers. Previous to

Constans, Tours had no church (Greg., Hist. Franc, x. 31; the church was restored by the rebuilding of a senator's house).

' At the same time, if even a small town like Die had a bishop in 325 (who was = the deacon Nicasius, at Aries 314? a personal friend of Constantineâ for this is the only natural explanation of the fact that he was the sole bishop from Gaul at the Nicene council), then we must assume that the episcopate was much more widely spread throughout Gaul than we are able to prove in detail. By the time of Hilary of Poitiers (359 A. D.) the episcopal organization of the country had made great strides, but there is certainly plenty of time between 312 and 359 for the addition of many bishoprics (according to Alhanasius, Aol c. Avian. 50, the orthodox resolutions of Sardica were approved by thirty-four Gallic bishops; he gives their names, but not, unfortunately, their dioceses). Important towns may have had Christian communities, without any bishops, for a long while, but one can scarcely appeal with much confidence in favour of this conjecture to the declaration of bishop Proculus of Marseilles before the synod of Turin (in 401 a. d.). In order to justify his claim to metropolitan rights over Narb. II., he speaks of " easdem ecclesias vel suas parochias fuisse vel episcopos a se in iisdem eccelsiis ordinatos." We do not know where these parishes (" parochise") are to be sought; they may have been small towns in the immediate vicinity of Marseilles. This holds good whether these Acts are genuine or, as is very likely, unauthentic.

- Wolfram (in k Jahrb. d. Gesellsch. f. Lothr. Geschichte tind Alterlmnskunde, xiv., 1902, pp, 348 f.) tries to show that a columnar structure in the local amphitheatre goes back to ci7-ca 300 A. D. and represents a Christian church. The latter is likely enough, but it is impossible to be sure that the structure dates from circa 300 A. D.

When Martin became bishop of Tours, there were martyrs' graves at a spot near the city (Sulpicius Severus, Vit. Mart, ii.), but he did not believe they were

The entire diocese was still almost wholly pagan about 375 a. d.; Q ' cp. Sulpic. Severus, Vita Mmiini, 13 ("Ante Martinum pauci admodum, immo paene nulli in illis regionibus Christi nomen receperant: quod adeo virtutibus illius exemploque convaluit, ut iam ibi nullus locus sit, qui non aut ecclesiis frequentissimis aut monasteriis sit repletus. nam ubi fana destruxerat, statim ibi aut ecclesias aut monasteria construebat " = Before Martin, few, indeed hardly any, had received the name of Christ in these regions. But his virtues and example gave such an impetus to Christianity that there is no district now which is not filled with numerous churches or monasteries. For where he destroyed the shrines, he built churches and monasteries at once). Were there martyrs at Amiens? or at Agen (Agannum)?-

Eusebius declares that Constantinus Chlorus did not destroy the church buildings in Gaul H. E., viii. 13. 13), so-JJialthere must have been buildings of this kind. Lactantius, however (de Mort. xv.), relates that he "allowed the churches, i. e., mere walls which could be restored, to be demolished" (" Conven-ticula, i. e., parietes, qui restitui poterant, dirui passus est""). His court in Gaul consisted partly of Christians (Eus., Vit. Const., i. 16-17).

By the opening of the fourth century the church must have come to play a role of its own in the towns of Southern Gaul. This is suggested by one consideration of a psychological nature. Would Constantine, it may be asked, have declared himself in favour of the church, if he had had always to associate with an infinitesimally small

Christendom during the years which he genuine and forbade the people to worship there. Probably it was an old pagan sacred shrine, so that it is precarious to infer the existence of Christians at Tours or in the neighbourhood prior to Constantine.

1 Martin of Tours, the bishop of war and peace, had the same weight in middle Gaul that Gregory Thaumaturgus, the astute philosophic bishop, had in N. E. Asia Minor. Over a century separates them, so far did the Christianizing of Gaul linger behind that of Asia Minor.

2 The martyrs of the Thebaic legion cannot even yet be left alone; I agree with Hauck Kirchengesch. Deiitschlands, I."2) p. 9) that the tradition about them is entirely unauthentic.

The best proof that Christians were not persecuted by this emperor personally is to be found in the address of the Donatist bishops (at the beginning of the controversy) to his son Constantine: "Pater tuus inter ceteros imperatores perse-cutionem non exercuit et ab hocfacinore imniunis est Gallia ' (Opt., i. 22).

spent in Gaul immediately previous to his great change of front? I doubt it. The Oriental traces of the church's early size are insufficient. But, in any case, one must not argue directly from its importance to its size,- nor must one forget the necessity of carefully distinguishing between the various towns (occasionally in process of transition from military encampments to actual towns) and districts, especially between those of the north and of the south. Certainly in Belgica the church was still in a very humble way about 300 a. d., as is plain from its most important town, Treves, a Roman colony," whose bishopric (first occupied by Eucharius and Valerius) was not founded till the second half of the third century. " Even by the opening of the fourth century, the number of members in this church was small. One little building sufficed for their worship down to 336 a. d., nor were steps taken towards the erection of a new edifice till Athanasius stayed there, during his banishment â " (Athan., Jpo. ad Constant. 15; cp. Hauck's KG. Deutschlands-', i. p. 28). Ti: e 'es ddÂ S-not seem tohava got 4ts second church till the beginning of the4fth-centmy (so Hauck, after Sulp. Sev., Vita Mart. 16,18, Dial. iii. 11). During all the fourth century the town remained substantially pagan, and what as true of Treves was practically true of Gaul itself, apart from the south-west and the region of the Rhone, to judge from the evidence furnished by the fourth and fifth centuries. A Christianizing movement upon a larger scale started during the second half of the fourth century (cp. the efforts of Martin of Tours), but it did not produce any far-reaching effects, nor was it till after the middle of the fifth

In earlier days a typically Gallic Christianity, such as that of Northern Africa, can hardly be said to have existed. Irenaeus is a Christian of Asia Minor, not of Latin Gaul, nor did the Gallic church, as a Latin church, produce any prominent figure till Hilary of Poitiers. Gallic rhetoric then made its way into the church, which it stamped with an impress of its own.

In spite of Arnobius (i. i6), who speaks of "innumerable Christians" in Gaul.

On the cantonal divisions of Gaul, see Mommsen, op. cil., pp. 8i f. (Eng. trans., i. pp. 90 f.).

Since Diocletian it was the capital of the entire West, and the imperial city. But we know nothing about its history prior to Diocletian.

' These are the only names known to us before Agroetius, for that of Maternus is probably to be deleted.

century that Gaul, i. e., its Roman population, became substan- M tially Christian. On the contrary, about 400 a. d. the world of W Gallic culture was still predominantly pagan. Then it was that r. o the legislation against paganism began to take effect (Honorius and Theodosius). All our witnesses for the period place this beyond dispute. The religion of the country no longer presented any serious obstacle to the church; but the Celtic element was overcome by Latin Christianity rather than by the German immigration (Mommsen, p. 92; Eng. trans., i. p. 103 f). The church-history of Germany begins with the well-known statement of Irenaeus, i. 10 (ovre at iv Tepfxanaig ispvmevat I ekKXfjcrlai awco ireiria-Tevkacnv 5) aaAo)? irapasisoacriv): " Nor were the faith and tradition of the churches planted in Germany note the plural in the Greek at all different." Irenaeus obviously refers to stable, i., episcopal churches; for only such churches could hand down any traditions. Hence it is certain that in the largest Roman towns of Germany (of which Cologne and Mainz at once occur to our minds) there were Christian communities and bishops as early as the year 185 A. D. Unluckily, all other evidence fails us at this point, nor are the episcopal lists of any value in this connection. All we know is that the bishop of Cologne was at Rome (in 313 A. D.; cp. Eus., x. 5. 19), while at Aries (314 a. d.) his deacon Macrinus was with him. Yet how small must the church have been, if even by 355 a. d. it had no more than one "little conventicle" ("conventiculum,"" Amm. Marc, xv.

For the overthrow of paganism in Gaul, see Schultze, op. cit., ii. pp. loi f.

"Cp. Kraus, Die christlichen Inschriften der Rheinlande (1890, f.). Philo had already mentioned the Rhine; the country between it and the Euphrates embraced "the most important part of the world, which could, strictly speaking, be called the world" Leg. ad Caiu? i, ii.).

Sozomen (ii. 6), referring to the age of Constantine, declares that Stj to o. fji. p rhu 'Prjvov (pvxa 6XP'""""""'C' '- â Maternus, bishop of Cologne, must have been Constantine's special confidential adviser, for it was he who, together with the bishops of Rome, Aries, and Autun, was entrusted with the preliminary investigation into the Donatist dispute. But the bishop's personal importance does not determine the size of his episcopate. From Theod. Cod., xvi. 8. 3, we find that there was a synagogue also at Cologne in the reign of Constantine.

"Silvanum extractum aedicula quo exanimatus confugerat, ad conventiculum ritus Christiani tendentem densis gladiorum ictibus trucidarunt."

5. 31). This of itself is enough to show that Christianity was an extremely weak plant all over Germany.

In Lower Germany, Tongern may still be claimed as a pre-Constantine bishopric; at any rate, not long after Constantine, the town had a bishop, Servatius, who is known from his connection with the Arian controversy (synod of Rimini, 359). The fact of the Cologne bishop Maternus appearing as the first bishop of Tongern also may be taken to mean that the bishopric was founded under Maternus himself. In Upper,, Germany there is no evidence of any bishopric or church before Constantine; but as it lay much nearer to Lyons than to Lower Germany, it is not necessary perhaps to restrict the range of Irenagus's statement to the latter district (cp. the instance of

Vesontio, already noted). The earliest evidence for a church at Mainz occurs in 368 a. d., when the greater part of the

Even the notices of martyrs in Germany (at Cologne and Treves) are quite uncertain, if not absolutely untrustworthy. Hauck op. cit., p. 25) considers that only the account of Clematius at Cologne is even " fairly authentic." It describes (in an inscription of the fourth or fifth century) the spot " where the holy virgins shed their blood for the name of Christ" (" ubi sanctae virgines pro nomine Christi sanguinem suum fuderunt"). It also mentions an old dilapidated basilica, or memorial chapel, perhaps built in honour of these virgins during the reign of Constantine, or shortly before then, which Clematius had entirely rebuilt. chdi QX Pfarrkhrhe u. Stift im deutschen Miiielalter, 1903, pp. 137 f) writes as follows: " It seems to me quite inadmissible for Hauck to argue from a remark of Ammianus the pagan about a ' conventiculum ritus Christiani' that only one conventicle of Christians then existed at Cologne. It is certain that by 355 a. d. there were the churches of (i) St Gereon, (2) St Ursula, and the cathedral of the pre-Constantine age (bishop Maternus and the ekK r Tiat ev to7s Ffpxaviais ISpvfievai of Irenaeus). How dangerous Hauck's interpretation of Ammianus may prove, is plain from Harnack's pages, which deduce important inferences from this passage as to the scanty diffusion of Christianity in the Rhine-land." On this I remark (i) that while St Gereon goes back to the Roman period, there is no evidence to prove that the church existed previous to Constantine; (2) St Ursula was entirely rebuilt by Clematius in the fourth or fifth centuryâ if the church was at that time entirely dilapidated, though it was a hundred years old, the older building probably was no more than a small martyr-chapel of light construction; (3) "the cathedral of the pre-Constantine age" belongs to the realm of Schjifer's imaginationâ in place of it we must supply the "conventiculum" which Ammianus mentions.â The small number of Christian inscriptions (Hauck, pp. 27, 34) also proves that the church at Cologne was small; Kraus, who enumerates 181 for Treves, gives only 17 for Cologne.

2 Tertullian mentions Christians among the Germans adv. Jud. vii.), but the rhetorical nature of the passage renders it unreliable as a piece of evidence.

inhabitants were already Christians (Amm. Marc, xxvii. 10). Jergjne Ep. cxxiii. 16) tells how ("multa milia hominum") " many thousands of people " were slain in the church, when the city was sacked by the Germans. This occurred, however, at the opening of the fifth century.

By the middle of the fourth century the ecclesiastical organization of the German provinces was complete. Hilarius Pict. addresses his treatise (composed in the winter of 358359) to " dilectissimis et beatissimis fratribus et coepiscopis pro-vinciae Germaniae primae the words "in qua est prima Moguntia" are a later addition et Germaniae secundae et primae Belgicae et Belgicae secundae, et Lugdunensis primae et Lugdunensis secundae et provinciae Aquitaniae et provinciae Novempopulanae et ex Narbonensi plebibus et clericis Tolesanis et provinciarum Britanniarum episcopis.""

As for. Rhastia we can trace Christian churches at Augsburg and Regensburg before Constantine; for the personality of

The exaggeration is obvious. There was not a single church throughout the entire West at that period, in which several thousands could be accommodated.â "The importance of Mainz," says Hauck (p. 34), "renders it likely that Christianity soon entered the town, but no records of this are extant, and it is not at all surprising that no bishop from Mainz attended the synod of Aries, or that none ever appeared during the Arian controversy. Possibly the tardy origin of the Mainz episcopate was connected with the fact that the military settlement of Mainz only slowly grew into a town." iug IIisl Zeiisckr., N. F., xxxi., 1891, p. 217) asserts that "the later Civitas Moguntiacum appears even in the second century as a group of villages In 276 A. D. we still find the Roman citizens of Moguntiacum merely organized as a corporation. Upon the other hand, Mainz, like Cologne, and Strassburg, like Bqnn, appear as the most important towns on the Rhine during the fourth and fifth centuries." "It is also surprising," Hauck continues, " that no absolutely certain primitive inscription is to be found among the Christian inscriptions of Mainz; Kraus, n. 33, is the only one probable; cp. also his note on n. 32." We have no evidence that there-Â v 0 4, Â-k.

were Christians at Strassburg either, before 325 a. d. We should have to point for evidence to the statement (of Arnobius, i. 16) that there were about 300 Christians among the Alemanni. 1 C trv, A0 2 Hauck oj. cit., pp. 346 f.) writes: "The scanty and scattered tribes who inhabited the Alpine valleys and upper plains of Rhsetia offered little resistance to the superior force of Rome (cp. ample proof of this in the large number of Roman place-names: 100 Roman to every 10 or 15 Rhsetian, according to Steub in Allg. Zeittmg, 1885, suppl. ii. No. 355). They adopted the Roman language, though of course they never acquired much of the Roman civilization." Cp. also Franciss, Bayern zur Romerzeit, 1905, and Rom, Quartalschr., xix. (1905), pp. 88 f.

- Cyuj–y KXM t—
St Afra the martyr is beyond doubt, and graves of martyrs have been discovered at Regensburg (cp. Hauck, p. 347). Beyond this, however, nothing can be proved.

Â 17. Britain

At first Christianity could not gain any firm footing in this far-off province, which was really a military province and only veneered with Roman civilization. Tertullian's notice (in adv. Jud. vii.) is of no consequence; the legend of a correspondence between the Roman bishop Eleutherus and an alleged king of Britain called Lucius Lib. Pontif., also Bede's Hist. Angl, i. 4) I have proved elsewhere to be irrelevant (cp. above, pp. 143 f); while Sozomen's statement (II. 6) that Christianity had been received even by the Celts dwelling on the remotest coasts during the reign of Constantine amounts to very little. Still, it is quite possible that Christians had arrived in Britain and laboured there by the end of the second century. We may assume that the accounts given by Gildas

The Martyr-Acts are of no use, but the fact of the martyrdom is well attested. The bishopric (only attested at a late date) shows an early and evident connection with Aquileia. Hence it is hardly older than the fourth century.

Even the third-century origin of the ancient bishopric of Sabiona (Seben, near Klausen) cannot be established. In the great enumeration of the ecclesiastical provinces given by Athanasius Apol. c. Arian. i.), Germany is never mentioned, although even Britain is included. This is the less accidental, as Germany is also passed over in the similar enumeration of Vita Const., iii. 19, where both Gaul and Britain are named. So still in Optatus, de Schism., ii. i and iii. 9. For Origen, see above, pp. 12 f.

Cp. Map IX., also the article on "The Celtic Church," by Zimmer, in the Protest. Real-Encykl. x. pp. 204 f.

â Early Christian inscriptions are totally lacking (cp. Hiibner's work).

â " Cp. Origen, vol. xi. p. i40(Lomm.): "in Britannia. in India."

8 "The language and customs that penetrated thither from Italy remained an exotic growth in the island even more than upon the continent" (Mommsen, op. cit., V. p. 176; Eng. trans, i. 193).

" Origen (Horn. iv. i in Ezech., xiv. p. 59, Lomm.) seems to know of British Christians: " Quando terra Britanniae ante adventum Christi in unius dei con-sensit religionem? quando terra Maurorum? quando totus semel orbis? nunc vero propter ecclesias, quae mundi limites tenant, universa terra cum laelitia clamat ad dominum Israel" ("When, prior to the advent of Christ, did the land of Britain agree to the worship of the one God? or the land of the Mauri? or the whole and Bede of the martyr Alban in Verulam (St Albans) and two others in Legionum Urbs (Caerleon)â during the Diocletian persecutionâ rest on some reliable tradition. But the British church emerges into daylight first of all through the fact of three bishops,"- from Lond on (Restitutus), York (Eborius; Constantius Chlorus died here), and IJncoln (though the name of this locality is uncertain: Colonia Lindiensium; the bishop is called Adelphius, and he was accompanied by the presbyter Saeerdos? and the deacon Arminius), having attended the synod of Aries in 314 a. d. Two of these bishops bear classical names, but the third is indigenous (Eborius). If three bishops from Britain were present at Aries, we are justified in concluding that the number of British bishoprics was more numerous still. Only, we have no information on this point. All we do know is that Britain was Christianized with remarkable rapidity in the course of the fourth century, when round earth? But now, thanks to the churches which occupy the earth's bounds, the whole earth shouts with joy to the Lord of Israel ").

' For other information about this legend of Albanus, cp. W. Meyer on "The Legend of St Albanus" in Abhandl. der Gott. Gesell. d, IViss., N. F., viii. i (1904). The utter silence of our sources upon the church-history of Britain during the third century is not inexplicable. " Hardly anything is told us about the fortunes of the island, from the third century" (Mommsen, p. 172; Eng. trans., i. 189).â The Mart dopi,. of Alban cannot be pronounced quite authentic, as the oldest i-"

sources declare that no martyrdoms occurred during the reign of Constantius Chlorus. Still, this statement does not preclude the occurrence of one or two. Even previous to Gildas (r. 430 a. d.), relics of the saint can be shown to have existed.

- In accordance with the division of the country into shires, the Latin towns of Britain rose just as gradually as those of Gaul. York was the headquarters of the army, while Camalodunum may have formed the civil capital. It is noticeable that traces of a bishop are to be found at the former town and at the trading centre of London at a comparatively early period. Also, the three other places where equally early traces of Christians are to be found are stations of the Roman army.

' It is perhaps worthy of notice that, when the synod of Rimini met (359 A. D.), with an attendance of over four hundred bishops, three British bishops alone accepted the imperial provision for the upkeep of members (Sulpic. Sever., Chron., ii. 41: " Inopia proprii publico usi sunt" = they availed themselves of the public fund, owing to lack of private meansâ which appeared unbecoming, "indecens," to their fellow bishops). This implies that their churches were still poor. There were other British bishops at Rimini, however. We find, from the law of Gratian (5th July 379 A. D.; Theod. Cod., xiii. i. 11), that the bishops of Italy and luyria were richer than those of Britain, Gaul, and Spain.

VOL. II. 18 the native population became practically Christian, while the tribes of Germany continued almost entirely pagan. Gildas Chron. Min., III. 32) states definitely that Arianism inflicted grievous wounds upon the church in Britain. It must have stood, therefore, in the stream of the general ecclesiastical movement. Zimmer has proved beyond doubt that Christianity reached Ireland from Britain as early as the fourth century, and it may have been there even earlier.

1 0 Â 18. Africa, Numidia, Mauretania, and
Tripolitana

The strip of coast lying between the sea and the mountain-range upon the southern coast of the western Mediterranean belongs to Europe, not to Africa. During the imperial age, the I most important province in this region, i. e. Afciciuprqconsularis, was a second Italy. The country, with Carthage its capital, 1 Nicholson (" Vinisius to Nigra: A fourth-century Christian Letter written in

V Southern Britain and discovered at Bath," London, 1904) has happily deciphered the puzzling sheet of lead unearthed at Bath, containing a letter from Vinisius to Nigra. The letter is said to belong to the fourth century, and it mentions Arius! There is no foundation for the idea that it was written during his lifetime, but it proves that Arianism threatened the British church at an early period. The letter is also printed in Â v. d'Aisl eccus., vi. (1905), pp. 691 f.

"Cp. Maps X. and XL â C. I. L., viii. 1881 f. (with supplement). Older works by Morcelli and Miinter. Cp. Tissot G ographie cotnpar e de la Prov. Rom. d Afrigiie, 2 vols., 1884, 18S8), Mommsen (v. pp. 620 f.; Eng. Trans., ii. pp. 320 f.), Toulotte (G i r. de PAfrique chr tietine, 4 vols., 1891 f.), Babelon, Cagnat, and Reinach Atlas arcmol. de la Tuttisie, 1892 f.), Schwarze Unt. iibei- die diissere Entw. d. afric. Kirche, 1892), Toutain (Les citis romaines de la Tunisie, 1895), Monceaux Hist. Litt. de VAfriqne chrh., 2 vols., 1901-2, and " Enquete sur l'epig. chret. d'Afrique " in Rev. arcjim. (1903 2'); PP- 59 f-i 240 f., (1904'"), 354 f.), Guignebert (Tertitllien, tude sur ses seutim. a figard de Vempire et de la sociiti civile, 1901), Audollent Carthage Romaiue, 146 B. C.-698 a. d., 1901), Leclercq VAfrique chr t., 2 vols., 1904). In no other province of the empire at that time have archaeological investigations been so thoroughly and successfully prosecuted as by the French explorers in Africa. For further literature on the subject, cp. Schwarze's article on "The Church of North Africa" in Protest Real- Enc kl. xiv.

Ter t. de Pallia, i.: " Principes semper Africae, viri Carthaginienses, vetustate nobiles, novitate felices" ("ever princes of Africa, men of Carthage, ennobled by antiquity, blessed with recent novelties") Salvian., de Gnbern., vii. 67: " Uni-versarum Africae urbium princeps et quasi mater, ilia scilicet Romanis arcibus semper aemula, armis quondam et fortitudine, post splendore ac dignitate, reached its zenith of prosperity between the end of the second and the close of the third century.

During this period, when the Romanizing of the country made its greatest advances, the Christian church attained a growtho vithi n this wide and fruitful province which was only

Carthaginem dico, et urbi Romano maxime adversariam et in Africano orbe quasi Romam " (" Cgrthage the. head and as it were the mother of all the African cities, that steady rival of Rome, once in arms and courage, afterwards in brilliance and dtgmty, the chief foe of the city of Rome, and herself a sort of Rome in the African world ").

The great emperor Septimius-Severus was an African! See further Tert., de 4ji- inia, XXX., a passage which refers primarily to Africa: " Certe quidem ipse orbis in promptu est, cultior de die et instructior pristino. omnia iam pervia, omnia nota, omnia negotiosa, solitudinas famosas retro fundi amoenissimi obliteraverunt, silvas arva domuerunt, feras pecora fugaverunt, harenae seruntur, sexa panguntur, paludes eliquantur, taniae urbes qtiantae non casae qit07idam. iam nee insulae horrent: ubique domus, ubique populus, ubique respublica, ubique vita, summum testimonium fre- quentiae humanae. onerosi sumus mundo, vix nobis elementa sufficiunt et necessitates artiores et querellae apud omnes, dum iam nos natura non sustinet," etc. (" Surely a glance at the wide world shows that it is daily being more cultivated and better peopled than before. All places are now accessible, well known, open to commerce. Delightful farms have now blotted out every trace of the dreadful wastes; cultivated fields have overcome woods; flocks and herds have driven out wild beasts; sandy spots are sown; rocks are planted; bogs are drained. Large cities now occupy land hardly tenanted before by cottages. Islands are no longer dreaded; houses, people, civil rule, civilization, are everywhere. Thick population meets the eye everywhere. We overcrowd the world. The elements can hardly support us. Our wants increase and our demands are keener, while Nature cannot bear us"). So in de Pallio, ii. (at the close). Salvian., de Gitbern., vii. 6o: " Tam divitem quondam Africam fuisse, ut mihi copia negotia-tionis suae non suos tantum sed etiam mundi thesauros videatur implesse " (" Africa was once so rich that its wealth of trade seems to me to have filled not only its own treasuries but those of the world ").

' Many natives even of the better classes still spoke Latin with reluctance in the'second century; cp. Apuleius, Apol. lxviii. (of a young man), "Loquitur numquam nisi punice, et si quid adhuc a matre graecissat; enim Latine neque vult neque potest" ("He never speaks anything but Punic or a smattering of Greek picked up from his mother; Latin he neither can nor will attempt "). The language of educated people, with which the superimposed Latin of these North, I '

African provinces had to reckon, was Greek. The " suaviludii," or lovers of the ' Q ' play, at Carthage in Tertullian's day (cp. de Corona, vi.), preferred to read Greek rather than Latin, and for their benefit Tertullian wrote his de Spectaculis in Greek (see Zahn's Gesch. des neutest, Kanons, i. p. 49). The Barbary vernacular had been long ago displaced from public usage by the Punic inhabitants. It waned still further under the Roman regime, though it survived amid the changes of foreign rulers. On the Latinizing of Africa by means of the settlement of Italian colonists in the country, see Mommsen's Kdm. Gesch., v, p. 647 (Eng. trans., ii. 332 f.).

paralleled in Asia Minor. But the church of Carthage, which IS the earliest of the great Latin churches, must have been of importance long before it emerges into the light of history. The early writings of Tertullian presuppose a large church in the capital as well as the extension of Christianity throughout Northern Africa. But it is surpi'ising that Tertullian tells us next to nothing of the early history of the Carthaginian ' Reasons for this rapid growth may be conjectured, but the question is, whether they are really relevant. Monceaux (i. lo) and Leclercq (i. p. 42) both hold, and adduce some evidence for their contention, that a monotheism lay sub-meri ed below the polytheism of Africa. But was not this also the case then in other provinces, especially during the third century? Leclercq replies, "Undoubtedly. But they these monotheistic traits do not appear to have been so strongly marked, nor above all so customary and popular, anywhere as in Africa, Theâ Christian propaganda must have profited by the deep affinities between Christianity and the local religions; it found a secret ally in the very conscience of its foes." This is possible, but uncertain. It is surprising, indeed, that the incontinent desertion of the shrines of Baal (the African Saturn) coincides with the growth and consolidation of the African church under Cyprian in the middle of the third century; cp. Toutain, De Saturni dei hi Africa romana cultu (1896), pp. 138 f., and the same writer's Les citis roniaines de la Tiinisie, pp. 228 f. ("It was the people, the lower classes and the poor, who were first converted. The first African bishops were, with very rare exceptions, plebeian. The religion of Christ was welcomed and confessed especially among the classes which remained most loyal to the old Carthaginian religion "). Leclercq further points out that " we find in the epigraphic texts material proof of this affinity between African terminology and Christian. Toutain ascribes to the worshippers of Saturn the dedicatory inscriptions which appear to us rather capable of being taken to favour Christian epigraphy". e. g., the inscriptions with " deus sanctus aeternus" or " aeternus"â are these all Christian or not?).

- Particular account must be taken of ad Sca. u. v.: " Tanta hominum multi-tudo, pars paene maior civitatis cuiusque"' " Such are our numbers, amounting almost to a majority of the citizens in every city"): "Tanta milia hominum, tot viri ac feminae omnis sexus, omnis aetatis, omnis dignitatis" ("So many thousands of people, so many men and women, people of both sexes, of every age, of every rank"): "Quid ipsa Carthago passura est, decimanda a te" ("What will Carthage herself suffer, if you must decimate her?"): " Parce Carthagini, si non tibi, parce provinciae, quae visa intentione tua obnoxia facta est concus-sionibus" ("Have mercy on Carthage, if not on yourself; have mercy on the province which, by the disclosure of your purpose, has been rendered liable to acts of extortion"). Similar remarks occur even in his earlier (197 A. D.) Apology; cp. chaps, ii. and xxxvii. In de Pnvscr. xx. he is able to declare that new churches were being founded everyday, and (xxix.) that " thousands upon thousands " had been baptized in vain, if the heretics were right. Both passages reflect his estimate of African Christendom, even in his outlook on Christianity as a whole.â Unfortunately, we have not the slightest information upon the relations subsisting between primitive AfricancRristianity and the numerous synagogues of church, and as little of the other churches in Africaâ even of their contemporary history. The reason is that Tertullian remained the citizen of a great city, even when he became a Christian. The country was no concern of his. Besides, he. lived wholly in the present and the future.!! A."rr

We know jiothing about the primitive (which was probably (c, ly the Greek) period of the African church.- We learn, however, J" ' f that Pergetua iioilversed in Greek with bishop Optatus and the iwV' " presbyter Aspasius, while Tertullian wrote in Greek as well as in Latin, The Greek versions of the primitive Acts of the African martyrs may be almost as old as the Acts themselves, and it is with martyrdoms, first f all in the year 180, that the church-history of Korthern Africa commences. At that period Namphamo of Madaura and several Christians from v '- ' ' the country. J udaism p enetrated the Berbej tribÂ S oi Txlpj2lls a. nd MQrqcco. We have disputes with Jews recorded (cp. Ten., adv. Jud. i.). Unlike Monceaux and Leclercq (i. pp. 39 f.), I would not lay any stress on the discovery of Jewish and Christian graves side by side in the cemetery of Djebel-Khaui.

Salvian de Gubern., vii. 79), at any rate, is wrong in saying that Carthage was "a Christian, an ecclesiastical city, which the apostles had once founded with their own doctrines" (urbs Christiana, urbs ecclesiastica, quam quondam doctrinis suis apostoli instituerant).

Mauretania really only half belonged to it; the western half gravitated always in the direction of Spain, to which it was afterwards assigned; cp. Aug., Ep. xciii. 24: " Mauretania Caesariensis nee Africam se vult dici."

" From its very foundation, a special tie must have bound the African church to that of Rome (Tertull., de Prascr. xxxvi.: " Roma unde nobis quoque auctoritas praesto est " = Rome, whence we too derive this our authority), but we know no details, and it does not necessarily follow (though it is natural to think so) that Roman Christians brought the gospel to Africa (according to late and worthless legends, Peter twice came to Carthageâ from Rome, of course). The original relations between Jerusalem and the " ecclesiae orientales," which Augustine asserts Ep. xliii. 7, etc.), are abstractions; and all conjectures about the originally direct connection between the African churches and the Eastern arc equally airj'. Naturally, there always was intercourse between them, partly direct, partly via Rome. Montanism, Praxeas the Modalist, and Hermogenes the lieretic, all came to Carthage trom the East. Tertullian knew Christian writings composed in Asia Minor (besides those of Rome and the great work of Irenasus), e. g., those of Melito of Sardis, the Acta Pauli, etc. Especially as a Montanist, he was well acquainted with the conditions of the Greek churches; he knew comparatively unimportant proceedings and features of their life. If the first African Christians really spoke Greek for the most part during several decades, we cannot infer that a direct Oriental mission went on in Africa. The African Jews also seem to have spoken more Greek than Latin, and Christianity all over the West found its first foothold among the more or less floating Greek jiopulation.

Scilium (a town which must have been situated in proconsular Nuniidia) were all put to death. We have thus evidence for Christians in Nuniidia as early as for Christians in Carthage.-The works of Tertullian prove the existence of Christian churches in four towns of Africa, and only four, viz., Had-jrumetuni, Thysdrus, Lambaese, and Uthina. All of these were places of importance, Lambajse in Numidia being the chief military depot in Africa. As Hadrumetum and Thysdrus lay in Byzacium ad Scap. iii.-iv.), the latter province must also

From the Vita Cypriani per Pontiuvt (i., cp. xix.) it follows that no-deiip was martyred at all in Africa, previous to Cyprian, i. e., to 258 a. d. This is very remarkable. The clergy knew how to live on good terms with the authorities, as is plain from the bitter complaints about the " deer-footed " clergy and their method of evading a threatening persecution by means of bribery (Tert., de Fuga in Persecut.). Tertullian's treatise ad Martyres shows that up till the date of its composition there had been very few martyrs in Africa. He refers not to early Christian martyrs, but to Lucretia, Regulus, etc.

The names of the martyrs of Scili are Speratus, Nartzalus, Cittinus, Donata, Secunda, and Vesliaâ plainly all plebeian. In the Acta Perpetiue (Vibia Perpetua) similar names occur, e. g., Revocatus, Felicitas, Saturninus, Secundulus, Optatus, Aspasius, Tertius, Pomponius, Dinocrates, Saturus, Jucundus, Artaxius, and Rusticus. As we can see, the Greek names are very few, and later on they disappear entirely. So far as regards the composition of the African churches, then, it is of very little moment to collect the large number of names of African Christians given by the writings of Cyprian and the primitive sources. The names of the eighty-seven bishops at the council of Carthage in 256 A. D. are for the most part Latin; but we get Polycarp, Nicomedes, Theogenes, Eucratius, Eugenius, Adelphius, Demetrius, Jader, Paul, Ahymnus, Irenaeus, Zosimus, Therapius, Peter, and Dioga (=Diogas, Diogenes?). The two bishops called Peter and Paul of course took their names from the apostles (so, possibly, Polycarp, from the famous bishop of Smyrna, but it is unlikely). None of the twelve who bore Greek names can be certainly said to have been Greek. Some of these names were by this time quite common even in the West among Latins (slaves and the lower classes). Jader and Ahymnus are Berber (Libyan) names (as, e. g., elsewhere, and even at a comparatively early period we get Christians called Baric, Mettun, Namphamo, Namgedde, Gudden feminine, Miggin, and Sanae). Thus we have no guarantee that there was only one native Greek among the bishops of that age. But there were hardly more than half a dozen. The Greek element was either absent or A vanishing. It is very remarkable that not a single Jewish name occurs among them. If the church had had originally a powerful Jewish Christian element, it

N. V had certainly been extinguished by about 256 A. D. In fact, it must have dis-Y V 1 appeared by Tertullian's day. Tertullian never treats of Christians who had been A Â iv V' Jews in all his numerous writings. The synagogue and the church must have been sharply divided from each other, even nationally.

Lambcese is meant in ad Scap. iv. ("Nam et nunc a praeside Legionis vexatur hoc nemen" = for even at present our Name is being harried by the governor of Legio), The Spaniards take it to be their Leon, which is impossible.

have contained Christians by this time. Even in Mauretania they were to be found, for Tertullian (op. cit. iv.) mentions a bloody persecution of the local Christians by the governor of Mauretania. We have his testimony, therefore, to the existence of Christians in Numidia, Byzacium, and Mauretania. Furthermore, Christianity had already reached the Gaetulians and the Southern Mauri (adv. Jtid. vii.). We have no information upon the strength of the Punic element in the church about the year 200 or during the course of the third century.- xj ' Tertullian and Cyprian tell us practically nothing about it, so 4 1 that we might even suppose it did not exist at all. But the fju fourth century (cp. especially the writings of Augustine) shows y 4) how strong it was; both bishops and parish priests had to know (â ' Punic in those days. We can quite understand how the Punic population (so far as it was not superficially Romanized) inclined less rapidly to Christianity than the Romanized Greco-Latin incomers, and how it remained decidedly retrograde even in the third century, during which period the names of the African bishops are almost entirely Latin. Yet from the very outset the Punic element was never quite absent. Punic names occur, e. g. among the martyrs; in fact, the first African martyr, Namphamo, was of Punic birth. On the other hand, no Punic version of the Bible, so far as we know, was ever issuedâ implying that the Christianizing of the Punic population meant at the same time their Romanizing more than ever. It did not prove, in the end either thorough or successful. 7 Â

The Latin Bible originated in Africa perhaps at an earlier y period than in Rome, and Africa formed the motherland of lt-

Cp. also the story of Vespronius Candidas in ad Scap. iv.; he was " legatus Augusti pro praetore" in Numidia C. I. L., vol. viii. n. 8782).

"The existence of quite a number of bishops in Africa as early as 200 A. D. is proved by several passages in Tertullian, e. g., that in de Fiiga, xi., which speaks of bishops who had fled during the persecution.â In Mauretania, Christianity was naturally more weak than elsewhere. The Martyr-Acts of Typasius Veteranus Anal. Bolland, ix., 1890, p. 116), which belong to this province, begin: "In temporibus Diocletiani. parva adhuc Christianitatis religio fuerat " (" In the days of Diocletian the Christian religion was still a small affair").

' On the Punic element in the African church, see Zahn's Gesch. des Neutest. Kanons, i. pp. 40 f. For the benefit of Christians who knew nothing but Punic, the Bible was translated during worship, and there was also preaching in Punic.

Latin Christian literature. In this sense the country possesses an epoch-making significance.

The strong military element in the vocabulary of the African church is a feature which deserves close attention. It can be verified as eari- as Tertuuian, who was a soldier's son. But it is far more surprising to find how prominent it is in the religious dialect of Qy priaii, which became authoritative afterwards. Was this accidental, we may ask? Or are we to suppose that relations were established at an early date between Christianity and the military camps in Africa? The very juristic element is not simply to be referred to Tertullian's influence; for it is natural to suppose that the ecclesiastical dialect which grew up in Africa was the work of immigrant officials and soldiers, in so far as it was not vernacular. But we have no thorough investigations of the problem.

Between 211 and 249 (Cyprian) a large increase in Christianity can be shown to have taken place at Carthage and throughout all the African provinces. Then it was that " so many thousands of heretics" (" tot milia haereticorum," Cypr., Epist. Ixxiii. 3) were brought over to the church. Even at the synod of Carthage held under Agrippinus (not later than 218-222 a. d.) to discuss the validity of heretical baptism, there were seventy African and Numidian bishops present, while ninety bishops attended a synod at Lambaese, presided

Does not even the pagan scoff at Christians which Tertuuian records (" Deus Christianus wokottijs " = The god of Christians lying in an ass's stall) go back to soldiers?

- Leclercq and others put it as early as circa 197 A. D., but the reasons for this date are inadequate (cp. my Cuonoogie, ii. pp. 286 f.).

I do not enter into the question of the political and ecclesiastical divisions of Africa, for which one must refer to the investigations of Mommsen and Schwarze (Unters. iiber die iiussere Entwickeliing der afriknnischeii Kiirhe, 1892). No certain solution can be given. There were synods for the separate provinces (though we do not know when these originated), and a general synod. The position of Carthage is quite plain from Cypr., Ep, xlviii. 3: " Quoniam latius fusa est nostra provincia, habet etiam Numidiam et Mauretaniam sibi cohaerentes" = Since our province has extended more widely, it has also Numidia and Mauretania within its sweep.

â â Augustine, de Unico Bapt. c. Petil. xiii. (xxii.); cp. Cypr., Ep. lxxi.

It is not certain whether they were entirely Numidian.

The passage may be read, however, in such a way as to leave the place of meeting an open question. In that case there were deliberations conducted also at Carthage.

I Cjm-J"

CHRISTIANITY DOWN TO 325 A. D. 281 over by Cyprian's Ep. lix. 10) predecessor Donatus ("ante inultos fere annos," says Cyprian, i. e., certainly not later than 240 A. D.). Unfortunately, we do not possess any lists of these two synods; but, when one bears in mind the well-known fact that only a certain proportion of bishops attended synods as a rule, the above numbers enable us to infer that a remarkable expansion of the church had occurred by the middle of the third century, although one must never forget that the organization of the church in Northern Africa evidently required a bishopric even when there were but a few Christians, i. e., in every township.

In Africa the episcopal organization was still more thoroughly.

worked out than in Asia Minor or Lower Italy. Of detached 1 presbyters and deacons we do not hear one syllable; even from 'â I

Cyprian's Ep. Ixii. 5 it is not necessary to infer that such l Cv functionaries existed. " y

From the writings and correspondence of Cyprian we can tv I u i discern the size of the Carthaginian church and the graduated order of the local clergy,- as well as the diffusion of Christianity throughout the provinces. His treatise de Lapsis shows that during the last thirty years the new j-eligion had become naturalized and secularized in the capital as a "religio licita," spreading through ajl ranks and classes. The victims of the l This episcopal organization in Africa was one result of the municifalxrganiza-tion of Northern Africa which was derived from the Phoenicians. " When the Roman rvile began in Africa, the C. territory then consisted in the main of urban communities, for the most part small in size, of which there were counted three hundred, each administered b)- its suffetes; in this matter the republic did not introduce any change" (Mummsen, Jidn. Gesch., v. p. 644; Eng. trans., ii. 329; on the transformation of this organization in Italian towns, see pp. 646 f.; Eng. trans., ii. pp. 332 f. Cp. also Barthel, Ziir Gesch. der r'om. Stddte in Africa, Greifswald, 1904). Among other reasons why the church J ailedâ to.-niqt,. ksejf atnong the Berbars, we may, perhaps, include this, that thesji Jjabasjield chiefly to the hills and steppes and lacked any municipal organization; they simply formed unions of natives, directly controlled by the provincial governors. Such conditions rendered any Christianizing process almost impossible. It was only in certain Celtic provinces, such as Ireland, that the church surmounted this obstacle, and she only did so after she had acquired in monasticism a fresh and more opportune instrument for her propaganda.

- Though these were not as large as in Rome. It held true, even within the Christian church, that " Rome must take precedence of Carthage, in virtue of her size" (" pro magnitudine sua debet Carthaginem Roma praecedere," Ep. lii. 3).

The large number of bishops may be inferred indirectly from their increasing secularization; cp. de Lapsis, vi. ("Episcopi plurimi, quos et hortamento esse

Decian persecution, i. e., those who succumbed by renouncing their faith, must have been counted by thousands. But, above all, the personality of Cyprian himself shows the importance which already attached to a bishop of Carthage. Read his letters and his martyrdom, and you get the impression that this was a– aan who enjoyed the repute, and wielded the authority, of a provincial governor ("praeses provinciae""). He is certainly not a whit inferior to Paul of Samosata (see above, pp. 106 f.). We can readily credit his statement (Ep. Ixvi. 5: " novus credentium populus" = a new host of believers) that numerous pagans were won over to Christianity under his episcopal rule.

For statistical purposes Cyprian's writings are of little service. According to Ep. Ixii. 5, he forwarded, along with his letter to some Numidian churches which had been laid waste by brigands, a list of all those members of the Carthaginian church who had contributed the large sum of a hundred thousand sesterces as ransom money! see above, vol. i. pp. 187 f. Unluckily, oportet ceteris at exemplo, divina procuratione contempta procuratores regum saecularium fieri, derelicta cathedra, plebe deserta per alienas provincias oberrantes negotiationes quaestuosae nundinas aucupari, esurientibus in ecclesia fratribus habere argentum largiter velle, fundos insidiosis fraudibus rapere, usuris multiph-cantibus foenus augere'" â A large number of bishops, who ought to exhort and give an example to others, despised their divine commission in order to undertake secular business, forsook their thrones, left their people, wandered over foreign provinces, and ransacked the markets for profitable trade, while the brethren were meanwhile starving in the church. Their craving was for hoards of money, they seized estates by deceitful frauds, and increased their gains by multiplying exorbitant interest).

We also see, of course, that he was surrounded by insignificant people, for the most part. Hardly one prominent layman occurs in the entire correspondence of Cyprian (for an earlier period, cp. "Vibia Perpetua, honeste nata, liberaliter instituta, matronaliter nupta " in the Acfa Perpehtce, above, vol. i. p. 396: also some passages in Tertullian). Cyprian is a king among plebeians. Or did he stand so high that there were no distinctions of rank below him? The repute of his writings almost equalled that of the Bible both in Africa and elsewhere. It was Augustine who first put a stop to this quasi-canonisation of Cyprian (cp. E-, xciii. 36, etc.), for all his veneration of the man.

The central position in Christendom occupied by Carthage about the middle of the third century is entirely due to Cyprian, who corresponded with bishops in Rome, Spain, Gaul, and Cappadocia, and took pains to bring his letters upon the question of apostates "to the notice of all the churches and all the brethren" ("in notitiam ecclesiis omnibus et universis fratribus," Â . Iv. 5). He governed the churches of Northern Africa from the Syrtes to Mauretania.

this list has not been engrossed along with the letter, so that we do not possess it. According to Ep. lix. 9, he furnished Cornelius of Rome with a list of all the African bishops who had held aloof from the Novatian schism. But this list also has been lost. No item can be gleaned from the records of the African synods which were held before the great synod upon heretical baptism. We learn nothing from the fact that an " ample number of bishops"" (" copiosus episcoporum numerus"), i. e., 42, QQ.) 37, 31 (from the proconsular province; 18 Numidian bishops are enumerated), and 71 attended these gatherings. On the other hand, great importance attaches to the protocol (in Cyprian's works) upon the synod of 256 or 257 a. d. (on the subject of heretical baptism). Here the votes of 87 bishops are verbally reported, and the sites of their bishoprics are given. At a single stroke we are thus informed of a large number of bishoprics which existed previous to 256-257. No doubt, a considerable proportion of these have not yet been identified, despite the remarkable advances made by explorers of Roman Africa. Still, the majority can be identified, with the aid of the later councils, the Corpus Inscript. Lat. (vol. viii.), and the investigations of Tissot and others (see below). Bishoprics already existed in all parts of Northern Africa (four, e. g., in Tripolitana), the greatest number being in the northern proconsular province, the smallest, as one might expect, in 1 Uhl horn Die christ. Liebestdtigkeit in der alien Kirche, p. 153; En '. trans., p. 158) writes thus: " The Carthaginian church cannot as yet i. e., in the days of Cyprian have been large. Cyprian remarks in passing that he knew every member of itâ which proves that at most it amounted to three or four thousand souls." Uhlhoin has Ep. xh'. 4 in view, but we cannot possibly infer from this passage that Cyprian knew all the members of the church. In my opinion, three or four thousand is too low an estimate. The passages upon the persecution, as well as others (including those upon the heretics), give one the impression that Uhlhorn's estimate is put too low, even were one to regard it as equivalent to the number of independent males, in which case it would need to be trebled or quadrupled. Still, Uhlhorn is right in pointing out that, to judge from the letters of Cyprian, the Carthaginian church cannot have numbered its members by tens of thousands. Statistical calculations such as those of Munter Primordia eccl. Afric, p. 24), which put the number of African Christians at the beginning of the third century at more than 100,000, are entirely baseless. It is also inadmissible to infer, as Renan does (Marc. Aurile, p. 451), from Tert., ad Scap. v., that the Christian population of Carthage amounted to one-tenth of the total population in 212 A. D.

284 MISSION AND EXPANSION OF CHRISTIANITY

Mauretania, while Numidia reveals quite a considerable number. We are justified also in assuming that this great African council was attended by the majority of the bishops in these provinces who were favourable to Cyprian, unless special circumstances prevented them from putting in an appearance. Those favourable to heretical baptism naturally absented themselves, and we do not know how strong they were.- But they were certainly not in the majority. As for the total number of African, bishops in the days of Cyprian we;â tn hardly put-that above a hundred and fifty.

i It is unfortunate that the Christian inscriptions of Africa, 1 V ' which in many respects are so unique and valuable, afford extremely little,. reliable. material for the pre-Constantine age.

As a rule, they are almost entirely undated, and consequently "Z almost entirely useless for our present purpose. The numerous inscriptions of the martyrs were almost without exception the - work of a later age, and in general they testify, not that a ji martyr suffered in such and such a place, but that he was ' â "7 reverenced there, or that his relics had been brought thither.

To work through the material furnished by the Christian inscriptions of Africa, therefore, yields little or nothing for the third century, although the results are so important for the fourth and fifth and sixth. As for the African Acts and narratives of the martyrs, they present a hard problem. Any tenable results to be got from them will be found collected at the close of our list of African towns.

Between the reign of Gallienus and the year 303, the church of Africa must have increased by a process of geometrical pro- ' Numidia proconsularis and Numidia itself, when put together, seem to have embraced hardly fewer bishoi:)rics than Africa proconsularis (?". t'., Zcugilana and Byzacium together). As we should expect a priori, the majority of the bishoprics which have been identified lie on the main routes.

- Cyprian merely speaks of " episcopi plurimi ex provincia Africa, Numidia, Mauretania," at the opening.

In the vicinity of Carthage there were a number of towns which sent no bishop to the council, but which nevertheless are not to be considered as having had no bishop. We may therefore conjecture that such bishops were opposed to Cyprian on the question of heretical baptism.

Cp. the sections in Leclercq (especially I. 3S1-432), who has made careful use of all the relevant material.

gression. The fragments of the Donatist Acts, relating to the earliest phase of the schism, almost give us the impression that Christianity had already become the religion of Northern Africa, and this impression is corroborated by a document of Constantin e (in Eus., H. E., x. 5), in which these "densely populated " provinces appear to be ranked as Christian. Moreover, if one considers (cp. the Gcsta apud Zenophihim) the clergy and ecclesiastical treasures of Tiiamugadi or the clergy of Cirtaathe verdict will be that the triumph of the chui'ch in Africa was imminent, owing to the internal development of the situation as well as to other causes. The Diocletian persecution only lasted two full years, though it certainly cost the church the loss of many martyrs and apostates (Eusebius himself, in far-off Palestinian Caesarea, bears in mind the martyrs in Africa and Mauretania y. E. y viii. 6). Once it was over, back flowed the crowd of apostates. But it is the Donatist movement which shows most plainly the extent to which the new religion had permeated the people, and even the Punic population. People actually began to represent it as a national palladium. Paganism, quite apart from the Berbers, was not of course 1 Several churches in Cyprian's day were certainly still poor, or very insignificant. Why, Cyprian deems it possible, and in fact likely, that the church in one town will be unable to furnish the minimum living wage to support a Christian (a teacher of the dramatic art, who was to abandon his profession)! The town is not named, but its bishop is called Eucratius; and a certain bishop of Thense, called Eucratius, occurs among the bishops of the Sentent. Ixxxvii. episcoportwi. Perhaps it was Thense which had so poor and small a church.

"Basilicas had been erected by this time in towns like Zama and Furni Acta Piirgai. Felic. iv.). When the Donatist controversy began, there were several churches, as we might expect, in Carthage. The city had special Christian churchyards by the end of the second century (Tert., Apol. xxxvii., ad Scap. iii.). The greatest activity in church-building throughout Africa prevailed in the fourth and the beginning of the fifth century, as we learn from the ruins. For a Christian "area" in Carthage and other African Christian " areas,"cp. Leclercq, I. pp. 55 f. Church-buildings must have been common on these "areas," even during the third century. An accurate description of the "area" in which Cyprian's corpse was laid is given in Acta proconsul. Cypnani, v.

â Seventy African bishops, e. g., apostatized (cp. August., Â p. xliii.). For the martyrs, cp. Aug., Ep. Ixxviii. 3: " Numquid non et Africa sanctorum martyrum corporibus plena est? " Note in passing that Cyprian's writings never mention any wxitship of the martyrs' bodies or relics; in this respect Africa was probably behind the East. But Cyprian's letters show that in Africa, as elsewhere, the martyred dead were worshipped and invoked.

extinct even by the fourth century, but the resistance encountered by Christianity seems upon the whole to have been less here than elsewhere. We must regard the pagan reactions at Calama and Sufes (Aug., Ep. xc, xci., 1.) as exceptional.

As for the number of bishoprics, almost, a hundred can be shown to have existed by 258 a. d., and by the beginning of the " ' ' fouiih century twenty-five more were added. But the places where bishops can be traced were not all the places where bishoprics existed (see above). This is shown by the following consideration. In his work against the Donatists, Optatus happens to mention seventeen towns in which there were bishoprics at the date of the great persecution. Of these seventeen, only eight occur in Cyprian. The other nine he vm never mentions. Hence it follows with some probability that A) the number of bishops in Africa was nearly doubled between 258 and 303 a. d.; while, if one postulates (see above) about 130 or 150 bishoprics in Cyprian's day, one will be disposed to enumerate about., 250 at, the opening of the fourth century. This hypothesis is corroborated by the fact that in the year 330 no fewer than 270 Donatist bishops were able to assemble at Carthage (Aug., Ep. xciii. 43). Consequently, if our calculations are correct, the growth of the episcopate in Northern Africa exhibits the following stages: circa 220 a. d. (Agrippinus), 70-90 bishoprics; circa 250 a. d. nearly 150; by the opening of the fourth century hardly less than 250; and at the beginning of the fifth century between 500 and 700.

I now proceed to enumerate the places where we know Christian churches existed previous to 325 a. d. They are as follows: â

Places mentioned previous to Cyprian.-â Carthage (Tertullian).

' Leclercq, I. pp. 79 f.: "It would be premature, in my opinion, to attempt here any classification of the ancient episcopates of Northern Africa; the investigations which have been undertaken in this field enable us to conclude that the numerous questions arising out of this problem do not yet admit of any definite settlement."

'â In marking the provinces in which the various towns lie, I have followed the map in C. I. L., vol. viii. Cp. the exact delimitation of the provinces in Leclercq, I. pp. 84 f.

adaura (in Numidia, whereâ according to Augustineâ the first African martyr perished).

Scilium (Acta Mah. Scil., hitherto unidentified, though it must4iave lain in proconsular Numidia; cp. Neumann's Rom. Staat U7id Kirche, i. p. 71; it is not the same as Cillium in Byzacium).

yihina (Tert., de Monog. xii.; in Africa procons. Zeug.).

Lambaese (Tert., ad Scap. iv. The heretic Privatus lived here not later than circa 240 a. d.; a Christian inscription in C. I. L., No. 18,488; martyrsâ Jacobus, Marianus, etc.; in Numidia).

Hadrumetum (Tert., ad Scap. iii.; in Africa procons. Byz.).

'rhysdi'us (Tert., ad Scap. iv.; iusafrica procons. Byz.).

Tipasa (in Mauj'et. Caes.; a dated Christian inscription of the year 238â Rasinia Secundaâ in C. I. L. viii. No. 9289, Suppl. 20,856. But its Christian character is not absolutely certain. Other traces of Christianity in the third century).

There were Christians in Tertullian's day in Mauretania; cp ad Scap. iv.: " Nam et nunc a praeside Mauretaniae vexatur hoc nomen.""'

Places mentioned (especially in the Sent. Ixxxvii. episcoporum) hy Cyprian': â

Abbir Germaniciana (identification uncertain; cp. Wilmanns

On the catacombs of Hadrumetum, cp. Wittig in Rom. Quartalschrift, xix. 1-2 (1905), pp. 83 f.: "Faint traces of frescoes can be made out on the tufa covering the walls, resembling those on the Callistus catacomb."

- A subterranean Christian graveyard has also been found here, as at Arch-Zara, in the vicinity of Sullectum, the ancient seaport in Byzacium. But we do not know if these belong to the preconstantine age.

In addition to some of those just mentioned, which he also notices.â The classification of the eighty-seven bishops at the council of Carthage is not according to their provinces, so that in cases where the seat of the bishopric has hitherto eluded identification, one cannot unfortunately determine from the order the precise province in which we are to look for it. Some help, however, is afforded by the lists of later Carthaginian councils, where the bishoprics are assigned to their provinces. A curious position at the former council was occupied by the bishopric of Tripolitana, which was represented by two members, one of whom voted also in the name of two absent bishops of Tripolitana. (It is remarkable, by the way, that Neapolis, along with Leptis magna, had a bishop of its own, and that the bishop of the latter place was represented by the bishop of Oea and not of Neapolis. Probably the former was an older man. Perhaps, too, by Neapolis we are meant to understand, not the Tripolitan town, but Neapolis in in C. I. L. viii. p. 102, and Tissofs Giogi-. de la province Roma'ine (TAfrique, ii. pp. 593, 771. Wilmanns identifies Abbir Cellense in Africa procons. Zeug. with Abbir mains south-west of Thimida, and our Abbir with Abbir minus, which is also to be sought in Africa procons.â near Germaniciana?).

Abitina (near Membressa in Africa procons. Zeug.; local martyrs, cp. vol. i. p. 397, and Ruinarfs Acta Mart., pp. 414 f.).

provincia Zeugitana, although it is mentioned after Oea.) These Tripolitan Christians voted (Nos. 83-86) at the conclusion of the division, apologizing for the non-appearance of their two colleagues, and then voting in their stead. As the opening of the protocol mentions Africa, Numidia, and Mauretania, without a word of Tripolitana, we may perhaps assume that the Tripolitan bishops were not at that time regular members of the general African synod, but held a kind of independent position, though they received on this occasion a special invitation to be present (which would also explain the unusual act of taking their votes m absentia). As the other bishops did not vote according to their provincesâ a proof that the ecclesiastical arrangement of the African provinces was still very imperfectâ it is obvious that they must have voted in order of seniority; and this conjecture is corroborated Xi) by the well-known fact that'Tn Numidia the oldest bishop always discharged the duties of the metropolitan; and (2) by the remark that the bishop (of Cuicul) who voted as No. 71 emphasized the "recent origin" ("novitas") of his episcopate ("Novitas episcopatus effecit, ut sustinerem quid niaiores iudicarent"), as did the seventy-eighth bishop ("quod et ipsi scitis, non olim sum episcopus constitutus "). A comparison of the names of the bishops at the earlier councils shows, however, that this principle of seniority cannot have been strictly adhered to in every case.â Monceaux (ii. pp. 7 f) remarks, on the list of the eighty-seven bishops, that "the majority of these bishoprics may be identified to-day with modern localities, which allows us to study the geographical redistribution and to draw up, at any rate in outline, a map of Christian Africa at the middle of the third century. If we first follow the coast from the great Syrtis to the frontier of Mauretania, we come upon nearly twenty bishoprics: Leptis magna, Sabrata, Oea, Girba, in Tripolitana; Macomades, Thense, Leptis minor, Hadrumetum, Horrea Cselia, in Byzacium; Neapolis and Carpis, on the peninsula of Cape Bon; then, north of Carthage, Utica, Thinisa, Hippo Diarrhytus; Thabraca and Hippo regius on the sea-board of Numidia proconsularis; with Rusicade and perhaps Tucca in Numidia proper. Pass now into the interior. The outskirts of Carthage show a host of bishoprics. On the south, in the valley of Oued-Melian or the neighbourhood, Uthina, Thimida Regia, Segermes, Medeli; on the west, in the lower valley of the Medjerda or its affluents, and on the adjoining plains, Thuburbo, Furni, Sicilibba, Membressa, Abitina, Thuccabor, Vaga, Thibaris, Agbia, Thugga, Zama, and Ausafa. Farther off, towards the south-west, on the plains of Byzacium, there are the bishoprics of Mactaris, Ammredara, Sufes, Marnzana, Sufetula, and Germaniciana; still farther south, at the entrance to the desert, Thelepte, Gemellre, and Capsa. In proconsular Numidiaâ Bulla, Sicca, Lares, Obba, and Assuras. Finally, in Numidia proper â in the north and centre, Milev, Cuicul, Cirta, Nova, and Gazaufala; on the southern slope of Aur s, Tubunse, Lamasba, Lambsese,

Aggva (= Acbia, = Agbia in Africa procons. Zeug.; Tissot, ii. pi 39, 341, 450).

Animedera (= Ad Medera, in Africa procons. Byz.; Tissot, ii. pp. 459 f., 816).

Assuras (Numid. procons.; Tissot, ii. pp. 568, 619, 818).

Ausafa (probably = Uzappa; cp. Tissot, ii. pp. 575, 586, 600, 791; in Africa procons. Byz., not far from the south-east corner of Numid. procons.).

Ausuaga (= Auzuaga; there were two places of this name in Africa procons., but neither, to my knowledge, has been identified; cp. Tissot, ii. p. 772).

Bagai (in Numid.; see Tissot, ii. p. 817).

Bamacorra (in Numid.; unidentified; called after the Bama-cures, Pliny, v. 4; cp. Tissot, ii. p. 777).

Biltha (unidentified; its bishop was the first speaker at Cyprian's great council. According to the list of the council of 411, we are to place it in Africa procons.).

Bulla (may be identified with Bulla Regia in Numid. procons., but there seems also to have been a Bulla in Africa procons.).

Buslacena (= Bisica Lucana in Africa procons. Zeug."' Hardly. The place is unknown).

Buruc (Burug; unknown. In procons.).

Capsa (= Gafsa in Africa procons. Byz.; cp. Tissot, ii. pp. 663, 783. But there seems also to have been a Capsa in Numidia; see Tissot, p. 777; so Monceaux).

Carpis (Africa procons. Zeug.). â

Castra Galbae (unidentified; in Numid.). p ' j

Cedias (in Numid.; cp. Tissot, ii. p. 817). j Vk

Chutlabi (unknown).

Cibaliana (unknown; procons.).

Cirta (in Numidia; the existence of several basilicas previous to the great persecution is proved by Optatus, i. 14. Native place of Caecilius Natalis, the disputant in the Octavius of Minucius Felix; see also C. I. L. viii., Nos. 7094-7098, and Dessau

Thamugadi, Mascula, Bagai, Cedias, and Theveste, with Badis to the south of Aures.â To these sixty-three bishoprics which can be located, we must add twenty-four others which have not been identified, twelve of them in provincia proconsularis, six in Numidia, and six which are quite indeterminate." Others identify Aggya with Oppidum Aggense, not with Agbia. VOL. II.

in Hei-nies, 1880, part 3. In the eighth consular year of Diocletian the " curator urbis" was Munatius Felix, the flamen, who drew up the report upon the results of the local persecution; cp. August., Ep. liii. 4).

Cuicul (in Numidia, on the borders of Mauretania; Tissot, ii. pp. 27, 409, 806, 815).

Curubis (Africa procons. Zeug.).

Diana (so Cypr., Ep. xxxiv. 1, according to codex Z: " Gaio Dianensi," MSS., or " Gaio Didensi." Possibly Diana Vetera-norum in Numidia; cp. Tissot, ii. pp. 484, 508, 817).

Dionysiana (Africa procons. Byz.; unidentified).

Furni (Africa procons. Zeug.; cp. Tissot, ii. pp. xvi, S22, 580)7

Gazaufala (= Gadiaufala, in Numidia; see Tissot, ii. pp. 385, 418).

Gemellae (either the Mlili in the extreme south-east of Numidia, or the Mauretanian Gemellae south-east of Sitifis; cp. Tissot, ii. pp. 28, 30, 507-509, 523, 807. A third Gemella? lay near Capsa in Byzac.; so Monceaux).

Germaniciana (Africa procons. Byz., between Aquae Regiae and Thysdrus; Tissot, ii. p. 589).

Girba (also Girha and Gibar in MSS.; identificatiqn tui-certain; probably the island Girba, Tripolitana).
Gorduba (MSS. al.: Gor, in Africa procons. Zeug.; cp. Tissot, ii. 555, 595).
Gurgites (Africa procons. Byz.; unidentified).
Hippo Regius (Numid. procons.).
Hippo Diarrhytus (Africa procons. Zeug.).
Horrea Caelia (Africa procons. Byz.; cp. Tissot, ii. pp. 145, 809).
Lamasba (Numidia).
Lares (Num. procons.; cp. Tissot. ii. pp. 454, 816).
Leptis maior (Tripol.; birthplace of Septimius Severus; cp. Tissot, ii. pp. 31, 219, 812). i

For some account of recent discoveries in the three Tripolitan towns of Leptis (= Lectis), Sabrata, and Oea, cp. Jahrb. d. A'ais. Dcutschen Archdol. Instituts, xix. 2. (1904), pp. 117 f.â In Leptis Achseus was the bishop; he wrote on the festival of Easter. Cp. my Litt.-Geschkhte, i. p. 776; Leclercq, IL p. 344. But the date is unknown.

licptis minor (Africa procons. Byz.; cp. Tissot, ii. pp. 49, 168, 171, 728, 810).
Luperciana (unknown).
Macoinades (Numid.; cp. Tissot, ii. p. 477; perhaps M. minores on the coast of Africa procons. Byz.; we are not to think of M. Syrtis).
Mactaris (Africa procons. Byz.; cp. Tissot, ii. pp. 586, 620, 819).
Marazana (Africa procons. Byz.; cp. Tissot, ii. p. 629).
Marcelliana (unknown).
Mascula (Nuniid.; cp. Aug., Eii. liii. 4; Tissot, ii. pp. 480 f., 505, 817).
Membressa (Africa procons. Zeug.; cp. Tissot, ii. pp. 325, 774, 812).
Midila (or Madili, Medeli, Medila. In the fifth century there was a Numidian bishopric of Midili, but here we are perhaps to think of the pagus Mercurialis Veteranorum Mede-litanorum lying not far from the modern Tunis; cp. Tissot, ii. p. 591).
Milev (in Numidia).
Misgirpa (or Miscirpa, Migiripa, Migirpa, in procons.; unknown).
Muguae near Cirta in Nuniidia (known through the Mart. Mariani et Jacobi).
Muzula (unknown; in procons.).
Neapolis (Tripolit.; cp. Barth, in Tissot, ii. p. 220. Though Neapolis was but a division of Leptis magna, it had a bishop of its own. Otherwise we must understand by it in this connection, as Monceaux does, the town of Neapolis in Africa procons. Zeug., despite the fact that Neapolis here stands immediately after Oea; cp. above, p. 288, and Tissot, ii. pp. 133 f).
Nova (Nova Sparsa, north of Diana in Numidia."' Tissot, ii. p. 509.
Obba (or Bobba; usually looked for in Mauretania, but it lay not far from Lares in Numid. procons.; cp. Tissot, ii. p. 459).

1 Cp. the description of the local ruins in von Eckhardt's Von Karthago nach Kairnan (1894), pp. 148 f.

Octavum (Num.; unidentified).
Oeai (Tripol.; cp. Tissot, ii. pp. 217, 812).
Rucuma (Africa procons; unidsntilied).

Rusicade (Numid.; Tissot, ii. pp. 103, 808).
Sabrata (Tripol.; Tissot, ii. pp. 209, 211).
Segermes (= Henchir Harat Bibae in Africa proccjji Â-Zeug.; cp. Tissot, ii. p. 558).
Sicca (= Sicca Veneria in Numid, procons.; Tissot, ii. pp. 7, 21, 375, 815).
Sicilibba (Africa procons. Zeug.; Tissot, ii. pp. xvi, 318, 437, 564).
- Signs (a mine near this town south-east of Cirta: Cypr., Ep. lxxix.; Tissot, ii. p. 424; cp, Leclercq, I. pp. 218 f.).
Sufes (Africa procons. Byz.; cp. Tissot, ii. p. 617).
Sufetulll(Afrit; a procons. Byz.; cp. Tissot, ii. pp. 613, 819).
Sutunurum, or rather Sutunurc (a); Cypr., Ep. lix. 10 (MSS., Sutunurcensis, Suturnucensis, Quoturnicensis, Uturnucensis. The town, as Dessau informs me, lay in A fries proroni bout 32 icilometres south of Tunis, near Henschir-el-Asker, 7 kilometres north of ancient Giufi; so inscriptions).
Thabraca (seaport on the African coast oÂ Num.,- PQcpns.; Tissot, ii. pp. 94, 808).
Thambi (unidentified).
Thamogade(= Thamugadi in Ntrmidia; cp. Tissot, ii. pp. 30, 487, 817; highly successful excavations have recently been made here).
Tharasa (in Numidia; unidentified).
Thasualthe (or Thasuathe,. perhaps the same as Thasarte in southern Byz,, on the borders of Tripolitana; cp. Tissot, ii. p. 656).
Thelebte (Africa proconsÂ Byz.; cp. Tissot, ii. pp. 49, 648 f., 676,783).
Thenae (Africa. Eir ocons. Byz.; cp. Tissot, ii. pp. 2, 16, 190, 811).
Thpj pstp (in Nnm ihia; see Mmi. Maximiliani, also Optatus, ii. 18).
Cp. the Life of Apuleius (A'ol. 72 f.).
' Known through the proceedings against Apuleius.
Thibaris (Africa procons. Zeug.; cp. Tissot, ii. p. 367).
Thimida. Begia (Africa procons. Zeug.; cp. Tissot, ii. p. 590)7'
Thinisa (probably Thunisa; Africa procons. Zeug.; cp. Tissot, ii. p. 86).
Thubunae (in extreme south-west of Numidia; cp. Tissot, ii. p. 719).
Thuburho-(either Th. minus in Africa procons. Zeug.; cp. Tissot, ii. pp. 247, 812; orâ less probablyâ Th. maius in the southern district of the same province; cp. Tissot, ii. p. 545. Augustine knew of martyrs in this town, who are grouped with Perpetua and Felicitas by the inferior class of MSS. of the Acta Perpet. et Felic.).
Thucca.(= Thugga; Africa procons. Zeug.).
JTucca (seaport on the borders of Numidia and Mauretania; Tissot, ii. pp. 411 f.; or Tucca Terebenthina in the north of Byzac.; Tissot, ii. p. 619; large excavations recently).
Thuccabor (Africa procons. Zeug.; cp. Tissot, ii. pp. 291, 812).
Badis = Vada, Bada (on the other side of the Atlas range, in the extreme south of Numidia).
Vaga (in Africa procons. Zeug.: cp. Tissot, ii. pp. 6, 302, 813).
Victoriana (in Numidia; unidentified).

Vicus Caesaris (unknown, perhaps in Numidia; hardly = Vicus Augusti south of Vaga in Africa procons. Zeug.; cp. Tissot, ii. pp. 257, 607, 770).

Ululis (unknown; are we to substitute for it Uzelis in Numidia or Uzalis near Utica?).

Utica (Africa procons Zeug.; Terl, de Pallio, i., "soror civitas "; Mart., " massa Candida ").

Zama (Zama Regia in Numidia procons.; cp. Tissot, ii. pp. 7, 571, 577 f., 586. We are not to think here of Zama minor Colonia Zama).

The father of Novatus died in a village ("vicus"; cp. Cypr., Â j. Hi. 3) which is not named. â We must look in Mauretania for the bishop " incerti loci" to whom Cyprian's seventy-first epistle is addressed (cp. Â . lxxii. 1); perhaps, too, for bishop Jubajan Â p. lxxiii.), who occupied a see at a great distance from Carthage.

Places mentioned after Cyprian, down to the council of Niccea: â

Abthugni (so more correctly than Aptungi, Acta Donat.). Now identified, Dessau informs me, by means of an inscription Bull. arch, du comite des ti-avaiuv historiqiies, 1893, p. 226); near Henschir es-Suar, due south of Carthage and west of Mediccera, on the southern frontier of Byzacium.

Aquae Tibilitanae (in Numid., on the borders of Numid. pro-cons., Acta Donat.; cp. Tissot, ii. p. 384).

A ioccala = Abiocatense oppidum (Africa procons.; the local bishop was murdered before the altar during the Donatist rising in 317 A. D.; cp. Acta ss. Donati et Advocati; Gsell, in M l. d"arch. et d"hist., 1899, p. 60, and previously Gauckler in Comptes rendus de PA cad. des inscr., 1898, pp. 499 f.; Rev. archeol., 1898, ii. p. 442), near Henschir el Khima in By c, not far east of Mactar (so Dessau informs me).

Calama (Acta Donat.; Aug., Ep. liii. 4; in Numid. procons.; unidentified; Tissot, ii. 43 f.).

Centurionis (Centurionensis, Acta Donat.; in Numidia, unidentified).

Garbe Acta Donat.; in Numidia; unidentified).

Limata Acta Donat.; in Numidia; unidentified).

Rotarium Acta Donat.; in Numidia; unidentified).

Casae Nigras Acta Donat.; in Numidia; cp. Aug., Retract., I. 20, and elsewhere; unidentified).

JTigisia. Numid. or Maur. Acta Donat. m Numidia; cp. Tissot, ii. pp. 420, 816).
" "?"

Caesarea Mauret., Cherchel (synod of Aries; martyrs, and inscriptions probably of third century, cp. C. I. L. viii. No. 9585).

Legisvolumen (in Numid., unknown; synod of Aries).

At Aries there were present the bishops of Carthage, Uthina, Utica, Bene-ventum this cannot be the Itahan town; even the bishop's name does not suit that. In 313 A. D. Theophilus was bishop of the Italian Beneventum; but where are we to look for an African town of that name?, Thuburbo, Pocofeltoe where is it?, Legisvolumen in Numidia unidentified, and Verum if this town belongs to Africa.

2 The town was still almost entirely Greek in Juba's day. Leclercq (I. p. 173) thinks that the local churchyard goes back to the age ot Septimius Severus. From Retract., II.

77, it follows that the town in Augustine's time had at least two churches (" ecclesia maior ").

Pocofeltae (synod of Aries; unknown).

Verum (synod of Aries; it is uncertain whether we are to look for this town in North Africa at all).

Alatina (or Alutina; unknown; a number of MSS. Mart. Satumini et Dativi write Abitina, a city mentioned also by Cyprian; cp. above, p. 288).

Ambiensis (in one MS. the martyr Maxim us is described as having been martyred in the province of Ambiensis Ruinart, p. 202; according to the Notitia eccl. Africance there was a bishop of Ambiensis in Mauretania. The place is unknown).

Bolitana civitas (local martyrs, according to Augustine; the place is unknown; perhaps = Ballis Vallis; cp. Optatus, ii. 4).

Cartenna (Mauret.; local martyrs; cp. Schwartze, Unters. iiber die Entivicmung der afrikanischen Kiixhe 1892, pp. 109 f.).

Cicabis (Ticabae; in Maur. Sitif.; unidentified; Mart. Typ. Veterani. Cp. Anal. Boll., ix. (1890), pp. 116 f.; Schwartze, p. 147).-

Maxula (Africa procons. Byz.; cp. Tissot, ii. pp. Ill, 719; local martyrs, according to Augustine).

Sitifis (Mauret.; martyrs; cp. Schwartze, pp. 145 f.).

Thagaste (Numid. procons.; August., de Mendacio, xiii.).

Thagura = Thagora (Numid. procons.; cp. Tissot, ii. pp. 382, 814; St Crispina was born here).

Thibiuca (not Thibiura; in Africa procons. Byz.; = Zuitina, 42 miles from Carthage, west, in valley of Bagradas, near Thuburbo minus; Mart. Felicis; cp. Tissot, ii. pp. 287 f.).

Tingi (Mauret., Acta Marcelli).

Tizica (Augustine observes that the bishop of this town, Novellus, was condemned by the Donatists in 313 a. d.; cp. ad Donat. post Collat. 38).

Uzalis (near Utica, orâ more probablyâ Uzelis in Numidia; Mah. Felicis et Gennadii).

Orleausville (near this town ruins of a basilica have been discovered, which was built in 324 a. d., according to an inscription in C. I. L. viii., No. 9708).

Monceaux (in J? ev. Archiol., fourth series, v., 1905, May-June, pp. 335 f.) shows that only the first part of this Martyrdom is genuine; the second part, which is unauthentic, is laid in Sicily and Italy.

Cephalitana possessio (near Thuburbo minus or maius; unknown; in Africa procons. Zeug.; Mart. Maximoe et Secundce, etc.).

Setting aside places which cannot be identified at all in connection with the province, as well as places which are doubtful, r n account of the similarity of their names or for other reasons,,, the remainder group themselves thus: Africa proconsularis and Numidia have the majority of the bishoprics: Tripolitana and

Mauretania have but a few. With map in hand we can see the equable distribution of Christianity over the various provinces (with the exception of Mauretania), equable, i. e., when we take into account the nature of the soil and the presumed density of 1 There is a dated (322 A. D.) Christian inscription in Satafis = Ain Kebira in Mauretania Sitif.

(cp. C. l. L. viii., Suppl. III. No. 20,305). Should we not also regard as Christian the inscription from Auzia in Mauretania Cses. loc. cit. No. 20,780), dated 318 A. D., with the formula D ' M ' S ', rendered as "donis memoriae spiritantium "? For Tipasa and its female martyr Salsa, see loc. cit., Nos. 20,914 and 20,903. Some Christian inscriptions (third century) are said to have been discovered at Henschir-Tambra, as well as one of Ain-Mziges near Zaghuan Acad, des Inscr. et Bell. Lettr., Cotnpte rendu 1904, pp. 186 f.), but I doubt if the third century inscriptions e. g., that of Giufi = Henschir-Mscherga, C. I. L., No. 870) which contain the name " Quodvultdeus " are necessarily Christian (otherwise Leclercq, I. p. 51). As the modelling of this inscription upon an expression in the Acta Perpetuce is quite uncertain, I would not afiirm that Pescennia Quodvultdeus, the wife of the proconsul C. Quintilius Metellus (before 227 A. D.), was a Christian. Near Sousse a catacomb has been discovered, after the Roman style, with inscriptions which are alleged to be pre-Constantine op. cit., 1903, pp. 637 f.; Rom. Quart., xviii. 2. 1904, p. 154). Catacombs are very rare in Africa; cp. Leclercq, I. p. 55. " In Numidia," the same writer declares (I. 390 f), "only three inscriptions can be held, with any show of probability to be prior to the peace of the church: one is an inscription of Ksar Sbai (the Gadiaufala of antiquity, south-east of Cirta), which is probably Christian, on a tomb erected to Corinthiadus, Theodora, and Chinitus by their parents Fidelis and Thallusa C. I. L., No. 4807); another is an inscription found near Tebessa C. l. L., No. 16,589: " Curtiae Saturninae quae hie fuit ann. Ix. Maevius Faustus coniugi fidelissimse, cum filiis fecit.â Maevii Octavianus Fortunatus Petrus Paulus Saturni-nus); finally, there is the curious inscription of Marinianus, in the museum of Philippeville (C.. Z., No. 8191: " Bono ispirito Mariniani deus refrigeret "). In Eastern Mauretania, at Setif (Sitifis), we find an epitaph of Sertoria (C.. Z., No. 8647). The other inscription recently discovered at Taksebt, in the Kabyles' country, near the site of Rusucurru, is the epitaph of a certain M. Julius Bassus, to whom his brother Paulus raised a pillar. This epitaph is dated the 6th of the Ides of November, in the year 260 (of the province) or 299 (of our era),â Of all the ruins of churches and basilicas discovered in the African provinces, I do not know one which can be traced back to the third century with any probability, not ; even the church of Henschir-el-Atech (= Ad Portum).

CHRISTIANITY DOWN TO 325 A. D. 297 the population. The only parallel to this diffusion occurs in some of the provinces of Asia Minor. Even before Constantine the Christianizing of the country had penetrated far. But though it penetrated far, it did not last. Rapidly as Christianity struck down its roots into the soil of Africa and spread itself abroad, it was as rapidly swept away by Islam. The "-T native Berber population was only superficially Christianized, 7 so far as it was Christianized at all. The next stratum, that of the Punic inhabitants, appears to have been Christianized for " vâ i4 the most part; but as the Punic language never embraced the 3 I. JJU Bible or any ecclesiastical dialect, the Christianizing process was f Â li not permanent. The third stratum, that of the Greco-Roman.

population, probably became entirely Christian by slow degrees. But it was too thin. Individual churches did manage to maintain their existence till far on in the Middle Ages, but they were scarce and sparse; the local Christians showed less tenacity than their far less numerous neighbours the Jews.

Â 19. Spain 2

"Here, also, the republic had from the very first contemplated the conquest of the whole peninsula." " If any preliminary steps had been taken by the republic which facilitated the Romanizing of the West,â that movement of world-wide significance which belonged to the subsequent imperial age,â these steps were taken in Spain." " In no other province, during the imperial age, was the Romanizing process so keenly urged by the authorities as in Spain," " When Augustus died, the Roman language and Roman customs predominated in Andalusia, Granada, Murcia, Valencia, Catalonia, and Arragon; and a

Only we must observe that Carthage retained the same importance for the Christianizing of Africa as for the Romanizing of the province. Churches were most numerous in the vicinity, near and remote, of the metropolis. 1A- 3

Cp. Map X.â No certain Christian inscriptions of the preconstantine period have as yet been found (cp. Hijbner's work on the inscriptions). Leclercq's work L'Espagne Ckrdtienne, 1906), which treats of the church-history of Spain down to the Arab invasion, I have been unable to use. But it provides no fresh material for the first three centuries. The appended map (" L'Espagne vers I'epoque de la yv t domination Gothique ") is most helpful.

large proportion of these results is to be attributed to a Romanizing, and not to a colonizing, process." " Monuments with native inscriptions, dating from the imperial age, can hardly be found in Spain." " No other province exhibits a Romanizing process of equal strength in matters of ritual." " Historically, the outstanding feature of importance in the Latin authors of Spain is the undeviating adherence of these provincials to the literary development which marked the mother-country. The Gallic rhetoricians and the great authors of the African church remained to some extent foreign, even as they wrote in Latin; but no one would judge, from their style and substance, that a Seneca or a Martial was a foreigner." " Lender Augustus, Tarraco was the headquarters of the Government." " The-'o headquarters of the Spanish troops lay between Lancia, the ancient metropolis of Asturia, and the new Asturica Augusta (Astorga) in Leon, which still bears his name." " Although elsewhere throughout the senatorial provinces it was unusual for imperial troops to be stationed, Italica (near Seville) formed an exception to the nile. It had a division of the Leon legion." " We find. Emerita (Merida), a colony of veterans founded by Augustus during his stay in Spain and elevated to be the capital of Lusitania. In the provincia Tarraconensis the burgess-towns are mainly on the coast; only one appears in the interior, viz., that of Csesaraugusta (Saragossa)."

The data known to us from the earliest history of the churches in Spain harmonize remarkably with these sentences from Mommsen's Rmn. Geschichte (v. pp. 57 f.; Eng. trans., i. 63 f.). For us, this history commencesâ apart from the doubtful journey of Paul, and notices in Irenaeus (i. 10) and ' Gams's work, Die Kirchengeschichte von Spanien (Bd. I. u. II., 1862, 1864), is extremely painstaking but uncritical, though the author is not so destitute of the critical faculty as several of his Spanish predecessors. Even he ignores the forged Christian inscriptions (I. pp. 387 f.). The coolest of these is one which Baronius holds to be genuine: " Neroni. Claudio. Cassari. Aug. Pont. Max. ob. provinciam. latronibus. et. his. qui. novam. generi. humano.

superstitionem. inculcabant. purgatam."" The inscriptions of Diocletian, with regard to the persecution of Christians, are hardly less audacious fabrications.

The voyage from Rome to Tarraco did not take more than from four to eight days. It was not a journey of any special distinction.

Tertullian (adv. Jud. vii., "Hispaniarum omnes termini"), which prove the existence of Christian churches (ekKXtjcrlai) in Spainâ with the letter Ep. Ixvii.) in which Cyprian replies to a Spanish communication. This letter shows that there were Christian communities at Leon, Astorga, Merida, and Saragossa, i. e., in the very spots where we would look for the earliest settlements. And there were others. We learn also that the Spanish Christian communities were already numerous, that their bishops formed a synod of their own, and that several of the Jaiahop-werÂ more secular than was the case elsewhere, whilst the sharp lines of demarcation between Christianity and the Roman cultus threatened to become obliterated (ch. 6). Finally, we learn that the earliest extant appeal of a foreign bishop to the bishop of Rome was one outcome of this crisis 1 Tertullian, it is to be noted, has just spoken of " Maurorum multi fines," so that we may assume that he intended to bring out a general diffusion of Christianity throughout Spain as compared with Mauretania.

It is a much disputed point, whether the churches in these two towns had only one bishop between them.

'â The letter also mentions other Spanish bishops, viz., those who had recommended Sabinus in writing, and those who maintained ecclesiastical intercourse with Basilides and Martialis after their reinstatement. Unfortunately, nothing is said about their places of residence.

"Quapropter cum, sicut scribilis, fratres dilectissimi, et ut Felix et Sabinus couegae nostri Spanish bishops, who had arrived at Carthage adseverant utque alius Felix de Caesaraugusta fidei cultor ac defensor veritatis litteris suis significat, Basilides et Martialis the accused bishops nefando idolatriae libello contaminati sint, Basilides adhuc insuper praeter libelli maculam the Decian persecution cum infirmitate decumberet, in deum blasphemaverit et se blasphemmasse confessus sit et episcopatum pro conscientiae suae vulnere sponte deponens ad agendam paeni-tentiam conversus sit deum deprecans et satis gratulans si sibi vel laico communi-care contingcret, Martialis quoque praeter gentilium turpia et lutulenta convivia in collegia diu freqiientata etfilios in eodein collegia exterariiin gentium ino7-e apud profana sepulcra depositos et alienigenis consceptiltos, actis etiam publics kabitis apud procuratorem ducenarium obtemperasse se idololatriae et Christum negasse contes-tatus sit cumque alia multa sint et gravia delicta quibus Basilides et Martialis implicati tenentur," etc, ("Wherefore, as you have written, dearly beloved brethren, and as our colleagues Felix and Sabinus maintain, and as another Felix of Caesaraugusta, who upholds the faith and defends the truth, has shown in his letter, Basilides and Martialis have been contaminated by the accursed certificate of idolatry; while Basilides, in addition to the stain of the certificate, blasphemed God when he was prostrated by sickness, and confessed that he had blasphemed; and then, owing to his wounded conscience, gave up his episcopate of his own accord, betaking himself to repentance and supplicating God, thankful even to be permitted to communicate as a layman. Martialis, too, besides his long-continued (ch. 5). Even in Spain people were Roman. If we examine further the chaos of Spanish legends relating to the martyrs, we can safely say that Tarragona (where Fructuosus the local bishop was martyred under Valerian), Seville, Cordova, Cala-horra, Complutum, and Saragossa were towns where Christian communities existed, while martyrdoms, and consequently Christian communities, may be probably assigned also to Italica, Barcelona, and Gerunda (= Gerona). A priori, we should expect this in the case of the majority of these towns. These scanty notices (together with the not very illuminating remark of Arnobius, i. 16, that there were " countless Christians " in Spain) would exhaust our knowledge of the Spanish church's history previous to Constantineâ a history with no famous bishop, not a single Christian author, and no trace whatever of independent life â had we not the good fortune to possess the Acts and signatures of a Spanish synod previous to Constantine, viz., the synod of Elvira (Illiberis = Granada).

attendance at the shameful and lewd feasts of the pagans in their halls, besides placing his sons there, in foreign fashion, among profane tombs and burying them beside strangers, has also admitted, in depositions before the ducenarian procurator, that he gave way to idolatry and denied Christ. Inasmuch, too, as there are many other grave crimes in which Basilides and Martialis are held to be implicated," etc.). When one recollects that this is the first appearance of the Spanish church in history, we are forced to admit that no other provincial church makes so poor a start. But this may be accidental.

It was in opposition to this appeal that the Spanish bishops turned first of all to the African synod.â The history of the church in Africa in other respects, however, stands entirely apart from that of the Spanish church. The Donatist movement did not pass beyond the Straits of Gibraltar; in fact, it barely reached Mauretania Tingitana. Upon the other hand, the Novatian movement penneated the Spanish church just as thoroughly as the other churches (cp. the writings of Pacian, bishop of Barcelona, at the close of the fourth century). It is not quite certain how far back the roots of Priscillia ni. sm- riscillian died c, 385), the special Spanish heresy, may. reach. So far as the history of literature is concerned, its beginnings lie in the apocryphal Acts of the Apostles. But it is quite possible that the heresy was. fij: st sown by Manichaeans in Spain. A gnostic syncretistic heretic called Marcus is expressly mentioned as Priscillian's teacher.

Compare some of the Acts of the martyrs, especially Prudentius irtpx fft((pdi'ai'. The Martyrdom of bishop Fructuosus of Tarragona I hold to be authentic.

One trace perhaps may be detected in Vigilantius along with Priscillian, at the close of the fourth century.

See Hefele, A'onziliengesch., 1."-' pp. 148 f. Eng. trans., i. p. 131 f.; Dale, 77ie Synod of Elvira (1882); and Duchesne, Le cone He ccElvire et les flamines

From these signatures (the names of course being almost entirely Greco-Latin, and unimportant) we learn that all the Spanish provinces (excepting Mauretania Tingitana, however) were represented at the synod.

Gallaecia: Leon (Legio).

Tarraconensis: Saragossa and Fibularia, i. e., probably the Calagurris Fibulariensis of Pliny, at the foot of the Pyrenees, not the better-known Calagurris Calahorra on the Ebro. (Tarragona and Barcelona are awanting.) jmsitotiior: Merida, Ossonova, Evora?

possibly Ebura in Baetica, or Elbora = Talavera near Toledo; but both identifications are precarious.

Carihaginiensi: Carthagena, Acci (Guadix), Castulo Caz-lona, Mentesa, Urci, Toledo, Lorca (Eliocrota), Basti.

Bcvticn: Cordova, Hispalis (Seville), Tucci Martos, Ipa-grum (Epagro), Illiberis (Elvira, Granada), Malaga, Ursona (Orsuna), Illiturgi, Carula, Astigi, Ategua (Ateva, Teba),

Chretiens (1886) Duchesne has shown that the synod probably took place not long before 303 A. D. Nineteen bishops and twenty-four presbyters (representing their bishops) are said to have attended it.

But cp the names of Sanagius and Evexes.

""The ecclesiasticalsituatjogjii-Ta xacoiiÂ nsis, thanks to Pliny's precise statements and their admirable elucidation by Detlefsen in Philologus (xxxii., 1873, pp. 606 f.), is. better known to us than any other province of the empire. It numbered 293 independent churches, 25 being colonies or municipalities with the rights of Roman citizenship and 268 being Latin, of which 124 are described as city-churches (oppida), the rest belonging to the country" (Momrasen in Hei-mes, xxxix., 1904, pp. 324 f.).

Instead of " Urcitanus," the variant " Corsicanus" has been preserved. But this is incredible. Corsica did not belong to the Spanish provinces.

â â The-episcopal seat of Hosius, the well-known court-bishop and "minister of religious affairs" under Constantine. He was the only Spanish bishop at 1,, 1, Nicsea. We do not know how he came to be in such close touch with the ', emperor. In Zosimus, II. 29, the pagan priests tell Constantine that his crimes J admit of no expiation, but "an Egyptian from Iberia who came to Rome and got intimate with the ladies of the court, had Constantine convinced by argument that the glory of Christians did away with every vice" hlyvirrios Tis â l rjpias els Trjf 'PciLi, r P ikoaiy Kal rais (Is to, fiacrlxela yvuai hi a-uviibtis yiyojxivos, ivrvx t K(iiv(na. vtivcf iratrrjs afxaprd os avaiperik u elvai T-i)i' rwv XpittTiavuiv Sie i aiwaato S6 av). If this refers to Hosiusâ which is anything but certainâ Hosius would be Egyptian by birth. This would nt in well with his mission to Alexandria, at the instance of Constantine, tn settle the Arian dispute, and his presidency at Nicasa. But our earliest sources simply call him a Spaniard, fc irj'

Acinipo, Igabrum (Gabra, Cabra), Ulia, Gemella, Ossigi, Epora (Montoro), Ajune (Arjona), Solia, Laurum, and Barbe.

To these fall to be added two other names in the list, which are either not to be identified or have been corrupted in the course of tradition." It is not surprising that, with a council held in Baetica, almost two-thirds of the bishops (or clergy) should be looked for in that province. But we may conjecture that Baetica was also the province in which the Christian population was most dense. At any rate, from those who took part in the council, it is plain that Christianity was diffused in all parts of the country about the year 300, as might readily be expected in the case of a province which had been so thoroughly Romanized. The mere fact of twenty-five Baetican churches and fourteen other churches being represented at Elvira proves that a considerable number of churches existed throughout the district. i y V 'X The earliest source available for the history of the Spanish church reveals a serious process of secularizing, and the eighty-

A comparison of the order of the Spanish signatures in the Acts of the council of Aries, in addition to some other evidence, suggests that the Spanish bishops at Elvira voted in the order of the age of their respective episcopates (cp. Gams, II. pp. 173 f; Dale, pp. 47 f.). Acci (Guadix) would then be the oldest, followed by Cordova, Seville, Tucci (Martos), etc.

Scgalvinia and Drona.â The signatures in the MSS. (leaving out the names of the bishops and clergy) run as follows:â Episcopus Accitanus, Cordubensis, Hispalensis, Tuccitanus, Egabrensis, Castulonensis Catraleucensis, Mentesanus, Iuiberitanus, Urcitanus Corsicanus, Emeritanus, Csesaraugustanus, Legionensis, Toletanus, de Fibularia (Salaria), Ossonobensis, Elborensis, de Eliocrota (Elio-croca), Bastitanus Bassitanus, Malacitanus. Presbyter de Epora, Ursona, Illiturgi, Carula, Astigi, (A)teva, Acinipo, Eliocrota (Eliocroca), Lauro, Barbe, a Gabro, ab Ajune, a Municipio (perhaps Elvira itself), Ulia, Segalvinia, Urci, Gemella, Castulo, Drona (Brana?), Baria, Solia, Ossigi, Caithagine, Corduba. Possibly by accident, Italica, the birthplace of Hadrian, quite near Seville (His-palis), is omitted. From the Rev. cthist. eccus., vi. (1905), pp. 709 f., I see that the Spanish Commission on Monuments is said to have discovered (M. M. F. Lopez) in Italica a Christian churchyard dating from the second century Excavaciones en Italica (ano 1903), Seville, 1904.

In the introduction to the Passio of S. Leocadia (Toletum, during the reign of Diocletiar the doctrine of Christianity is said to have reached Spain late. But this introduction is modelled upon that of the Passio of S. Satuminus of Toulouse; cp. Gams, I. pp. 337 f.

The Spanish churches had not all bishops; several, indeed, were governed by a single deacon. Cp. the seventy-seventh canon of Elvira. Of the 37 churches represented at Elvira, 19 sent their bishops (some of whom also brought a pres- one canons of the synod amply corroborate this. At the same time they are a striking illustration of that contrast between coarse worldliness and fanatical strictness which has characterized thetiistory of the Spanish church in every age. The dreadful state of matters which Sulpicius Severus has pictured in the Spanish church of his own day, here throws its shadow across the earlier history. i ".

The worldliness of the Spanish church and the danger which it incurred of compromising with pagan rites, may be seen from ' 'V p Â the remarkable fact that local Christians discharged the office of uV-A. flamen and other pagan priestly offices (whose religious character had faded), besides the duumvirate (cp. canons ii.-iv., Iv., Ivi.), as well as from the misdeeds perpetrated by Christians themselvesâ such as Christian mistresses who flog their handmaids to death (canon v.), Christian murderers, " qui maleficio inter-ficiunt" (vi.), the coarsest forms of lechery, adultery, and laxity in marriage (vii.-x., xxx., xxxi., xlvii., Ixiii., Ixiv., Ixvi.-lxxii.), Christian pimps and procuresses (xii.), adulterous consecrated virgins (xiii.), parents who marry their daughters to pagan priests (xvii.), whorish and adulterous bishops and clergy (xviii.), Cav Ci adulteresses among the wives of the clergy (Ixv.), clergy who trade and frequent fairs (xix.), clerical usurers (xx,), and so forth. Further evidence of secularization is afforded by the prohibition of lighted candles by day in cemeteries, " lest the spirits of the saintly dead be disquieted" (xxxiv.), and of women spending the night there, "since they often make prayer the pretext for secretly committing sin" (" eo quod saepe sub obtentu orationis latenter scelera committunt," xxxv.). The byter), while i8 were represented only by presbyters. These i8 all belonged to Baetica and the adjoining eastern districts; i. e., the remote districts sent only bishops to the council. We cannot therefore form any idea of the strength of Christianity in Tarraconensis and Lusitania; all we can infer from the fact that, with all their detail, the canons draw no distinction between the various provinces, is that a certain amount of uniformity prevailed.â Acci appears in legend as the oldest Spanish bishopric (see p. 302, note i).

1 This canon, however, shows the poverty of many Spanish clerics and churches: " Episcopi, presbyteres, et diacones de locis suis negotiandi causa non discedant, nee circumeuntes provincias quaestuosas nundinas sectentur; sane ad victum sibi conquirendum aut filium aut libertum aut mercenarium aut amicum aut quemlibet mittant, et si voluerint negotiari, intra provinciam negotientur" (cp. above, vol. i. p. 307).

304 MISSION AND EXPANSION OF CHRISTIANITY prohibition which forbids any paintings in the churches may be designed against gorgeous basilicas and pagan abuse of pictures (xxxvi.: " Ne quod cohtur et adoratur in parietibus depingatur," where one expects " ne quod in parietibus depingitur colatur et adoretur"). Lampoons were already affixed to churches (lii.). A secularizing tendency is also implied even in the provision of canon xxxix., that "if pagans in their sickness wish hands to be laid on them, and if their life has been at all respectable, it is resolved that they shall receive the imposition of hands and be made Christians"(" Gentiles si in infirmitate desideraverint sibi manum imponi, si fuerit eorum ex aliqua parte honesta vita, placuit eis manum imponi et fieri Christianos "); for this means that Christianity has been adopted as a " viaticum mortis." The fortieth canon presupposes a class of Christians who are great landed proprietors, and who permit their tenants to deduct from their rent monies laid out in honour of the god of agriculture. The forty-first canon (" si vim metuunt servorum, vel se ipsos puros conservent") presupposes people who let their slaves retain their idols, while canon xlix. relates to those who have their fields blessed by Jews. Slackness or utter neglect of church attendance (xxi,, xlvi.); catechumens who for a long while (" per infinita tempora,"' xlv.) never came near the church; Christians who lent their clothes to deck out secular pageants (" qui vestimenta sua ad ornandam saeculariter pompam dant," Ivii.); Christians who go up, like very pagans, to sacrifice to the idol and to look on (" qui ut gentiles ad idolum Capitolii causa sacrificandi ascendunt et vident," lix.); gamesters (Ixxix.), etc.â these are other features of the situation.

These samples must suffice to indicate the extent to which Spanish Christianity had become domiciled in the world, as well as diffused, before the days of Constantine. But one other canon is particularly significant in this connection, viz., the canon (Ix.) which declares that no one is to be counted a martyr who has demolished images and perished for this offence. Here and there throughout Spain, Christians must therefore have

It is evident from this canon, moreover, that lists of catechumens were kept no longer, owing to their large numbers and their loose connection with the church. Yet they were held to be already Christians (cp. canon xxxix.).

attacked the pagan cultus by force, a fact which imphes a wide diffusion of the faith. One further proof of this may be noted in the apphcation of the name "faithful" ("fideles") even to hereticsâ which, so far as I know, was confined to Spain. It was applied thus by the very orthodox themselves (canon li.), so that the terxn " fidelis " must have lost much of its pristine force. Heretics must have become very numerous already in Spain, and the church must have been imperilled thereby, as is shown by the decision of canon xvi., which condemns intermarriage with heretics more severely than intermarriage with heathens. The Jews, too, were a danger to the Spanish Christians, and a number of canons show that a certain Judaizing tendency threatened the local Christians. But whether this was so from the outset, we cannot tell.â As for the severity of these penalties, we have only to glance at the regulations of the other provincial churches to get a standard of comparison.

The history of the Spanish church, whose characteristics are so vividly brought out by these synodal canons, is totally unk nown to us, as far as its origins are concerned. The canons present it as already an " old" church. In the " Roman" territory, to which even the apostle Paul (according to Clemens Romanus and the Muratorian Fragment) made his way, the church may have arisen almost as early as in Rome itself, but for a long while it did nothing to bring itself into notice, and on its ultimate entrance into the daylight of history no glorious things were spoken of it. Not a single author or famous bishop is mentioned in the pre-Constantine age. How different this church was from that of Africa! The first Spanish Christian writer is the poet and presbyter Q. Ve ttius A quilinus Juvencus. (about 330 a. d.), who composed an epicâ the first Latin Christian epicâ in due form out of the gospels. The rigorous discipline) imposed by the synod of Elvira upon the churches may look im-

In canon xv. we read: " Propter copiam puellarum gentibus minime in matrimonium dandae sunt virgines Christianae, ne aetas in flore tumens in ad-ulterium animae resolvatur" see above, pp. 82 f. But no punishment is threatened as in the case of marriages with heretics and Jews. It is noticeable that the female sex in Spain, as elsewhere, appears to have taken a keener interest in Christianity than did the men.

VOL. II. 20 pressive to many people, but we are quite ignorant of its effects, or rather we are not ignorant that by the close of the fourth century the Spanish church was in a very bad way. No country offered such resistance as did Spain and her clergy to that monastic asceticism which formed the contemporary expression of all that was most earnest in Christianity.

Sulpicius Severus portrays the Spanish bishop Ithacius as follows Chron. II. 50): " Certe Ithacium nihil pensi, nihil sancti habuisse definio: fuit enim audax, loquax, impudens, sumptuosus, ventri et gulae plurimum impertiens. hie stultitiae eo usque processerat, ut omnes etiam sanctos viros, quibus aut studium inerat lectionis aut propositum erat certare ieiuniis, tamquam Priscilliani socios aut dis-cipulos in crimen arcesseret." He concludes Chron. II. 51) with the following scathing words upon the state of the Spanish churches: " Inter nostros perpetuum discordiam bellum exarserat, quod iam per xv annos focdis dissensionibus agitatum nuuo modo sopiri poterat.

et nunc, cum maxima discordiis episcoporum omnia turbari ac misceri cernerentur cunctaque per eos odio aut gratia, metu, inconstantia, invidia, factione, libidine, avaritia, arrogantia, somno, desidia depravata, postremo plures adversum paucos bene consulentes insanis consiliis et pertinacibus studiis certabant: inter haec plebs dei et optimus unusquisque probro atque ludibrio habebatur."

The spread of heretical unions and of sehismatical churches hardly possesses any independent value for the history of the expansion of Christianity; in the first place, these invariably follow the church and appear embedded in the same great tratum, while, in the second place, several of them, i. e., the"" Gnostic, are distinctly said to have directed their propaganda to Christians rather than to the heathen. " De verbi autem-h– ' administratione," says Tertulliail of. all Gnostics and Marcionites de Proescr. Hceret. xlii.), " quid dicam, cum hoc sit negotium illis non ethnicos convertendi, sed nostros evertendi? banc magis gloriam captant, si stantibus ruinam, non si iacentibus eleva-tionem operentur. ita fit, ut ruinas facilius operentur stantium aedificiorum quern exstructiones iacentium ruinarum " (" But what shall I say of the administration of the word, since they make it their business to subvert our people, not to convert heretics? This is the glory they seekâ to compass the ruin of those who stand erect, not the elevation of the fallen

Accordingly, they accomplish the ruin of standing edifices more easily than the erection of ruins which are fallen "). Similarly, he says of the Vjllentinians j(2;. Val. i.): " Valentiniani, frequentissimum plane collegium inter haereticos, quia plurimum ex apostatis veritatis" (" the Valentinians, no doubt a very numerous body of heretics, including a large number of apostates from the truth"). Compare, e. g., the conversion of the Roman presbyter Florinus, the erstwhile friend of Irenaeus.

Tertullian is hardlv exaggerating when he speaks thus. The principles and doctrines of these Gnostic communities were such that it was not easy for them to gain any adhe rents except where some Christianity had gone before them. This is true of the Manichaean movement in the fourth century. It won most of its adherents among Christians or Christian catechumens (cp. above, vol. i. pp. 26 f., for the attractive power of Gnostic ideas in connection with Christian). It is not necessary, therefore, to enter into any details at this point upon the spread of the Simonians (cp. p. 105), the adherents of Menander (ibid.), of Basilides, of Valentinus (cp. Julian's Ep. xliii., ed. Hertlein), of Marcion (they spread from the East, during the days of Irenasus, as far as the Rhone valley), of Carpocrates, or of the Ophite sects. It is enough for us to know that they (especially those mentioned third, fourth, and seventh in our list) were to be found everywhere, though in small numbers, throughout numerous provinces which had been evangelized by Christians, from the last thirty years of the second century onwards; that they took advantage of the vital intercourse kept up by the churches; that they all made for Rome; and that from the end of the third century they gradually disappeared in the West, either ensconcing themselves within the church or going over to Manichaeanism, which was also spreading throughout the West about 300 A. D. Thus Optatus (i. 9) writes, circa 380 a. d.: " Haereticorum per provincias Africanas non solum vitia sed etiam nomina videbantur ignota" ("Throughout the African provinces the very names, much more the vices, of the heretics seemed unknown""). How different it was in Cyprian's day! Optatus proceeds to instance Marcion, Praxeas,

Sabellius, Valentinus, " and the rest, down to the very Cataphrygians." Ambrosiaster and Augustine bear the same testimony. Phil-astrius of Brescia (c. 390 a. d.), in his great work, holds really a triumphal last judgment on over one hundi-ed and fifty dead heresies; for by that time the old heresies had almost entirely disappeared in the West. It was otherwise in the East, yet even there only in the extreme eastern regions. Within the metropolitan sphere of Antioch to the borders of the empire the old heretical unions maintained and propagated themselves much longer. We get an accurate picture of them in the extensive anti-heretical work of Epiphanius, as well as in the works, fetters, and regulations of Chrysostom, Nestorius, and Theodoret. Some of these unions, as we learn both from Clement of Alexandria and Tertullian (Scorpiace), avoided any conflict with the state from the outset, and refused to recognize the duty of martyrdom in the Christian's duty of confession (so the followers of Valentinus and Prodicus, cp. above, vol. i. p. 493). Yet even so, esoteric companies, as these unions were, couldjnotattain any great size or importance. Finally, several items of evidence e. g., the Abercius inscription, the existence of worshippers of Oeo? v' ia-TO'i, the father of Gregory Naz., etc.) prove that in Asia Minor (and possibly elsewhere) there were many supporters of serai-Christian unions, who were well organized, and who were at the same time semi-pagans. Still, we know no particulars about such popular "churches'" or about their significance. The laws against heretical gatherings for worship begin with Constantine's decree (Vita, III. 65), which orders their buildings to be demolished and forbids even meetings in private houses.

It would be entirely misleading to discuss the Montanist movement and its wide diffusion. Montanism must be viewedm.â- Â ' ' always as an inevitable movement within Christianity, which " every provincial church had to meet. Still, it is significant ur L x,. for the history of the spread of Christianity that a Phrygian prophet, together with two prophetesses, could gain such an enormous influence. By about 200 a. d. the names of the new prophets were as well known to Christians in Syria and Egypt, Home, North Africa, and Gaul as in Phrygia and Asia; thousands of Christians in the East and in the West alike believed the claim of Tyniion and Pepuza to have been born in Nazareth and Jerusalem. Still, this appears to illustrate not the diffusion of Christianity but the vitality of Christian intercommunication and the opportuneness of the Phrygian prophetic utterances.

I shall merely give a brief account here of two movements outside the church, characterized by special width of range and energy, viz., the Marcionite and the Novatian. Marcion, who came from Sinope (see above, p. 188) to Rome about 140 a. d., was'attacked by Polycarp of Smyrna. Justin, about 150 a. d., says that the Marcionite movement was to be met with everywhere in the empire (09 Kara irav yevo? avopcowwv Siu ryj? twu Saifxoi'cov crvwf Jyeco ttoxXou? ireirolrjke BXact rjmlag Xeyeiv â " who, by aid of demons, has caused many of every race to blaspheme," Apol. I. 26). We can verify its existence towards the close of the second century in almost all the provinces of the church; Philip of Gortyna (Crete), Dionysius in Corinth, Irenaeus in Lyons, Clement of Alexandria, Theophilus of Antioch, Tertullian in Carthage, Hippolytus and Rhodon in Rome, and Bardesanes in Edessa, all wrote against the Marci-onites. Even in the course of the third century they were still refuted or noticed by many writers. Epiphanius observes that this heresy was to be found " still in Rome and Italy, Egypt and Palestine, Arabia and Syria, Cyprus and the Thebais, as well as even in Persia this is corroborated by the polemic of Aphraates in the fourth century and elsewhere"" (evt KOI vvu ev re Foofxt kui ev rr Itoxui, ev Kiyvirru) re Kai ev TIaxai(TTivr, ev 'Apa ia. re kqc ev Ttj Hvpia, ev ls. v7rpw re Kai Qtj atsi, ov juLrjv axXa Kai ev rr) Tiepaisi Kai ev uwoi totto?, Hasr. xlii. 1). Theodoret tells Ep. lxxxi.) how he converted no fewer than eight villages and their surrounding districts Ka Tct? irepi Keijuevai;) from Marcionitism (note that the Marcionites had gone back from the town to the country, and erected villages of their own). In Ep. cxiii. the same bishop says that he converted over a thousand Marcionites, and similar exploits are told in connection with Nestorius and Chrysostom. Even in Armenia there were Marcionites; in fact, as the polemic of Esnik in the fifth century proves, they were a danger to the local church. Possibly they reached Armenia from Eastern Syria (Edessa), where Ephraem Syrus had vigorously disputed with them in the fourth century. The Arabic author Fihrist described them as quite a respectable church with a literature of their own. Of all the primitive heretical churches, the Marcionite is the only one which has left an inscription behind it (cp. above, p. 124), belonging to the beginning of the fourth century. The bishops and martyrs of the Marcionite church are mentioned by early catholic writers (cp. Acta Pioniif xxi.; along with Pionius a Marcionite presbyter called Metro-dorus was put to death, Eus,, H. E. iv. 15. 46; cp. also Mart. Pal, p. 73, ed. Violet, Asclepius the bishop and martyr of the Marcionites; and finally a woman martyr at Caesarea, Eus., vii. 12).

The Npyatian church, which had a fully equipped hierarchy on the lines of the catholic organization, arose in 250 a. d., and gradually fused itself with the remains of Montanism, especially in Phrygia. We can prove its existejnce in Rome " infelicissimi pauci" is its name in Sixtus II."s phrase (ad Novat. 2), but they were quite numerous; they had several churches in Rome even by-the ppening of the fifth century, and of course a bishop of their own; there is ample evidence to attest their importance during the fourth century, Afric a (even in Mauretania; cp. I eo I., Ep. xii. 6), Spain (Pacian), aul (Marcian of Aries, Reticius of Autun, the letter of Innocent I. to Rouen, Ep. ii. 11), Upper Italy (Ambrose, de Pceyiit.), Alexandria where they had several churches, and where they were numerous in the days of bishop Cyril, Syria (cp. the refutation of Novatianism by Eusebius of Emesa), and above all in Asia Minor, particularly in Phxygia, where they had almost complete control of large districts cp. the Church History of Socrates, and in the Hellespont. Their bishops were occasionally of high repute under Constantine and his successors, and in the case of one or two churches (e. g., that of Constantinople) we can draw up a list of Novatian bishops. Socrates even mentions one in Scythia.

To sketch the spread of Manichaeanism lies outside the purview of the present work; it did not originate till the last quarter of the third century, and even then, even during the first quarter of the fourth, it remained, so to speak, latent in the church.

One of the most practical ideals of the leading bishops and theologians was to secure the unity and integrity of Christendom as a whole; and this ideal, in its essence, sprang from the Christian idea of a close bond of the brotherhood (cp. Paul, John, Ignatius; eiptjvt koi ei eocn?, " peace and unity '"). As against Montanism and gngsticism, this idea passed over into the sphere of doctrine and organization, where it was carried out almost to the verge of uniformity. The consequence was that the church became a great social, political, and intellectual force within an empire which was crumbling away both outwardly and inwardly.

No unity, however, was reached at two pointsâ either in the matter of language or of customs (or of discipline).

(1) As regards language, Christianity was a Greek movement ' almost to the end of the second century. Even in the following century, despite the conflict with Hellenism, it reinforced the Greek spirit in many regions of the East where several languages were spoken, and in this way it carried on the work of Alexander the Great. The fact that it had to make room for Latin after the close of the second century did not mean any cleavage, either at first or for some time to come. The Latin spirit was dependent on the Greek everywhere in the intellectual sphere, and it could not injure the latter. The characteristic element of authority which it embraced meant no more during the early centuries than a reinforcement of the

Greco-Roman spirit, which was still unbroken and still all- rvading.

But the Christian Greeks could not Hellenize the Syrians, Copts, Armenians, and Goths, even while they Christianized them. These nations had to make versions of the Bible for themselves and to create a liturgical speech of their own, and this meant a steady weakening of Hellenism; it involved very serious loss to Christianity in the future. No one gained by this development. The nations themselves, with the exception of the Goths, had eventually to reckon the increase of their ecclesiastical nationality at the cost of a melancholy deterioration, which perhaps the Armenians alone were able to avoid. If we could imagine them Hellenized by the influence of the church, the course of the world's history would have been very different, and Islam would probably have never spread beyond Arabia.

The course of affairs in the West went otherwise. Here Latin xvas the one Biblical and lituj-gical language for a thousand years and more. Now why was this."' Cumont has recently raised and answered this question finally. In the West, as he points out, " the paganism" which the church encountered in the provinces (Gaul, Spain, Africa, etc.) was either already Latinized, or at any rate was so rough, barbarian, and therefore insignificant, that it did not represent any serious factor in history. " When idolatry disappeared, I doubt if there was a single temple in all the provinces of Italy or Gaul where the ceremonies wei-e performed by the priests in a local tongue. The catholic clergy naturally did not care to use any dialect save that which was in universal use, and in this way the force of habit and of tradition gradually led to the principle that the distinctive language of the Roman church was Latin." This

They did so at once, as soon as Christianity penetrated their life. We often hear of bishops who preached in Greek and Syriac, Greek and Gothic, Greek and Coptic, etc. Socrates H. E., v. 23) tells of a bishop who preached in Greek and Phrygian.

"Pourquoi le latin fut la seule langue liturgique de l'occident" Extrait de Milanges Paul Fredericq, Brussels, 1904).

This is true of Africa as well: Saturnus and Asclepius were the new names given to the old gods.

remark is borne out by a study of the Western controversial writers against paganism in the fourth and fifth and sixth centuries. Wherever they wrote, at Tours or Bracara or elsewhere, their blows were struck at Jupiter, Juno, Venus, etc., i. e., against the Latin gods. When the devil appeared to tempt the saints in Gaul or Germany, he was in the guise not of a Gallic or German god but of Jupiter, Mercury, Venus, or Minerva (cp. Vita Martini., 22). Hence, in Christianizing the nations subsequently (viz. the Franks, the Anglo-Saxons, the Upper and Lower Germans), both popes and bishops availed themselves of a principle which had been long established and which was consequently a matter of course. The rigorous ecclesiastical process of Romanizing all converts rested not on any " lust of power" or sacerdotal despotism but on an extremely elementary basisâ on the insignificance of all Western cults, and the victory ' won by the Roman religion over these cults prior to the Christian mission. In the East, upon the contrary, when Christianity-came upon the scene the local cults (which were occasionally of great influence and at any rate most impressive) had been bai'ely Hellenized; their liturgical language was the vernacular. In Lydia, in the temples of Anahita, the priests sang Sdp apa Kol ovsajum? uvâ Tu "EXXtjaiv (" hymns which were barbaric and quite unintelligible to Greeks""); Elagabalus spoke Syriac, the Armenian gods spoke Armenian, and Mithra was ovse ewijvl oou Tt (poovrj. It was the same in Egypt. The Copts who became Christians were for the most part untouched by the Greek spirit. Even when the Oriental deities migrated to foreign countries, they frequently retained their language and compelled their worshippers either to learn it or to worship in dumb show. When the church won her great triumphs in Syria and Phoenicia, Edessa and Armenia, Egypt and the Thebais, she drove out the local gods and desecrated their shrines. But she failed to substitute Greek for the vernacular of these new believers, who retained part of their former worship under the new modes

Cumont has certainly shown, in his work on Mithraism, that Greek was the normal language of that cult; but it is doubtful whether this was so from the first in regions where Greek was not spoken; cp. Roese, der Mtthrasdienst (1905), p. 20.

DIFFERExnCES IN PROVINCIAL CHURCHES 315 of religion. She tried everywhere to achieve this result, and her efforts were not entirely unsuccessful. But the preliminary conditions were awanting. '" In founding their churches beside the temples of the barbarian gods, Christians preserved the idiom in which prayer had always been offered. Thus the multiplicity of languages which prevailed in the Eastern church perpetuated the variety of those which had been employed by the pagan cults." It was no accident which led afterwards to the emergence of doctrinal differences between the Greek Byzantine church and the Eastern church; this was directly due to the differences which were already in existence. The future history of Rome and Constantinople is already foreshadowed in the fact that during the pre-Constantine age, while the Bible was translated into Syriac and Coptic (and shortly afeef rards into Armenian), it was never rendered into the Punic, Celtic, or Basque vernacular.

(2) Along with the linguistic differences, the variety. oiflocal customs formed an increasing peril to the unity and power of the church, as that made itself felt in the propaganda. These differences related to the cele bration of feasts e. g., Easter) and fasts, xiiual, discipline, the local and provincial organization of the churches, the popular religious customs of each district, and even the schools of learning. With regard to the first five, the Roman bishops took great pains (so, even in the second century, Anicetus and Victor) to maintain uniformity (after the Roman model, of

course), while large synods in the middle of the third century and shortly after the presecution of Diocletian attempted not unsuccessfully to enforce discipline and order in the most important matters under dispute. But the majority of the bishops were of the opinion of Irenaeus, that, provided there was unity in doctrine, and provided love was supreme, any difference of customs was irrelevant or had to be put up with. Cyprian, indeed carried this principle so far that he would even have opposite views on the validity of heretical baptism tolerated by the church. Firmilian of Caesarea (in Cypr., Ep. lxxv.) writes, circa 250 a. d.: " Nee observari Romae omnia aequaliter quae ' But Cumont underestimates, I think, the efforts made by the church in the direction of Hellenizing.

Hierosolymis observantur, secundum quod in caeteris quoque provinciis multa pro locorum et hominum diversitate variantur " ("All things are not observed at Rome alike which are observed at Jerusalem, just as in many other provinces also there are great varieties due to the variety of places and of people"). He does not take umbrage at this. Incidentally we learn from Sozomen (v. 3) that Gaza and its port of Majuma had a festal calendar of their own; while it is clear, from August., Ep. xxxvi. 32, that there were differences in the observance of fasts within the African churches of a single district. The result was that even by the fourth century there was a great variety of liturgical and other customs in the churches of the various provinces; Socrates (v. 22) and Sozomen (vii, 19) give a list of these which is by no means complete. Particularly in the supreme act of worship liturgical differences of no small moment made their appearance as early as the third century, while the regulations for the various feasts and fasts were by no means uniform. Still more divisive must have been the local religious usages which passed into the church from earlier popular traditions and pagan cults in various provinces, and were then re-consecrated. These, more than anything else, stamped the national and provincial churches with their idiosyncrasies; they were the presuppositions of subsequent differences in doctrine; they separated the churches one from another, and finally broke up the unity of the church catholic. Their centrifugal tendency was also accelerated by the schools of learning. A large amount of the controversies over dogma was determined by the differences between one school and another. Arius himself was a Syrian, and he laboured at Alexandria in the spirit of the school of Antioch.

1 He does not sanction, however, the preference of new arrangements in any individual provincial church, in opposition to the authority of the church at Carthage, or any refusal to fall in with a decree of the central church Ep. xxii. 4).

Thanks to Cumonfs fine work, Les Mysteres de Mithra (1900, with a map illustrating the diffusion of the cult throughout the Roman empire), we now know the main features, as completely as possible, of the history of Mithraism and the extent of its diffusion. It is instructive to compare its spread with that of Christianity, for (i.) both religions were Oriental;.(ii.) both entered the Roman empire abqut the same time, to run a parallel coui'se; (ih.) both were propagated at first among the lower classes; and (iv.) both agreed in several important features. A glance at Cumont's map, however, reveals at once the sharpest difference between the two religions; in fact, it shows why the cult of Mithra could not gain the day, and why its religion could not but be weak, despite the wide extent of its diffusion. For almost the entire domain of Hellenism was closed to it, and consequently Hellenism itself Greece, Macedonia, Thrace, L rxx Bithynia, Asia, the central provinces of Asia Minor (apart from.,.,

Cp. German ed. by Gehrich (1903); Dieterich, Et'fie Mithraslitiu-i ie (1903); and Roese, Uber Mithrasdienst (Stralsunder Programm, 1905). For attempts to connect Peter's primacy with Mithra, cp. Grill, Der Pritnat ' n (1904).

Eng. ed. and trans, of his smaller work by T. J. M'Cormack (1903; London: Kegan Paul, Trench, Trtibner Co.).

The oldest dedicatory inscription to Mithra comes from a freedman of the Flavian house, circa 80 A. D., when Commagene and Armenia Minor, after Cappa-docia and Pontus, had been added by Vespasian to the empire (cp. Roese, p. 27). It is a remarkable coincidence that the earliest Roman Christian writer, Clement, was also, in all probability, a freedman of the Flavians; cp. also the consul F. Flavius Clemens and his wife Domitilla, and also the fact that a Mithrseum underlies the ancient Clementine church at Rome.

3)i)
318 MISSION AND EXPANSION OF CHRISTIANITY

Cappadocia), Syria, Palestine, and Egypt â none of these ever had any craving for the cult of Mithra. And these were the civilized countries kut' e oxw- They were closed to Mithra, and as he thus failed to get into touch at all, or at an early stage at any rate, with Hellenism, his cult was condemned to the position of a barbarous sect or conventicle. Now these were the very regions in which Christianity found an immediate and open welcome, the result being that the latter religion came at once into a vital contact with Hellenism, which led before long to a fusion of the two. Lay a map of the spread of Mithraism (in the East) beside a map of the spread of Christianity, and you will observe that what is marked white in the one is black in the other, and vice versa. The historian at once sees that the former had to perish, and the latter to survive. Throughout the regions lying between the south coast of the Adriatic and the Taurus, between Pontus and the cataracts of the Nile, there was never any struggle at all between Mithraism and Christianity. Nowhere within these bounds, apart from a few towns upon the coast, was anything known of Mithra.

It was otherwise in the West. There Mithraism is not visible till after the close of the first century, and even during the second century its diffusion is still limited. But after the reign of Commodus it increases at a rapid rate, occupying province after province. From Cumont s map we can plainly see that soldiers were the real supporters or missionaries of the cult. Adherents of Mithra are most numerous in Dacia, Moesia, Noricum, Rhaetia, and Germany, always on the boundaries of these provincesâ as well as in remote Britain and in the military Cappadocia. Next to the soldiers, it was Syrian traders, and especially Oriental slaves (as we learn from the ancient inscriptions), who spread the cult. But a diffusion of this kind counts for very little, and, as a matter of fact, while Mithraism permeated almost all the Western empire, it was of no importance as a universal religion until about 180 a. d. This change occurred as soon as it was recognized at Rome that the imperial

With the exception of the cosmopolitan Alexandria.

â â ' VVhen he finally got into touch with it, somewhere during the second half of the third century, when Mithra became Demiurgus, Logos, etc., it was too late.

cultus and Mithraism were calculated to afford each other mutual support. Cumont has rightly brought this out in pp. 33-41 of his monograph (the section entitled "Mithra et le pouvoir imperial"), pp. 13-32 having been already devoted to a survey of the spread of the religion. The cult of Mithra now passed beyond the soldiers' tents and the settlements of the veterans, to reach the officers of the army and to penetrate the world where people were socially connected with officials of high rank and with the emperor. And it vivified the imperial cultus as it went (this cultus of the holy, the blessed, the invincible, the eternal One, the sun-king). In the third century Rome was simply the headquarters of the Mithra-cult, in which and with which the emperor was worshipped as co-essential with the sun, " consubstantivum soli." Middle and Upper Italy also, as well as the capital, had a large share in the cult. Vvvr

Did it form, we may ask, any real rival to Christianity H oli Aa-v throughout the West.? To this question, in spite of the swift and wide expansion of the cult, I cannot give an affirmative answer. In the first place, we know nothing about the number of its adherents in the different localities; we have much more accurate information upon the numerical strength of the"

Christian churches. Secondly, despite the deep significance of n ' A. y-A.,. its mysteries and conceptionsâ which, on a superficial view, X,, reveal many points of resemblance to those of Christianity â

The fathers of the church do not seem to me (as against Roese, p. 28) to display any serious apprehensions about Mithraism, auhough of course they are astonished at several points of resemblance between it and Christianity. See, e. g., Tert., de Prcescr. xl.: " Tingit diabolus quosdam, utique credentes et fideles suos, expositionem delictorum de lavacro repromittit: et si adhuc memini, Mithra signat illic in frontibus milites suos; celebrat et panis oblationem et imaginem resurrectionis inducit et sub gladio redimit coronam. quid quod et summum pontificem in unius nuptiis statuit? habet et virgines, habet et continentes" ("The devil baptizes certain folk, his believers and faithful ones, promising remission of sins after immersion. And if I still recollect aright, Mithra there sets a mark on the forehead of his soldiers, celebrates the oblation of bread, introduces a symbol of the resurrection, and wins a crown under the sword. And what are we to say of Satan restricting his high-priest to one marriage? The devil, too, has his virgins, and his chaste celibates "); also, de Corona, xv., and particularly a number of earlier passages in the Apology and Dialogue of Justin. As for the relation between Mithraism and Christianity, I would sum up my conclusions as follows. (i.) As religions of redemption, both had certain vital principles in common, which stretched far back (perhaps to the influence of despite its flexibility and powers of assimilation, Mithraism seldom managed to rise, even in the West (so far as I know), to the higher levels of intellectual cultm'e. Even when it- td so, it was comparatively late in the day; and by that time Christianity was no longer in fear of any rival. The emperor and the army supported it, and this lent it an importance in wider circles. But a religion whose influence, properly speaking, was confined to the capital and to the outer circumference of the empireâ a circumference of which large sections soon lapsed

Persian religion on Judaism; but how far?). Yet (ii.) the historical and Biblical conceptions of Christianity had nothing to do with Mithraism. (iii.) The rites an4 worship of the church show no trace of Mithra's influence; any coincidences are either specious or, so to speak, natural (due to the essence of both religions and to contemporary feeling, as well as to the religious substratum common to both). (iv.) So far as there is anything more than coincidences, it is more likely that

Mithraism borrowed from the church than vice versa. This is Roese's opinion also. He writes as follows (pp. 28 f.), after depicting the coincidences and resemblances e. g., the mystery of a divine sacrificial death, eternal bliss won by

Ca conflict with fleshly lusts, crypts, priests, church, candles, lamps, catechumens, baptism, the meal of brotherhood with bread and wine, the reckoning of the A V J ' week, Sunday, dies solis invicti = 25th December, birth in cave, the shepherds,-' apotheosis, etc.: "What was the origin of these resemblances? In both re-

U ligions the fundamental idea of a redemption is so essential, in its similarities and diff"erences alike, to the origin and characteristic nature of each, that any derivation seems out of the question. With regard to the details of the sacred tradition and the external forms of worship, further investigation is needed to l 'i prove whether Mithraism borrowed from Christianity or Christianity from vi vi V Mithraism, and if so to what extent. Two reasons, in my opinion, favour the. I '. conclusion (in spite of Cumont's and Dietcrich's scepticism) that the scale will Y incline in favour of Christianity in this new sphere of inquiry: (i) the extra- . "I ordinary adaptation of Mithraism to the religions of those countries, from (V" " H, Babylonia to Italy, through which it hurried in triumph (2) as regards details, Â â the circumstance that, e. g., the representation of shepherds at the birth of Mithra occurs only on sporadic large altar-pictures of the cult, and even there only furtively, whereas, had it been a genuine part of the Mithra-legend, it would occur more or less plainly in all the crypts. Further, although the celebration l of a mystic meal can be shown to have formed part of other Oriental forms of worship e. g., that of Jupiter Dolicheus), still, the religious celebration of a love-feast of believers in Christianity, which went back to the Lord's supper, appears to be almost foreign to the primitive Iranian tradition as well as to the Chaldean."

' It must be admitted, however, that we still know very little about the content of the cultus; the literary tradition is extremely reticent upon this point, though Dieterich's discovery of a liturgy i. e., the liturgy of the sacrament of immortality) has certainly extended our knowledge to a surprising and significant degree. It is probable, though of course not certain, that we have here an actual liturgy of Mithra.

definitely into barbarian handsâ such a reb'gion could not possibly win a decisive triumph over the world. Galerius would fain have enforced Mithraism, at the instigation of its priests. The "cult had become a shield and safeguard for all the rest of the decaying cults. But the attempt failed, and Coaajtantliie gav e the (quietus to anj hopes cherished by the priests of Mithra. Certainly, Julian's philosophic worship of the sun, with which even philosophic Hellenism finally tried to establish some points of contact, would have favoured Mithraism. Only, it proved itself abortive.

If Mithraism, as such, is not to be regarded either as a very dangerous rival, or as the rival, to Christianity, it is idle to look for any special pagan religionâ except the imperial cultus of the state-religion â which would seriously threaten the Christian propaganda. The Fathers of the church must have known if any special religion was their chief opponent, and if so what. But they are silent on the subject. Tlwir opposition is directed against the state-religion i. e., against the state and its idea of rrltgion. Everything else was more or less u7ie quantite negligeahle which might excite anger or ridicule, but nothing more. Even the widely spread religion of Egypt forms no exception to this rule; for in my opinion Domaszewski is wrong in holding that it formed the unifying element in the East since the days of Hadrian Mitteil. des rdm. Institnts, xvii. pp. 333 f). We may adduce Celsus at this point. What sort of religion does he set in motion against Christianity, in his elaborate 'AXrjorjg Aoyo?? None and all! He is too much of a philosopher to oppose the imperial cultus simpuciter to Christianity; hence he could not go too far against the Christians. But to make play with a special religion!â only a fanatic could do that! Such religions only survived in con- 1 Von Wilamowitz-Moellendorff (G irj- z. der grieck. Religion, reprinted from the Jahrbuch der Fr. Dentschen Hochstifs, 1904, pp. 23 f.) has brilliantly shown how this is to be understood and appreciated.

- Cp. Erman Die Aegyptische Relii; ion, 1905, pp. 240 f.) on the religion of Egypt, its diffusion throughout Europe, its simplification, and its spiritualization.

As Reitzenstein has shown Poimandres, 1904), the significance of this religion has hitherto been underestimated, but I do not think its influence upon the best kind of Christianity was serious.

venticles and as superstitions, since the day when the Romans vanquished the country and its deity. There was nothing for it then but to recommend all pagan religions impartially " which existed by favour of the state." Choose which you pleaseâ none is exclusive. Or rather, Celsus impartially refused to recommend an '. He would appeal to the patriotism which could not tolerate any aoeortj? (" atheism "), but which prescribed nothing beyond the cult of the imperial Divus.

A complete history of the Christian propaganda would include the history of the spread of each religion (Egyptian, Syrian, etc.) during the imperial period. But this would not furnish much material for church history. Such cults were inwardly on the point of death. The sort of religion to which they had given expression in their classic phase was perishing. Once it came to be a question of combining religion with a confession, a question of personal religion, of religious philosophy and public worship, then Christianity, with its foothold on Hellenistic Judaism and its possession of the Bible, easily surpassed them. It was a struggle between dwarfs and a giant. Even their united forces failed to subdue their rival, and the more they tried to imitate his armour, the weaker grew their opposition.

But what of Neoplatonism? What did it lack.? Was it not monotheism, the cult of the sun, philosophy, and personal faith in one? Was it not in touch with all the earlier re- y ligions, and did it not take possession of the heritage left by ry- 'â, civilization as a whole? It certainly had all these elements. It "" took possession of many important cults, recognized the sun-god in all, and hailed even the " deus philosophorum "" under his

A," ' name. This made it about 300 a. d. really the most dangerous yt j. opponent of the church. Did its cardinal weakness consist in jlv the fact that it came too late upon the scene, since the church

I i T.-! already appropriated the idealist philosophy as its own, had vvwvr Cw already shaped its organization and penetrated deeply into the

Vj r r masses of the people? Or was it that Neoplatonism lacked the

I P' v-'l Origen (Horn. xiv. 3, in Genes,, t. 8, p. 255) has given a very characteristic T l 'v'. Lr V opinion on the relation of Christian theologians to the idealist philosophy: " j ys. " Philosophy is not in all points opposed to the law of God, nor in accord with

IV w it. For many philosophers write that there is one God, the Creator of all things.

11 1 S:'" y agree with the law of God. Some add that God made and rules all exclusive note? To exclude Christianity alone was no use; the vagueness remained irreparable. Or again, was it weak because it was in a sense esoteric, though it vainly tried to throw off this esoteric element? Was it really unable to reach the common people? Was it a philosophy rather than a religion? Or, finally, did it lack a " praesens numen," ' the Son of God made son of man (filius dei factus filius hominis)? This was Augustine's conviction. But the previous factors we have mentioned all cooperated. Perhaps, however, the matter was still more simple. Perhaps it was not a question of one religion against another but simply of the state. The state withdrew its state-religion, and this meant the downfall of every religion which had hitherto been protected, together with its philosophy. All that was left was the religion which hitherto had neither been a state-religion nor enjoyed the protection of the state. The opposition party became now the ruling party. And yetâ the great revolution was not carried out quite so smoothly. We have good reason to define precisely the content and the value of the rival powers. Nevertheless it remains true that while the church encountered opposition from other religions, none of them was specially dangerous to her, whilst her strongest opponent, Neoplatonism, came too late upon the scene and proved too aristocratic.

things by His word, and that it is by the word of God that all things are regulated. In this their arguments agree not only with the law of God, but with the gospels. Nay, moral and so-called physical philosophies agree in nearly all respects with us. But they differ from us in asserting that matter is co-eternal with the deity, in denying that God cares for mortal affairs, but that His providence is restricted to spheres above the moon. They differ from us in making the lives of men at birth depend on the courses of the stars, and in alleging that this world is eternal, and destined to no end. In many other respects they agree with us or differ from us" ("Philosophia neque in omnibus legi dei contraria est, neque in omnibus consona. multi enim philosophorum unum esse deum, qui cuncta creaverit, scribunt. In hoc consentiunt legi dei. Aliquanti etiam hoc addiderunt, quod deus cuncta per verbum suum et fecerit et regat, et verbum dei sit, quo cuncta moderentur. in hoc non solum legi, sed etiam evangeliis consona scribunt. moralis vero et physica quae dicitur philosophia pene omnia, quae nostra sunt, sentiunt. dissident vero a nobis, cum dec dicunt esse materiam coaeternam. dissident, cum negant deum curare mortalia, sed providentiam eius supra lunaris globi spatia cohiberi. dissident a nobis, cum vitas nascentium ex stellarum cursibus pendunt. dissident, cum sempiternam dicunt hunc mundum et nullo fine claudendum. sed et alia plurima sunt, in quibus nobiscum vel dissident vel concordant"). Origen says nothing about the incarnation or the resurrection.

Do the materials thus amassed permit of any conckisions being drawn from them with reference to the statistics of Christianity? Can we get any idea, even approximately, of what was the i imbeÂ joÂ-Chrtstiaft at-. thel-period-wheil-Constantine ventured on the extraordinary step of recognizing the religion of the church and of granting privileges to the church itself?"

Definite figures are, of course, out of the question. It is htghly Tecaitous to form any estimate of how large was the population in the separate provinces of the empire and throughout the empire as a whole about the beginning of the fourth century, and how much harder, it may be argued, would it be to calculate, even approximately, the number of Christians? Despite all this, however, we need not give up all attempts at statistics as hopeless. For arelatikeâ methoi of calculation pcqinises, J: a-yield important results, if only one is careful to distinguish one province from another. To form wholesale calculations by lumping everything together, is no manner of

In this case, to be recognized was to obtain privileges, just as in modern times the full recognition of the Catholic church is equivalent to granting it a privileged position; admit it with all its pretensions and claims, and you thereby concede it supreme authority.

Unfortunately, as has been already noted, the inscriÂ tions are of hardly-ajiy use fo r our present purpose. Apart from Rome, their number appears to be quite small till we come down to the beginning of the third century. After that they may be of some importance (as is fairly certain, e. g., in the case of Asia Minor), but we are not in a position to distinguish between those of the third and the fourth century; hardly any of them are dated, while the internal criteria which have been drawn up with regard to those of Rome, Asia Minor, and North Africa are not quite so reliable from the positive side as they are from the negative.

use. Thus (jiiibpn thought he could estimate the number of Christians in the reign of Decius at about a twentieth of the i entire population. JEiiedliibder only raises this figure very" slightly, even for the reign of Constantine, while LisL-Bastie and y Burckhaxdt calculate about a twelfth for the same period. x-Chastets total for the East is about a tenth, for the West a fifteenth, thus leaving on an average a twelfth as well. Matte r thought of a fifth, Staildlin even of a half.

The last-named estimate is decidedly to be rejected. Beyond ' all question, the number of Christians, even in the East; upvpr anifiiinted td half-the population. Even at the opening of the (y 7 fourth century, Lucian speaks of Christians as constituting "by If this time almost a majority in the world" ("pars paene mundi iam maior"); that is, even a Christian of Antioch, who was surveying one section of Asia Minor, did not dream of asserting that Christians already formed half of the local population.

On the other hand, as we shall see, it is highly probable that in-one or two provinces Christianity did embrace a hal MJrjvery nea rly a half, j)f the population by the opening of the fourth ' century, while in several cities Christians already formed the krrr majority, and in fact the large majority, of the inhabitants. ' tw-Furthermore, Eusebi ys who is not much given to exaggeration, desgribes CJiristians as " the most populous of peoples" (see above, p. 21), evidently under the impression that there was no people of equal numbers. One Roman writer (see above, p. 4), not long after the middle of the second century, declares that they outnumbered the Jews; and although this statement may have originally applied to Rome and Italy alone, it was undoubtedly true of the whole empire, ere a century and a half

Richter Das ivestrd? fnsche Reich, 1865, p. 79) calculates that there were about isoo bishoprics throughout the 120 provinces of the empire at the cloae-of Constantine's reign. For the period circa 312 A. D. we must lower this number (in the West), but otherwise it is scarcely too high. I calculate that about 312 a. d. there were between 800 and 900 bishoprics in the East, and between 600 and 700 in the Westâ though even here one cannot get beyond the region of surmises. At the synod of Rimini (359 a. d.) more than 400 Western bishops took part (Sulpic. Sever., Chroti., ii. 41).

2 Hence we are able to fix the outside limits within which the number of the Christians is to be sought. It must lie somewhere between three and four millions, on the one handâ since even the Jews cannot be reckoned at less than had passed. Christianity must therefore have exceeded its first million long ago.

One important fact must not be overlooked, viz., that as late as the reign of Philip the Arabian the far-ti'avelled Origen found the number of Christians upon the whole extremely small compared to the total population (see above, p. 28). Shch is the opinion of a level-headed observer. It is corroborated by the evidence of Cyprian, and it serves to check all those exaggerated outbursts of an earlier age e. g-t in Tertullian) which frequently depict the external, geographical spread of Christianity as if it involved a corresponding increase in numbers. It would be unwise, therefore, to raise any question at all about what percentage of the population was Christian, circa 245 a. d. But when seventy or eighty years had passed, the council of Nicaea was held. Now it was during these seventy or eighty years or during thejlfty or sixty years previotis to Dio-cktiaics persecution) that the first considerable expansion of the church took place. By the end of this period Christianity had at all events ceased to be of small account. Thanks to its very numbers, it now constituted a weighty factor in the Roman empire.

The precise weight of this factor I propose to try and indicate, in the following pages, by means of a brief survey of the various provinces. It must be borne in mind, however, that numerical strength and real influence need not coincide in every case; quite a small circle may exercise a very powerful influence if its members are largely drawn from the leading classes, just as a large number may represent quite an inferior this, at the opening of the third century (cp. vol. i. pp. 3 f.)â and considerably short of half the entire population of the empire on the other. In the East, the number rose above the former limit; while in the West, as will be evident, we must put it considerably lower than the latter.

' "Syprian c jrroborates this j-adgaient of Origen to this extent, that we may infer from his correspondence that the church at Carthage cannot have amounted to many tens of thousands. Including women and children, it may have been from ten to fifteen thousand strong. This enables us to form a rough idea of the strength of Christianity in Proconsular Africa and in Numidia during the days of Cyprian; perhaps it may have amounted to something between three and five per cent, of the population in the cities. Xfituiihan s flourishes,, of, cours e, rea ch a far higher percentage; but no reliance is to be placed on him.

amount of influence if it is recruited from the lower classes or in the main from the country districts. â Ckdmianmy.–' was a religion of tozans and cities; the larger the town or city, the larger "(even relatively, it is probable) was the number of the Christians. This gave it an extraordinary advantage. But besides this, Christianity naj already "puseeci Tax into the country districts throughout a large number of the provinces, as we know definitely with regard to the majority of the provinces in Asig Minor, no less than as regards Armenia, Syria, Egypt, Palestine, and Northe ft Africa (with its country towns). WHerever we possess sources bearing on the inner history of the churches in a given province, we light upon a series-oÂ-small placesj iiijierwige unknown, with Christian inhabitants, or villages which either contain Christians or are themselves entirely Christian. Compare, for example, the history of Montanism in Phrygia, the " Sententice Ixxxvii episcopo?"um " in the works of Cyprian, the treatise of Eusebius upon the Palestinian martyrs, the Testament of the Forty Martyrs in Armenia, and the Meletian Acts (for Egypt). All this shows Jiaa!â deeplyâ Christianity- had penetrated the country districts in a number of provinces during the course of the third century, while at the same time it warns us to multiply considerably the number of such places as we happen to know of, if we want to get any idea of the extent to which Christianity had diffused itself locally.

Instead of attempting to give actual percentages, I shall rather try to draw up ur categories or. classes-of provinces and districts: (1) Those in which Christianity numbered nearly one half of the population and represented the most widely spread or even the standard religion, by the opening of the fourth century; (2) those in which Christianity formed a very important section of the population, influencing the leading s-classes and the general civilization of the people, and being' capable of holding its own with other religions; (3) those in which Christianity was thinly scattered; and (4) finally, those in which the spread of Christianity was extremely slender, or where it was hardly to be found at all.

The first of these categories includes (1) the entire extent of j j mo dern As ia Minor â loith the exception of some out-qf-the-' wai districts, which were then, as they still are, of small account in the matter of civilization. The process of Christianizing went on apace in the west, the north-west, and certain districts of the interior, at an earlier period than in the east, north-east, and south, the local conditions varying here and there; but by the opening of the fourth century the latter districts appear to have equalled the former, and to have become almost entirely Christian. The proofs of this have been collected above, on pp. 182 f. In Ehrygia, Bithynia, and Pontus there were districts which by this time were practically Christian through and through; also there were now towns and villages which contained few if any pagans. Furthermore, as the numerous chor-episcopi indicate, the Lq vlands fai' and wide liad been extensively Christianized. Most probably the network of the episcopal organization throughout all the Asiatic provinces was almost complete by circa 300 a. d., and in these provinces the reaction under Julian was unable to make any headway. (2) It includes the regio i j)f Thrace opposite Bithynia, i. e., Europe L) (so called); and (3) Armenia. It baffles us to estimate the actual diffusion of Christianity in this country; all we can say is that the Christian religion had by this time become the official religion, and that the royal household was Christian. Eusebius treats the country as a Christian land, and regards the war waged by Maximinus Daza against the Armenians as a religious conflict. (4) Cyjprus. (5) Finally, there is. dessa, a city which, according to Eusebius, was entirely Christian. I do not venture to group any other places under this category.

The second category includes (1) Antioch and Coele-Syria â y (?) not merely the maritime towns of Syria and the Greek cities, observe, for by this time Christianity must have also penetrated deep into the Syriac population. Also (2) Alea'andria, together jwith Egypt and the Thebais. The episcopal organization of Egypt as a whole, which did not start till the close of the second century, was substantially finished by the opening of the fourth century, when the new religion had also penetrated far into the lower non-Hellenic classes, as is proved by the origin

RESULTS 329 and extraordinary spread of monasticism in these circles after the close of the third century, no less than by the production of the Coptic Bible and the ecclesiastical dialect. (3) Then came Jiome, Loma'- Italy and ce? ia'm parts' of Aliddle Italy (i. e., the coasts). In Rome itself the majority of the upper classes still held aloof, and the events of the next sixty years show that we must not overestimate the Christianization of the city by the opening of the fourth century. On the other hand, it is a well-established fact that Christianity was widely represeiited amon the upper-and even the highest ranks of society. Thus Eusebius was able to describe how Maxentius began by assuming the mask of friendship towards the Christians (though, of course, he soon changed his tactics), " in order to flatter the people of Rome," while the subsequent elevation of the cross by Constantine within the capital itself met with no opposition. Furthermore, the large ij umber nf c. hnrrhes in Rome, and the way in which the city was divided up for ecclesiastical purposes, yl-show how thoroughly it was interspersed with Christians. By 0 A. D. the number of Christians in Rome cannot well have been less than 30,000 (see above, p. 247). Subsequently, by the beginning of the fourth century it was probably doubled, perhaps quadrupled. As for Lower Italy and the districts of Middle Italy which adjoined Rome, the fact that sixty Italian bishops could be got together as early as 251 a. d. â bishops who resided in out-of-the-way districtsâ enables us to argue the existence of quite a considerable Christian population circa 300 A. D. This population would be denser wherever Greeks forniedan appreciable percentage of the inhabitants, i. e., in the maritime towns of Lower Italy and Sicily, although the Latin-speaking population would still remain for the most part pagan. The fact that the Christian church of Rome was predominantly Greek till shortly before the middle of the third century, is proof positive that up till then the Christianizing of the Latin population in Middle and Lower Italy must have been still in an inchoate stage, although it certainly made rapid strides between 250 and 320. (4) Africa proconsularis and Numidia. â We may unhesitatingly reckon these provinces in the present category, since the facts prove that the majority of these towns contained Christian communities by the opening of the fourth century, and that the whole country was divided over the Donatist controversy. One might even be disposed to add these provinces to those of the first category, were it not for the inscriptions, which warn us against over-estimating the amount of Christianity in individual towns during the third century. True, the inscriptions are no reliable guide even here. How much Christianity, nay, how much early Christianity even, may lie hid in them! Only, we are no longer able to lay hands on it.-J S S pain. â The canons of the synod of

Elvira, together with the lists of that synod, justify us (though upon this point I am not quite certain) in including the Spanish provinces within this category, since these canons show the extent to which Spanish Christianity had become mixed up with local civilization by the year 300, and also how deeply it had made its way into all the relationships of life, ifi) The overwhelming probability isâ to judge from the situation as we find it in the fourth centuryâ that certain (i. g., the maritime) parts of J ijmia, Thessaly, Macedonia, and the islmtds are similarly to be reckoned in this category, as well as the southern coast of Gaul.

Our third category will embrace (1) Palestine, where some Greek towns like Caesarea had a considerable number of Christians, as well as one or two purely Christian localities. Upon the whole, however, the country offered a stout resistance to Christianity. (2) Phoemcia, where the Greek cities on the coast had Christian communities, while the interior, dominated by a powerful and hostile religion, continued to be but slightly affected by Christianity. (3) Arabia, where Christianity of a kind unfolded itself amid the Greco-Latin cities with their distinctive civilization. (4) Certain districts in Mesopokmiia, j(5-12) the interior of Achaia, of Macedonia, and of Thessaly, with Ep'irus, Dardania, Dalmatia, Moes'm, and Pannonia. The two last-named large provinces adopted Christianity at a comparatively late period (see above, pp. 236 f), but it must have shot up rapidly once it entered them. (13) The northe? districts of Middle Italy and the eastern region of Upper Italy. (14) and (15), Mauretania and Tripolitana.

Finally, our fourth category includesâ apart from regions outside the empire such as Persia, India, and Scythia (though Western Persia at the opening of the fourth century may be included more accurately, perhaps, in our third category)â (1) the toxm of ancient Philistia; (2) the nohh and noi-ih-ivest coasts of the Black Sea; (3) xcestern Upper Italy â Piedmont having no ecclesiastical organization even by the opening of the fourth century; (4) Middle and Upper Gaul; (5) Belgica; (6) Genimm; and (7) Wicetia To get some idea of the sparseness of Christianity in Belgica, and consequently in Middle and Upper Gaul, as well as in Germany and Rhsetia, one has only to recollect what has been already said upon the church of Treves (p. 268), and also to compare the facts noted with regard to the church of Cologne. But let me at this point set a small problem in arithmetic. Treves was the most important city in all these provinces, and yet the sole church there certainly cannot have included more than from 500 to 1000 members. Probably an even smaller total is to be fixed. Now, if we assume that twelve bishops, at the very outside, may be counted in Middle and Northern Gaul, Germany, Belgica, and Rhsetia put together, and if we multiply this number by 500-700, adding also soldiers and some natives to our total, we get a membership of not more than 10,000 Christians for all these provinces. From which it follows that in a statistical account of the church for the opening of the fourth century, these provinces, together with the rest of those grouped under our fourth category, might be omitted altogether, without any serious loss.

The radical difference between the eastern and the western sections of the empire is particularly striking. Indeed, if one makes the employment of Greek or I atin a principle of differentiation, the relative percentage of Christians in the former j. l case becomes higher still. And the explanation is simple enough. While a Greek

Christianity had been in existence since the apostolic age, any Latin Christianity worth mentioning dated probably from the reign of Mai'cus Aurelius. Since the days when the adherents of the Christian faith had got their ' I do not venture to pronounce any opinion at all on Britain and Noricum, or upon Cyrenaica and Crete.

MISSION AND EXPANSION OF CHRISTIANITY name in Antioch, Christianity had ceased to be a Jewish body. Strictly speaking, it had never been such, for it was rooted in what was a counter-movement to the Jewish church, being Hellenistic from the outset. It never divested itself entirely of this Hellenism, neither on Latin nor on Syrian soil. Wherever it went, until the close of the second century at any rate, it tended jto romote the Hellenizing movement, and even at a later period it retained a strongly marked Hellenistic element which clung to it and urged it on. The transference of the empire's headquarters to the East also preserved and accentuated tlie Greek character of the church as an influence telling upon the western section of the empireâ and that at a time when East and West already stood apart, and when a distinctive Latin Christianity had already begun to develop with vigour. But it was the Hellenism of Asia Minor, not that of Egypt, which now dominated the situation, a Hellenism with elements and associations stretching as far back as the civilization of Persia. There lay the headquarte7's of the Christian church at the opening of the fourth century.

There is ample evidence (from inscriptions, lists of names, connection of most western provincial churches with Rome) to show that the c hurch ope rated as a Romanizing force in the JWest, just as she proved a Hellenizing force in the East; so that, in this light, the state and the Greco-Roman civilization were really waging an internecine war against each other when

Compare the significant sentences with which Mommsen-begins his article on "The Country of Gregorianus" Zeitschrift der Savigny-Stifhmg, Rom, Abt., vol. xxii., 1901, pp. 139 f.): "Since Rome had ceased to be, not the capital of the empire, but the residence of its ruler, i. e., since the days of Diocletian, the eastern division of the empire, the gÂ ZÂ il 2?? Â iy. fj took the lead in every depa rt: . ment. This tardy victory of Hellenism over the Latins is perhaps nowhere more surprising than in the sphere of juristic authorship." We may go further without any hesitation, and add "and in the sphere of theological authorship." Thanks to the Hellenism of Hilary, Ambrose, Rufinus, Jerome, Victorinus, and Augustine, . this acquired an entirely new stamp throughout the West; the East simply thrust its problems upon the West during the fourth century, but it also brought the West the wealth of its own gifts. Even by the close of the fourth century, the Latins in the churchâ apart, of course, from Rome and the Roman bishopâ felt themselves quite inferior in many respects to the Greeks. Rufinus writes the closing books of his church-history as though the history of the Greek church were really the one thing that mattered, all else being a quantity n gligeable.

they attacked a church which, so far from checking, rather accentuated and accelerated the process of Hellenizing and Romanizing the provincials.

We cannot procure any rough and ready figures giving the total percentages of Christians for the eastern and the western divisions of the empire; and even were such figures available, they would be valueless, for the separate provinces or groups of provinces are far too varied. More weight attaches to such proofs as we have already led. From these we find that—Asiar- XÂ.–Minor was jtkeâ most Christian country (with Armenia- and Edessax-that, in short, it was practically Christianized; that, in the second place, it is closely followed by Coele-Syria with An ioch Egypt (and Alexandria), Rome (and Lower Italy), Africa proconsularis and Numidia, and lastly, the maritime districts of Southern Gaul (perhaps Spain too)â as regards the strength of their Christian element. The resultant picture tells its own tale to the historical expert. If Christianity in these hifluential provinces not merely existed, but existed in large numbers, and existed as a jjower (which, as we have seen, was actually the case); if it had already become the dominant power in Asia Minor especially, and if it had already (as has been shown) made its way into the very heart of the army, then it is a matter joÂ-ahnost- entire indiffei-ence how it fared in the other provinces, or how vigorous was the Christian element in these districts. Moreover, the church was international. Consequently, it was latent, so to speak, as a powerful force even in provinces that were but thinly Christianized. Behind the tiniest and most isolated church stood the church collective;

The first edition of this book was read, chapter after chapter, by Mommsen, who communicated his opinions to me by word and letter. When he finished it, he remarked (on 27th October 1902) to me that it contained a serious indictment of Christianity. Christianity first destroyed the empire; then and thereby it destroyed nationalityâ in that sense it is indeed to be understood as "the third race." All the distinctions created by the state and nationality were to be overthrown, and only religious distinctions were now to be valid. It meant the setting-up of a theocracy, or ratherâ as Mommsen finally put itâ "the Centre" party was founded even at that period. This is quite true, but it is equally true that the church fostered the Hellenizing and Romanizing process, and that the state would have been unable to carry it on in the fourth century had it not been for the church. The church was only responsible to a slight degree, if at all, for the weakness of the former during the third century.

and this, so far from being a fanciful idea, was a supreme reality.

For a number of years previous to his epoch-making "flight" to Gaul, Cons tan t ine stayed at the court of Diocletian in Nicomedia. In our sense of the term, he was no longer a youth when he lived there. He kept his eyes open in a city and a province in which he was confronted everywhere with a church, with her episcopate, and with her sway over the minds of men. Jl is Asiati c impi ioris accompanied him to Ganl where they reappeared in the form of political considerations which led to his decisive resolve. His chief oppon ent, Maximinus D aza, the Augustus of the East, was unteachable; but that verymct made him the most useful tutor Constantine could have had. For the career of Daza showed Constantine in capital letters what were the methods which could not, and therefore must not, any longer be employed in dealing with Christianity.

It is idle to ask whether the church would have triumphed even apart from Constantine. Sjonve Constantine-Â)râ-other would have had to come upon the scene. Only, as one decade succeeded another, it would be all the easier for anyone to be that Constantine. Throughout Asia Miimr,â atâ any rate, the victory of Christianity was achieved before Con stant ine came on the scene at all, whilst it was assured throughout the countries mentioned in our second class. It is quite enough to know these facts regarding the spread of Christianity. It

As Delbriick shows in his military history, the Roman army and the Roman legions, in the ancient sense of the term, had long ceased to exist. Upon what then was any ruler to depend, who aimed at something better than reigning only from one day to another, or over a single province? Even Constantine only possessed regiments; they had no traditions. Now the church and the episcopate were fixed and powerful; they had traditions, authority, and an obedient people behind them. There still remained one city indeed, where remnants of the power wielded by the ancient state and the ancient gods still survived as a great memory. But Constantine could not at the outset ally himself with this authority; his aim was to conquer Rome, and his one hope of vanquishing the city lay in bringing a stronger force into play against it. This stronger force of Christianity had numerous adherents within Rome itself. When Constantine attached the cross to the Roman colours before the battle at the Milvian bridge, he told the Christian priests that henceforth he would reign with them; he told the Christians in Kome that he came to deliver them, and that Christ was to triumph over Jupiter Capitolinus.

required no special illumination and no celestial army-chaplain (to quote the saying of Lactantius about him) to disclose this, or to realize what was already in existence. All that was nee ded was an ac ute and forceful statesmau and one zciho at the sam time had a vital interest in the religious situation. Such a man was Constantine. His genius lay in the fact that he clearly recog nized and iirmly grasped wjiat avÂ, s- inevitable. It was not by any artificial or arbitrary means that he laid down the basal principles of his imperial state church; he simply allowed the leading provinces to have the religion they desired." Whereupon other provinces had to follow suit.

Was thexa-anything. remarkable, it may be- asked, in the rapidity-jÂ; ith which the Christian religion spread? We have only, it is true, a small amount of parallel material relating to the other religions in the empire, which might serve the purpose of such a comparison; still, my reply to such a question would be in the affirmative. The facts of the case do justify the impression of the church-fat hers in the fourth century, of men like Arnobius and Eusebius and Augustineâ the impression that their faith had spread from generation to generation with inconceiiiablÂ L i: a iity. Seventy years after the foundation of the very first Gentile Christian church in Syrian Antioch, Pliny wrote in the strongest terms about the spread of Christianity throughout remote Bithynia; in his view it already threatened the stability of other cults throughout the province. Seventy

Intolerance was among their desires, for intolerance is inseparable from the exclusiveness of the catholic religion. But the emperor shared this feeling. In this way, he would be lord of men's souls as he was lord of their bodies. To recognize the catholic church with all its claims meant to grant it a privileged position. Constantine at once lent his aid to suppress any "heresy"; cp. the law of 1st September 326 A. D. Theodos. Codex, xvi. 5. i): " Privilegia, quae contemplatione religionis indulta sunt, catholicae tantum legis observatoribus prodesse oportet. haereticos autem (atque schismaticos?) non solum ab his privilegiis alienos esse volumus, sed etiam diversis muneribus constringi et subici " (" Privileges granted in the matter of religious observance must only profit adherents of the catholic legislation. It is our pleasure that heretics (and schismatics?) should not only be deprived of such privileges, but be restrained and held in check," etc.).

Augustine, in his rhetorical fashion, thinks Christianity must have reproduced itself by means of miracles, for the greatest miracle of all would have been the extraordinary extension of the religion apart from any miracles. See what has been said above (pp. 21 f., the passage from the Theophany of Eusebius).

years latei' still, the Paschal controversy reveals the existence of a Christian federation of churches, stretching from Lyons to Edessa, with its headquarters at Rome. Seventy years later, again, the emperor Decius declared he would sooner have a rival emperor in Rome than a Christian bishop vol. i. p. 277. And ere another seventy years had passed, the cross was attached to the Roman colours.

It has been our task to decipher the reasons for this astonishing expansion. These reasons, on the one hand, were native to the very essence of the new religion (as vital monotheism and as evangel). On the other hand, they lay in its versatility and amazing powers of adaptation. To say that the victory of Christianity was a victory of Christ is true; but it is also true to say that Christianity simply supplied the form in which syncretistic monotheism won the day. It baffles us to determine the relative amount of impetus lent by each of the forces which characterized Christianity. We cannot ascertain, e. g., how much was due to its spiritual monotheism, to its preaching of Jesus Christ, to its consciousness of redemption and its hope of immortality, to its active charity and system of social aid, to its discipline and organization, to its syncretistic capacity and contour, or to the skill which it showed during the third century in surpassing the fascinations of any contemporary superstition. Christianity was a religion which proclaimed the living God, for whom man was made. It searched and shook the human conscience. It also brought men life and knowledge, unity and multiplicity, the known and the unknown. It allied itself to Greek philosophy, knowing how to criticize it and also how to complete it. It was able (in an age of decline, of course) to assume command of the intellectual movement and to subdue Platonism. Born of the spirit, it soon learnt to consecrate the earthly. To the simple it was simple; to the sublime, sublime. It was a universal religion, in the sense that it imposed precepts which were binding upon all men, and also in the sense that it brought men what each individual specially craved. Christianity became a church, and a church for the world; thereby it secured everv possible means of authority, under the sword itself. It continued to be exclusive, and yet it drew to itself any outside factor of any value. By this sign it conquered; for on all things human, on what was eternal and on what was transient alike, Christianity had set the cross, and thereby subdued all to the world to come.

The question may be asked, however, how did it actually influence the course of things on earth? What share is to be assigned to it in the protracted changes which revolutionized the ranks and classes of society, labour and workmen, organizations and the various social groups? It is impossible to answer this query for the pre-Constantine age. Down to the close of the second century, the church was too small numerically to exert any influence worth mentioning upon the main currents of life, while the task of adjusting itself to the world claimed all its energy during the third century. Only after it had broken down the party-wall which it had itself raised, and which separated it from " the world," could it become a factor in civilization. Hence the entire pre-Constantine period is the embryonic phase of the church. Thanks to Constantine, it was born into the world for the first time. Now, it was in the world; now, it was in possession and power. It took possession of the world, and it exercised its power, by proclaiming a spiritual authority which had hitherto been undreamt of, and at the same time by pro-mulffatino; monasticism. Such were the standards under which it led the nations forward into the Middle Ages.

1 A brilliant example of how to treat the lofty problems set by the influence of the moral and religious consciousness upon the material conditions of life, with adequate breadth and insight, is given by Max Weber in his essays upon "Protestant Ethics and the 'Spirit' of Capitalism" Archiv fiir Soziahviss. u. Sozialpolitik, vol. xx. No. i, vol. xxi. No. i, 1904-1905).

VOL. n.

Vol. i. p. 355, line 23 from top, after " Hermas " add: " A whole series of teachers is mentioned by Clement of Alexandria, in a passage Strom., i. 11) which also shows how international they were: My work is meant to give a simple outline and sketch of those clear, vital discourses and of those blessed and truly notable men whom I have been privileged to hear. Of these, one, an Ionian, was in Greece; two others were in Magna Graeciaâ one of them came from Ccele-Syria, the other from Egypt. Others, again, I met in the East: one came from Assyria, the other was a Hebrew by birth, in Palestine. When I came across the last (though in importance he was first of all), I found rest. I found him concealed in Egypt, that Sicilian bee.""

(a) NEW TESTAMENT PASSAGES b) GENERAL

Abgar of Edessa, i. 71, 90, 102; ii.

50, 143-"Abraham's seed," i. 402. Adam, Christ the second, i. 243. sculapius, the cult of, i. 105 f., 118 f.; ii. 181. Esthetic, early Christian, i. 116, 218. "Agape," the, i. 156; ii. 320. Agapetus, bishop, ii. 219. "A7iot (" saints "), i. 404 f. Alban, St, ii. 273. Alke, ii. 45, 70. Allegorical interpretations, i. 286 f., 498. Alms, Christian, i. 121, 150, 154 f., 348, etc. Andrew, the apostle, ii. 152, 234. Angels, worship of, i. 232. Anti-Semitism, i. 11 f. Aphraates, ii. 148. Apocalyptic elements, i. 256 f., 288 f. Apollos, i. 79,321,32 5, 331; ii. 159 f Apologists and Christian apologetic, i. 208 f., 226 f., 363 f Apostates, i. 440 f., 496 f.; ii. 285. Apostles, Christian, i. 319 f., 445 f. Apostles, Jewish, i. 3, 15, 58 f., 327 f. Apostolic Council, i. 60 f. Apotheosis, i. 238 f, 295 f., 298 f. Aquila and Priscilla, i. 79; ii. 66 f., 205, etc. Arcadia, ii. 234. Arianism, ii. 274. Aristides, the orator, i. 500 f Army, Christianity in the, i. 308 f; ii. 52 f. Asceticism, i. 32, 91 f, 98 f., 216 f., 384 f.; ii. 139, 148, 161, etc. Astrology, i. 305 f. Atheism, Christians charged with, i. 266 f., 297; ii. 322. Augustine, i. 169 (home), 398 (home), 505 (on Porphyry); ii. 'J2i' 282, 315 f., 335.

Augustus, i. 20, 259 f, 262; ii. 182 f., 186. Authority of the church, i. 219 f., 223.

Baptism, i. 228 f., 387 f.; ii. 76 f. Baptism of heretics, ii. 283 f. Baptism of infants, i. 388 f. Bardesanes, ii. 143. Barnabas, i. 52 f., 78 f., 321, 237 ii. 126, 140, 290. Barnabas, epistle of, i. 67 f.

Baffiaeus, i. 259.

Basilicas, ii. 88, 259, 270, 285, 289, 295 f Basilides, ii. 160 f " Believers," i. 255, 403 f. Beryllus of Bostra, ii. 154. Bible, knowledge of, i. 87, 285 f. Bible, translations of, i. 378; ii. 119, 145 f-, 279 f-, etc. j Birth, narratives of Christ's, i. 71, I 95-Bishops, i. 114 f, 120 f (physicians), 223 f., 361 f., 436 f, 445 f.; ii. 89 f. Book, the religion of a, i. 221 f., 278 f. Books, censorship of, i. 306. " Brethren," i. 405 f., 421. Buildings, church, ii. 85 f, 109, 285, etc. Burials, Christian interest in, i. 165 f.

"Ccesariani," ii. 38, 49, 51. Calamities, Christians and, i. 271, 499 f-Callistus and marriage-laws, i. 171; ii. 31, 246. Catacombs, ii. 179, 230, 243 f., 254 f., 296, etc. Catechumens, i. 391 f.; ii. 304. Catholic epistles, i. 342 f. " Catholic," the term, i. 409 f. Celibacy, i. 212 f; ii. 148. Celsus, i. 104, 242, 501 f.; ii. 321 f, etc. Cemeteries, i. 203; ii. 249, 254 f., 277, 287, 294. Charity, i. 121 f., 150 f.; ii. 248. Chiliasm, i. 92-93. Chloe, ii. 66. Chor-episcopi, i. 472 f. "Christian science," i. 124. " Christian," the name of, i. 410 f.; ii. 125. Christianity, a city-religion, ii. 327. Christianity, a superstition, i. 267. Christianity, cosmopohtan, i. 245 f., 263-. Christianity, simple yet complex, i.

84 f. 513-Christians, charges against, i. 498 f. Chronography, Christian, i. 254. Church, as an authority, the, i. 223 f. Church, as a federation, the, i. 483 f. Church and churches, the, ii. 80 f., 87, 312 f., 333 f. Church, heightened value of, i. 435 f. Church, social power of, ii. 337. " Church," use of term, i. 407 f. Churches, schismatical, ii. 307 f. Collection, the Pauline, i. 182 f., 330; ii. 98. Communism, early Christian, i. 151 f. Confession, duty of open, i. 292 f., 493-Confessors, glory of, i. 492. Constantine, i. 223 f., 227, 497; ii.

235 (founding of Constantinople),
Constantius Chlorus, ii. 51.
Coptic Christianity, ii. 177 f.
Counsels of perfection, i. 216 f.
Court, the imperial, ii. 42 f.
Cremation, i. 166.
Cross, the, i. 96, 233.
Culture, Christian, i. 87, 209 f., 378 f.; ii. 33 f., 106 f., 175 f., 194.
Cyprian, i. 192 f. (flies in persecution), 378 f. (style of), 425 (name); ii. 282 f. (influence of).

Daza, Maximinus, i. 495 f.; ii. 118, 189, 334-Deaconesses, i. 161. Deacons, i. 122 f, 161. Decalogue, i. 282. Deism, i. 99.

Demetrius, bishop, i. 361. Demons, belief in, i. 125 f. Diaspora, Jews in, i. 4 f., 49 f., 329 f.

Diatessaron, ii. 143 f.
"Didascalia Apost.," ii. 157 f.
Aisaffkakela, Christian, i. 255, 358, .443-Diognetus, epistle to, i. 247, 253; ii. 5. Disciples, see under juasrjtoi. " Disciplina Arcani," i. 230, 390 f. Diseases of the soul, i. 111 f. Domestic life. Christians and, i.

393 f-Domitian, ii. 46. Dreams, i. 200. Dualism, i. 33 f.
Ebionites, i. 402; ii. 100 f.
Ecstasy, i. 200 f.

Editing of Christian writings, i.

Egyptian religion, ii. 178, 321. Egyptian versions, ii. 176 f. 'EKK r (riatTikvi, 01, i. 410. Elkesaites, ii. 103-104, 126. Elvira, synod of, ii. 300 f. Employments, secular, i. 303 f.; ii.

303-

Epictetus, i. 212.

Epiphanius, ii. 230.

Episcopate, see under Bishop.

Episcopate, the monarchical,!. 439f-

Eschatology, i. 96 f.

Essenes, i. 151, 332.

Essential Christianity, i. 43, 96 f., 511 f.; ii. 336.

"Eduv, 1. 59 f-, 243 f-

Eusebius, i. 59, 119 (on statue of Jesus), 427 (on names of Christians), 464 f. (on Egyptian bishoprics); ii. 18 f. (on spread of Christianity), etc.

Evangelists, i. 338, 348 f.

Exclusiveness of Christianity, i.

313; ii- 335-Exorcists, i. 132 f. Expansion of Christianity, stages in, i. 512 f.; ii. 280 f. Extension of Christianity, rapidity of, ii. 32 f., 257, 335.

Faith, power of blind, i. 213 f., 219 f. Festivals, Christian, ii. 315 f. Festivals, pagan, ii. 207 f. " Fideles," i. 404; ii. 305. Firmilian, ii. 194.

"Flamines," ii. 40.

Flight in persecution, i. 192 f.; ii.

207, 278. Florian, St, ii. 238. Foreign churches, care for, i. 178 f. Forgeries, i. 217, 365, 377 f. Francis of Assisi, i. 38. " Friends," use of term, i. 419 f

Galen, i. 212 f., 268. Galerius, ii. 54, 321. "Galileans," i. 401 f. Games, the pagan, i. 300 f. Genesis, the book of, i. 282, 286. Gnosticism (see also Syncretism), i.

93f- 316 f. Goethe, i. 218. Gospel, individual and social, i.

149 f. Gospels in Egypt, ii. 160 f. Greek, use of, i. 19; ii. 100, 119, 127, 241, 274 f. Gregory Thaumaturgus, ii. 196 f.; 206 f Guardian spirits, belief in, i. 136.

Hall-churches, ii. 87.

Healing, Christianity as a religion of, i. loi f. Hebrews, epistle to the, i. 53; ii.

66-69. Helena of Adiabene, i. 2. Hellenism, influence of, i. 11 f.

(on Jews), 19 f, 31, 34 (syncre- tistic); 64. (on Christianity); ii.

99, 124 f., 182 f., 313, 317 f., 332. Hellenists in Jerusalem, i. 49 f. Heresy and heretics, i. 250; ii.

307 f. Hermas, view of" prophets," i. 339 f. Heroes, spiritual, i. 216, 359, etc. Holiness, development of idea of, i. 211 f. Hospitality, i. 177 f. House-churches, i. 443; ii. 85 f. Huguenots, ii. 189. Hypsistarii, i. 3; ii. 195, 309.

Idolatry, attacks on, i. 138, 290 f., 304 f Ignatius, i. 189 f., 196, 470, etc. Imitation of Christ, i. 88. Immorality, crusade against, i. 205 f.,

Impostors, Christian, i. 180, 203 f., 353 f-. Incarnation, i. 317, 507 f. Inscriptions, i. 3, 426; ii. 42, 45, 183, 229, 270, 271, 284, 296, 298, 324-

Irenceus, i. 70 (on Old Testament), 72 (on apostles), 135 f. (on demons), 204 (on spiritual gifts), 248, 460; ii. 26 (on spread of Christianity), 263 f., etc.
Israel, the true, i. 241 f.
Islam, i. 64, 279; ii. 297.
Ithacius, bishop, ii. 306.
Itinerants, i. 52 f., 341 f.
James, the Lord's brother, ii. 97. Jesus, relatives of, ii. 91 f, 99. Jesus and universalism, i. 36 f Jewish Christians, i. 48 f, 60 f., 65 f.; ii. 102 f., etc. Jews, attitude of, i. 58 f., 487; ii. 43. Jews, mission to the, i. 45 f. Jews, Roman, i. 3, 5 f. John, the presbyter, i. 81 f. Josephus, on Christianity, i. yo; ii. I. Judaism, a philosophy, i. 11 f, 267. Judaism, a universal religion, i. 9 f., 16 f. Judaism and public opinion, i. 266 f. Judaism, numbers, i. 2 f.; ii. 4 f. Judaism, Palestinian, i. 16 f. Judaism, propaganda of, i. 9 f.; ii.

199 f., 277, etc. Judaism, the state and, i. i f., 257 f. Julian, i. 161 f, 215, 276 f.; ii. 196. Justin Martyr, i. 89,134 (on demons), 254 (school), 357; ii. 4 f. (on spread of Christianity).

Kadapol 01, ii. 218.

Labour, emphasis on, i. 173 f. Language, the problem of, ii. 312 f. Latin Christianity, ii. 275 f, 313 f., 331 f-Laxity, Christian, i. 311, 509 f.; ii. 299 f. Laymen, functions of, i. 361, 441; ii. 214. Letters, function of, i. 191, 372 f. Library at lia, ii. 106, 194; (at

Csesarea), i. 375. Literature, circulation of, i. 376 f.

Love, Christian, i. 123, 149. Lucian (the Christian), i. 357, 361; ii. 16, 29. Lucian (the pagan), i. 178, 188 f.; ii. 225. Luke, i. 80, 412; ii. 234. Luther, i. 13. Luxury, i. 166, 303; ii. 78.

Macaritis Magnes, i. 34 (on monotheism), 155, 212, 222, 276, 299 f., 317, etc.

Magic, i. 233 f.

Manichjeans, i. 313 f.; ii. 147, 308, 311-Marcion, i. 69, 156; ii. 188, 307 f., 309 f. Mark, i. 46, 80, 174. Marriages, mixed, i. 385 f.; ii. 65 f., 81 f., 216, 303 f. Marriages, regulations for, i. 171; ii. 303 f. Martin of Tours, ii. 267. Martyrdom, justification of, i. 210, 293 f, 492 f.; ii. 304 f Martyrs, i. 210 f., 367 f., 492 f.; ii.

120, etc. Mathematics, i. 305. Ma077Ta, i. 399 f. Maxentius, li. 250 f. (cp. 31 f). Medicinal metaphors, i. 113 f. Melito, i. 261 f. (views of state and church). Menander, ii. 105. " Metaphysics," Christian, i. 237. Methods of Christian propaganda, i. 381 f. Metropolitans, ii. 106 f., 240, etc. Military metaphors, i. 414 f; ii. 55. Ministry, support of, i. 158 f, 415. Miracles, i. 203, 205. Missionaries, the Christian, i. 349 f Missionary preaching, i. 86 f, 239. Mithraism, i. 417 f.; ii. 314, 317 f. Monasticism, ii. 120, 148, 204, 209, 267, 306. Monica, i. 169, 200. Monotheism, i. 34 f.; ii. 276, 336. Montanism, i. 135 f., 437 f.; ii. 75 f., 213 f, 309. Morality, i. 207 f. Mysteries, the Christian, i. 255 f., 263. Mysteries, the pagan, i. 235 f Myths, i. 30 f.

Names of Christians, i. 422 f. Names of Nicene bishops, i. 428 f.; ii. 90 f. Names of Persian Christians, ii.

2 50 f. Narcissiani, ii. 45. " Nazarenes," i. 402 f; ii. 100. Neoplatonism, i. 27, 313 f.; ii.

322 f. New Testament, i. 288. Novatians, ii. 212, 248 f., 264 f., 311. Numenius, i. 498, 506. "Nutrimenta spiritus" (Scriptures as), i. 285.

Oaths, i. 308 f.

Offices, civil, i. 307 i.; ii. 40 f.

'Oioko'itTis, ii. 280.

Ordination, i. 445 f.; ii. 129, 164 f., 249, etc. Organization of church, i. 431 f. " Orientalism," i. 29 f. Origen, i. 20, 98, 104, 109 f., 117 f., 201 f., 263 f., 361, 510, 512; ii.

10 f. (on spread of Christianity), 165, 194 (early life), etc.

"Pagan," origin of term, i. 416 f.

Paganism, survivals of, in Christianity, i. 316 f.; ii. 184, 195 f., 207 f., 217.

Pamphilus, i. 285.

Pantaenus, i. 351.

Papylus, i. 351; ii. 224.

Paschal controversy, ii. 225, 315 f.

Patriarch, Jewish, i. 14, 329.

Patriarchs, Christian, i. 469 f.

Patriotism, i. 4, 267, 295.

Paul, i. 48 f., 54 f., 73 f., 221 f, 238 f, 243 f., 331 (a Jewish "apostle"?), 381 f.

Paul of Samosata, ii. 130 f.

Paulinism, i. 56.

Pentecost, ii. 23.

Peratae, ii. 104.

"Perfect," the, i. 216, 224.

Perpetua, i. 396 f

Persecutions, i. 192 f, 487 f.

Peter, i. 61 f.

Pharisees, i. 17 f.

Philo, i. II, 13.

Philosophers, Christians as, i. 254 f., 36s f-Philosophers, pagan, see under Celsus, Porphyry, etc.

Philosophic schools, i. 357, 420. Philosophy, Christian view of, i.

294 f., 365 f.; ii. 322 f. Phoebe, ii. 66. Pionius, ii. 224. " Pistores," i. 403 f. Plagiarisms, i. 254 f., 276. Platonism, i. 295. PHny, i. 211 f., 488; ii. 3, 186 f. Polemic, anti-Christian, i. 260 f. Political standpoint of Christians, i.

296 f. Polytheism, i. 24 f., 290 f. Poor, care of the, i. 157 f; ii. 165 f, 248. Porphyry (the Christian), i. 169. Porphyry (the pagan), i. 34 f., 105 f, 229., 268, 316, 389 f, 498, 504 f (see also Macarins Magnes). Posidonius (the philosopher), i. 27, 315-Posidonius (physician), i. 146. Prayers of the church, i. 297 f. Presbyters, i. 446 f, 474 (in Egypt), 480 f.; ii. 163 f, 198. Priesthood, i. 439 f. Priscillian, ii. 300. Prisoners, care of, i. 163 f.; ii. 117. Prophecy, fulfilment of, i. 283 f Prophets, the Christian, i. 331 f Prophets, the Jewish, i. 332. Prophets, women as, i. 135, 353; ii.

69 f, 194. Proselytes, i. 10 f. Provincial bishops, i. 450 f. Provincial churches, i. 437 f.; ii.

312 f. Pythagoreans, i. 420.

Quietism, i. 310.
Rabbis, the, i. 333-334-
Race, Christianity as the third, i.
266 f. Raising the dead, i. 135. Rationalism, early Christian, i.
225 f. Reactions against Christianity, i.
57 f-, 487 f. Reader, office of the, i. 362. Recompense, idea of, i. 96. Religion, natural, i. 225. Resurrection, i. 44, 91 f. Rhodon, i. 357.
Riches, i. 97 f.
Rome, Jews in, i. 5 f.
Rome, prestige of church at, i.
178 f, 372, 485 f; ii. 240 f, 334, 336.
"Sabbatistes,"' i. 3.
"Sacrament," i. 416.
Sacraments, attractiveness of, i.
99 f, 228 f. Sadducees, i. 332. Sampsasans, ii. 103, 104. " Sarmaticii," i. 418. Schools, in Christianity, see under
Teachers. " Sect," i. 409. Sibylline oracles, i. 201. Sick, visiting the, i. 160 f. Sign of the cross, making the, i.
124; ii. 54. Silas, i. 178 f. Simon of Cyrene, ii. 178. Simon Magus, adherents of, i. 45 135, 246; ii. 15, 105. Sins, forgiveness of, i. 96, 214 f., 268 f Slaves, Christian, i. 23, 167 f. Socrates, i. 209, 295, 420. Soldiers, see under Army. Sc TTjp, i. 103 f, 259. Speculation, early Christian, i. 93 f.,
Spirit, activities of the Holy, i. 200 f.
Spyridon, ii. 175 i.
State, the, i. 21 f, 256 f., 309 f; ii. 199 f., 333.
Statistics, of Judaism (i. 2 f.), Jewish Christians (ii. 104 f.), Roman clergy (ii. 247 f.), African clergy and Christians (ii. 282 f.). Christians in general (ii. 324 f), etc.
Stephen, i. 49 f.
"Strangers and pilgrims," i. 252, 438. " Sunday Christianity," i. 309. Supper, the Lord's, i. 228 f. Symbolism, i. 228 f. Symmachus, i. 62. Synagogue, Jewish, i. i, 47. Synagogue, Christian, i. 407 f. Syncretism, i. 33 f, 312 f.; ii. 196. Synods, church, i. 197, 441 f.; ii.
129, 185, 215 f. Syriac versions, ii. 119 f., 144. Syrians, ii. 140.
Tacitus, i. 5 (on Judaism), 413 f.
(on Christianity). Tatian, i. 137, 281 f., (school) 357-Teacher, Christ the, i. 399 f. Teachers, Christian, i. 226 f., 255, 332f., 354f., 443f-
Teachers, Christians as, i. 305 f.
Temple, destruction of the, i. 63.
Tertuuian, i. 126 (on visions), 137 (on demons), 167, 220 f. (on philosophy), 257, 269 f. (defence of Christian character), 297 (on emperors), 300 f. (on worldli-ness), 362 (on proselytizing); ii. 7 f. (on spread of Christianity), 55 f. (on the army), 71 (on women), 78 (on luxury), 319 (on Mith-raism), etc.
Testament, the Old, i. 52, 65 f., 279 f., 284 f.; ii. III.
Thaumaturgus, Gregory, i. 315 f.
Theatres, i. 300 f.

Thekla, i. 163, 395; ii. 73, 227.
Themison, i. 342.
Theodore of Mopsuestia, i. 445 ff.
Thomas, Acts of, ii. 129, 152.
Timothy, i. 79 f.
Titus, i. 80; ii. 93.
Trade, i. 175, 304 f., 307; ii. 281 f.
Travels, Christian, i. 20, 179, 369 f.
Trinity, idea of the, i. 35.
Twelve apostles, traditions of the, i. 71-72,224, 350; ii. 23, 149.
Ulfilas, i. 417 f.; ii. 193, 239. Ulpian, i. 128; ii. 121. Unity of the church, ii. 312 f. Universalism, Christian, i. 36 f., 513. Upper classes, Christianity among, ii. 33 f-Usury, forbidden, ii. 281 f.
Valentinus, i. 345, 392, 409, 421; ii. 36, 161 f., 307 f. Varro, i. 275. "Vernaculi ecclesiae," i. 388. Virgin Mary, ii. 156, 206, 236. Virgins (church), ii. 75 f. Visions, i. 200, 367; ii. 75, 204, 206.
Widows, care of, i. 159 f.
Women and Christianity, i. 363 f., 368 f.; ii. 64 f., 305. Women, workers in church, i. 122 f., 161 f., 368. Work, obligation to, i. 173 f. World, Christian estimates of history of the, i. 244 f World, stern attitude to, i. 96 f.; ii.
158, 215 f. Worldliness, see under Paganism. Worship, Christian, i. 434 f. Worship of emperors, i. 295 f.; ii.
183. Worship of saints, i. 298 f., 430; ii. I 208 f., 321 f.
i Xenocrates, i. 129.

(r) GEOGRAPHICAL
Abbir Cellense, ii. 288.
â Germaniciana, ii. 287 f.
â maius, ii. 288.
â minus, ii. 288. Abila, ii. 99. Abiocatense oppidum, ii. 294. Abitini(-a), 1. 363, 397; ii. 288,295. Abthugni, ii. 294. Abyssinia, ii. 157, 179. Acbia, ii. 289. Acci, ii. 301, 302. Achaia, ii. 89 f., 234, 330-Acinipo, ii. 302. Adana, ii. 181. Adiabene, i. i f.; ii.
142 f. Ad Medera, ii. 288 f. Adraa, ii. 103. Adramyttium, ii. 183 Adriani, ii. 212. Adrianopolis, ii. 235. JEgse, ii. 181 f. yegina, ii. 230. lia, see Jerusalem.(â Â milia, ii. 258. zani, ii. 219. Africa, i. 3; ii. 274 f., 308, 326, 329 f. Agbia, ii. 289. Agen (Agaunum), ii.
267. Agense oppidum, ii.
289. Aggya, ii. 289. Aila, ii. 115, 119. Ain Kebira, ii. 296. AYn-Mziges, ii. 296. Ajune, ii. 302. Akmonia, ii. 215. Alalis, ii. 122. Alassus, ii. 122. Alatina, ii. 295.
Alba, ii. 258. Albanians, ii. 210. Albano(-um), ii. 253. Albans, St, ii. 273. Alcheis (?), ii. 135. Alemanni, ii. 17, 271. Aleppo, ii. 139. Alexander-Insula, ii.
167. Alexandreiopolis, ii.
161 f. Alexandretta, ii. 180 f. Alexandria, i. 4 f., 357 f.; ii. 38f., 56f., 158 f., 328. Alpho-kranon, ii. 172. Alpine provinces, ii.

258, 271. Alutina, see Alatina. Amasceunites, ii. 228. Amasia, ii. 187,190,205. Amastris, i. 455 f.; ii.
187 f., 203. Ambiensis, ii. 295. Amblada, ii. 221. Amida (= Diarbekir), ii. 149. Amiens, ii. 267. Amisus, ii. 92, 188, 205. Amiternum, ii. 253. Ammjedera, ii. 288 f. Ammoniace, ii. 165. Amorium, ii. 219 f. Amphipolis, ii. 93. Anab, ii. 116 f. Anacipolis, ii. 171. Anaea, ii. 226. Anazarbus, ii. 181 f. Anchialus, ii. 234. Ancona, ii. 255. Ancyra, i. 454 f.; ii.
188 f., 215, 216 ff. Ancyra ferrea, ii. 226. Andalusia, ii. 297. Andaval (Andabilis), ii. 195.
Andrapolis, ii. 152. Anea, ii. 116-117. Angers, ii. 266. Anim, ii. 108, 116. Antaeopolis, ii. 173. Antaradus, ii. 122. Anthedon, ii 99. Antinoe, ii. 166, 171 f., 177. Antioch (Isaur.). ii. 227. â (Car.), ii. 226. â (Pisid.), ii. 220 â (Syrian), i. 52
Antiochia Mygdonia, ii. 146. Antipatris, ii. 99. Antipyrgos, ii. 173. Antium, ii. 253. Apamea (Bithyn.,) ii. 212. â (Phrygian) =
Cibotus, ii, 188, 218. (Pisid.) = Ce-lasnae, ii. 221. â (Syrian), ii.
136, 137 f-Aphaka, ii. 124. Aphrodisias, ii. 226. Aphroditon, ii. 174. Apollonia, ii. 93, 99. Apouonias (Bithyn.), ii.
212.,, (Carian), ii.
226. Apollonopolis inf., ii.
174. Aprocavictum, ii. 137. Apta, ii. 265. Aptungi, ii. 294. Apulia, ii. 255. Aquie regime, ii. 290.
Aquae Tibilitanae, ii.
294. Aquila ii. 255. Aquileia, ii. 259-260. Aquitania, i. 452. Arabia, i. 373; ii. 152 f-, 330-Arabissus, ii. 199.
Aradus, i. 2; ii. 121. Arbela, ii. 150. Arbokadama, ii. 137. Arcadia, ii. 234. Archipelago, the Greek, ii. 229, 330. Ardabau, ii. 188, 218. Areh-Zara, ii. 287. Areopohs, see Rabba, ii. 156. Arethusa, ii. 137, 138. Argos, ii. 231. Ariace, ii. 12 f., 152. Aricia, ii. 253. Arimathea, ii. 114. Arjona, ii. 302. Aries, i. 452 f., ii. 264 f. Armenia, ii. 196 f., 328. Arnem, ii. loi f. Arpiensium civitas, ii.
255. Arragon, ii. 297. Arsinoe (and district), ii. 161 f., 171 Arycanda, ii. 226. Ascalon, ii. 99, 112, 115. Aschtischat, ii. 202 f. Ascoli Pic, ii. 255. Ashdod, ii. 93. Asia (Asia Minor), i.
74 f., 81 f., 261; ii.
328 f., 333-Asia, seven churches of, ii. 92, 183. 'Asker, see Sichar. Aspendus, ii. 227. Assisi, ii. 255. Assuras, ii. 288-289. Assus, ii. 93. Assyria (see Syria). Astaroth, ii. loi f. Astigi, ii. 301. Asturica (Astorga), ii.
298 f. Ategua (Ateva), ii. 301.
Athens, i. 265; ii. 231-232.
Athribitis (Athribis, Athribe, Atripa; also town of this name in Upper Egypt), ii. 161 f., 172.
Attalia, ii. 93, 227.
Attica, ii. 231.
Attil, ii. 108.
Augsburg, ii. 271 f.
Augustoeuphratesia, ii.

Aulana, ii. 108. Aulona, ii. 117. Auranitis, ii. 120. Aurelianopolis, ii. 226. Aureus Mons, ii. 254. Ausafa, ii. 288-289. Ausuaga, ii. 289. Autumni, see Aptungi. Autun, ii. 265. Auxerre, ii. 266. Auzia, ii., 296. Avellino, ii. 255. Avioccala, ii. 294. Axiupolis, ii. 236. Axum, ii. 100, 152. Azotus, ii. 99, 115.

Babylon, ii. 93-94, 146. Babylonia, i. 4. Bacata, ii. 155. Baccanae, ii. 255. Bactria, ii. 147. Bada (Badis), ii. 289, 293-Baetica, ii. 301 f. Bagai, ii. 289. Bagis, ii. 226. Bagravan in Bagre- vand, ii. 202 f. Baischan (Besan), see Scythopolis. Bakathus, ii. 115. Balanese, ii. 137. Balkan peninsula, ii. 230 f. Ballis, ii. 295. Bamacorra, ii. 289. Banea, see Batanea. Barata, ii. 227 f. Barbe, ii. 302. Barce, ii. 173. Barcelona, ii. 300 f.

Baria, ii. 302. Baris, ii. 221. Basanitis, ii. loi f. Bassano, ii. 255. Basti, ii. 301. Batana, ii. 149 f. Batanea, ii. 102 f., 120. â (near Cies.

Pal)., ii. 108, 117. Bath, ii. 274. Beauvais, ii. 266. Belgica, ii. 266 f., 331. Beneventum, ii. 254, -94-Bereitan (Berothai), ii.

Berenice, ii. 168, 173. Bergamo, ii. 259. Beritana, ii. 156. Beroea (Maced.), ii. 232.

â (Syrian), ii. loif., 139. Bertinoro (Brictino- rium), ii. 256. Berytus, ii. 122 f., 141, 212. Besanduke, ii. 115. Beter-Ras, ii. 115. Bethabara, ii. 117. Beth-'Alam, ii. 117. Bethelia, ii. no. Beth Gubrin, ii. 117. Beth Lapath, ii. 149. Bethlehem, ii. 108, 116. Bethphage, ii. 109. Bethsaida, ii. 99. Bethzabde, ii. 147. Bettona, ii. 255. Biltha, ii. 289. Bisica Lucana, ii. 289. Bithynia, ii. 186 f., 210 f., 328. Black Sea, i. i f.; ii.

239 f-, 331-Blaundus, see Stan- dus. Bobba, see Obba. Bolitana civitas, ii. 295. Bologna, ii. 259. Bomotheus, ii. 174. Bonn, ii. 271. Bordeaux, ii. 265 f. Borissus, ii. 195.

Bosphorus, ii. 239 f. Bostra, ii. 154 f. Bourges, ii. 266. Brana, ii. 302. Brescia, ii. 259. Bretagne, ii. 96. Brindisi, ii. 254. Britain, see England. Brittium (Bruttium), ii.

257. Bruzus, ii. 219. Bubastus, ii. 172. Bucolia, ii. 174, 177. Bulla, ii. 288-289. Buruc, ii. 289. Busiris, ii. 172. Buslacena, ii. 289. Buththrotum, ii. 235. Butis, see Bella. Byblus, ii. 123, Byzacena (Byzacium), ii. 278 f. Byzantium, ii. 95, 234 f.

Cabra, ii. 300. Caerleon, ii. 273. Csesaraugusta, ii. 298. Caesarea (Bithyn.), ii. 212. â (Cappadoc), 193 f-â (Ma u ret.), ii. 294. â (Palest.), ii.

ii3f., ii5, 33Â-â (Philippi), see Pan-eas. Cagliari, ii. 255. Calabria, ii. 240. Calagurris- Fibularia, ii. 301. Calahorra, ii. 301. Calama, ii. 286, 294. Calytis (Canytis?), ii.

221. Camalodunum, ii. 273. Camerino, ii. 255. Campania, ii. 251. Campsas, ii. 212. Camulia, ii. 192. Capernaum, ii, 109,146.

Capitolias, ii. 99. 115. Cappadocia, i. 165 f.; ii. 192 f., 239 f. Capparetea, ii. 114. Capsa, ii. 288, 289. Capua, ii. 254. Cardaba, see Ardabau. Caria, ii. 226. Cariathaim, ii. 155. Carnaim, ii. loi f. Carpis, ii. 288, 289. Carrhai, ii. 63, 145. Cartenna, ii. 295. Carthage, i. 165, f., 172 f., 377; ii. 8f.,274f., 280 f., 286, 326. Carthagena, ii. 301. Carthagena (Span.

prov.), ii. 301. Carula, ii. 301 f. Carystus, ii. 231. Casae Nigrse, ii. 294. Castabala, ii. 181. Castra Galbae, ii. 289. Castulo, ii. 301. Catalonia, ii. 297.

Catania, ii. 255. Caucasus, ii. 77. Cazlona, ii. 301. Cedias, ii. 289. Ceima, ii. 230. Celasnas, ii. 221. Celts, ii. 263 f. Cenchrcee, i. 463; ii.
    233-Centumcellae, ii. 255. Centurionis, ii. 294. Cephallenia, ii. 230. Cephallitanapossessio, ii. 296. Cephro, ii. 167. Cesena, ii. 254. Cetis, ii. 195. Chabolo, ii. 115. Chaduthi, ii. 198. Chalcedon, ii. 211. Chalcis, ii. 231, 235. Chalons, ii. 266. Charisphone, ii. 198. Chartres, ii. 266. Chenebri, 174. Chenoboscium, ii. 169. Cherchel, ii. 294. Cheretapa, ii. 220. Cherson, ii. 240.
    Chios, ii. 230. Chulabbi, ii. 289. Cibaliana, ii. 289. Cibalis, ii. 237. Cibyra, ii. 226. Cicabis (Ticabae), ii.
    .295-Cilicia, i. 164, 329 f.; ii. 180 f. Cillium, ii. 287. Cirta, ii. 285, 288 f. Civita Vecchia, ii. 255. Claudiopolis, ii. 227 f. Cleopatris, ii. 171. Clermont, ii. 264, 266. Clusium, ii. 256. Clysona, ii. 174. Cnidos, i. 2. Cnossus, i. 197; ii. 95, 229. Coele-Syria, see Syria. Couuthion, ii. 167. Cologne, ii. 269-270. Colonia (Capp.), ii. 192. Colossae, ii. 218. Coma, ii. 173. Comana, (Capp.), ii. 192. â (Pont.), ii.
    205. Commagene, ii. 182. Como, ii. 259. Complutum, ii. 300. Constantia, ii. 115. Constantinople, ii. 184, 235-Coptus, ii. 171. Coracesion, ii. 228. Corcyra, ii. 230. Cordova, ii. 240, 301, 3?–Corinth, i. 194 f.; ii.
    231 f. Corna, ii. 229. Coronia, ii. 231. Coropissus, ii. 221, 227. Corsica, ii. 301. Cos, i. 107; ii. 171, 230. Cotiaium, ii. 219. Cremona, ii. 259. Crete, ii. 95 f., 229 f. Ctesiphon, ii. 150. Cuicul, ii. 288 f. Cumce, ii. 256.
    Cumane, ii. i88, 215,
    Curubis, ii. 290. Custe, ii. 171. Cybistra, ii. 192. Cynopolis (Cynos) sup. et inf., ii. 171 f. Cyprus, i. 4 f.; ii. 140 f., 328. Cyrene (Cyrenaica, Pentapolis), i. 4; ii.
    95 f., 178 f. Cyrrhus, ii. 137. Cyzikus, ii. 192 f., 225.
    Dacia, ii. 236 f. Dalmatia, ii. 93, 238, 33Â-Damascus, i. 4; ii. 99, 103 f., 125. Dantu, ii. 170. Dara, ii. 150. Dardania, ii. 330. Darnis (Dardanis), ii.
    173-Daroma, ii. 166. Uascylium, ii. 226, Debeltum, i. 459; li.
    234-
Decapolis, ii 99 f.
Deir Ali, ii. 123.
Delos, i. 2.
Der'at, ii. 103.
Derbe, ii. 221.
Diana (Veteranorum), ii. 290.
Diarbekir, ii. 149.
Didensis, ii. 290.
Die (Gaul), ii. 265 f.
Digne, ii, 266.
Dikella, ii. 174.
Diocaesarea (Capp.), see Nazi-anzus. â (Isaur.)
C h e r e-tapa, ii. 220. (Pal.)Sep-phoris, ii.
Diodoris, ii. 150.
Dionysiana, ii. 290.
Dionysias, ii. 156.

Dioskome, ii. 219. Diosphacus, ii. 174. Diospolis (Egypt), ii. 169, 171. (Pal), see Lydda. Dirschaba, ii. 170. Dium, ii. 99. Djebel Khaui, ii. 277. Dokimion, ii. 215. Doliche, ii. 137 f. Dora, ii. 99. Dorla, ii. 229. Dorostorum, ii. 236. Dorylkum, ii. 219. Drepana, ii. 212. Drizipara (Drusipara), ii. 235. Drona, ii 302. Dschuren, ii. 103. Duja, see Die. Dumanli, ii. 218.

Eauze, ii. 266. Ebura, ii. 301. Edessa, i. 2 f.; ii. 86, 142 f., 201 f., 328. Egypt, i. 8 f., 73, 360 f., 464 f., 482; ii. 158 f, 321, 328. Ekdaumana, ii. 217. Elataea, ii. 231. Elbora, ii. 301. Eleutheropolis, ii. 99, 115 f., 144. Eliocrota, ii. 301. Elvira (Illiberis, Granada), ii. 301. Embrun, ii. 266. Emerita, see Merida. Emesa, i. 464 f.; ii. 122 f. Emmaus, ii. 99, 114. England, ii. 272 f. Epagro, ii. 301. Ephesus, i. 75 f.; ii. 222 f. Epibata, ii. 235. Epidaurus, i. 107. Epiphania (Cilic.) ii. 181. â (Syr.) ii. 137. Epirus, n. 330, Epora, ii. 302, Erment (Ermont), ii. 171. Esbon (Esbus, Hes- bon), ii. 99, 155. Esneh, ii. 169. Es-Suweda, ii. 115. Ethiopia, ii. 179. Etruria, ii. 256. Etschmiadzin, ii. 202. Eubcea, ii. 231, 235. Eucarpia, ii. 219. Eumenea (Phryg.), ii. 188, 190, 219. "Europe," ii. 231, 328. Evora, ii. 301.

Faenza, ii. 254. Fano, ii. 256. Ferentino, ii. 256. Fermo, ii. 256. Fibularia, ii. 301. Flavia duorum, ii. 265. Flavias, ii. 181. Florence, ii. 254. Foligno, ii. 256. Forli, ii. 256. Forlimpopoli, ii. 256. Forum Claudii, ii. 254. Fruschka Gora, ii 238. Fundi, ii. 253. Furni, i. 474; ii. 285, 288, 290.

Gaba, ii. 99. Gabbala, ii. 137. Gabra, ii, 302. Gabula, ii. 137. Gadamaua (Gdmaua), ii. 217. Gadara, ii. 99, 115. Gadiaufala, ii. 290, 296. Gasta, ii. 255. Ga tuli, ii. 9. Gafsa, ii. 289. Gagje, ii. 226. Galaaditis, ii. loi. Galatia, i. 454 f.; ii. 92, 212 f, 216, 261. Galilee, i. 45 f. Galltecia, ii. 301. Gangra, ii. 204. Garbe, ii. 294. Garyatis orient. et Merid., ii. 174.

Gaul, i. 452 f.; ii. 260 f., 330 f., 334. Gaza, i. 464 f.; ii. 99, no, 112 f., 115, 316. Gazaufala, ii. 288, 290. Gelae, ii. 247. Gemella (Africa), ii. 288, 290. â (Spain), ii. 302. Genoa, ii. 259. Georgia (Iberia), ii. 210. Gerasa, ii. 99, 156. Germania, ii. 269 f., 272,331-Germanicia, ii. 137. Germaniciana, ii. 288, 290. Gerunda (Gerona), ii. 300 f. Ghuwin, ii. 116. Gibar, see Girba. Gindaron, ii. 137. Girba (Girha), ii. 288, 290. Girgenti, ii. 255 f. Gitta, ii. 114. Giufi, ii. 292. Gor, ii. 290. Gorduba, ii. 290. Gortyna, i.2,196,445 f.; ii. 229 f. Gothia (Goths), ii. 239 f. Granada, ii. 300 f. Greece, see Achaia. â (Greater, see also Italy), ii. 96. Grenoble, ii. 266. Grimenothyree, ii. 219. Guadix, ii. 301. Gundeschabur, ii. 149 f. Gurgites, ii. 290. Gustra (= Ostra?), ii. 149.

Hadrianopolis (Pis.), li. 221. Hadrumetum, ii. 278, 287 f. Halicarnassus, i. 2. Hamath, ii. 134.

VOL. II.

Haran, ii. 145 f. Harba Q'dam, ii. 137. Harbath Glal, ii. 150. Hebron, ii. 116. Helenopolis, see Dre- pana Helenopontus, ii. 213. Heliopolis (Egypt), ii. 171. â (Phoen.), ii. 122. Hellespontus, ii. 222. Henschir-el-Asker, ii. 292. â Atech, ii. 296.,, Khima, ii.
294. â es-Suar, ii.
294. â Harat, ii.
292., Mscherga, ii. 296. â Tambra, ii.
296. Hephaestia, ii. 230. Heraclea, ii. 235. Heracleopolis magna et parva, ii. 170 f. Hermethes, ii. 171. Hermopolis magna et parva, ii. 167, 171. Hesbon, see Esbon. Hierapolis (Phryg.), i. 369; ii. 75, 188, 218 â (Syr.), ii.
137-Hierocsesarea, ii. 226. Hieropolis, ii. 218. Hippo, i. 3.
â Regius, ii. 288, 290.
,, Diarrhytus, ii. 288, 290. Hippus, ii. 99. Hispalis, ii. 301 f. Horrea Caelia, ii. 288, 290. Humanades, ii. 220 f., 227. Hybla maior, ii. 256. Hypaepa, ii. 226.
Hypselis, ii. 174. Hyrgalis, ii. 219.
Iberia, i. 460; ii. ' ', 210. Iconium, ii. 'j') 213 f., 216. Idumea, ii. 154. Igabrum, ii. 302. Ilistra, ii. 227. Ilium, ii. 225. Ilium aliud, ii. 225- 226. Illiberis, ii. 301. Illiturgi, ii. 301 f. Illyria, i. 73 f.; ii. 93, 238. Imola, ii. 259. India, ii. 100, 150, 152. i Ionia, i. 3. lonopolis, ii. 203. Ipagrum, ii. 301. Ireland, ii. 274, 281. Irenopolis, see Nero- nias. Isaura pal. et nova (Isauropolis), i. 420; ii. 228-229. Isauria, ii. 227 f. Isbunda, ii. 155. Italica, near Seville, ii.
300 f Italy, i. 474, ii. 255 f., 329 f. Ituraea, ii. 103.
Jabne, see Jamnia. Jamnia, ii. 99, 109, 115. Jattir, ii. 108, 116. Jericho, ii. 115. Jerusalem, i. 44 f., 182 113, etc. Jether, see Jattir. Joppa, ii. 99, 108, 114. Judsea, ii. 99 f. Julias, ii. 99. Julias (= Livias), ii. 99. Juliopolis, ii. 218. Juvavum, ii. 238.
Kabiil, ii. 115. Kabun, ii. 103, 124. Kakab, ii. 102. Kanata, ii. 99.
Kanatha (= Kanawat), ii. 99. Kardaba, ii. 1S8. Kariatha, ii. 155. Karina, ii. 224. Karkha dh Bheth
Slokh, ii. 150. Karnaim Astaroth, ii.
103. Kaschkar, ii. 147, 150. Kephar Sechanja, ii.
109. Keramon Agora, ii. 220. Kerioth, ii. 155 f. Kerkuk, ii. 150. Kharaba, ii. 103. Khirbet Bethan, ii. 108. Khoba, ii. 103, 124. Khoraba, ii. loi. Kina, ii. 217. Kius, ii. 212. Kochba, ii. loi f. Kokab, ii. 103. Kokab el Hawa, ii. 102. Ksar Sbai, ii. 296. Kurejat, ii. 155. Kysis, ii. 168.
Lacedeemon, ii. 231, 233-Lamasba, ii. 288, 290. Lamba; se, ii. 278 f., 287, 288. Lampe, ii. 219. Lampsacus, ii. 226. Lancia, ii. 298. Langres, ii. 266. Laodicea (Phryg.), ii. â 186 f., 218. â (Syr.), ii. 138. Laranda, ii.95,2i4,227. Lares, ii. 288, 290, 291. Larisa (Syr.), ii. 137. Larissa (Maced.), ii.
234-Lasom, ii. 150. Latopolis, ii. 174. Lauriacum see
Lorsch), ii. 238. Laurum, ii. 302. Lebaba, ii. 123-124. Lebanon (villages), ii. 138. Ledrai, ii. 141. Ledscha, ii. 103.
Legionum urbs, ii. 273. Legisvolumen, ii. 294. Lemnos, ii. 230. Leon, ii. 278, 299. Leontion, ii. 256. Leontopolis, ii. 171. Leptis magna (maior), ii. 287 f., 290. â minor, ii. 288, 291. Lesbos, ii. 230. Letopolis, ii. 171. Libyse, ii. 163 f. Liguria, ii.

258 f. Lilybceum, ii. 256. Limata, ii. 294. Limenas, ii. 221. Limoges, ii. 264, 266. Lincoln (Lindiensium
Colonia), ii. 273. Livias, ii. 99. London, ii. 273 f. Lorca, ii. 301. Lorsch, ii. 238. Lucania, ii. 257. Lucca, ii. 256. Lud, see Lydda. Lugdunensis, ii. 265 f. Luna, ii. 242. Lunda, ii. 219. Luperciana, ii. 291. Lusitania, ii. 301 f. Lycaonia, ii. 220 f. Lycia, ii. 226 f. Lycopolis, ii. 171 f. Lydda, ii. 99, io8 f., 114. Lydia, ii. 92, 182 f. Lyons, i. 452 f.; ii.
261 f. Lyrbe, ii. 227. Lystra, ii. 221.
Mabug, see Hierapolis (Syr.). Macedonia, ii. 92, 330. Macedonopolis, ii. 146. Macellum, ii. 194. Macomades, ii. 288, 291. Mactaris, ii. 288, 291. Madaba, ii. 155. Madaura, ii. 277 f., 287. Madili, see Midila.
Magnesia, ii. 185 f. Magydus, ii. 50, 102, 227. Mainz, ii. 270 f. Majuma, ii. no, 115, 316. Malaga, ii. 301. Malta, ii. 93. Malus, ii. 217. Mamre, ii. 110. Mangan ea, see Ba- tanea. Mantinium, ii. 205. Marasch, see German icia. Marazana, ii. 288, 291. Marcelliana, ii. 291. Marcianopolis, ii. 236. Marcomanni, the, ii. 7, etc. Mareotis, ii. 167. Margaritatum, ii. 137. Marmarika, ii. 173. Mar Mattai, ii. 148. Marseilles, ii. 261,266. Martos, ii. 301. Mascula, ii. 289, 291. Masil, ii. 170. Mauretania, ii. 277 f., 287, 296 f., 330. Maximianopolis (Egypt), ii. 171.
â (Pal.), ii. 115.
„ (Pamph.), ii. 227. Maxula, ii. 295. Medeli, see Midila. Mediccera, ii. 294. Medicones, ii. 217. Media, i. i; ii. 146. Medila, see Midila. Megalopolis, ii. 231. Megara, ii. 231. Melitene, ii. 55, 60 f., 138, 193, 197 f. Melos (Malus), ii. 230. Membressa, ii. 288, 291. Memphis, i.- yj; ii.
172 f. Mende, ii, 266. Mentesa, ii. 301. Mercurialis pagus ve-ter. Medelitanorum, ii. 291. Merida, ii. 298 f.
Merus, ii. 219. Mesopotamia, ii. 144 f, 146 f., 330. Messina, ii. 256.
â (Peleponn.), ii. 231. Metapontum, i 264. Metelis, ii. 172. Metropolis (Isaur.), ii. 227 f. â (Pisid.), ii.
221. Metz, ii. 266. Midila, ii. 288, 291. Milan, ii. 23, 258-260. Miletus, ii. 93. Milev, ii. 288, 291. Misgirpa, ii. 291. Mitylene, ii. 93. Mlili, ii. 290. Moabitis, ii. 103. Modena, ii. 259. Moesia, ii. 236 f., 330. Montoro, ii. 302. Mopsuestia, ii. 181. Motella, 219. Moxiane, ii. 219. Muguae, ii. 291. Municipium, ii. 302. Murcia, ii. 297. Mursa, ii. 237. Muzula, ii. 291. Myndus, i. 2. Myrrha (Lye), ii. 95, 188, 226. Myrsine, ii. 174. Mysia, ii. 182 f. Mytilene, ii. 230.
Nabatitis, ii. 102. Naissus, ii. 237. Nantes, ii. 266. Naples, ii. 253. Narbonensis, i. 445 f.; ii. 264, f. Narbonne, ii. 264, 266. Naro, i. 3. Naupactus, ii. 231. Nazareth, i. 402, f.; ii.
109, 113. Nazianzus, ii. 193. Neapolis (Pisid.), ii.
221. â (Tripol.), ii.
287, 291.
Neapolis (Zeug.), ii.
288, 291.
â (= Sichem), ii. 99, 114.
Nehardea, ii. 142.
Neo-Cassarea (Pont.), ii.2o6f.

â (Syr.), ii.
137-Nepi, ii. 256. Neronias, ii. 181. Nicaea, ii. 211 f. Niciopolis, ii. 171. Nikomedia, ii. 29, 51, 188 f., 211 f., 334-Nikopolis (Arm.), ii. 197. â (Epir.), n. 93) 234. â (Pal.), see
Emmaus. Nilus (Nilopolis), ii.
. 7; 171-Nisibis, ii. 146. Nitrian desert, i. 377; ii. 170. Nizza, ii. 265. Nocera, ii. 256. Nola, ii. 256. Noricum, i. 404; ii.
237, f-Nova (Sparsa), ii. 288, 291. Novempopulana, ii. Noviodunum, ii. 236. Noyon, ii. 266. Numidia, i. 185; ii. 279 f., 284 f., 326,
Oases, small and great, ii. 155. Obba, ii. 288, 291. Octavum, ii. 292. Oea, ii. 287 f., 290, 292. Olba, ii. 195 f. Olympus (Lycia), ii. 226 f. â (Bithynia), ii. 212. Opus, ii. 231. Orange, ii. 265.
Orba (Olba, Urba,
Urbanopolis), ii.
195 f. Oriolo, ii. 254. Orleans, ii. 266. Orleansville, ii. 295. Orthosia, ii. 121. Osrhoene, ii. 143 f. Ossigi, ii. 302. Ossonova, ii. 301. Ossuna (Orsuna), ii.
301. Ostia, ii. 253. Ostra, ii. 149. Otrus, ii. 188, 218. Oxyrhynchus, ii. 168, 171.
Padua, ii. 259. Pagae, see Gagse. Palermo, ii. 256. Palestine, ii. 97 f., 330 f. Palmyra, ii. 125, 151. Paltus, ii. 121. Pamphylia, ii, 227. Pandataria, ii. 93. Paneas, i. 119 f; ii. 99, 102 f., 122. Panemon Teichos, ii.
227. Panephysis, ii. 172. Pannonia, ii. 2365, 330. Panopolis, ii. 173. Panormus (Palermo). Paphlagonia, ii. 182 f. Paphos, ii. 140. Pappa, ii. 221. Paraitonium, ii. 173. Paralus, ii. 174. Parembole, ii. 172. Parethia (?), ii. 224. Paris, ii. 264 f. Parium, ii. 188, 224. Parnassus, li. 192. Parthia, i. i f.; ii. 152. Pasmasus (Pasa, Paspassa. Villa Pom- pali), ii. 195. Passala, ii. 221. Patara, ii. 227, 228. Patmos, ii. 230. Patras, ii. 231. Pavia, ii. 259. Pazus, ii. 219. Pbow, ii. 169.
Pele, ii. 235. Pella, ii. 98, 99, 100 f. Pelusium, ii. 172 f. Pentapolis(j-ifi? Cyrene), f., lysf. Pepuza, ii. 188, 218. Peraea, ii. 100 f. Perdikia, ii, 227. Pergamum, i. 107; ii.
224. Perge. ii 227. Perinthus, see Her- aclea, ii. 235. Persa(= Perra), ii. 146. Persia, ii. 146 f., 310, 33I-. Perugia, ii. 256. Pesaro, ii. 256. Pessinus, ii. 218. Petra, ii. 156. Pettau, ii. 237. Phaeno, ii. 108, 117. Phakusa, ii. 172. Pharbaethus, ii. 166. Phasaelis, ii. 99. Phasko, ii. 174. Philadelphia (Egypt), ii. 167. (Arab.), 11. 99, 155-â (Asian), i. 463. Phils, ii. 177 f. Philippi, ii. 68, 231 f. Philippopolis (Arabia), ii. 153. â (Maced.), ii. 234. Philistia, ii. no, 331. Philomelium, ii. 188, 221. Phoenicia, ii. 120 f., 330. Phrebonitis, ii. 161. Phrygia, i.3,73f., i9if.; ii. 29, 190 f., 212 f., 218, 311, 328. Phthenegys, ii. 172. Phydela, ii. 198. Piacenza, ii. 259. Picenum, ii. 255. Piedmont, ii. 258 f., 33'-Pisa, ii. 254.
Pisidia, ii. 212 f. Pispir, ii. 173. Pityus, ii. 210. Platsea, ii. 231. Pocofeltas, ii. 294 f. Pompeia (Alba), ii. 258. Pompeii, ii. 93. Pompeiopolis (Cil.), ii. 181 f. â (Pontus), ii. 203 f. Pontia, ii. 93. Pontus, i.454 f.; ii. 186 f., 203 f., 328. Pontus Polemoniacus, ii- 213. Porphyritis, ii. 168. Porthmus, ii. 231. Portus, ii. 253. Prasneste, ii. 254. Priene, ii. 183. Proconsularis, see

Africa. Prosopitis, ii. 161 f., 174. Prusa (Prusias), ii. 212. Prusa (another), ii. 212. Prymnessus, ii. 220. Ptolemais (Cyr.), ii. 167 f. â (Phcen.), ii. 99, 121 f. â (Theb.), n. 171, 173 f. Puni, ii. 279 f. Puteoli, ii. 253, 257. Pydna, ii. 235. Quintianum, ii. 254. Quoturnicensis, ii. 292.

Rabba, ii. 156. Raphana (Raphaneas), ii. 99, 137. Raphia, ii. 99, 112. Ravenna, ii. 259-260. Regensburg, ii. 271 f. Resaina, ii. 146. Rha; tia, ii. 271 f., 331. Rheims, ii. 266. Rhinocorura, ii. 174. Rhodes, ii. 229 f. Rhone, the, ii. 76, 260 f. Rhossus, ii. 139. Rimini, ii. 254,257,273.

Romagna, ii. 257. Rome, i. 5 f., 105 f., 357, 369f.,485f.; ii.24of., 308 f., 329. Rostoces, ii. 167. Rotarium, ii. 294. Rouen, ii. 265. Rucuma, ii. 292. Rusicade, ii. 288, 292. Rusucurru, ii. 296. Ruwen, ii. 116.

Sabaria, ii, 237. Sabiona (Seben), ii. 272. Sabrata, ii. 288, 290, 292. Sabulon, ii. 115. Sadagolthina, ii. 192 f. Sagalassus, ii. 220. Sais, ii. 161 f., 174. Salamis, ii. 140. Salaria, ii. 302. Salerno, ii. 256. Salona, ii. 238. Salzburg, ii. 238. Samaria, i. 45; ii. 108. Same (Cephallenia), ii.

230. Samnium, ii. 251. Samos, i. 2. Samosata, ii. 137 f. Sampsame, i. 2. Sanaus, ii. 219. Sansorum, ii. 212. Saragossa, see Caesar- augusta, ii. 299. f. Sardica, ii. 236. Sardinia, i. 5, 7 f., 164; ii. 255. Sardis, ii. 224. Sarin, ii. 198. Sarmatia, ii. 9. Saron, ii. 108, 114. Satafis, ii 296. Satala, ii. 198-199. Scarabantia, ii. 237. Scarphia, ii. 231. Scetic desert, ii. 170. Schedia, ii. 173. Schenesit, ii. 169. Schenute, ii. 177. Scili (Scilium), ii. 278 f., 287. Scupi, ii. 235.

Scythia, ii. 152, 239. Scythopolis, ii. 98, 99, 114, 119. S baste (Arm.), ii. 197. (Phryg.), ii.2i9. see Samaria), ii. 99, 114, etc. S astopolis (Pont, et olch.), ii. 199, 205, 40. Sepennytus, ii. 172. Sebulon, ii. 108. Sejalvinia, ii. 302. Se ermes, ii. 288, 292, Segni, ii. 254. Seleucia (Isaur.), ii. 227.; (Pamphyl.), ii.

227. â (Pisid. = Sid-era), ii. 221. (Syr.), ii. I37f. â Ctesiphon, ii.

'49-Senlis, ii. 266. Sens, ii. 265. Sepphoris, see Diocaes- area (Pal.). Sequani, i. 455. Serae, ii. 12 f. Sethroitis, ii. 172. Sethron, ii. 172. Seville, see Hispalis. Shargerd, ii. 150. Sibapolis, ii. 150. Siblianoi, ii. 219. Sicca (Veneria), ii. 292. Sichar-'Asker, ii. 108,

Sichem, ii. 114. Sicilibba, ii. 288, 292. Sicily, ii. 254 f., 329. Sicyon, i. 2. Side, ii. 227. Sidon, ii. 122. Siena, ii. 254. Sigus, ii. 292. Silandus, see Standus. Simitta, i. 3. Singidunum, ii. 237. Sinna, ii. 254. Sinope, ii. 188, 205. Sipontum, ii. 256. Sirmium, i. 397; ii.237.

Siscia, ii. 237. Sitifis, ii. 295, 296. Smyrna, i. 3, 189 f.; ii. 69 f., 186 f., 223 f. Sodom, ii. 155. Soissons, ii. 266. Solia, ii. 302. Sousse, ii. 296. Spain, i. 76 f.; ii. 94, 297 f., 330. Spania (= Spalia), ii.

192. Sparta, see Lacedse- mon. Spasinu Charax, ii. 150. Spoleto, ii. 256. Standus, ii. 226. Stathma, ii. 174. Stektorion, ii. 219. Stobi, ii. 235. Strassburg, li. 271. Straton's Tower, see

Ceesarea (Pal.). Sufes, ii. 286, 288, 292. Sufetula, ii. 288, 292. Sullectum, ii. 287. Sutri, ii. 256. Sutunurum (Sutu- nurca), ii. 292. Syarba, ii. 227. Syedra, ii.

227. Syene, ii. 168, 174. Synnada, ii. 214, 219. Syracuse, ii. 254. Syria, i. 188 f.; ii. 125 f., 328. Syrtes, ii. 179, 288 f.
Tabatha, ii. 115. Tabennisi, ii. 63, 169. Taksebt, ii. 296. Talavera, ii. 301. Tanagra, ii. 231. Tanis, ii. 172. Taormina, ii. 355 f. Taposiris, ii. 167, 174. Taron, ii. 202. Tarraconensis, ii. 301. Tarragona(Tarraco), ii.
298. Tarsus, ii. i8of. Tauche, ii. 173. Tauric peninsula, ii.
239-240. Tavium, ii. 217.
Teano, ii. 256. Teba (Teva), ii. 301. Tebessa, ii. 296. Tegasa, ii. 231. Tell Astura, ii. 103. Tell-el-Asch'ari, ii. 103. Tentyrse, ii. 171. Tecs, ii. 224. Termessus, ii. 227. Terni, ii. 256. Terracina, ii. 254. Teurnia, ii. 238. Thabraca, ii. 288, 292. Thagaste, ii. 295. Thagura, ii. 295. Thambi, ii. 292. Thamogadi (Thamu- gadi), ii. 285, 287, 292. Thana, ii. 156. Tharasa, ii. 292. Thasualthe (Thasarte), ii. 292. Thebais see Egypt), ii. 161 f., 328. Thebes (Diospolis magna), ii. 174. (Greek), 11. 231, 235-Thebeste, see The- veste. Thelea (Thelseje?), ii.
122. Thelebte (Thelepte), ii.
288, 292. Themisonium, ii. 220. Thenae, ii. 285, 288, 292. Thera, ii. 229 f. Therasia, ii. 230. Thespiae, ii. 231. Thessalonika, ii. 231 f. Thessaly, ii. 330. Theveste, ii. 61, 289, 292. Thibaris, i. 474; ii.
288, 293. Thibiuca, ii. 295. Thimida Regia, ii.
288, 293. Thinisa, ii. 288, 293. Thmuis, ii. 166, 172. Thrace, ii. 236, 328.
Thubun e (Tubunas), ii. 288, 293. Thuburbo (minus? maius?), ii. 288, 293. Thucca (Thugga), ii.
288, 293. Thuccabor, ii. 288, 293. Thunisa see Thinisa), ii. 288, 293. Tliyatira, ii. 190, 215. Tliysdrus, ii. 278, 287. Tiberias, ii. 99, 109. Tiber-insula, i. 105. Tiberiopolis, ii. 220. Tibur, ii. 253. Tiburnia, ii. 238. Ticabas (Tigab e), ii.
295. Tigisis (Numid.), ii.
294. Tingi, n. 295. Tingitana see Maure- tania), ii. 61. Tipasa, ii. 287, 296. Tizica, ii. 295. Todi, ii. 256. Toledo, ii. 301. Tomi, ii. 236, 239. Tongern, ii. 270. Toul, ii. 266. Toulouse, ii. 264 f. Tours, ii. 264, 266. Trachonitis, ii. 120. Trajanopolis, ii. 219, 220. Tralles, ii. 185 f. Trani, ii. 256. Trapezus, ii. 210. Trastevere, i. 6. Tres Tabernas, ii. 254. Treves, ii. 266, 268,331.
Tricca, i. 107; ii. 235. Trimithus, ii. 141. Tripolis (Asian), ii. 226, 236. â (Phoen.), ii.
122 f. Tripolitana, ii. 287 f., 330. Troas, ii. 220. Troyes, ii. 266. Tucca, ii. 288, 293. â (Terebenthina), ii. 293. Tucci, ii. 301 f. Tuscany, ii. 259. Tyana, ii. 192. Tymion, ii. 188, 218. Tyre, i. 502; ii. 121 f.
Uarba, ii. 227. Ulia, ii. 302. Ululis, ii. 293. Umanada, see Hu- manades. Upper Italy, ii. 257 f. Urba (Urbanopolis), see Orba. Urbinum, ii. 254. Urci, ii. 301. Urhai, ii. 142 f. Ursinum, ii. 254. Ursona, ii. 301 f. Usada (= Vasada), ii.
221, 227. Usduin, ii. 155. Uskiib (Scnpi), ii. 235. Uthina, ii. 278 f., 287 f. Utica, ii. 288, 293. Uturnucensis, ii. 292. Uzalis, ii. 293, 295. Uzappa, ii. 289. Uzelis, ii. 293, 295.
Vada, ii. 293. Vaga, ii. 288, 293. Vaison, ii. 265. Valarschapat, ii. 202. Valencia, ii. 297. Valentia, see Sanaus â (Gaul), ii. 263. Vallis, ii. 295. Vasada, ii. 227. Vaspurakan, ii. 197, Venetia, ii. 258. Venosa, ii. 257. Vercelli, ii. 258. Verdun,

ii. 266. Verona, ii. 259. Verulam, ii. 273. Verum, ii. 294 f. Vesontio, ii. 263. Victoriana, ii. 293 Vicus (Augusti), ii. 293; (Cccsaris), ii. 293. Vienna, i. 452 f.; ii. 261 f. Viviers, ii. 266. Volubilis, i. 3.

Xois, ii. 174.

York, ii. 273 f.

Zabulon, see Sabulon. Zaghuan, ii. 298. Zama (Regia), ii. 285, 288, 293. Zanaatha, ii. 156. Zeita, ii. 108. Zela, ii. 198, 205. Zeugitana, ii. 284 f. Zeugma, ii. 137. Zimara, ii. 198. Zoar, ii. 117. Zuitina, ii. 295.

PRINTEU BY NEII. L AND CO., LTD., EDINBURGH m-Yt ' onuiuta.

nl-st

JEL-YL

Lightning Source UK Ltd.
Milton Keynes UK
178179UK00002B/67/P